A CULTURAL HISTORY
OF IDEAS

VOLUME 1

A Cultural History of Ideas
General Editors: Sophia Rosenfeld and Peter T. Struck

Volume 1
A Cultural History of Ideas in Classical Antiquity
Edited by Clifford Ando, Thomas Habinek, and Giulia Sissa

Volume 2
A Cultural History of Ideas in the Medieval Age
Edited by Dallas G. Denery II

Volume 3
A Cultural History of Ideas in the Renaissance
Edited by Jill Kraye

Volume 4
A Cultural History of Ideas in the Age of Enlightenment
Edited by Jack R. Censer

Volume 5
A Cultural History of Ideas in the Age of Empire
Edited by James H. Johnson

Volume 6
A Cultural History of Ideas in the Modern Age
Edited by Stefanos Geroulanos

A CULTURAL HISTORY
OF IDEAS

IN CLASSICAL
ANTIQUITY

Edited by Clifford Ando, Thomas Habinek,
and Giulia Sissa

BLOOMSBURY ACADEMIC
LONDON · NEW YORK · OXFORD · NEW DELHI · SYDNEY

BLOOMSBURY ACADEMIC
Bloomsbury Publishing Plc
50 Bedford Square, London, WC1B 3DP, UK
1385 Broadway, New York, NY 10018, USA
29 Earlsfort Terrace, Dublin 2, Ireland

BLOOMSBURY, BLOOMSBURY ACADEMIC and the Diana logo are trademarks of
Bloomsbury Publishing Plc

First published in Great Britain 2022

A catalogue record for this book is available from the British Library.

A catalog record for this book is available from the Library of Congress.

ISBN: HB: 978-1-3500-0737-6
         Set: 978-1-3500-0755-0

Series: The Cultural Histories Series

Typeset by Integra Software Services Pvt. Ltd.
Printed and bound in Great Britain

To find out more about our authors and books visit www.bloomsbury.com
and sign up for our newsletters.

CONTENTS

ILLUSTRATIONS

ACKNOWLEDGMENTS

The planning for this volume and the commissioning of its first essays were the work of our dear colleague, Tom Habinek. Tom's final years included a long struggle with cancer, but were defined by a late and brilliant body of work, as well as ongoing dedication to the departmental community at USC that he had led for many years. When Tom passed away on January 19, 2019, he had read and commented on several drafts, but some chapters had yet to be submitted; his own chapter existed in a rough draft but with only memoranda to himself about its annotation; and he had written a half-dozen sentences about topics an introduction might cover. Tom's was a polemical and brilliant voice in the Classics community. We have undertaken to bring this work to completion, not in imitation of what he might have done—Tom was inimitable—but out of the deepest respect for the unique combination of critical engagement and philological rigor that he practiced.

Finally, this work would have been impossible without the cooperation of Hector Reyes, and the patience of Sophie Rosenfeld and Peter Struck; to them, we offer our deepest thanks.

We dedicate the volume to Tom, in memory of long friendship.

Clifford Ando and Giulia Sissa,
Volume Editors

GENERAL EDITORS' PREFACE

When Arthur Lovejoy introduced the field of the history of ideas to his listeners in the 1933 William James lectures, later published as *The Great Chain of Being*, he compared ideas to molecules. As he explained it, molecules combine and recombine to make compounds that vary over time. Yet the underlying stuff abides. The comparison gave him a way to capture the dynamic properties of ideas themselves and to forestall this or that thinker's eagerness to claim novelty. Further, since the periodic table has only so many elements, Lovejoy's conceit suggested that a person could, retroactively, make sensible statements about the whole.

In this book series devoted to the history of ideas, we hope to be able to make sensible judgements about the whole, but we are also convinced that the analogy needs rethinking. When Lovejoy accorded agency to the elements, with their pent-up interactive energies, he left out of focus the solution or medium in which those chemicals do their interacting. The non-noetic factors for which Lovejoy allowed come only from thinkers' internal dispositions, personal habits and preferences that might vary from person to person or from time to time. These volumes aim to widen considerably the intellectual historian's conception of how ideas emerge and move through the world.

A Cultural History of Ideas sweeps over 2,800 years of evidence. It proceeds on the premise that certain broad areas of inquiry have held humans' collective attention across a segment of the globe over all of this time. These nine topics are not presented as ideas in any simple sense. G. E. R. Lloyd's treatment of "Nature" in antiquity in volume 1 will already belie any confidence in a singular, perduring core even in this one-ninth of the terrain these volumes lay out. We propose this taxonomy instead as a set of general areas of investigation focused on comparable subjects across the ages. As historians of ideas, we aim to trace in this book series prominent lines of thought in each of these various realms—chapter by chapter, in the same order across volumes, from antiquity to the present—with close attention to constancy, change, and variation alike.

The first of these areas is "Knowledge" itself: what are we to make of the immaterial notions stored in our minds? Which ones count as true? How are such truths found, divided into new categories, conveyed, and used? After all, it is only in the twentieth century that anyone could speak meaningfully of the humanistic, social, biological, and physical sciences as distinct branches of knowledge. Many other systems came before. From "Knowledge," we turn to one of its central foci and the other starting point of this series: "The Human Self" in all its dimensions, physical, intellectual, emotional, and more. For it is the self that is the knower.

Then, moving outward from the singular self, we shift to "Ethics and Social Relations," or humans in concert with one another, and "Politics and Economies," or systems for organizing that collective existence legally and materially. "Nature" follows, including the human body, but also encompassing the earth that humans share with other animals, plants, and minerals, as well as the atmosphere and celestial bodies. Continuing to widen our lens, "Religion and the Divine" then takes the focus to the world beyond nature and to thinking about our origins, our afterlives, and our beliefs, which also means at times the limits of human knowledge.

The final categories take up, in close conversation with all of these previous domains, the realm of representation. "Language, Poetry, Rhetoric" concerns thinking about words in their many forms and uses. "The Arts" expands those questions into other symbolic systems employed in music, dance, theatre, fashion, architecture, design, and especially the visual arts, with a focus too on conceptions of beauty. Finally, "History" draws our attention to the representation of time itself, including notions of past, present, and future that simultaneously bring us full circle back to the understandings of knowledge and the self where we began.

Some specific ideas or concepts—freedom, dreams, power, difference, the environment, anger, to pick a random assortment—cross these many areas of inquiry and will appear more than once. But we take these nine broad categories to be proxies for some of the most fundamental areas to which humans in the domains of our focus—from so-called great thinkers like Plato or Locke or Einstein, to political leaders from Augustus to Charlemagne to Catherine the Great or Gandhi, to now-nameless scribes or teachers or midwives or bricklayers—have, over the centuries, applied their minds, alone and together.

But what is a *cultural* history of ideas? There are two distinguishing features of this approach, and both begin from the premise that the history of ideas is not, as some earlier historians including Lovejoy would have it, best understood as the record of a perennial conversation that largely transcends the specifics of space and time. Rather, we posit that just as the answers to big questions change depending on where and when we look, so do the questions themselves along with their stakes. "What is freedom?" means something very different to an enslaved Celt living in ancient Rome, a twelfth-century French monk, an aspiring merchant involved in transatlantic trade in seventeenth-century London, and a political theorist working in a US university in the era of late capitalism.

A cultural history of ideas is thus imagined, first, as a way to demonstrate the proposition that even the most innovative ideas to emerge from such queries, as well as the uses and impact of those ideas, have varied enormously depending on a host of contingent and contextual features extrinsic to the intellects that gave birth to them. These external features go well beyond other, competing ideas, or even competing texts in which other ideas are housed, despite the arguments of Quentin Skinner and much of what is thought of today as contextualized intellectual history. Cultural historians of ideas, to understand the thought of the past, necessarily look considerably more widely at a range of different domains of human life—or culture in the broadest sense.

Those cultural factors include changes in technology, media, and the economics of production and distribution; the authors in these volumes consider the evolution of ideas in relation to the emergence of alphabetic script and scribal culture, the printing press, photography, the computer, and other methods of communication that shaped their respective eras, as well as the commerce established around them. Our list also includes differing social structures and kinds of hierarchies and status markers, from race and gender, to estate, wealth, patronage, and credentialing, that have brought new kinds of thinkers to the fore and turned others into enemies or nonentities. In these pages we will meet, and also identify the support systems behind, philosophers, physicians, librarians, clerics, writers, artists, state officials, and only from the nineteenth century onward, "scientists," "experts," and, indeed, "intellectuals," as well as those denied these appellations. Other factors shaping ideas—including those of the most influential thinkers of every era—have been changes to laws; to religious practice and identity; to the distribution of resources; to patterns of migration, settlement, and urbanization; to notions of taste and manners; and to literacy rates, education, and intellectual life itself. So, too, do we need to study encounters between different peoples, whether through war, conquest, travel and exploration, exploitation, or peaceful cultural and commercial exchange. Then there is space in another sense. Historically specific settings, whether they be market places, monasteries, universities, salons, courts, coffee houses, medical clinics, port city docks, or think tanks, have inflected how ideas have been forged, disseminated, and debated and, ultimately, the form they have taken. So have modes of sociability. How can we understand the power of the ideas of Demosthenes or Horace or Lord Byron or Sarah Bernhardt without accounting for the social practices in which they were embedded, be that public oration, letter writing, listening to sermons or novels read out loud, or attending public performances, but also the material infrastructure behind those endeavors, from road construction to the microphone? And scaffolding everything else in the realm of ideas have, of course, always been geopolitics and the apparatuses of power: empires, nations, regions, city states, kingdoms, dioceses, and villages, but also competition about and between ideologies, factions and parties, and policies, whether established by vote, by decree, or by physical coercion.

In approaching ideas in this deeply contextual way, the cultural history of ideas could be said to be borrowing from the subfield known as the sociology of knowledge. Both share an interest in uncovering the structures, including practices and institutions, that allow for the varied means by which knowledge has been invented, organized, kept secret, exchanged, transformed, and weaponized to accomplish various goals, from acts of radical imagination and liberation to keeping people in their place. Equally, though, the approach employed in these volumes could be said to draw on histories of reading, of looking, and of hearing, that is, of interpretation and reinterpretation, or hermeneutics and textual exegesis, across genres, languages, and eras—all modes long associated with histories of the arts and literature and philosophy. Moreover, a cultural history of ideas should equally be a history of dissent and of forms of censorship and repression instituted in response. Historians also need to establish the evolving boundaries between the sayable and the unsayable, the representable and the unrepresentable, and why and how they have been enforced or not. That means paying attention to conflicts and forms of violence over just these questions as well as networks and modes of intellectual collaboration. Part of the interest in looking at the history of thought embedded in ever-shifting contexts over such a long period of time is discovering how some ideas—say, ideas about gender difference or modes of seeing others—persist across moments of social and political fracture, such as major wars. Another part is discovering how ideas are transformed by— or help transform—larger movements in the worlds that produced them; consider, for example, how much the ideas of Jean-Jacques Rousseau shaped political and religious practice in the context of the French Revolution, from republicanism to the institution of a civil religion, but also how his conceptual innovations were blamed for the revolution's excesses and thus delegitimized afterward. Some ideas, of course, fail to create any kind of traction until long after their moment of invention. Or they never do. All this is of interest to the historian of ideas too.

Yet there is a second sense in which these volumes function as a *cultural* history of ideas. Grasping this aspect requires looking more to anthropology than to sociology or literary theory. It also demands taking seriously the ideas and representations that animate everyday life, which is another meaning of culture. This approach turns our attention at least partly away from the ideas associated with philosophers, famous thinkers, or even major social movements or modern "isms" like nationalism or communism in their larger contexts. It does so in favor of a focus on collective habits, rituals, patterns of speech and behavior, and customary forms of representation operative in social, political, and economic experience, seeing them as imbued with, and productive of, a vital, culturally specific landscape of ideas. Some scholars call these ideas, taken together, folk knowledge or folk logic. From the Annaliste tradition of history writing in France, others have adopted the term *mentalité*. Included under its purview are, potentially, studies of the history of collective memory, of values, of popular and mass culture, and of the senses and emotions and decision-making in all their historical particularity.

Importantly for our purposes, sometimes the realm or realms of *mentalité* have operated to uphold the dominant ideology of the moment or to boost an ascendant one; Jack Censer and Gary Kates's introduction to the volume on the Enlightenment, for example, highlights the way eighteenth-century advertising circulars, the so-called *Affiches*, subtly bolstered the intellectual currents associated with Enlightenment philosophy without ever drawing directly on the work of any of its key thinkers. But other times folk knowledge has worked to undergird marginalized people's efforts to resist, circumvent, or revise dominant thinking, whether that has been in order to preserve traditions under pressure or to try to break free of various forms of repression. Consider craftworkers or Black revolutionaries of various eras deploying vernacular notions and forms of protest to challenge those with political and material power, including those who own the means of production. Often these commonplace and quotidian ideas, even as they structure collective life, are so routine and taken-for-granted within the culture where they exist that they go largely unremarked upon in any of the standard modes of conveying thought that are the focus of most histories of ideas. It is only when such everyday ideas collapse or get deployed in new ways that we tend to see that they belong to history too—and bear some relationship to the better-known history of explicit ideas.

What this means is that a cultural history of ideas in the second sense must extend its source base well beyond great books or texts of any kind; relevant ideas are just as likely to be embedded in visual, material, or somatic forms as they are in writing. Coin collections, garden designs, bits of code, temple complex plans, dance patterns, even habits of greeting: all become potential sites for uncovering foundational ideas in past moments and varied places. It also means thinking beyond traditional notions of thinker or audience to encompass the voices, eyes, and ears of those traditionally excluded from the tribe of "intellectuals," including women, people of color, and the nonliterate, as they can be unearthed from these varied sources. The volumes and individual chapters of this series will have succeeded if readers come away with an ability to take recognizable ideas or ideologies (i.e., those of Karl Marx and, subsequently, Marxism) or recognizable moments in intellectual history (i.e., "the Middle Ages") and see them as doubly imbricated in culture as ideational context and culture as the realm of everyday meaning-making and representation.

One risk, of course, is that this collection, with its cultural approach to ideas, ends up reinforcing an obsolete ideological construction paid lavish attention, particularly in the last century: that of "Western Civilization." The primary focus of these volumes is indeed the part of the globe, the temporal range, and much of the subject matter that scholars have inconsistently labeled and identified with "the West." But not content just to reject this terminology, we aim in these volumes to avoid the trap of its logic too, and we do so in several ways. The authors of these chapters do not take their geography to be bounded in any *a priori* way; their terrain stretches variously beyond Europe to the Near East, to China and other parts of Asia, to Russia, to Africa, and, unevenly over the last half millennium to North, Central, and South America. It is also important that every volume pushes back on the idea that the subject at hand can be described as constituting some unified cultural ethos. Radical intellectual pluralism exists in every era, and links of commonality also reach across whatever temporal and geographical boundaries we might construct. At the same time, we advocate a kind of geographical awareness that keeps us from losing sight of the fact that the histories under primary scrutiny here have been both carefully constructed and profoundly shaped by fantasies about, as well as dehumanizations of, varieties of others, whether labeled barbarians, foreigners, exotics, or heathens, whether near or far. This kind of thinking, in turn, is inseparable from an often violent history of the extraction of resources and commercial practices around the globe, of missionary activity and evangelization within and well beyond Christendom, of the enslavement of, particularly, African peoples, and of the conquest and colonization of various Indigenous peoples from the Americas to the South Seas. Advocacy for social justice is a distinct project from this one, but exposing the blinding legacies of injustice stemming from every era is very much a part of it. These volumes embrace the idea that a cultural history of ideas is necessarily a "connected history," with a focus on circulation and hybridity, along with serious attention to disparities of power.

But even more, perhaps, a cultural history of ideas potentially offers a conceptual way out of the trap of Western Civilization precisely because it historicizes, indeed "provincializes" (to borrow Dipesh Chakrabarty's term), the very categories long used to bolster it. Of particular pertinence here is "progress." Rather than treat techno-scientific or moral-political progress across time as a given, this series sees conceptions of progress, as well as those of newness and modernity, as polemical claims invented to serve different purposes at different moments (see especially the introductions to the volumes on the Enlightenment and the Age of Empire, but also the Middle Ages). The same could be said for periodization, including the very terms into which these volumes are carved up; Jill Kraye, in her volume on "the Renaissance," starts off not by guiding a tour of this arena but by showing us how this category was invented in the first place and then exposing its retrospective ideological functions. Indeed, the authors in this collection uniformly work hard to take up the intellectual pillars of standard accounts of what has been called Western Civilization and embed them, as ideas, in history. In addition to the notion of progress, these include the idea of the individual genius thinker, the advent of intellectual tolerance, the mastery of nature, secularization or the ultimate triumph of scientific reason over the enchantment of the world, and a firm distinction between past and present.

Moreover, despite the fact that this set of volumes ties ways of thinking to particular circumstances in the past, it is also designed to make the case that no one era or people or place owns those ideas going forward. Even the pointed anxieties of today, which Stefanos Geroulanos lists in the introduction to the final volume as including "dehumanization, species extinction, climate catastrophe, economic indifference to individual suffering, and artificial [forms of] intelligence," are in some sense variants of old concerns. We can thus treat previous responses to them as a storehouse from which people anywhere can continue to build new answers even as those ideas' initial relationship to particular conditions and situations remains important to understanding their full complexity. If this collection of the work of sixty-two scholars from multiple humanistic disciplines has a central goal, it is to remind us that inherited ways of thinking and our ever-changing lived experiences are constantly pushing against one another in productive ways, generating refreshed responses or, indeed, ideas as a result. We all aim to continue this endeavor.

Sophia Rosenfeld and Peter T. Struck,
General Editors

Introduction

CLIFFORD ANDO AND GIULIA SISSA

In writing histories of ideas, it is conventional—and appropriate—to acknowledge the extraordinary influence of Greece and Rome on subsequent thought and practice. This is so even if we recognize and duly and consistently acknowledge the extraordinary influence of the multicultural Mediterranean on the cultures and literatures that we have come to call "classical."[1] In launching Bloomsbury's *Cultural Histories of Ideas*, this volume naturally participates in that tradition, with the essential revision that we seek, at every turn, not to burnish antiquity's "legacy," but rather to locate the culture and thought of antiquity precisely and specifically in their many contexts. In this way, good historicism is a necessary (if not sufficient) corrective to bad history.

In a project as broadly conceived as this one, it seems appropriate to begin by reflecting on how capacious were the notions of history and, indeed, of cultural history held already by the ancients themselves. This way of proceeding brings three benefits. For one, it is essential to the design of any large-scale endeavor that one proceed on the basis of the fullest possible awareness, both historical and comparative, of how others have traversed the same terrain. This is particularly true in this instance because in our writing of cultural history we rely necessarily and essentially on the evidence supplied through the intellectual endeavors of the ancients—not simply in what we might term primary cultural production, but especially in the efforts of successive generations in antiquity to synthesize and comprehend what had already been produced. In short, we will do our work better if we study carefully how the ancients did theirs.

As a second matter, related to the first, we need always to be aware that modern studies of Greek and Roman culture do not proceed, and cannot proceed, through a simple first-order collation of the evidences of antiquity. This is true for the simple reason that no modern has access to antiquity that is unmediated by a prior history of reception and interpretation. It is also—essentially and importantly—true that much of what we "know" of antiquity results from efforts made already in that period to gather, sort, distill, preserve, and interpret the remains of prior cultural production. For example, we know nothing of the reforms of Cleisthenes, or of the early history of Roman religious festivals, that has not been delivered to us through efforts of historical recuperation and understanding made by the ancients themselves. In a very real sense, then, a modern "cultural history of the ideas of the ancients" can only be prepared in the form of a "cultural history of the ideas of persons in later antiquity about earlier ideas." To read later classical literatures responsibly as sources for earlier times, we must first locate those later texts in their context of production.[2] What sources were available to them? What were their methods and biases? Only when we have addressed these and similar questions can we begin to treat any text as evidence for that which it claims to recall.

Finally, a third benefit of thinking hard, openly, and at the start about Greeks' and Romans' own projects of cultural history is that we are brought thereby to confront some essential, material aspects of their world that some versions of the history of ideas once sought to occlude. This includes some pressing, perhaps uncomfortable, truths about our knowledge of antiquity. How comprehensive is our knowledge? What cultural forces have shaped historical processes of selection and evaluation, as materials from antiquity were read and preserved, or ignored and lost? What problems arise for us as historians, from a considered evaluation of how we know what we think we know?

Approximately a quarter of a billion words of Latin and Greek remain from between the earliest surviving epigraphic material and the end of antiquity. (For the present purpose, the scale of the estimate is not hugely changed by the endpoint, whether the loss of England, Spain, and North Africa to invaders from outside the Roman Empire, or the final failure of eastern Roman efforts to reconquer the western Mediterranean, or the rise of Islam.) Many estimates have been made of what proportion of ancient textual production this surviving material represents or, adopting another index, what proportion of ancient authors are still meaningfully known to us, or even known to have existed.[3] But the meaning of these numbers is clear enough. By the late third century BCE, to say nothing of the third century CE, Greek and Roman intellectuals felt deeply their belatedness in respect to the vast cultural production that had preceded them. They were likewise aware that they and their fellow Greeks and Romans—meaning, of course, Hellenizing and Romanizing elites of whatever background—had received and interpreted that prior culture, and had generated new ideas and new culture, across political, ecological, and demographic spaces that stretched from the Firth of Forth to the Atlas Mountains, and from Spain to Afghanistan. The consequence of their grappling with these impressions of scale was remarkable efforts to sort this material: to build a notion of "the classical" and construct canons around it; to identify eras, or places, or persons of importance to allow for a mapping of a terrain that was always too big to comprehend. "Classical Athens," "Athens in the age of Pericles," and the "golden age of Latin literature" are all products of ancient efforts along these lines.

A final and hugely important effort to make sense of the volume and diversity of ancient cultural production took the form of literary and intellectual experimentation, that is, to devise forms of literature that made cognition of the world feasible. The dictionary; the encyclopedia; the natural history; grammars of dialects and histories of language; handbooks and histories of doctrines and genealogies of philosophical schools; booklets containing prose summaries of earlier books; and literary dialogues in which characters discuss such subjects as the long history of scholarly study in a given topic, or their favorite lines of poetry, or the history of the reception and interpretation of their favorite lines of poetry. All these and more are products of classical antiquity. They are among the "ideas" that we have received from that era. They are the ineluctable means by which antiquity is known to us today.

The chapters in this volume express diverse scholarly voices. A shared concern, however, links them all: the authors heed the complexity of normative arguments, the emergence of novel ideas about how the world, the self, or a song ought to be, and the subtlety of semantic shifts over time, from ethics to politics to the aesthetic experience, with a constant awareness of the genres of discourse, the intellectual milieux, and the circumstances and contexts in which these discourses are embedded. The writing of a specifically *cultural* history has inspired the contributors to value the embodiment of agents, thinkers, and speakers; the concrete media of intellectual creativity; the sensory aspects of performance and perception; and the variable circulation of forms of knowledge among ordinary people. Although Michel Foucault's critique of the very project of a history of ideas has neither deterred any of us nor framed our approach, the imperative to focus on domains of knowledge (*savoirs*) and situated utterances (*énonciations*) runs through the entire volume.[4] Although the import of anthropology into the study of ancient history is not a programmatic choice for most contributors, still the fundamental lesson of this social science has been heard. Culture means society.[5] More precisely, it means how we live our own lives in a society.

Knowledge, the topic of the opening chapter in this volume, illustrates perfectly the nature of the legacy that we have received from classical antiquity, as well as the potential of a more open, specifically cultural form of history. Already in antiquity, there developed a tradition of self-identified "lovers of wisdom"—philosophers—who concerned themselves with the nature, possibility, and security of knowledge; the relationship of knowledge to the stability of its objects; the nature of things we know only on the basis of the report of others; and so forth. Motivating questions in their work were, for example, whether information concerning things in this world deserved the name of "knowledge" at all, it being presupposed that knowledge is eternal, while things of this world are subject to change. Can an object in flux be known at all? This body of inquiry has been enormously influential over the centuries that have followed; indeed, there are few domains of philosophy where the legacy of classical thought is more apparent. But, as Thomas Habinek shows in his chapter, a vast range of literature beyond the philosophical attests to the wrestling by Greeks and Romans with questions of knowledge, and this literature is not concerned, as philosophy was, with whether knowledge was possible, but merely with how to acquire it and whether to trust those who claimed to have it.

In the chapter on the human self, Giulia Sissa takes the anthropology of ancient societies in a new direction. In most ancient genres of narrative and normative thinking, humankind is the object of keen attention and systematic comparison with other living beings. Humans can be described in contrast with other bodies and behaviors. While sharing animal features, they occupy an anthropocentric position in the cosmos. They think, speak, act, and socialize in their own way. Being human can also be seen, however, as a lived experience. Then, the awareness of the human self, namely the consciousness of what it means and what it feels like to be a woman or a man—for a person who acts, speaks, and thinks in a society—emerges as a challenge. Then, the very fact of being in the world appears to be a source not of taxonomic reassurance, but of anxiety. We are thrown into the cosmos, and yet nothing is given to us. We are doomed to care, in the double meaning of occupation and preoccupation, business and anguish. We care for ourselves and for everything else. The philosophy of existence that flourished in Europe in the twentieth century harks back to the Greek poets and thinkers who have emphasized precisely this apprehensive consciousness of oneself. The care of the self and the care of the world that Seneca, and later Herder, Goethe, and Heidegger theorize as distinctively human—we are the "Children of Care"—was right there, embedded in narrative and normative writings about life in society, war and peace. Human beings reflect on their own identity as a matter of relentless concern: this is a culturally rich idea, available to be rethought in successive moments of deliberate reception ever since these antique formulations.

In contrast with knowledge, the field of ethics and social relations resisted from the start both the temptations of metaphysics and the simplicity of doxography. The issue, as James Ker reveals, is that ancient ethics was concerned with evaluation and guidance with respect to conduct in this world. There was no escaping the imperfections and foibles of human beings; nor would it do to wish away the regularity of social, cultural, political, and material change. The translation of philosophical concepts across languages from Greek to Latin, and their transposition from Greece to Rome, cannot be appreciated without paying appropriate regard to such factors as the discrepant conventions that regulated the elite *oikos*, or household, to its context in Athens and the vast webs and rituals of social dependency that bound individuals both inside and outside of the Roman *familia* to its *paterfamilias*, its patriarch. Likewise, efforts to hone catalogs of cardinal virtues had always to be nuanced by the recognition that humans cannot be considered, evaluated, or advised without regard for their social position, or the wider array of positions afforded by any given, wholly contingent network of social relations. In this domain, cultural history may be the only responsible form of history.

The fields of politics and economics present a challenge of a different kind. The ancients did craft traditions of theory in these areas, and a history might be told of their content and development. But in no domain of ancient theory—of ancient *ideas*, on a narrow conception—was the gap between theory and practice greater, or so Clifford Ando seeks to show. To consider one example from the domain of politics, democratic theory was concerned above all with the distribution of power among institutions, the allocation of public office to individuals, contests for power among classes and factions, and the mitigation of the effects of group interest for the running of the democracy. Left wholly out of account were those who were deemed non-political but whose exploitation was necessary for the oligarchic *demos*, the minority of male citizens, to conduct normative politics: slaves, women, resident aliens, and children, to name but four salient categories. Similarly, ancient writings on economics overwhelmingly treat economic conduct within frameworks of evaluation that moderns, conditioned by the ideologies of market capitalism, would consider extraneous to economic analysis. For them, the use of money was an arena for ethical display and the cultivation of social relations (among other things). In these fields, a cultural history must consider not only the ideas immanent in their practice but also the wider causes and effects of this gap between their practice and theory.

Nature may be thought of as a simple and stable domain of phenomena, namely what happens regularly, "always or for the most part." But this idea has a history in a particular culture. It is the outcome of two innovative moves: firstly, the debates on the causes of illness in the Hippocratic corpus (fifth and fourth centuries BCE), especially in the treatise *On the Sacred Disease*; secondly, Aristotle's classification of distinct kinds of beings and multiple fields of knowledge. Then, *phusis* becomes the vast repertoire of what is neither contrived by divine intervention nor manufactured thanks to art and craft, *technê*. Then, the natural becomes the object of observation, experience, and science. This is the major premise of Geoffrey Lloyd's contribution to this volume. Before those epistemic turns, we cannot project a generic notion of "nature" onto the cultural universe of ancient societies. We need to take a radically genealogical approach to its very definition. We also need to take stock of its extension. The same Aristotle who draws a line between nature and artifice theorizes the natural foundation of social relations, especially rapports of hierarchy and domination among human beings. It is by nature that the free adult male must rule slaves, women, and children. It is by nature that, in all gendered species, the male must be embodied in an anatomical fabric, separate from that of the female. Sexual difference fits the superiority of this particular animal, of which the female is an approximative and imperfect version. With Aristotle, nature becomes fundamentally ambivalent: it is both what happens to be on a regular basis, and what represents the ideal accomplishment of any given entity. To enhance even more the complexity of a historical understanding of the natural order, Lloyd draws attention to the benefits we can derive from comparing the peoples of Greece and Rome with those of ancient Mesopotamia, China, and the Americas. Anthropologists such as Eduardo Viveiros de Castro and Philippe Descola have called into question the very distinction of nature *versus* culture.[6] They have argued that different cultures may produce different ontologies. We, modern, Western-educated people, are "naturalists" because our sciences teach us that human beings are made up of the same elements and molecules as the other components of the world, and this is our shared "nature." But we behave differently from nonhuman animals, plants, or minerals. This is our "culture." There exist, however, other notions of what is either cultural or natural. Animism implies that, across multiple species that are anatomically diverse, subjectivities are the same. While we may not share those perspectives and although we may reject the principle of incommensurability, we should be aware of how profoundly different ideas about the natural world can be.

The meaning of what it means to write a cultural history of ideas has specific relevance—and importance—when one writes on religion and the divine, as Zsuzsanna Várhelyi explains in her chapter. In recent decades, scholars have come to understand that common understandings of the term "religion" in twentieth-century scholarship were culturally specific and extraordinarily narrow. They were not simply oriented toward Christianity; they derived very specifically from Protestant critiques of Catholic ritualism. The result, where scholarship on Greek and Roman antiquity is concerned, has been a remarkable efflorescence in the study of religions as systems of ritual or embedded and embodied networks of cultural practices. Since then, elite writings on religion have continued to be studied and read, of course, but they are now more regularly viewed through models of intellectual history, or read as contributions to philosophy rather than data in the history of religion, or interpreted as intellectualizing efforts at Weberian rationalization, and so forth. Várhelyi's chapter seeks to bring the histories of practice and ideas into dialogue and, most importantly, to locate areas where discourse and practice, which for so long were analytically differentiated, actually shaped each other. This is an important ambition of a cultural history of ideas.

Language, and normative discourses about linguistic theories, performances, and techniques, are the object of Sean Gurd's chapter in this volume. The starting point is the liquid ontology that Heraclitus sees as an unstable foundation of our experience of the world. Since everything is in a state of flux, the meaning of words is also fluctuating. Political sedition (*stasis*), Thucydides warns us, has an especially destabilizing effect upon language. It is against this threat that, firstly, Plato and, later, Aristotle deploy "countermeasures." The former opposes the enduring conceptual entities we have come to call Forms or "Ideas" to the lability of our perceptions and our words; the latter moves the attention from concepts to propositions. We can think correctly about the world. We can also convey our logically and dialectically interconnected thoughts to others. The success of discourse is communication: what we say can be understood by others in social interactions. The challenge of getting to know concepts and to learn how to reason, Gurd argues, is experienced in the speaking situation. It happens out there, in a vocal and aural culture. The second focus of this cultural approach to language is the technique of fabricating speech, namely poetics and rhetoric. *Poiesis* is a manner of shaping an aesthetic object, by assembling words thanks to "meter," namely rhythm, parallelisms, and euphonic, sensorial effects. In its Platonic version, this object, be it a text or a song, may be mimetically anchored to the ideas. In the Aristotelian reformulation of *mimesis*, the verbal/musical artifact may be appreciated on account of its narrative structure. It is this objective composition that gives it proper meaning, makes it susceptible of generalization, and endows it with affective power. This thing produces a sensory impact, especially upon people who live in a theatrical and auditory culture. Later development of this theorization can be found in Hellenistic philosophy. Finally, Gurd looks at the receiving side of performance. *Aisthêsis*, perception, can be refined in a manner of self-transformation: on the one hand, Dionysius of Halicarnassus prescribes how a discriminating listener can improve his or her sensitivity; on the other, Longinus sees a spontaneous, universal response to sudden and striking words as proof of the sublime. But this too can be learned.

What we may call "the Arts" cannot be apprehended as a unified domain of cultural creativity, argues Ruth Webb. A core of normative ideas, however, underpins the aesthetic experience. The most salient is *mimêsis*, imitation or, more precisely, representation or enactment. From archaic poetry to Plato, Aristotle, and later philosophers in the Greco-Roman world, fiction is meant to elicit pleasure thanks to all manner of craftsmanship, *technê*. Different media can be used, such as sound, colors, metals, or stones, but the human body is also thought to be a versatile instrument of performance in acting, singing, and dancing. Emphasis is placed on the process of fashioning, the acting like, the mimicking of somebody or something, this being more important, Webb argues, than the final, ready-made, product of fabrication. Hence the paradigmatic importance of the theater. The contrast of Plato and Aristotle comes to the fore. Plato blames *mimêsis* on account of two arguments: its remoteness from the Form, on the one hand, and its vivid, contagious, durable effects upon the souls of the audience, on the other. Aristotle deflates the danger of becoming a tragic or comic character. He circumscribes the impact of a play to the time and space of the theater, and radically rethinks the powers of fiction, thus redeeming *mimesis* from Plato's charges. In dialogue with the chapters by Sean Gurd and Giulia Sissa, Ruth Webb focuses on how ancient discourses drew attention not only to the ritual settings and the social situations in which mimetic work is done but also to the senses involved in its reception.

We turn, finally, to history. In conventional histories of the historical sciences, the writing of complex narratives of human events, undertaken with a critical attitude to the gathering of information and a rationalist approach to causation, commences in ancient Greece. Nor is this incorrect. The first products of Greek historical writing, the large-scale works of Herodotus and Thucydides, rightly remain among the classics of historiography and exemplify, in their contrasting ambitions and intellectual styles, nodal points on any mapping of historical inquiry. Lucas Herchenroeder and Clifford Ando give these due attention in their chapter. But they also observe several further features of the function of history in culture, not least the essential role played by representations of the past in affirming the ongoing operation of social institutions and, collectively, society itself. The multiplicity of the contexts of need and use for historical memory—from genealogies of aristocratic houses, to lists of donations to particular cults, to the memorial of victories and losses in battle, to records of proceedings from the trials of religious dissidents—gave rise in the ancient world to a bewildering array of technologies and genres for preserving historical information, as well as a bravura sense of what might count as data in support of those projects. This vast ecology forms a fitting object of cultural history, and an appropriate close to the volume.

CHAPTER ONE

Knowledge

THOMAS HABINEK

The key issues that inform ancient approaches to knowledge are anticipated in the earliest remains of Greek epic poetry. The central concerns underlying early references to truth, falsehood, and knowledge are, first, a quest for strategic information that will allow individuals and communities to survive and flourish in the world and, second, a concern with the reliability of information transmitted by others. The archaic texts show little interest in debating the possibility of knowledge or in accumulating information for its own sake—even Odysseus' renowned curiosity is deployed toward instrumental acquisition or finding his way home to Ithaka.[1] They take it for granted that everything is known or knowable, at least by the gods. The problem for the average mortal is how to gain access to knowledge and whether to trust those who claim to have it already. These concerns are as we would expect for human societies in general, given the human need and capacity for creative interaction with the surrounding world, including other human beings. But they were perhaps of special relevance to inhabitants of the ancient Mediterranean, with its distinctively varied and unpredictable physical environment.[2]

The human need for reliable information underlies the earliest programmatic pronouncements concerning truth and knowledge. Thus, in book two of the *Iliad*, just prior to reciting the catalog of Greek forces that invaded Troy, Homer calls upon the Muses who "are present at everything and know everything, while we [mortals] hear only what is reported by tradition and know nothing at all."[3] Hesiod, in his roughly contemporary *Theogony*, describes the Muses as proclaiming their own access to truth, which is characterized as both strategic information and reliable report. As they put it,

> We know many lies (*pseudea*) that resemble verifiable statements (*etumoisin*);
> But we also know, when we choose, how to transmit truths (*alêthea*).[4]

More precisely, the truth (*alêthea*) transmitted by the Muses consists, in essence, of "things that do not escape attention"; while the lies (*pseudea*) to which they refer are better understood as "unreliable statements" that potentially confuse the mortal listener with their resemblance to verifiable claims (*etumoisin*).[5] In other words, the Muses have access to all necessary information (nothing escapes their notice), and they are also free of the human anxiety over the reliability or unreliability of information provided by others inasmuch as they preside over that very distinction. The extent and quality of their knowledge mark by contrast the limitations upon human knowledge.

Access to information and, in particular, invulnerability to deceit, also characterize the god Zeus, whose triumphant establishment of the present cosmic order is the main theme of the *Theogony*. Zeus, who, like the Muses, sees all, prevents the birth of a successor and rival by ingesting the goddess Metis, or "cunning intelligence," whom he has impregnated. The outcome is the emergence of Athena, goddess of wisdom, from the head of Zeus. The story seems less concerned with Zeus' acquisition of Metis' knowledge (after all, he sees everything anyway), than with his self-inoculation against her power to deceive, that is, her cunning. Metis' knowledge (*eiduian*) enables her to mislead, and Zeus overcomes her through his own treachery (*doloi, exapatesas, haimulioisi logoisin*).[6]

A similar concern motivates Zeus' encounter with Prometheus, which is also narrated in the *Theogony*. There we are told that Prometheus both deceived and did not deceive Zeus when he concealed the edible parts of an ox under offal (stomach, belly, paunch) and dressed or disguised bones in shining fat. Whatever the theological implications of the encounter, it is a struggle pitting knowledge (*medea eidos*) against cunning and deceit, with each deity apparently trying to deceive or outwit the other.[7] The nature of the conflict is made explicit in a version of the encounter narrated in *Works and Days*, where Prometheus and Zeus trade *apate* and *dolos* (deceit and trickery), the latter taking the form of the false female Pandora, whose entrance into the world of men allows for the proliferation of unreliable representations, or *pseudea*. Among humans, limited access to knowledge of how to make a living[8] and vulnerability to deceit (as embodied in Pandora) are Zeus' retribution for Prometheus' use of treachery on behalf of mankind. As the narrative progresses, Zeus' capacity to see and cognize all[9] stands in marked contrast to the poet's anxiety about the false oaths of men, not least his brother Perses.[10] The vital human capacity for linguistic and other forms of symbolic communication always carries with it the danger of deceit or misrepresentation.

The remainder of this chapter explores ancient approaches to knowledge as a series of strategies for addressing the human limitations already identified in archaic poetry, namely, lack of access to the full range of necessary information for operating successfully in the world, and uncertainty over the knowledge claims made by others. Both the problems addressed and the strategies adopted spill over from one historical period to another and across discursive and pragmatic genres (e.g., religion, rhetoric, science, philosophy, folkways) that are usually treated separately in the scholarly tradition. Philosophy has no monopoly on epistemological self-awareness, nor can cognition be understood as a purely intellectual or disembodied practice. Although discussion of each strategy will generally move from earlier to later sources, taking note of the ways in which later sources reflect on and respond to earlier, the structure of presentation employed here is by no means intended to suggest a progressive or teleological narrative. To the contrary, the strategies adopted in late antiquity in pursuit of reliable information bear a strong resemblance to those attested for the earliest epochs of the classical world.

DIRECT ENCOUNTER

Perhaps the most straightforward way of acquiring reliable information is through direct encounter of the relevant person, object, or event. This of course is the special power of the Muses, who are present to everything, and of Zeus, who sees all; but it is also available to humans in limited contexts, especially if they are willing to explore and inquire. Already in *Works and Days* (293–7), Hesiod proposes personal inspection (as well as reliance on a trustworthy source, to which we will return) as a solution to the problem of ignorance. As he explains,

> That man is altogether best who perceives all himself
> And considers what will be better next and in the end.
> That man is also good who listens to one who speaks well.
> But as for the man who neither perceives for himself nor takes to heart
> What he hears from another, he is useless.[11]

For Hesiod's brother Perses, at whom the advice is directed, the failure thus to secure the necessary information will lead, quite literally, to starvation. Gathering information oneself is the best antidote to human ignorance, although listening to a reliable source can also be productive. Otherwise, it would seem, a man is of no use to himself or to the community to which he belongs.

The epic tradition can be quite precise about what exactly is learned through direct sensory contact. Thus when Aeneas encounters Achilles on the battlefield outside Troy, he declares

> We know each other's genealogy, we know each other's begetters
> By hearing the renowned words of mortal men
> Though I do not know yours by sight nor you mine.[12]

In effect, it is the relationship of parents to offspring that Aeneas and Achilles are said to "know," having heard it directly. But without direct visual contact they do not know the parents themselves.

In Homer's *Odyssey*, personal examination or autopsy is the primary motivation for a number of Odysseus' adventures. At the outset of the poem the hero is described in balanced verses as one who "saw the settlements and became familiar with the mindset of many people" even as he "endured many sufferings on the open sea."[13] Observation and endurance (*idein* and *pathein*) are complementaries, just like land and sea. In his own account of his adventures later in the poem Odysseus refers repeatedly to his pursuit of direct sensory experience. For example, even though he can infer from the contents of the Cyclops' dwelling that the inhabitant is a monster of some sort (*pelorios*),[14] Odysseus presses on in his quest for direct encounter (*peirasomai, hoi tines eisin*)[15] and observation (*oisato*),[16] with dire consequences for his men. When confronted with the Sirens, whose song lures mortals to their destruction, he has himself bound to the mast so that he can listen with impunity (Figure 1.1).[17] So strong is the hero's desire to be present to the Sirens that he signals to his companions to free him from his bonds, fortunately to no avail. Later in the poem, Odysseus' wife Penelope matches her husband's insistence on autopsy as she seeks direct encounter with the mysterious beggar who has attached himself to her household; and indeed, it is the maidservant Eurykleia's visual and tactile recognition of an old scar that reveals Odysseus' identity.[18] Key steps leading to the successful outcome of the Odyssean plot depend on direct sensory encounter, even as the hero makes his way past many obstacles in large part through his ability to fool others with trickery, disguise, and unreliable stories.

Direct sensory encounter never loses its appeal, despite many ancient philosophers' insistence on its unreliability as a means of access to "real" knowledge. Indeed, two of the founding figures of the philosophical tradition, Parmenides and Empedocles, recount

FIGURE 1.1 Odysseus tied to the mast listening to the Sirens. Athenian vase, early fifth century BCE. © Alamy Stock Photos.

their own direct encounters with goddesses, on analogy with Hesiod's initiation by the Muses. Parmenides describes the experience as involving sight, touch, sound, and a sense of movement. Empedocles suggests that the Muse has been present to him more than once (*nun aute paristaso*)[19] and invites her on the occasion of his poem to activate whichever sense is best suited for understanding a given object (*noêsai, noei*).[20] As in archaic epic, so here, *noêsis*, that is, an understanding that is not limited to a specific sensation, is nonetheless taken as an extension or outcome of sensation, an ancient anticipation, it would seem, of what contemporary cognitive science refers to as "event recognition" or "binding."[21]

The quest for direct observation carries over from mythical narrative to actual practice. The word *histôr*, from the verbal root meaning "to see," is twice used of an official who verifies by his presence and observation the claims and wagers of participants in a dispute.[22] In later texts the term refers to a range of inquiries that entail direct sensory encounter with people, places, or things. For example, Heraclitus mocks Pythagoras' mode of inquiry (*historia*) as consisting of a cut-and-paste job on the writings of others,[23] presumably as opposed to direct observation or some other mode of information gathering. Herodotus' exposition of his own inquiry or research (*historia*)[24] begins with a report of conflicting stories reported by Persian and Greek sources, but goes on to include numerous instances of authorial examination of sites and objects. He specifies the aim of his narrative as keeping human achievements from fading from sight or sound (*exitela, aklea*). Thucydides seeks to improve upon Herodotus in part by writing a history of contemporary events, which allows him to rely on direct observation by himself or by other participants. For example, in his account of the plague that devastated Athens shortly after the outbreak of the Peloponnesian War, he declines to speculate as to causes, but instead lays out the symptoms in detail, a task for which he tells us he is well suited, having had the disease himself and observed (*idon*) the experiences of others.[25] Even when his narrative requires him to write of affairs prior to his lifetime, he relies heavily on personal inspection of sites and remains, and inference therefrom.

Thucydides' account of the plague parallels the descriptive practices of early doctors as reported in the Hippocratic corpus, especially the compilation called *Epidemics*, which describes both communal and individual experiences of illness, including weather at the time of the outbreak, the age and gender of patients, the timing and sequence of symptoms, and so on.[26] The Hippocratic treatises frequently emphasize the doctor's direct sensory encounter with the individual patient, even when allowance is made for the value of accumulated case studies and of a more theoretical understanding of the human constitution. Indeed, the author of the Hippocratic *Art* defends the reality of the art of medicine against skeptics on the grounds that it can be seen with the eyes and recognized by means of judgment (*opthalmoisin idein/ gnomei noêsai*).[27] According to the author of another Hippocratic treatise, *The Ancient Medicine*, the methodical ordering (*hodos*) of investigation (*zêtêsis*) provided by medical art keeps the practitioner from deceiving and being deceived.[28] More generally, Greek and Roman authors attribute the creation of arts or *tekhnai* to the systematization of perceptions acquired through experience. In one influential Stoic definition, "art is a system of perceptions organized toward some useful goal in life."[29] Epicureans, as well as Stoics and some Academics, persist in the conviction that perception is not just necessary but sufficient for knowledge, against strong opposition from other philosophical sects. In the opinion of later writers on rhetoric, one of the greatest achievements of the speaker or writer is to place narrated events "before the eyes" of the audience, in a practice called *ekphrasis* (Greek) or *evidentia* (Latin).[30] Even Aristotle's *Posterior Analytics*, often regarded as a foundational document of "scientific method," recommends passive observation of phenomena rather than active experimentation.[31]

AUTHORITY AND SIGNS

As indicated by a number of passages already cited, reliance on physical presence and accompanying sensation can include direct encounter with authorities, whether divine or human. Often the human authorities are regarded (or regard themselves) as such due to their own privileged access to divine omniscience. Early poets claim to transmit knowledge supplied by divinities (e.g., Hesiod or Homer and the Muses, or Empedocles, who explicitly presents the utterance he has heard from the goddess as antidote to unreliability [*mêtis*] and deceit [*apatê*]),[32] but many other claimants can be found both within and beyond their texts. Individual heroes in epic poetry seek access to especially pertinent information from their divine friends and mentors (e.g., Achilles and his mother Thetis, Odysseus and his divine guide Athena). When the Achaeans at Troy are struck by a plague, Achilles consults the seer Calchas (Figure 1.2) who, like the Muses, "knew all things that were, the things to come and the things past."[33] He is asked to

FIGURE 1.2 Relief with the seer Calchas, along the Via Appia, Rome, *c*. second century CE.
© Image courtesy of the Getty's Open Content Program.

provide strategic information in a moment of crisis in part because of his prior success in guiding the Greek fleet on its voyage to Troy—his reliability is thus both asserted and observed.

Such appeals to authority or tradition never really disappear from ancient intellectual life. Among the early medical writers, the author of the Hippocratic *On Ancient Medicine* already speaks respectfully of "the many and excellent [medical] discoveries made over a long period."[34] Centuries later Galen will defend earlier writers on the grounds that oftentimes they are not wrong, just misunderstood. As one commentator puts it, "arguments from authority have considerable value for Galen."[35]

One of the most common strategies of interpretation in ancient literary, philosophical, and theological discourse was allegorical reading, which sought to find beneath the surface, as it were, of an older text, a still valid truth, especially about the physical nature of the universe. In use from at least the fifth century BCE through and beyond the end of antiquity, the technique has rightly been understood as an attempt to preserve cultural continuity in the face of inevitable changes in knowledge.[36] It does so by confirming the reliability of authorities that might otherwise seem to mislead.

Even seemingly irrational actions, such as consulting oracles or diviners, can be interpreted as rational attempts to reduce uncertainty. As we have seen, Achilles' reliance on Calchas is due not just to the latter's claim to special knowledge but also to the value of his advice on past occasions. To consult a famous oracle at Delphi, the inquirer had to channel his uncertainties into a single, focused question. Even an ambiguous answer could facilitate decision-making, especially when the enquirer was a collectivity or leading political figure, as was often the case. From the period of the Roman Empire numerous dice, alphabet, and textualized oracles provide the worried user with answers to questions concerning uncertain situations such as commercial ventures, life expectancy, and legal procedures (Figure 1.3). With dice oracles, for example, the user asked a question, rolled the dice, then read the answer corresponding to the number shown. Interestingly, for questions on which we have outside information (for example, the failure rate of business ventures, life expectancy), the probability suggested by the oracles roughly corresponds to real-life experience. As one scholar has recently argued, consulting such oracles was a way of "playing the odds. It focused energies on the probable, not the possible."[37] Greek diviners, too, "with very few exceptions ... produce incremental advice on tactical matters in the proximate future."[38]

The authority generated by access to knowledge is often political in nature; and in turn political authorities can be regarded as sources of reliable knowledge. One scholar calls attention to the figure of Nereus, or the old man of the sea, in Hesiod's *Theogony*, who neither misleads nor overlooks (*apseudês, alethês*).[39] His knowledge of justice and of mild counsels (*dikaia kai epia denea oiden*)[40] marks him as a mythic prototype of the just king who is honored by the Muses and to whom the common people turn for judgments and for skillful or knowing (*epistamenos*) resolutions of conflict.[41] Political discretion thus embodies one type of strategic information necessary for the survival and flourishing of human communities (indeed the Latin term for wisdom, *sapientia*, often refers to excellence in military or political strategy).[42] Its distinction from or overlap with other types of knowledge becomes a point of discussion and disagreement throughout antiquity. The legendary seven sages are characterized by their ability to perform certain types of political or social wisdom.[43] Plato's philosopher kings are intended to have preeminent political authority owing to their mastery of a new, distinctly philosophical and disembodied type of knowledge. The Pythagoreans took the leadership in writing new constitutions for south Italian city-states based on their mathematical knowledge.[44] There is some indication that Stoic teachings may have played a part in the organization of the short-lived Sun-City, or Heliopolis, refuge of escaped slaves during the late Roman republic.[45] Individual philosophers served as advisers and "friends" to figures as diverse as Alexander of Macedon, Mithridates of Pontus, the young Nero, and the emperor Constantine.[46]

FIGURE 1.3 Twenty-sided die from Ptolemaic or Roman Egypt, made of serpentinite and inscribed with Greek letters. © Courtesy of the Metropolitan Museum (public domain).

DELIBERATION, PERSUASION, AND SHARED REASONING

Ancient discussions of political authority provide access to yet another widespread strategy for overcoming human ignorance and susceptibility to deceit. There is an implicit recognition of what is today known as distributed cognition, a term that loosely covers a variety of ways in which human thought extends beyond the individual mind to include external objects and, in particular, other individuals.[47] In one view, the term is best used of situations in which a system has access to more information—and generates more reliable information—than any individual participant within it. Awareness of this human capacity to generate knowledge collaboratively is present already in the fragments of Heraclitus, who describes *logos* or reason as a common possession or property,[48] notes that thinking (*to phronein*) is common to all,[49] and seems to prefer the collective play of children to the stratified discourse and institutions of adults.[50] According to one ancient report, Heraclitus "declares quite explicitly that the common reason is the standard, and the things that appear in common are reliable as we judge by the common reason, but the things that appear to each person individually are false."[51] Although there is little if any reason for associating Heraclitus with incipient democracy, his emphasis on the close connection between shared acceptance and what is true and reliable (*aletheia, pistos*) highlights a nexus of concerns that will underlie civic discourse in subsequent centuries.

Peitho, or persuasion, which functions in archaic epic as both an accompaniment of erotic seduction and a means of determining a course of action in military assemblies, can also be a means of developing ideas and plans collectively. For Democritus it stands in opposition to the strictures of law and necessity,[52] while Parmenides describes truth (*aletheia*) as itself persuasive.[53] In one instance the sophist Gorgias describes Peitho as making everything become its slave willingly rather than by force,[54] thus giving a negative connotation to Peitho's nonviolence (and anticipating modern theories of the effectiveness of symbolic, as well as physical, violence). Gorgias also provides a striking reversal of the Parmenidean association of Peitho with truth when, in his display speech in defense of Helen, he says,

> Everyone who has persuaded anyone about anything persuades him fashioning false speech (*pseudê logon*). For if everyone had concerning everything memory of the past, <awareness> of the present, and foresight of the future, speech would not be like it is in actuality, now that it is not easy to remember the past, examine the present, or divine the future.[55]

Persuading (*peisas*) and deceiving (*apatêsas*) are treated in the passage as virtual synonyms.[56] On this account, the persuasive speaker takes unfair advantage of the audience's lack of complete and reliable information, namely, the fact that we are not in the position of the gods and (perhaps) no longer believe we have access to their knowledge, to deceive and overpower.

But persuasion can also describe the constructive work of deliberation, especially in the civic assemblies that replace the archaic soldiers' councils. In the mainstream rhetorical tradition, which comes to form the primary basis of elite education from roughly the fourth century BCE through the end of antiquity, persuasion is aligned with knowledge, both as a means of sharing information among participants and as a form of collective knowledge construction. For example, when Aristotle describes the responsibilities of the deliberative or symbouleutic orator, that is, one who (literally) "takes counsel with" others, Aristotle specifies that he must have knowledge (*eidenai*) of relevant matters, such as the expenses, resources, military capacity, and laws of the city he is advising.[57] Adopting an even more collaborative or distributed model of information exchange, the dialogues of Cicero enact the construction of knowledge through shared conversation, with diverse participants bringing their skills and experience to bear on the issue at hand to generate a type of knowledge unavailable to any of them individually.[58] For Cicero, conversations of the sort presented in his philosophical treatises extend into the realm of the social practices that are familiar from the civic gatherings of the Roman republic. In his massive compendium of rhetorical theory and practice, the Roman educator Quintilian, writing a century and a half after Cicero, describes certainty (*certum*), which he regards as the aim of reasoned discourse, as the outcome of a shared construction of knowledge or understanding of a situation.[59] Quintilian is responding to philosophical attacks on the possibility of knowledge by asserting the power of collective judgment or wisdom. For him, as for the rhetorical tradition more generally, consensus based upon deliberation is the most effective antidote to individual human ignorance. He seems to have anticipated by some seventeen centuries Condorcet's theorem whereby a slight statistical probability that any given judge of a situation is correct becomes a virtual mathematical certainty the greater the number of judges.[60]

For at least one recent scholar, the certainty attributed to rhetorical discourse is not just a theoretical ideal but also the practical outcome of the procedures of the classical city-state, especially in its democratic form, more generally. The competitive success of democratic Athens, on this account, is due to its structures of participation that facilitate the aggregation, alignment, and codification of the social, technical, and latent knowledge of individual actors. As he puts it, "ancient Athenian democracy harnessed the power of dispersed knowledge through the free choices of many people ... The Athenians' capacity to make effective use of knowledge dispersed across a large and diverse population enabled democratic Athens to compete well against non-democratic rivals."[61] Although the circle of participants in the decision-making processes of the aristocratic Roman republic was narrower than in democratic Athens, a similar capacity to aggregate and align the dispersed knowledge of individual senators through something resembling democratic deliberation was crucial to Rome's success in adapting to the "interstate anarchy" that characterized the Mediterranean world.[62]

MEMORY AND THE ARCHIVE

Another hedge against the insufficiency and unreliability of information is production of an archive. In claiming that nothing escapes their attention, the Muses, whose mythical mother is the goddess Mnemosyne, or Memory, present themselves as guardians of memory. Human (or semi-human) advisers such as Nestor, Phoenix, and the centaur Chiron are valued for their ability to bring recollection to bear upon present situations. With the diffusion of writing, texts of various sorts become records of past events and prompts to recollection. City-states in particular foster the textualization of memory as a means of constructing knowledge that will be available beyond the aristocratic circuits of oral, embodied communication. Socrates' reservations about writing as a source of knowledge go hand in hand with his objections to democratic governance. In the Roman republic, the aristocratic general and politician Scipio Africanus discounts written documents that contradict his own memory: a clear example of the ongoing struggle between personal and communal control of the archive of relevant information.[63]

Despite resistance, archives of texts proliferated, in storage spaces on impermanent media such as papyrus, wax, and wood, and in public spaces in monumental inscribed form on stone or bronze. This occurred especially as peoples and communities became interconnected across space and time. The great library/museum established at Alexandria under the Ptolemies set the pattern for the assemblage of dispersed knowledge, and its directors became prototypes of scholars as gatherers and preservers of information (Figure 1.4). Public libraries were fairly commonplace in the Roman world, with several especially prominent collections housed within the city of Rome itself. Such institutions seem to have contained both administrative documents and literary texts of various sorts; in Alexandria, at least, they also preserved the learning of non-Greek peoples, such as Babylonians and Jews.

Libraries and archives carried on the protection against oblivion previously associated with the gods. Heraclitus is said to have deposited his books in a temple of Artemis; the library of Alexandria took its name from the Muses; republican-era temples at Rome are thought to have maintained collections of religious materials; and the great public libraries of the early principate were all affiliated with religious sites (i.e., the Temple of Apollo on

FIGURE 1.4 A nineteenth-century engraving, imagining the Library of Alexandria. © Getty Images.

the Palatine, the Temple of Peace, the Atrium Libertatis, the Forum of Trajan).[64] Although book-collecting necessarily entailed selection, intentional exclusion seems to have been the exception rather than the rule. The major libraries included books in diverse languages and from various eras, authors, locales, and genres. Although "ancient libraries did not spin off academies, like those founded in European nations from the seventeenth century on,"[65] they were the site of various sorts of learned activities, including comparison of variant copies of texts, production of translations from one language to another, scholarly discussion and debate, and composition of new works of poetry and prose.

Alongside the construction and maintenance of libraries as physical archives of learning, single texts that incorporated earlier learning, often verbatim, became increasingly commonplace. Already in the fourth century BCE Xenophon depicts Socrates and a group of youths unrolling scrolls and copying choice excerpts from earlier authors.[66] About a century and a half later, Eratosthenes, third librarian at Alexandria, supervised the duplication of every older book he could get his hands on, which in turn served as a prompt to his own creative investigations in mathematics, geography, and chronology.[67]

In late first-century BCE Rome, the scholar Marcus Terentius Varro is reported to have composed over five hundred books, the majority of them compilations of material from earlier writers and sources in danger of being lost to memory. Of Varro's works on Roman history and culture, Cicero declared, "we were wandering like foreigners in our own city until your books brought us home, allowing us to know at last who we are and where we dwell."[68]

Such compilations could be organized thematically, as in the case of Pliny the Elder's *Natural History*, or adopt a seemingly random or miscellaneous structure, for example, Aulus Gellius' *Attic Nights* (Latin) or Plutarch's *Sympotic Questions* (Greek). The act of compilation could serve as the basis for what later came to be regarded as a new discipline or scholarly field, as when Vitruvius assembles scattered information and personal reminiscences into a manual of architecture and structural engineering, or writers such as Verrius Flaccus, Cloatius Verus, Julius Pollux, Festus, and Isidore seem to invent a field of lexicography. Even more so than libraries, such textual compilations were open to knowledge transmitted by other than elite writers. The lexicographers, for example, frequently cite spoken dialectal variants; Pliny the Elder relies at times on the lore of peasants or knowledge particular to women;[69] Galen records the experience of numerous unnamed medical practitioners even as he debunks many of their inferences. Just as with libraries, textual compilations rarely if ever lay out a program for future research. Underlying all of them is the age-old sense that everything of importance to human existence is already known by someone somewhere. The true expert is the person who can mobilize such knowledge in the relevant context. A similar confidence in knowledge transmitted from the past helps account for the widespread practice of allegorical or etymologizing reading of earlier texts, mentioned above: even when an author such as Homer or Hesiod seems patently wrong, his reliability can be recuperated through techniques of reading that reveal the true sense of his words.

The urge to preserve an archive of critical information underlies much of the surviving writing on stone and bronze of Greece and Rome as well. Records of tribute, treaties, donations, and political offices, etched in bronze or carved in stone, constituted a civic or national archive available to successive generations and thus fostering a sense of identity over time. More ephemeral, but still of importance, were paintings of battles, often carried in triumphal processions. Maps informed users of faraway locales, while milestones marked distances to and from key locations. Diagrams amplified the knowledge transmitted by scientific and mathematical treatises. Ancestor masks and accompanying laudatory literature differentiated noble Roman homes from those of commoners while preserving the memory of past achievements. Portrait images and slogans engraved on coins provided a ready means of circulating basic knowledge about political leadership, identity, and ideology across time and space.

EPISTEMOLOGY; *OR,* KNOWLEDGE AS A TOPIC OF PHILOSOPHICAL INQUIRY

Many of the hedges against ignorance and deceit discussed thus far would have been loosely grouped by Greeks and Romans under the heading of wisdom (Greek *sophia*, Latin *sapientia*). Wisdom was understood as a way of operating successfully in the world, of overcoming obstacles to personal and communal happiness. The transfer of the Greek term *sophia* from craftsmanship makes this understanding clear: wisdom is a craft of living or, in dire circumstances, of surviving.

The goal of much of what comes to be known as ancient philosophy is to professionalize the quest for wisdom, to make it the purview of some experts and methods of inquiry as opposed to others. A redefinition of knowledge becomes a key strategy in the quest for professional supremacy. By arguing that the wisdom, or functionality, of others is not based on genuine knowledge, philosophers can grant poets, artists, orators, diviners, and so forth their competencies while assigning to themselves a superior mode of cognition and, depending on the philosopher, access to a superior type of knowledge. In effect, philosophers such as Plato, Aristotle, and their successors seek to attain, as far as is humanly possible, the epistemological status of the archaic gods whose knowledge consists of an unmediated and secure access to reality. As Gerson explains in his survey of ancient (philosophical) epistemology, unlike in more recent epistemology (what he calls the "standard account"), where knowledge is a matter of justification of propositions, for the ancient philosophers, knowledge or *epistêmê* is of things as they really are.[70] But this in turn implies that reality, or some aspect of it, is indeed knowable, with the result that philosophical discussions of knowing (i.e., epistemology) are consistently intertwined with discussions of the nature and knowability of the world (i.e., ontology, physics, metaphysics). In the words of yet another scholar, "a determinate description of knowledge determines a distinction between the types of entities that can be known and those that cannot."[71]

Because of their professional ambitions, philosophers end up fighting a double battle. On the one hand, they seek to diminish, belittle, or subsume non-philosophical claims to wisdom by advancing a distinctive notion of knowledge to which only they can provide access; on the other hand, they must struggle against a persistent strain of skepticism that argues that knowledge of the sort advocated by philosophers is simply not attainable by human beings, thereby calling into question the whole enterprise of philosophy. This double struggle produces an odd tension, especially evident in the works of Aristotle, between philosophy as an encyclopedic, almost comprehensive ordering of the information gathered by other types of inquiry, and philosophy as a mode of abstraction so carefully circumscribed and so far removed from everyday reality as to seem a type of mathematics, and therefore impervious to skeptical critique.

The contours of debate within the later philosophical tradition are to some extent determined by the pre-Socratics, even though they would not have regarded themselves as professional philosophers. Thales, according to one anecdote, demonstrated the potential usefulness of his theoretical knowledge of weather signs when he made a killing on olive presses as a result of his ability to anticipate an unusually large harvest. Heraclitus suggests that men who aspire to wisdom (*philosophoi andres*) are quite naturally inquirers (*histores*). Parmenides' goddess, in contrast, clearly differentiates between "the unshaken heart of persuasive Truth" and "the opinions of mortals, in which there is no true reliance," even as she proclaims that it is right for the initiate to learn both.[72] Her introduction of a distinction between atemporal Being and unstable Becoming implies and is implied by a contrast between knowing the truth and holding opinions.

With Plato the emphasis in the (English) expression "knowing the truth" will shift from truth as object of knowing, to knowledge as possession of the knower. Key elements of Plato's epistemological project are evident already in the early dialogue *Euthyphro*, in which Socrates confronts Euthyphro over his decision to prosecute his own father for murder of a laborer. Euthyphro is made to seem befuddled as he fails to respond adequately to Socrates' insistence that he provide a clear definition that grasps the unchanging essence of piety or holiness, namely, shows that he *knows* what piety is. Euthyphro is never given the chance to make the argument that what matters is his knowledge of the right way to act in present circumstances and his awareness of the likely *social* consequence of a failure to do so, namely, that a murderer will go free. By becoming entangled in Socrates' attempt to define knowledge in abstract intellectual terms, he inadvertently participates in the larger project of privileging philosophical inquiry over other sources of wisdom, that is, of operating successfully in the world. (No wonder he parts company with Socrates at the end of the dialogue.)

Plato's epistemology entails postulating not just distinct objects of knowing (specifically the Forms), of intellection (intelligibles, or *noêta*), and of perception (perceptibles or *orata*, *aisthêta*), but also distinct processes of cognition associated with them and distinct categories of cognizing subjects. He supplies a vocabulary that crystallizes his distinctions and allows them to shape subsequent philosophical discourse, often uninterrogated. Thus in *Republic* book seven we are invited to distinguish among knowledge or science (*epistêmê*), understanding (*dianoia*), belief (*pistis*), and imagination (*eikasia*), with the first two jointly designated as intellection (*noêsis*), and the latter two as opinion (*doxa*).[73] Ultimately it is philosophers—and only philosophers—who can acquire knowledge, which is understood as direct presence to the known entity, without intermediary representations, the way sight is taken to be a direct encounter with the object seen.[74] In an apparent repudiation of Heraclitus' description of philosophical men as investigators or witnesses[75] and of Pythagoras' likening of philosophers to observers at a festival, Plato specifically differentiates philosophers, in their quest for true knowledge, from "lovers of sights and sounds." In so writing, Plato endowed the term *philosophos* with a new valence, one that ultimately proved determinative. Uses of the term prior to Plato relate to information gathering and observation.

Although there is some disagreement over the matter, it seems clear that the *Republic*'s account of knowledge in relation to other types of cognition is generally confirmed by a subsequent dialogue, *Theatetus*, which is devoted to explaining what knowledge is not.[76] Socrates is presented as successfully refuting claims that secure knowledge can be obtained through perception and that true belief is itself a type of knowledge, while seemingly allowing for the possibility that knowledge might be true belief accompanied by an account or *logos*, provided the account is of the right sort. Sustaining the argument almost from the outset is the unexamined (in this dialogue) claim that wisdom (*sophia*) and knowledge (*epistêmê*) are the same thing.[77] Socrates also makes the strong claim that if Heraclitus' account of the flux of reality is correct, then "no assertion whatever can properly be made."[78] In effect, the dialogue reinforces the view presented in the *Republic*, and widespread in antiquity, that knowledge is of a different type of entity or essence than the entities understood or perceived by other modes of cognition. It is hard to tell which comes first, logically or historically: the assumption that there is a stable, timeless Being, which can only be known in a certain way; or the privileging of a certain type of cognition that, like that of the gods, grants access to past, present, and future.

In Aristotle, the distinction between different types of objects and, additionally, different types of cognition, is maintained, but with greater energy devoted to explaining, analyzing, and practicing forms of cognition other than pure intellection.[79] Aristotle writes respectfully of craft, or *tekhnê*, not so much the practical aspect of making things happen as the intellectual process of judgment (*hypolêpsis*): "Craft (*tekhnê*) occurs when there is judgement of the single universal arising from the many thoughts that come from the experience of things that are the same."[80] Indeed, his treatises lay the groundwork for investigation of a diverse range of what we would consider arts and sciences, including biology, physics, politics, ethics, and poetics. In each, there is great concern to define the topic of inquiry owing in part to a need for division of intellectual labor but also to the underlying principle that knowing (a broader category than Platonic *epistêmê* of the Forms) requires grasping the essential nature (*ti esti*) of an entity. Grasping the essence is the work of definition, which in turn provides the premises for demonstration.[81]

For Aristotle, who rejects Plato's theory of Forms, induction or abstraction from experience is the ultimate basis of productive knowledge. But once this process of induction leads to the formulation of mathematical principles, they become decisive criteria for evaluating and developing other sorts of claims about the natural world. Thus Aristotle rejects atomist physics on the grounds that it violates a principle of geometry (i.e., that lines are infinitely divisible); and argues that the cosmos has three and only three dimensions on the grounds that "magnitudes in general cannot be more than three-dimensional."[82] As to the source of mathematical principles themselves, Aristotle at times seems to imply that they are abstractions from physical reality that correspond to it in an exact way.[83] At other times, he claims that intellect (*nous*) "is separable, incapable of being affected, unmixed, and its essence is actuality."[84] This idealized intellect, namely, intellect separated from the body, is identical with the intelligibles it thinks: it seems to come always already equipped with this identity. Ordinary thinking involves accessing intellect and its self-identical intelligibles through images, thoughts, and arguments. Insofar as mathematical principles are the quintessential intelligibles, then it would seem that nous comes equipped with them. Induction is a means of gaining access to preexistent principles of deduction.

Philosophers working in the wake of Aristotle, especially Epicureans and Stoics, were unwilling to resort to appeals to disembodied intellect as a basis or explanation for the knowability of the world, especially in the face of persistent attacks on the part of Skeptics. The rejection of disembodied intellect is not surprising in that both Epicureans and Stoics adhere to a materialist physics: for the Epicureans nothing exists but atoms and void, for the Stoics the universe is a dynamic material continuum, "god" referring only to the energizing principle thereof. There is nothing of the Aristotelian eternal, supralunary realm in either school of thought. Knowing is a human capacity, and the possibility of knowledge arises from the composition of the material realm, including human bodies. Each school develops standards of knowledge, called *canon* by the Epicureans, *criterion* by the Stoics. For the Epicureans, there are three standards: sensation, preconception (*prolepsis*), and feeling. Thus we can test a claim by determining whether it is in accord with past sensations, both our own and those of others. We can also measure it against preconception, that is, "a generic notion of any type of object of experience, the concept naturally evoked by the name of that thing."[85] Sensation thus can tell us whether the man before us is Plato or not; preconception is what allows us to reject the claim that he is in fact a dog. Feeling is especially relevant to ethical claims, as might be expected of a philosophical system that posits pleasure as the highest goal of human existence: the feeling of pleasure or pain associated with an activity can help us to know whether the activity ought to be pursued or not. With respect to sensation the Epicureans also develop an important principle of non-contestation that helps them to advance knowledge claims about entities not accessible to the senses. In a remarkable reversal of the Platonic-Aristotelian position that knowledge is only accessible to intellection, for the Epicureans certain claims can be accepted as true if, although not based on sensation per se, they follow from sensory experience and there is no further sensory basis for contesting them.

For the Stoics the criterion of truth is the so-called cognitive impression or *phantasia kataleptikê*. The Greek expression is more literally translated as the appearance that grasps—that is, a sense-presentation that both grasps the reality of its corresponding object and, if assented to by the perceiver, that is, if the perceiver aligns himself with it, allows him or her to grasp reality in turn.[86] The cognitive impression or grasping appearance was defined by Zeno, the earliest Stoic, as "an appearance that arises from what is and is stamped and impressed exactly in accordance with what is, of such a kind that it could not arise from what is not."[87] Knowledge, or *epistêmê*, is grasp or *katalêpsis* "made secure and firm and unchangeable by [counter]argument."[88] For the Stoics, the potential unreliability of *katalêpsis* has to do not with the ability or inability of the senses to grasp reality, but with the possibility that a given human being's assent to a grasping appearance may itself be changeable or weak—a failure that training in the withholding and granting of assent can counteract.

Stoic epistemology thus allows for the everyday grasp of reality, a capacity it regards as evidence of the underlying rationality or orderliness of a cosmos that gives entities the means necessary for flourishing in their environment, a process known as *oikeiôsis* in the case of humans. As Long and Sedley put it, "Throughout their history the Stoics did not budge from the thesis, first adumbrated by Zeno, that infallible knowledge of the world is possible, and that all normal human beings have a natural faculty to make secure discriminations between discoverable truths and falsehoods."[89] It is this adaptation of creature to context through the accumulation and systematization of cognitive impressions that constitutes *tekhnê*, which can be translated as art, or science, or skill, or expertise. In contrast, say, to Plato, with his strict distinction between *tekhnê* and *epistêmê*, in which the former is at best a manifestation of "true opinion," for the Stoics artistic knowledge is always valid as a means of flourishing in the world and, if held by the right kind of knower (i.e., one who is steadfast in his or her assents), can legitimately be deemed *epistêmê*. The Stoic concept of cognitive grasp, and of its systematization through art as a means of functioning in the world, comes closest of any of the ancient philosophical schools to the modern anthropological emphasis on the human quest for strategic information.[90] This also helps to explain why Stoicism, to a greater extent than other philosophical schools, became closely entwined with rhetoric, medicine, law, and artistic theory in antiquity and beyond.[91]

For Plotinus, who can be taken as the founder of the Neoplatonic movement that arose in later antiquity, knowledge is already present within the individual soul, which is itself an aspect of the universal soul.[92] Like Plato's remembering slave, the Plotinian knower accesses what he already knows; only when he has forgotten, "stupefied as the result of a disaster, and the victim of a Lethe calling for constant reminding," does he rely upon sense-impressions to grasp external reality.[93] Plotinus speaks of the process whereby the higher levels of reality supply the human soul with knowledge in terms of "illumination,"[94] a concept and metaphor put to great use by early Christian writers, such as Augustine of Hippo and several of the Greek fathers. As light is a necessary condition for the operation of vision, so, in their view, illumination enables the mind to have "direct acquaintance with intelligible objects."[95] Although such a process may seem far removed from the necessary quest for information to function in the world, Augustine presents it as a kind of psychological survival technique. "Unlike the perspectival and private realm of sense perception, illumination holds out the prospect of fulfilling the yearning to which Augustine's eudaimonism gives such prominence, the yearning to find a realm wherein we can overcome the vulnerability that besets us and the moral distance that divides us from one another."[96]

While most Greek fathers deny that a human being can ever know the essence of God (although knowledge that God exists and of the attributes of God is considered possible), they are generally rather optimistic about other types of human knowledge. For example Gregory of Nyssa, in an account reminiscent of Stoic *oikeiôsis*, celebrates the intellectual and sensory capacities that allow for the "perfection" of bodily life.[97] For Gregory of Nazianzen, humans' ability to develop productive knowledge of the natural world is an extension of animals' adaptive capacities to build nests, hives, and storehouses, and to attract mates with song and other displays.[98] For him the beauty of the natural world becomes not just evidence of divine providence but also an invitation to the exercise of human intelligence through scientific inquiry and artistic production. Unlike Plato and Aristotle, for whom knowledge can only be of stable, eternal objects, ancient Christian philosophers make room for the knowledge of nature by denying the knowability of the divine. They implicitly (and at times explicitly) adopt the Stoic criterion of the kataleptic impression and/or the rhetorical commitment to the possibility of certainty in worldly affairs. In the hands of such writers, the archaic anxiety over human limitations becomes a celebration of human possibility.[99]

Concurrent with their participation in traditional philosophical inquiry, many late antique writers remain open to alternative, seemingly irrational ways of knowing. For writers such as Plotinus, Proclus, and Iamblichus, "certain 'non-rational' practices, such as oracular testimonies, theurgic rituals, erotic passion, poetic inspiration, metaphors, and myths, were reckoned as reliable as reasoned argument, or better still."[100] Although emerging Christian orthodoxy frowned on many such practices, theologians were of course committed to the "non-rational" authority of divine revelation and far from averse to reliance on myth, ritual, and metaphor. To some extent, the late antique return to a more expansive understanding of knowledge can be attributed to intensified interaction with non-Greco-Roman traditions, including Egyptian, Jewish, Mesopotamian, and Indian.[101] Yet it is equally true that the mainstream Greco-Roman philosophical tradition had never really lost interest in the wide range of strategies for acquiring reliable information that characterized ancient societies more generally, such as direct encounter, reliance on authority, compilation of an archive, and collective reasoning. Even instances of overt hostility to such procedures can be understood as implicit acknowledgment of their social force.

CONCLUSION

The range of knowledge practices surveyed in this chapter is of use for a richer understanding of the intellectual life of the ancient cultures that developed them. But they also provided resources that later generations could draw upon in their own quest for strategic information that would allow human beings to flourish in new and changing circumstances. Although scholars have sometimes sought to compress such diverse modes of knowing into a narrow account of the triumph of philosophical reason, ancient thinkers and their successors demonstrate remarkable and steadfast creativity in finding a variety of ways to cope with the uncertainties of existence.

FURTHER READING

[Editors' Note: The bibliography prepared by Habinek left out many works cited by author's last name in the notes but also included several items that were not cited in the fragmentary and provisional notes that he had prepared. As these seem clearly to have been items he was reading while writing the chapter, we list them here for interested readers.]

Brisson, Luc. "Myth and Knowledge." In *Greek Thought: A Guide to Classical Knowledge*, edited by Jacques Brunschwig and Geoffrey E. R. Lloyd, 39–50. Cambridge, MA: Harvard University Press, 2000.

Cooper, John M. "Plato, Isocrates, and Cicero on the Independence of Oratory from Philosophy." In *Knowledge, Nature, and the Good: Essays on Ancient Philosophy*, edited by John M. Cooper, 65–80. Princeton, NJ: Princeton University Press, 2009.

Detienne, Marcel, and Jean-Pierre Vernant. *Cunning Intelligence in Greek Culture and Society*. Translated by Janet Lloyd. Chicago: University of Chicago Press, 1991.

Dillon, John "The Question of Being." In *Greek Thought: A Guide to Classical Knowledge*, edited by Jacques Brunschwig and Geoffrey E. R. Lloyd, 51–71. Cambridge, MA: The Belknap Press of Harvard University Press, 2000.

Formisano, Marco, and Philip Van der Eijk, eds. *Knowledge, Text and Practice in Ancient Technical Writing*. Cambridge: Cambridge University Press, 2017.

König, Jason, and Tim Whitmarsh, eds. *Ordering Knowledge in the Roman Empire*. Cambridge: Cambridge University Press, 2007.

Lehoux, Daryn. *What Did the Romans Know? An Inquiry into Science and Worldmaking*. Chicago: University of Chicago Press, 2012.

Lloyd, G. E. R. *Methods and Problems in Greek Science*. Cambridge: Cambridge University Press, 1991.

Lloyd, G. E. R. *Cognitive Variations: Reflections on the Unity and Diversity of the Human Mind*. Oxford: Oxford University Press, 2007.

Rihll, T. E. "Introduction: Greek Science in Context." In *Science and Mathematics in Ancient Greek Culture*, edited by C. J. Tuplin and T. E. Rihll, 1–34. Oxford: Oxford University Press, 2002.

Silverman, Allan. "Plato's Middle Period Metaphysics and Epistemology." *The Stanford Encyclopedia of Philosophy*, edited by Edward N. Zalta. Fall 2014. https://plato.stanford.edu/archives/fall2014/entries/plato-metaphysics (accessed January 9, 2022).

Uzdavinys, Algis. "Animation of Statues in Ancient Civilizations and Neoplatonism." In *Late Antique Epistemology: Other Ways to Truth*, edited by Panayiota Vassilopoulou and Stephen R. L. Clark, 118–40. London: Palgrave Macmillan, 2009.

Wills, Bernard. "Ancient Skepticism and the *Contra Academicos* of St. Augustine." *Animus* 4 (1999): 108–23.

CHAPTER TWO

The Human Self

GIULIA SISSA

An *anthrôpos* is a living being. But what kind of life does he or she live?

A history of the definition of humanity would take us from Aristotle's political animal, whose *logos*, as opposed to mere *phônê*, makes possible the creation of a reasonable moral community, to the Stoic focalization on rationality, and to the increasingly unflattering characterizations of modern and contemporary philosophy. We are sinful creatures, for Christians; working agents, for Karl Marx; narrative neurotics, for Sigmund Freud; speaking subjects, for Jacques Lacan; self-transcending nothingness, for Jean-Paul Sartre; or self-interpreting beings-in-the-world, for Martin Heidegger. We might be tempted to emphasize the abysmal gap between antiquity and modernity, but we should rather take stock of a theoretical thread that runs through our philosophical anthropology.

We are the "children of Care," we exist as *caring* animals.[1] Care bears a double meaning. We care *for* others and ourselves, but at the same time, we care *about* things and people. Attention and apprehension, curiosity and concern go together. We are anxious beings. In its unobvious and yet crucial understanding of what it means to be human, the philosophy of existence that has emerged in the twentieth century resonates with archaic Greek poetry and Hellenistic philosophy. To be sure, from the very beginning, ancient cultures have tried to organize their worlds into taxonomies, and place humans in these encompassing classifications. From the narrative thinking we call "mythology" to medicine and philosophy, different domains of knowledge draw lines of demarcation between stones, plants, and nonhuman and human animals. Bodies and habits add specificity to the members of these groups. Human beings belong in a vast network of entities to which they relate in a variety of manners, such as worshipping the immortal gods, hunting, domesticating or eating other living beings, and moreover, distinguishing themselves in ethnic and social groups. We are taxonomic animals.

The anthropology of ancient societies has brought to light many fundamental ideas about the identity and difference of this particular kind of living beings—humans—from others. But the notion of a human *self* goes beyond descriptive arrangements of the cosmos. A more sensitive account of the experience of our being in the world is required. Humanity is lived consciously and felt emotionally. The Homeric characters who fight at Troy, or those who till the Hesiodic fields, are phenomenologically aware of their peculiar condition. This is not merely a private perception of one's unique vicissitudes. It is rather an insight into a common destiny, shared through cultural practices, such as work, marriage, sacrifice, sorrow, mourning, or poetic performances. The human self is an object of socialized anxiety.

It is this deep line of thought that I wish to bring to the fore in this chapter.

KÊDEA LYGRA

Humanity is not a given. In archaic poetry, Hesiod narrates how humans came into being. In one version, it was a disruptive event that made human beings properly human by bringing into the world the "baneful cares" (*kêdea lygra*) that would, henceforth, be men's constant companions.[2] This event is the fabrication of the first woman. The manufacturing of this new being is the result of a chain of actions and reactions. The god Prometheus tricked Zeus, who was his cousin and the father of the Olympians. While carving an ox, cunning Prometheus offered to Zeus only a bunch of bones concealed under layers of fat. Zeus grew frightfully angry and struck back, not by punishing the culprit of the prank, namely, Prometheus himself, but by confiscating fire from the mortal men who already dwelled on earth. In response, Prometheus attempted to retrieve that precious good, fire, on their behalf. He was successful. It was to retaliate once again not against Prometheus himself, but at the expense of the primeval males of whom Prometheus was the champion, that Zeus ultimately asked Hephaestus, Athena, Aphrodite, and Hermes to make a "beautiful evil" (*kalon kakon*).[3]

This narrative occurs both in *Theogony* and in *Works and Days*, but only the latter poem gives a proper name to the first human female. She is called "Pandora" (All-gifts, Hes., *WD* 81) (Figure 2.1). Pandora comes to life equipped with a huge jar, which she has been warned not to open. As it is to be expected in any mythological tale, a hero who receives an ominous prohibition cannot wait to disobey. Pandora opens the jar, and lets the contents spread out into the world. All of a sudden, "baneful cares" become the lot of humankind.

Temporality is all that matters: there was a time before the trick, during which generations of human beings had already been living on earth. They could, of course, only be all males, as the introduction of gender difference is a supplemental, catastrophic addition to a primeval human life. These uncomplicated early men were "free from ills and hard toil" (*ater kakôn kai ater chalepoio ponoio*), and free from the "troublesome sicknesses" (*nousôn t'argaleôn*) that the Keres give to men (*andrasi*).[4] But this was before Woman made her fatal gesture. With her hands she removes (*aphelusa*) the great lid of the jar and, instantaneously, everything that is undesirable—grueling effort, annoying illnesses, and old age—comes to life.[5] In misery (*en kakotêti*), mortals (*brotoi*) grow old quickly.[6] Pandora is not responsible for mortality itself. The *anthrôpoi, brotoi, andres* of the past were already exposed to death, which distinguished them from the everlasting Olympians. But Pandora makes their finitude into hardship. She arranges "baneful cares for men" (*anthrôpoisi d'emêsato kêdea lygra*),[7] thus bringing to fruition Zeus' vindictive design, for it is the father of the Olympian gods who had prepared those "baneful cares for men" in the first place.[8]

In *Works and Days*, Hesiod also offers an alternative version of the genesis of humanity, even more focalized upon decline and deterioration. The point of this new storyline is that divine and human individuals belong to one *genos*. Originally, they lived very similar lives. The gods themselves had created a first generation of human beings (*anthrôpoi*), made up of gold. They lived like gods, and this divine way of life consisted of "being apart from toil and hardship" (*nosphin ater te ponou kai oizyos*) for they "lived with a carefree spirit" (*ezôon akêdea thymon echontes*).[9] They did not grow old, but with their feet and hands they could dance incessantly, "away from all ills" (*kakôn ektosthen hapantôn*).[10] When they died, it was as though they were falling asleep. "They had all good things," for the earth produced abundant food for them, out of an unprompted drive (*automatê*).[11] Being voluntarily tranquil (*ethelêmoi hêsychoi*), they distributed tasks

FIGURE 2.1 Giulio Romano, *Pandora*, painting, sixteenth century. Galleria Nazionale d'Arte Antica di Palazzo Barberini, Rome. © DeAgostini / Getty Images.

"among many good cities" (*esthloisin poleessin*).[12] They were "rich in flocks" and dear to the gods.[13] But suddenly, this godlike, serene, idle, light-hearted, pastoral generation of men are terminated by a decision of the gods. The golden ancestors of humankind become its "guardians." Four other races follow on earth, each made of increasingly less-precious metals: silver, bronze, and finally iron. Between bronze and iron, however, Hesiod inserts a fourth generation, that of the heroes who fought at Troy and Thebes, at the time of Agamemnon and Oedipus.[14] In Hesiod's mythological history, the present breed of human beings is the worst of all.

Both these variations of an anthropogonic narrative revolve around "care." In Pandora's story, the plural word *kêdea*, qualified as *lygra*, "baneful," synthetizes the variety of ills that weigh upon a fallen humanity: firstly, our vulnerability to sickness and painful death, and secondly, the inevitability of labor and fatigue (*ponos*) for, after Pandora's mindless deed, men have to work hard to survive. Farming replaces the spontaneous generation of nutritious vegetables. More generally, the bundle of "baneful cares" that Woman has brought about determines men's submission to a regime of "bad things" (*kaka*) and "badness" (*kakotês*). All that was good is gone. But this badness, let me insist, is filled with arduousness. All that was easy is also gone. Men are left with the need to conquer at a high cost everything they need and may desire—foodstuff and sustenance in the first place. Agriculture, marriage, the responsibility of a family: all this is Pandora's legacy. Men cannot live in peace and idleness, indifferent to what has to be done. They have to make a constant effort, just to stay alive. They have to take care of themselves. *Kêdos* (the singular form of *kêdea*) is the most distinctive feature of humankind, the very condition of its existence.

MODIFICATIONS OF CARE

In Hesiod's *logos* about the metallic generations, these same ideas resurface, but reassembled in a different storyline. Since the focus is on the common origin and, therefore, the initial alikeness of Immortals and Mortals, great emphasis is placed on this blissful condition. Once again, it is a mode of existence unscathed by *kêdos*. The golden humans "lived like gods having a carefree spirit" (*hôste theoi d'ezôon akêdea thymon echontes*), free from "toil and hardship" (*ponou kai oizyos*).[15] They danced, remaining forever young, until death came to them under the anesthesia of sleep. They did not have to work at all for edible goods grew, once again, by spontaneous generation, ready to be effortlessly collected.[16] They enjoyed a lifestyle that was the exact opposite of what men endure in the agrarian world of *Works and Days*, where heavy-duty, labor-intensive, hazardous farming is now in order. The present time of the poem is diametrically different from that original past, for a carefree humanity has yielded to one that lives in a time of never-ending cares. Not for a single day can men escape fatigue and hardship (*pausontai kamatou kai oizyos*).[17] The gods now provide them with nothing but "hard cares" (*chalepas* [...] *merimnas*).[18] Like *kêdos*, *merimna* means "care," understood in the double meaning of occupation and *preoccupation*. Now, the end of this anthropogonic tale is a perfect reversal of its beginning: restless, anguished work instead of the enjoyment of an automatically produced livelihood. In between, however, the human condition undergoes a complicated transformation. At every single step, the deterioration of human life is a matter of how individuals engage with the world, either earnestly or inattentively. From gold to iron, from bliss to anxious fatigue, they experience different forms of care, either defective or excessive.

The humans of the silver generation lived in a permanent state of childhood. These infantile men failed to attend to anything, not even to the cult due to the Olympians.[19] To describe this kind of dutiful concern, Hesiod uses the verb *therapeuein*. From a condition of semidivine nonchalance, mankind slips into one of complete negligence. A careless, inconsiderate humanity replaces one that was light-heartedly unworried. This form of disregard is deeply offensive to the gods. For this crime, Zeus brings the silver race to an end. In their place he makes a race of bronze, which has yet another problem with care. Instead of being utterly neglectful, they are obsessed with one preoccupation: warfare.[20]

The verb used to denote these men's incessant activity is *melô*, which also belongs to the semantic field of care. Bronze human beings concern themselves only with quarrels, battles, and reciprocal violence. But such a destructive lifestyle can only come to an end: these individuals fight each other until they are all exterminated. Then comes the race of heroes, the half-gods (*hêmitheoi*) who take part in the wars at Troy and Thebes, where they fall on the battlefield.[21] Some of them, after death, have settled on the Islands of the Blessed, where they now enjoy perfect happiness. Their souls are no longer burdened by any care whatsoever. In their afterlife, the poet tells us, these noble warriors become as untroubled as the men of the golden race. Like them, they are now endowed "with a carefree spirit" (*akêdea thymon echontes*).[22] There the story ends in the present time, with the race of iron. Now, as we have said, everything is toil, trouble, and "hard cares" (*chalepas* […] *merimnas*).[23] At this point the poem offers an even more pessimistic prediction for the future. Not a single divinity will remain on earth, not even *Aidôs* (Respect) or *Nemesis* (Indignation). Human beings will be left entirely alone, at the mercy of "baneful sufferings" (*algea lygra*).[24] This unhappy ending rejoins that of Pandora's story, with the spreading of *kêdea lygra*, according to Zeus' plan.[25]

The vicissitudes of our being in the world take us from an obsolete, idealized, optimal bliss to multiple modifications of care that include the extreme unconcern of the silver race, and the wrong kind of concern, typical of the bronze and iron generations. The

FIGURE 2.2 Andrea Mantegna, *Minerva Expelling the Vices from the Garden of Virtue*, painting, *c.* 1500–1502, Louvre, Paris. © Fine Art Images / Heritage Images / Getty Images.

thematic coherence transpires in the vocabulary of *kêdos*, *akêdês*, *therapeia*, *epimeleia*, *melein*, *meletê*, *ponos*, *merimna*.

This language structures the narrative. Care comes across as the touchstone of human life, whichever form it may take. The good life hinges on it, both in its materiality and its felt experience. Care may well be good and productive, but it implies unease. For the golden race, earth's artless gift of food created an absolute certainty about one's ability to remain alive. The blooming and ripening of nutritious plants was not only automatic and, therefore, guaranteed but also overabundant. There was neither lack nor *fear* of lack. Now, on the contrary, a man has laboriously to make a living, day after day, without ever knowing whether there will be enough to eat for himself and his family. Humans can no longer count on the spontaneous cooperation of nature for their survival. Not only do they have to extract food from the soil, but their very environment has itself become hostile. What happens tends to be obnoxious. A destructive automaticity has replaced the bountiful spontaneity of the origins. Whereas, for the golden men, the earth used to generate fruits all by herself (*automatê*), after Pandora, it is every kind of sickness that falls upon human beings, all by themselves (*automatoi*).[26]

In *Works and Days*, the narrator constantly urges his addressee, a farmer, to manage scarce supplies, preempt famine, strategize about tasks according to the seasons, and navigate the aleatory circumstances of the weather. Nature is a nightmare of draughts, storms, heat, cold, bugs, and drudgery.[27] Every single day, a peasant is liable to make a fatal mistake. Do's and don'ts fill the poem with notoriously prosaic lessons about the need to be careful, and the consequences of carelessness. Agriculture is a struggle. The farmer has to accumulate stuff and consume his stocks little by little to keep at bay "fiery hunger" (*aithopa limon*).[28] Whereas it is excellent to count on what one has in store, "to need what is not there is a calamity for your spirit" (*pêma de thymôi chrêizein apeontos*).[29] The good farmer has to measure what he should draw from the jars where he stows his food so that "what is there at home does not cause care to a man" (*oude to g'ein oikôi katakeimenon anera kêdei*).[30] "I bid you to ponder carefully the following!" (*ha se phrazesthai anôga*), the poet goes on to say.[31] There is a remedy to the apprehensive feeling of care: it is more care still, in the form of mindful solicitude. Whereas the simple awareness that time goes by causes fear of want, that trepidation can be converted into a prudent strategy of consumption. You must not put your tasks off until the following day. Labor is not enough: one needs to care about what one does, for "it is care that makes work successful" (*meletê de to ergon ophellei*).[32] In the possible—and very realistic— world of this epic, life is not merely exhausting. It is full of anxiety.

THE GIFT OF PLEASURE

This philosophy of existence is rooted in an economic perspective but is attentive to feelings and intentions. We have become living beings subjected to mortality, frailty, dearth, hunger, and hard work. This is what defines our being in the world. We are peasants, coping with the materiality of Earth, a power we experience not as a divine, supportive, generative, nurturing source of life, as it was the case in the *Theogony*, but as a tremendously unforgiving soil. Nature is no longer automatic. We, however, are also embodied, sentient, and thoughtful subjects. We live our own condition by apprehending the unknown, by worrying about tomorrow, and by constantly trying to master the natural world. Nature challenges us. We take up the challenge. Preoccupation becomes occupation. Like Marx, Hesiod sees a human being as a working animal. Like

Heidegger, Hesiod also recognizes that a human being is a "child of care." Hesiod's poetic anthropology understands the human engagement with the ecosphere both as a mode of production and as an experience. It is, furthermore, a twofold experience: we suffer what worryingly concerns us, and we feel solicitously concerned *for* that. We *are in trouble* and we *take the trouble*.

In this anthropology, the taxonomic specificity of a human life is at stake. Not all living beings have to be "careful." Within Zeus' design, Pandora's "baneful cares" (*kêdea lygra*) are destined for the *anthrôpoi*.[33] The Immortals, in contrast, are endowed "with a carefree spirit" (*akêdea thymon echontes*).[34] This is precisely the similarity between the Olympians and the blithe humans of the golden race, or the heroes surviving in the Islands of the Blessed. But in this same universe there are also divine figures whose carefree character is uniquely significant: the Muses (Figure 2.3).

The Muses too are endowed "with a carefree spirit" (*akêdea thymon echousais*).[35] Unlike other deities, however, the Muses are not simply immune from care; they are also capable of altering the human experience of care. The arts, and sung epic poetry in particular, enchant, charm, and seduce us (*terpousi*).[36] Through fiction, the Muses give pleasure, and a very particular kind of pleasure: "a forgetfulness of ills and a rest from cares" (*lêsmosynên te kakôn ampauma te mermêraôn*).[37] The voice flowing from their mouths, and from that of their "servants," the poets, is so sweet (*glykerê*) that if a man suffers in his "newly-troubled spirit" (*neokêdei thymôi*) and if he "groans being distressed in his heart" (*azêtai kradiên akachêmenos*), by merely listening to the performance of a poem, he will remember nothing at all of his cares (*oude ti kêdeôn memnêtai*).[38] These goddesses offer gifts (*dôra*) to human beings, which distract them—if only temporarily—from all those woes.[39]

Archaic poetry represents a society in which the aesthetic experience is pervasive. There is a profound reason for this fact. Since *kêdea* are essential to being human, and since the Muses deliver men from those cares (*kêdea*), nothing can be more fundamental than the seemingly superfluous enjoyment of the Muses' gifts. Music relieves the defining feature of humanity. The therapeutic power of musical performance alleviates nothing less than the human condition.

Let us unravel these semantic connections. To feel with a "newly-troubled spirit" one has to remember. Memory is not merely the cognitive awareness of the past but also our affective experience of it. Music buffers the disturbing and provoking effects of an event. The Muses do not bring fun or excitement to their audience, therefore, but trigger a pleasure negatively defined: the pure and simple fact of not worrying about what would normally cause pain. More to the point, the Muses disable our preparedness to do something in response to what has happened. Death itself is an appropriate example. One of the specific meanings of *kêdos* is "mourning." To pay respect to a dead body is quintessentially "care." There is a perfect consistency between the personal character of the Muses—their being "endowed with a carefree spirit" (*akêdea thymon echousais*)—and the influence of their songs upon the spectators: being themselves carefree and careless, they make you, albeit for a brief period of time, exactly like them.[40] They infect you with their own ataraxy. Thanks to music, *kêdos* simply ceases to be felt. The event is still there but does not matter in the least.

In the narrative thinking of archaic poetry, pleasure is the antidote to care.[41] The Muses do nothing less than obliterate the innumerable manifestations of the baneful cares (*kêdea lygra*) that plague humanity. Their "gifts" (*dôra*) are the exact opposite of "all the gifts" that the gods offer to the first Woman, aptly named Pan-*dôra*. Those *dôra* are "a calamity

FIGURE 2.3 Gustave Moreau, *Hesiod and the Muses*, painting, 1860, Musée Gustave Moreau, Paris. © Christophel Fine Art / Universal Images Group via Getty Images.

for the enterprising men" (*pêm' andrasin alphêstêisin*).[42] Pandora receives enchanting grace from Aphrodite, beguiling finery from Athena, sparkling jewelry from Persuasion and the Graces, and a crown of flowers from the *Hôrai*. Hermes adds a deceiving mind and fallacious speech. Pandora is the embodiment of untruth. She promises delight but, ultimately, disseminates troubles. She is a "beautiful evil."[43] Her erotic attractiveness is especially significant, as it is meant to provoke a longing desire that is "troubling" (*pothon argaleon*) and to cause "cares that devour the limbs" (*gyioborus meledônas*).[44] *Meledônê*, a word akin to *meletê* and *epimeleia*, belongs to the semantic area of "care." Pandora's overall sensuality announces just that: cares. It is the forebear of the opening of the jar, and the propagation of *kêdea lygra*. In contrast, the honeyed voice of the Muses neutralizes all these troubles. The Muses counteract Pandora. Fiction is the true pleasure that remedies the false one. Fiction relieves the human self.

There is more to this poetic anthropology. The anesthetic effect of the Muses extends to the very content of their songs. The Muses know the present, the past, and the future. They chant "the glories of the first human beings and the blissful gods who have Olympus" (*kleia proterôn anthrôpôn hymnêsei makaras te theous hoi Olympon echousin*).[45] They celebrate a heroic humankind, in tales of prowess, war, passion, violence, carnage, and death. Epic poetry is far from rosy. *Kleos* is won with difficulty, at the price of risk, self-sacrifice, and immense suffering. Think of the *Iliad*! And yet the Muses make their audience immune from the very pain the poets themselves sing about. The feelings of fictional creatures do not bleed onto the listeners. Pity, as a sorrow that would mimic the characters' own sorrows, is not the expected response to poetry. Once again, far from erasing the memory of the deeds of those grand, remote, illustrious humans and of the terrible things that happened to them, the Muses reveal precisely those acts and those events, but in doing so, they disable any sympathetic, anguished response. Once again, they cure care.

This is counterintuitive. Precisely when a contagious transmission of grief might be expected (think of Plato), or when an apprehensive, empathetic response might be in order (think of Aristotle), Hesiod's Muses fail to transfer the heroes' suffering to their audience. On the contrary, they preempt the very possibility of our sympathy for those *anthrôpoi*. There is no pity. Now, this pitiless enjoyment of other people's pain complicates our understanding of archaic poetics. The song has the power to "deflect" the mind[46] and gives aesthetic pleasure on account of two features: it sings what other people went through and it does so "vividly." As Andrew Ford has argued, "the audience is interested in epic song not because it happened but because it happened to others. The delight in the tale is not the satisfaction of accuracy or the communication of some higher truth but the pleasurableness of a convincingly full picture."[47] All this is true: epic song is indeed pleasurable as it discloses to the audience what "happened to others," thus turning away its listeners from what may have happened to them. But there is more to this distraction. Songs are not merely vivid: they sound "sweet" (*glykerê*).[48] This emphatic characterization of the Muses' voice as *glykerê*, a quality that we should understand as a synesthetic metaphor—the perception of musical poetry being blended with that of succulent, flavorsome, honey-tasting food—tells us how and why these goddesses give pleasure rather than pain or, more to the point, how they give pleasure instead of making us share the characters' misery. On the one hand, if we care for other human beings, then we will be profoundly concerned for them and will experience *kêdea* on their behalf. This is the meaning of Hesiod's hypothesis that a death may be felt with a "newly-troubled spirit" (*neokêdei thymôi*).[49] We will grieve the loss, and feel compelled to mourn the dead, which is a form of *kêdos*. But, on the other hand, the Muses reenact other people's troubles in such a dulcet, soothing, singing voice that the performance itself forestalls our empathetically worried response. Fictional troubles do not trouble us. We could not care less. We not only cease to feel with a "newly-troubled spirit" what we may have suffered in person but also are unable to feel for the woes of others. We are both carefree and careless. This is the specific effect of the Muses whose defining feature is, precisely, to have a "carefree spirit." Thanks to them, we too become momentarily unconcerned for the very pain that the poems describe. Musical sweetness, therefore, sweetens the upsetting content of poetry. It blunts the feelings that, should we care for the characters, we might share with trepidation. The aesthetic experience is paradoxically anesthetic. To take pleasure is to savor the pure delight of not taking care.[50]

ODYSSEUS *KÊDOMENOS*

Hesiod echoes the *Odyssey*.

Odysseus' sojourn in Scheria, among the Phaeacians, is a very long period of rest, conviviality, and remembrance, which spans seven books.[51] In this pivotal episode, the poem offers a dramatic, and autobiographic, meditation on the human self. Odysseus emphatically casts himself as a man, not a god.[52] On his arrival, confronted with king Alcinous, who believes him to be a deity in disguise, he claims that this is absolutely not the case. He is not in any way similar to the Immortals who own the wide sky! On the contrary, he is a mortal who has suffered innumerable pains (*en algesi*) and many ills (*kaka*).[53] Were he to say who he truly was, this is the tale (*mythos*) he would have to tell. This is the story of his life. More to the point, he calls himself "*kêdomenos*," literally "someone who cares."[54] Later, when talking to Arete, the queen of the Phaeacians, he repeats that to recount his biography from beginning to end would amount to reciting the countless *kêdea* that the gods have allotted to him.[55] These gloomy words resonate with Athena's reminder of Odysseus' situation when he dwelled in Ogygia, at the mercy of Poseidon, at the beginning of the poem. The man, Athena had told Zeus and the other Olympians, was living through many *kêdea*.[56] Now, in Arete's and Alcinous's royal palace, Odysseus starts his tale right away, with the wreckage that brought him to the island Ogygia, where Calypso tried to retain him forever, against his stubborn intent to go home to his wife. And Odysseus recounts the other multiple "baneful cares" (*kêdea lygra*) he has been going through with his companions.[57] Odysseus' cares include the misfortunes inflicted by the gods, namely, Poseidon, but also his own unwavering resolve to stick to his plan: he must return, this is all that matters to him. He cares for his future. He cares about his past. Odysseus' existence is made up of nothing but *kêdea lygra*. He has nothing else to say for himself. The *Odyssey* is all about *kêdea*.

Now, Odysseus' long tale to the Phaeacian royals includes his descent into the realm of Hades, where he encounters the dead heroes and heroines from the Trojan past. In Hades, Odysseus empathizes both with the warriors who have lost their lives on the battlefield and with their women. While listening to the account of Agamemnon's pitiful death at the hands of Clytemnestra, Odysseus cries together with him.[58] He can easily relate to the tragic end of a husband returning home to an unfaithful wife. But now, at the court of Arete and Alcinous, when he describes in detail all those moments of compassionate concern, the Phaeacian listeners feel only enchantment: "So he spoke, and they were all hushed in silence, and were held spellbound [*kêlêthmôi*] throughout the shadowy halls."[59] Odysseus admits to his own pity. But pity is not contagious. We might surmise that poetry does what Hesiod says: impairing the ability to feel other people's pain. But Homeric poetics are subtler.

There is an epic poet in the palace, Demodocos. Prompted by the king, he starts to chant the glories of men of old. Of all the stories he could choose, of all the characters he could portray, he has to pick one particular scene: a quarrel between Achilles and Odysseus.[60] Once again, the Phaeacians take pleasure (*terpsis*), but Odysseus does not. While listening to a chapter of his own biography, Odysseus breaks into tears (Figure 2.4).[61]

FIGURE 2.4 Odysseus weeps at the song of Demodocus. Illustration after *The Odyssey Of Homer Engraved By Thomas Piroli From The Compositions Of John Flaxman Sculptor Rome 1793.* © Culture Club / Getty Images.

Alcinous is still unaware of his guest's identity, but realizes that the song makes him unhappy. He tries to find a way to lift his spirit. Let all compete in athletic tournaments and cheerful dances! Odysseus is reluctant to participate. His *kêdea*, now rehearsed in Demodocos' song, are too present.[62] He cannot let go. Only after the games, when the minstrel goes on to sing the loves of Ares and Aphrodite, a story in which the Olympians themselves laugh at Hephaestus' attempt to punish his wife and her lover. Like the gods in the song, Odysseus now rejoices in his heart.[63] For a moment, he allows himself to be distracted. But only for a brief moment. At Odysseus' own request, Demodocos reverts to a serious story: the trick of the wooden horse and the conquest of Troy.[64] Rather than enjoying himself at more cruel laughter, Odysseus chooses to reactivate his own suffering. This detail is revealing. Odysseus wants to hear Demodocos sing not any old story, but the account of his own most memorable feat. He wants to go back to himself, to his most authentic self—that of the warrior who puts himself in extreme danger, for his own life and that of his companions. That was care. Now he is overwhelmed by as irresistible a grief as the tumultuous sobbing of a wife clinging to the body of her dead husband. This is care. Once again, he faces himself alone. The other guests take pleasure in the song (*terpsis*).[65]

From this sequence of performances, we reckon that poetry (sung by a poet or a narrator) may well act as an anesthetic for a detached audience, but not at all for an individual who has undergone in person the very vicissitudes described in the poem. The aesthetic experience is not an automatic response to the sweet voice of the Muses, but a reflective awareness of one's own concerns. The same narrative may trigger empathy for someone who feels anxiously concerned while causing mere amusement for those who have no reasons to care. Whereas Odysseus may well relish the comedic adultery of Ares and Aphrodite, with no pity for Hephaestus' humiliation, he sheds tears for Agamemnon's tragic death at the hands of his wife and her lover. A denouement that could potentially be also his own is not funny in the least. In the same logic, Odysseus cries about himself at Troy. He cannot possibly forget his own *kêdea*, be they past, present, or plausible. He deliberately asks to be reminded of them. This is why Odysseus' insistence that he is a human being, and not a god, is so significant. He is a paradigmatically *kêdomenos* man, a mortal whose interactions with others and whose conscience of himself depend entirely on his *kêdea*. This is also why, in this long episode, the poem is so focalized on songs, storytelling, and fictions. It is not a matter of metaliterary indulgence. Since the Muses have the power to disable the pressure of memory, the urgency of mourning, and the mindfulness of agency, situations of musical pleasure test the persistency of Odysseus' care—his care of himself as the man who never forgets his experiences and his resolve to accomplish his consuming project. He passes the test.

As he has resisted the enchanting voice of the Sirens, the seductive entreaties of Calypso, or the fare of the Lotus-eaters, so Odysseus remains impervious to the charm of the Muses. As he endeavors to sail back home against the odds of his tormented journey, so he tries not to lose the thread of the memory of himself, notwithstanding Alcinous' attempts to sidetrack him. Those particular troubles—his part in the Trojan War— matter so much to him that he cannot remain apathetic, let alone enjoy the performance. However dulcet the voice of the poet, Demodocos' sung version of his life could not possibly be "music" to his ears.

Unlike Hesiod's poems, the Homeric poems do not offer an etiological account of how care came to shape the human condition. Nevertheless, the vocabulary of *kêdos* and *kêdesthai* is massively present in the *Iliad* and the *Odyssey*. The Mortals are affected by *kêdesthai*, whenever they feel the obligation to do something for others, and on their behalf. Family solidarity, friendship, and mourning are the typical situations in which one accepts *kêdos*.[66] Odysseus is affected by *kêdos*. Odysseus is engaged in *kêdos*. Odysseus returns to *kêdos*. From the beginning to the end of the poem, he impersonates the many nuances of care. He is curious, attentive, resourceful. He is also concerned for his comrades, his wife, his son, his father, his servants, and his dog. He is, furthermore, deliberately aware of his own unforgettable woes. He is a champion of the "baneful cares" (*kêdea lygra*) he keeps reciting and against which, for him, there is no remedy.

CARE OF THE *POLIS*

The human self exists in time as a constant experience of care. The Muses can act through a contagious anesthesia. This distraction can happen in Hesiod's poems, but not necessarily in the *Odyssey*. Odysseus is a man who goes through life with a "newly-troubled spirit" (*neokêdei thymôi*), as Hesiod would say.[67] He is a man who never stops rehearsing his own *kêdea* and who even insists that Demodocos should sing precisely those *kêdea*. Poetry refreshes his mindfulness of the past. Song is not about what happened to others, but to himself.

This conception of selfhood resurfaces in the political philosophy of the classical period. Plato places care at the heart of the narrative accounts of civilization. In the *Statesman*, Socrates defines the art of governing as a form of care and concern (*epimeleia*). We call *politikê* the *technê* that is concerned with, and thus cares for, the *polis*. Government is "the common care/concern of creatures in herds" (*tên de koinêi tôn en tais agelais thremmatôn epimeleian*).[68] Monarchy is the care/concern of the entire human community (*epimeleia de ge anthrôpinês sympasês koinônias*).[69] This pastoral metaphor extends to all gregarious living beings. As a generic activity of tending to, protecting, and watching, *epimeleia* becomes "nurturing" (*trophê*). But when we speak about human beings, Socrates adds, we should specifically say "care" (*epimeleia*).[70] Human politics goes far beyond food. In conclusion: "should we declare that the man who has such an art and a care is the true king and statesman?" (*ton echonta au technên tautên kai epimeleian ontôs onta basilea kai politikon apophainômetha?*).[71] The answer is yes. Government is an art as well as a form of care and concern. In the *Laws*, the idiom of care / protection / watchfulness permeates the description of what government is, and what figures of authority do, especially the "Guardians of the laws" (*nomophylakes*).

But it is in the *Republic* that Plato organizes the project of his best city, Kallipolis, in view of an ultimate end, that of a community of citizens who "care (*kêdesthai*) for each other and the polis."[72] All should be bound together by this particular kind of interaction: a mutual concern that spreads to the city itself. The rulers, namely, the philosopher-kings and the warriors especially "care (*epimeleisthai*) for themselves and for the polis."[73] They are aptly called "Guardians" (*phylakes*). The Guardians exercise their mission in the best possible way, thus becoming even superlative guardians, *phylakikôtatoi*.[74] They look after the body politic like watchful dogs.[75] They are, literally, the "caregivers of the city" (*kêdemonas tês poleôs*).[76] They care for the belief that they should endeavor to do what is best for the *polis*, with "total, wholehearted eagerness" (*pasêi prothymiai*).[77] They care to care.

Plato plays with the semantic resources of the language of care to make clear that a primordial intentionality must orient the expertise required to rule a state. Care becomes a normative political value. Hesiod's poetry is not far away. To make the citizens of Kallipolis care for each other and for the *polis*, a "noble lie" is needed. They should be made to believe that their souls have all been fashioned in the earth, but in different metals. Golden souls make the kings; silver souls, the warriors; and bronze/iron, the producers. Socrates reworks the "metallic" anthropogony in *Works and Days*, in which, as we have seen, human degradation depends on how different races, from gold to iron, deal with care. The humans of the golden age become the guardians (*phylakes*) of humankind, and this is a kingly privilege.[78] In Kallipolis, the metallic races coexist. All these more or less precious human beings should cultivate proper concern for each other and for the city. This is the purpose of the myth itself. Politics is nothing but care. We will not be surprised that, in a world where care must be so highly valued, the aesthetic experience should become suspicious. The enjoyment of both tragedy and comedy is a pleasure (*hêdonê*). It is the "filling up" (*pimplêmi*) and the "pleasing" (*chairô*) of a part of the soul that strongly desires such pleasure.[79] As for Hesiod, so for Plato, pleasure threatens care: *hêdonê* has the power to wash away all form of dedication.[80] The sweet voice of Muses relieves the *kêdea lygra* of their listeners. Poetry transforms human beings into individuals who permanently indulge in weeping or laughing. We should also be attentive, however, to the fact that the political culture of democracy encourages as a matter of routine the earnest commitment to the public good that Plato attributes exclusively to his Kallipolis.[81]

AT THE HANDS OF CURA

A much later anthropogony is to be found among the myths that a Roman grammarian and mythographer, Caius Julius Hyginus (67 BCE–17 CE), collected in his *Fabulae*.[82] Hyginus makes of Cura herself—the very personification of care—the casual, absent-minded creator of what we call *homo*.[83]

Once upon a time, Cura crossed a river. She saw the mud (*cretosum lutum*) under the water, and thoughtfully (*cogitabunda*) took a handful of sludge, which she started to mold.[84] By giving shape to a lump of wet dirt, she manufactured (*fingere*) the first human being.[85] Seemingly uncertain as to what she had done, she started to wonder about her own creation. At that moment, Jupiter came by. Cura asked him to infuse this new object with spirit (*spiritus*), which the god readily accepted to do. But when Cura wanted to give her name to the artifact, Zeus objected. The two deities began to fight. Tellus (Earth) leaped into action and claimed that as it was she who had provided the material, it was she who had the right to give this new being her name. Finally, Saturn intervened and determined that the name had to be "Homo," a neologism derived from *humus* (mud). The three powers involved in the craftmanship would be rewarded. Tellus was to receive Homo's dead body, whereas Jupiter would recover the soul. Cura, who had fashioned this new thing in the first place, was allowed to hold fast (*possideat*) to Homo as long as it lived.[86] During our time in this world, therefore, we are at the hands of Cura. We are the humble creatures of Care.

One of Seneca's *Epistles to Lucilius* reiterates the same claim about our allegiance to Cura, but in different language.[87] Whereas the perfection of god is achieved by nature, Seneca argues, it is *cura* that brings to fruition (*perficit*) the Good (*bonum*) of human beings.[88] Only thanks to *cura* we realize our potential, thus becoming the best we can be. Our very specificity as humans is a matter of perfectionism. This is a normative meditation on our being in the world. Seneca's argument starts from the premise that the Good is the free and complete use of reason. The Good "is a free mind, an upright mind, subjecting other things to itself and itself to nothing" (*liber animus, erectus, alia subiciens sibi, se nulli*).[89] But this is not a given, quite the contrary: we strive toward this full rationality, in a dynamic tension that elevates us above irrational animals, and places us on a level with God. More precisely, our Good is a clear and pure mind, "which emulates a god and raises far above human things" (*aemulator dei, super humana se extollens*).[90] Humanity, therefore, is a sort of asymptotic ambition to come closer to divinity. We are meant to soar.

Cura, according to Seneca, is not any form of existential anguish that holds on to us as long as we live, as it is the case in Homer's and Hesiod's poems and in Hyginus' fable. It is rather a kind of aspirational anxiety: the eagerness to transcend the less rational aspects of our being in the world, namely, the sensory and emotional experience we share with nonhuman animals and plants. Paradoxically, we fulfill the promises of humanity by actually going *beyond* humanity. Through *cura* we can divinize ourselves, so to speak, as we endeavor to attain the quality that a god enjoys by nature. *Cura* is anxious perfectibility.

ANXIETY IS THERE

This poetic anthropology has become highly influential in the philosophy of the twentieth century. In *Being and Time*, Martin Heidegger quotes and comments both Hyginus' *fabula* and Seneca's *Epistle* in a crucial chapter: "Confirmation of the Existential Interpretation of Dasein as Care in terms of Dasein's Pre-ontological Way of Interpreting Itself." Here, Heidegger sets out his theory of *Dasein* (Being there), as the "Being-in-the-World" that is proper to humanity.[91] A human being can be studied as a type of living creature, endowed with specific qualities, within a larger taxonomy. This is how the natural and social sciences operate. But *being human* should be understood, philosophically, as a particular way of being in the world. The former approach to the human is "ontic," for it takes for granted the simple fact that there exist entities (*ta onta*) to be distinguished and described; the latter is "ontological," for it questions the very possibility of being there, that is, of existing. Why is there such a phenomenon as "being," rather than not? This is the foundational question of philosophy. Humans ask this question about themselves all the time, although they may not formulate it in explicit terms.

Two aspects of this question are crucial: uncertainty and timeliness. Firstly, humans are "thrown" into the world and experience their "thrownness" with an anxiety (*Angst*) that takes all sorts of forms such as daring projects, a busy daily life, *divertissement*, addiction, or sheer existential anguish. However we may live, we are always dealing with the contingency of our being (as opposed to not being at all), in ways that we have to figure out. Our being is an issue for us. We are troubled, self-interpreting animals. Secondly, the being of humans is situated *there* (*Da-sein*) in the world, in unchosen circumstances— which means that, whatever we do, we are always, already, somehow engaged in our environment. But this engagement in the world is also always an experience of time. Now, for Heidegger, all this—our anxiety and our awareness of time—bears a name: *Sorge* (Care). *Die Sorge* is the inescapable attitude toward ourselves and the world, one that we may want to deny or willingly accept to recognize, try to flee or own up to. In any case, she is there. A condition of possibility for any form of being in the world, Care is "a state of Being which is already underlying in every case. ... The existential condition for the possibility of 'the cares of life' and 'devotedness', must be conceived as care, in a sense which is primordial [*ursprünglich*]—that is ontological."[92] In Hyginus' story, Cura is responsible for the coming into existence of human beings. She holds on to us as long as we live. "This pre-ontological document" delivers a profound truth: "*Cura prima finxit*" means that, as a new entity, *homo* "has the 'source' of its Being" in care.[93] "*Cura teneat, quamdiu vixerit*" means that "the entity is not released from this source but is held fast, dominated by it through and through as long as this entity 'is in the world.'"[94] Whatever we do, *die Sorge* never lets us go. Care is the key to Heidegger's existential/ontological interpretation of being human.

Heidegger derives his insight from the most canonical German literature of the eighteenth century. Goethe's *Faust*, a landmark philosophical play about the illusion of escaping the human situation, ends with the triumph of care, namely *die Sorge*.[95] But even more deeply, Heidegger harks back to classical antiquity.[96] It is in this remote past that emerges a conceptualization of being human, which is not merely ontic, but pre-ontological. The ancients had already understood that our being in the world is always an experience of care.[97] We can only *exist* as care.

Heidegger builds his deep genealogy of Care upon an article by Konrad Burdach, "Faust und die Sorge."[98] Burdach argues that the meaning of Goethe's *Faust* hinges on the final scene of the play. Four eerie ghosts come to haunt Faust in his palace. One of them is die Sorge. The man who has struck a covenant with Mephistopheles, in the hope of living immune from any trouble, discovers that, after all, Care has insinuated herself through the keyhole. Now, Sorge in person is there. "Do you recognize me?", she asks. Faust replies that he does not, therefore she introduces herself. She is Sorge! And nobody can possibly send her away, she explains, because she is at home in every single human house. Care is *there*, in her appropriate place.[99] She is there because she is everywhere, at all times endlessly taking on the most varied appearances. She is as ubiquitous as she is persistent. Human beings, Sorge reveals to Faust, cannot possibly be carefree. Our experience of time is intrinsically busy and apprehensive. Faust actually knew that already. As he acknowledges at the beginning of the play, in language reminiscent of the Hesiodic world,

> Care [Sorge] has nested in the heart's depths,
> Restless, she rocks there [*wiegt sie sich*], spoiling joy and rest [*Ruh*],
> There she works her secret pain,
> And wears new masks, ever and again,
> Appears as wife and child, fields and houses,
> As water, fire, or knife or poison:
> Still you tremble for what never strikes us,
> And must still cry for what has not yet gone.[100]

Goethe dramatizes the twofold nature of Care. When we take responsibility for "wife and child, fields and houses," we are mindful of the ends, the means, the efforts necessary to succeed, but also of the infinite accidents that may occur. We inevitably feel uneasy, worried, if not angst-ridden. Alertness and apprehension are inseparable. The very condition of a man (*das Menschenlos*), Faust knows only too well, is uncertain (*ungewisse*).[101] Hence Sorge's metamorphosis into "water, fire, or knife or poison." A child and a wife might die, a house can burn into ashes, and storms never cease to threaten the fields. No "rest" (*Ruh*) is to be hoped for. The temporality of our life oscillates between "trembling" for the future and feeling the painful memory of the past. There is no experience of the present, except in the form of care. Deep down in our heart, Sorge restlessly "rocks" (*wiegt sie sich*). Faust's discovery is that we may well try to avoid her, but to no avail. Sooner or later, she will catch up with us. When Faust refuses to recognize her, Sorge breathes on his face and makes him blind.[102] "Anxiety is there" (*Die Angst ist da*), echoes Heidegger, "It is only sleeping. Its breath [*Atem*] quivers perpetually through Dasein."[103] In *The Child of Care* (*Das Kind der Sorge*), a poetic remake of Hyginus' fable, Johann Gottfried Herder writes that Man (*der Mensch*), "in his life belongs to Care."[104]

Burdach places Hyginus and Seneca in the background of Herder and Goethe. Heidegger follows through, being ostensibly fascinated by their intuition that Cura is there, before any such thing as a human being ever comes into existence. Hyginus' narrative thinking is able to capture the historicity of being human: we have emerged out of nothing. It is she, Cura, who first makes *homo* exist of out the most insignificant stuff, mud, and then holds fast to it. Seneca acknowledges that it is *cura* and nothing else, who accomplishes our truly human—not divine, not natural—good.

In the wake of Heidegger, Michel Foucault, who in his latest works grew attentive to the Stoic turn of Hellenistic and Roman thought, placed the care of the self at the heart of moral philosophy in late antiquity.[105] While giving due importance to Seneca's theory of *cura*, Foucault misses two ideas that are essential to the history of care: the aspirational aspect of the care of the self, and the pervasiveness of an insight which already permeates archaic Greek poetry. The first point has been raised by Pierre Hadot.[106] As it appears in the *Epistle to Lucilius*, discussed above, human beings, by cultivating their reason, strive to rise above their mortal nature to surpass themselves. Their *cura* is not a concern with their bodily or worldly self. Both Foucault and Heidegger fail to see the Stoic, perfectionist effort to overcome human nature.[107] The second blind spot in Foucault's account of the care of the self is the much longer duration of this anthropological theme. In Hesiod's poetry, Pandora thoughtlessly lifts a lid and spreads the *kêdea lygra* that

FIGURE 2.5 Michelangelo (school), *The Dream of Human Life*, painting, after 1533. National Gallery, London. © Fine Art Images / Heritage Images/Getty Images.

were there, in a jar. She makes us what we are. A family, a household, and an economic activity require uneasy attention. The sense that human life is burdened by "baneful cares" resonates with Goethe's words about Sorge's "secret pain" and about her "new masks," from wife to child, from house to field. In Homeric poetry, Odysseus is the man who cares (*kêdomenos*), the man whose life is nothing but an uninterrupted sequel of *kêdea*, the man who may well indulge in a fleeting moment of solace, but then goes back to his own daring business, namely, the one project that truly matters to him: going back to the house, the wife, the child. Anxiety is not an accident or a pathology. "Nested in the heart's depth," it is primordial, relentless, and always ready to be converted into the drudgery, or the heroism, of daily life. Life is anxious. The human self is anxious. Anxiety is there.

CONCLUSION

Selfhood is experienced as concern. This is true in ancient cultures. If we make ourselves attuned to care, we can better read Homer with an eye to the theme of *kêdos/kêdesthai* as the grief, the distress, and the effort humans are bound to go through as they live in the world. We can read Hesiod's anthropology, a taxonomy that places us in comparison with the other beings that live in our ecosphere, but that also acknowledges our intentional and reflective self. The world is indeed an "object of care," even of "baneful cares" (*kêdea lygra*). Only intermittently, and thanks to the Muses, can we be distracted and relieved (*paratrepô*).[108] Only in this perspective can we fully understand that the purpose of aesthetic pleasure is not decorative, but existential: if care defines our human condition, by enjoying music we stop minding our own selves. Poetry does nothing less. Pleasure is nothing less. By interrupting the pressure of "baneful cares," the children of Memory make us forget that we are the children of Care. Following the same guiding question, we can read classical political theory and Hellenistic ethics.

Heidegger's focus on care as the quintessentially human Dasein, however, may prove misleading. Divine powers too feel *kêdos*. Contrary to the Epicurean definition of divinity as blissful, thus necessarily carefree, the goddesses and the gods of Greek and Roman polytheism busy themselves with innumerable cares.[109] At the beginning of the *Iliad*, Athena stops Achilles in his attempt to kill Agamemnon. It is Hera who sends her, because she loves this irascible hero and cares for him (*phileousa te kêdomenê te*).[110] This intervention sets in motion the action of the poem. In response to her child's sorrow, Thetis, "for all [her] concern, [has] an unforgotten grief in [her] heart" (*kêdomenê per, penthos alaston echousa meta phresin*).[111] It is her maternal solicitude (*kêdos*) for her son, Achilles, that makes the goddess suffer, and, as a further consequence, makes her want to protect him. Care is not the prerogative of human beings. The anthropomorphism of the gods culminates in their being in the world as subjects of care.[112] In the same logic, according to Seneca, *cura* may well distinguish mortals and immortals, but it also bridges the gap between them. Whereas both Hesiod's anthropogonies emphasize the disjunction between the Olympians and the generations of post-Pandora, iron-made humans, affected by baneful cares, the Stoics echo Homer's fluid anthropology. We may very well look like gods, and the gods do care like us.

CHAPTER THREE

Ethics and Social Relations

JAMES KER

The goal of this chapter is to assemble a cultural history of the heterogeneous and changing field of ethical thinking in relation to social relationships in the ancient Greek and Roman world. It would, however, be both daunting *and* simplistic to document a progression from the heroic ethos of the Homeric age to the contests of elite and democratic values in the archaic and classical *polis*, the birth of philosophy that followed from Socrates' scrutiny of those values, the multiplication of philosophical schools in the Hellenistic era, the Romans' selective adaptation of these doctrines into more practical directives for private and political life, and lastly to the early Christians, who adopted philosophy's ethical systems to organize their ascetic spiritual lives. A more realistic and also more relevant approach for us will be to survey some of the most generative interactions between ethical ideas and social forms and practices, including the significant mediating role played by Greek and Latin literature.[1]

MAKING MORAL EXPERTISE

To trace ethical thought in antiquity is in part to trace the history of philosophy and philosophers, who formulated precise assertions about the best forms of human conduct. One early "student of nature" (*phusiologos*) was Democritus of Abdera (*c.* 460–360 BCE), whose fragmentary writings show an interest in characterizing the psychological experiences that accompany people's ethical choices: "The smooth-spirited (*euthumos*) person, who is inclined toward just and lawful deeds, feels joy and is strong and is free from concern, … but one who gives no thought to justice and does not do the things that are right—to this person all things of this sort bring no joy when he recalls them, and he feels fear and reproaches himself" (fr. 174).[2] Democritus' notion of *euthumia* gives a more precise characterization to the workings of the *thumos* (spirit), which had featured as a locus of cognition and emotion in the epics of Homer. Following Democritus, and then Socrates in late fifth-century BCE Athens, we see the evolution and divergence of precise claims about the world and how to live in it, as well as how these questions relate to our minds, particularly in the succession of thinkers and writers who formally identified themselves as "lovers of wisdom" (*philosophoi*), from Plato to Aristotle to their various successors and critics in the Hellenistic, Roman, and early Christian periods (see Figure 3.1).

Democritus' early thought, for example, inspired the doctrine of Epicurus (341–270 BCE), which also emphasized a utilitarian connection between social institutions such as justice and psychological benefits such as freedom from anxiety or fear (*ataraxia*). The notion of *euthumia* also evolved in Latin philosophy into a striking metaphor. In his *On Tranquillity of Mind*, the Roman Stoic author Seneca the Younger (*c.* 4 BCE–65 CE)

FIGURE 3.1 Raphael, *The School of Athens*, fresco, 1511. Vatican Museums. © Incamerastock / Alamy Stock Photo.

compares the mind of his troubled friend (conveniently, his name is Serenus) to a sea that is becoming placid after a storm but remains vulnerable to further fluctuation,[3] and then explains to him the different areas of a person's social relationships in which one's tranquil state of mind is most vulnerable, and how it can be protected.

It is also possible to trace, over a much longer time span and a broader sphere of influence, a history of institutions and ideologies in which various social ideas were enshrined. Hesiod's poem *Works and Days* (c. 700 BCE) alludes to civic procedures for dispute resolution that at their best serve a superordinate ideal of justice that the poet associates directly with Zeus, but are also vulnerable to bribery and wrongful judgment by "gift-devouring kings."[4] Teaching his estranged brother, Perses, Hesiod prescribes household harmony and productivity: "Perses, you should store these things up in your mind (*thumos*), and do not let Strife who takes joy in evil keep your mind away from work as you stare at disputes and listen to the marketplace."[5] The poem gives us an early glimpse of a popular culture in which the workings of the world are parsed, and moral paths recommended, no less than in philosophy.

Even the most quotidian interactions of Greek and Roman civic life were encoded with moral presuppositions. One Roman routine was the everyday morning greeting (*salutatio*) in which socially inferior "clients" submitted to the inconvenience of rising early and waiting at the door of the socially superior "patron," whose house served as a public representation of self. Such interactions could validate a patron's social authority through an ostentatious etiquette of "friendship" (*amicitia*), though from the perspective of a critical client they could be construed as a pageant of social humiliation. The poet Horace (65–8 BCE) sketches a nostalgic view of morning patronage as a patron might have imagined it, in which "it was sweet and solemn to wake early in the morning and open one's home, provide justice to one's client, dispense judicious loans to solvent persons, to take advice from elders, and to those younger to explain how one's substance could grow and ruinous greed be reduced."[6] The epigrammatist Martial (*c*. 38–104 CE), by contrast, channels the client's viewpoint by complaining about the indignities of rising early: "You wretch, Titullus: … you go as a greeter wearing out every doorstep; you sweat out the morning, dripping with a whole city's kisses."[7]

The moral authority par excellence was the "wise person"—in Greek, *sophos*, and in Latin, *sapiens*. That label became something of a technical term in philosophy, being attached to a hypothetical morally perfect person and, among historical individuals, reserved for Socrates (*c*. 470–399 BCE) and those (if any) who met the standard. One Roman Socrates existed, for some, in the figure of Cato the Younger (94–46 BCE), the Stoic statesman whose suicide after the ascendance of Julius Caesar in some sense matched the Athenian philosopher's virtuous death by hemlock.[8] But before philosophy, or beyond philosophy's margins, the terms *sophos* (wise) or *sophistēs* (expert) had also been applied in a less technical sense to a variety of figures: to Odysseus or Heracles, whose heroism manifested ideals of cunning intelligence or community-saving valor; to the Seven Sages, the legendary archaic Greek figures whose combination of statesmanship, verbal art, and wisdom made them a favorite milieu in which profound political or moral concepts were debated; or to the "sophists," the fifth-century intellectuals whose expertise in fields such as rhetoric and constitution-making Plato treated as a negative foil due to their supposedly relativistic approach to moral questions. Further authorities of moral knowledge included the poet, the orator, and the *theios anēr* (holy man)—whether traveling philosopher, divine-born military hero, or Christian ascetic.

It is essential to recognize, however, that normative ethical representations, whether in philosophy or in social institutions more generally, often functioned to justify or rationalize the social position of a selective and ambitious set of social actors. Thus, for example, in his *On Duties*, written in the weeks following the assassination of Caesar in March of 44 BCE, the republican orator Cicero (106–43 BCE) adapted the pragmatic ethics of the Stoic philosopher Panaetius (*c*. 185–109 BCE) to articulate the relationship between the "useful" (*utile*) and the "virtuous" (*honestum*), both with a view to justifying Caesar's assassination and with a view to locating his own moral authority in a now profoundly uncertain political world.

MAPPING SOCIAL LIFE

One recurring form of quasi-scientific social analysis came in the form of ancient culture-histories, which presented a diachronic account of the origins of civic society, usually in strongly moralizing and teleological terms. In his *Politics,* Aristotle (384–322 BCE) charts the stages of human "associations" (*koinōniai*), such as the household (*oikia*) and the village (*kōmē*), that predated the invention of the city (*polis*).[9] For Aristotle, the city was at once a gift of nature, reflecting the fact that "the city is both natural and prior to the individual," and a felicitous human invention: "the one who first organized [a city] is responsible for the greatest benefits."[10] Aeschylus (*c*. 525–456 BCE), in the final play of his *Oresteia* trilogy entitled *Eumenides*, has the young matricide Orestes saved from a retributive killing through the intervention of Athena and Zeus, who impose a form of justice associated with the votes of an Athenian civic jury—a conclusion that is democratic, though also patriarchal. Such genealogies as a rule show technology and morality progressing hand in hand, but they can be contrasted both with the many pessimistic portraits of human decline from a putative mythical golden age and with more utilitarian accounts in which civic development is a series of practical human innovations.

One complementary form of analysis was the mapping of human social relationships ranging from the most proximate to the most distant, as seen in a fragment from the Stoic philosophical writer Hierocles (second century CE):

> Each of us is as it were surrounded by many circles, some smaller, some larger. ... For the first and tightest circle is the one that someone has drawn around his mind as if around a center. In this circle the body is encompassed as well as the things taken for the sake of the body. ... The second from this, standing further from the center and encompassing the first, is the one in which are arranged one's parents, siblings, wife, children. ... [Then there is] the one encompassing one's other relatives. In order from this one is the one encompassing those in the same deme, those in the same tribe, and then fellow-citizens, and so on in this way those from neighboring cities but from the same descent-group (*ethnos*). But the furthest and greatest, and encompassing all the circles, is the one encompassing the entire race of human beings.[11]

Within this schematic model of social relations Hierocles endeavors to decrease our sense of the distance between the circles: "Contemplating these circles, then," he instructs, "it is right ... to draw these circles together somehow, as if toward the center, and always to endeavor to transpose the encompassing circles to the encompassed circles"—for example, by "calling one's cousins and uncles and aunts 'brothers'." But such schemas are also interesting for what they exclude, and in Hierocles' case the exclusive emphasis on gradations of kinship and social proximity elides the question of social status, since although some of the terms he uses are gender-inclusive, the model nevertheless implies a married male subject who is a parent, and enslaved persons are not mentioned at all as ones to whom "we" might correspond or relate. The question of how enslavers should relate to the enslaved, and vice versa, was typically addressed as a separate topic with different ethical criteria.

This ranking of social relationships in terms of proximity and distance was sometimes integrated into a model of the human lifecourse. In the Stoic theory of "appropriation" (*oikeiōsis*) that is presupposed in Hierocles' advice discussed above and is also explained by Seneca in his *Moral Letters*, after infancy a person progresses from self-preservation to other-directed concern, as soon as maturation and social encounters facilitate the growth of the "foundations and seed of virtue" that nature has given it.[12] Such conceptions were not limited to philosophy: numerous rites of passage, such as the Athenian *ephēbeia* (rite of manhood) or the Roman male's assumption of the *toga virilis* (toga of manhood), involved normative assumptions about the young person's progression beyond the household and into civic life. Seneca, discussing the capacity of mirrors to facilitate our self-knowledge, reflects upon moral advice that is specific to one's stage in the lifecourse: "The young adult is reminded, by his youthful flourishing, that this is the time for learning and for daring brave deeds. The old person is reminded to put aside things unbefitting the greyhaired, to give some thought to death."[13]

Ethical theory, at least as this is retold by philosophical writers, emerges in part through an interrogation or redefinition of cultural conventions. The earliest and most prolific representations of this encounter are Plato's Socratic dialogues, a subtle reconfiguration of Athenian literary genres, especially public drama.[14] In these mimetic scenes that turn the reader into an eavesdropper or eyewitness, the philosopher converses with other Athenians on friendly terms, but insistently questions their knowledge about fundamental ethical concepts. In *Euthyphro*, for example, Socrates challenges a young man to explain how he knows for certain that a controversial decision he has made—to prosecute his own father for homicide after he caused the death of a hired worker—is founded on a firm knowledge of "the nature of the divine (*theion*) concerning what is pious (*hosion*) and impious" (*anosion*).[15] Although Euthyphro's successive attempts to define holiness conclude in frustration and perplexity (*aporia*) after repeated challenges by Socrates who protests his own ignorance, the dialogue calls into question certain ethical notions institutionalized in Athenian custom or law—resonating with the charges for which Socrates himself was facing trial, of challenging traditional thought about nature and ethics and "not even believing in the gods."[16] Much of the Greeks' and Romans' creative thinking about ethics unfolds either in variations of this scenario or in other pageants it inspired, such as the more extreme pose of the Cynic Diogenes (*c.* 412–324 BCE), who sought to "deface the currency" of social norms in Athens,[17] and schoolroom philosophizing such as that of the Stoic Epictetus (*c.* 55–135 CE), who interrogated the young elite Romans of the imperial era in a blend of Socratic questioning and instruction in the Stoic ethical system.[18]

Ethical profiles and habits were bundled together as a taxonomy of lifestyles (Gk. *bioi*; Lat. *genera vitae*), either in terms of specific philosophical schools or in broader sets of categories such as the difference between honors, wealth, or pleasure as the focus of one's life. In an anecdote about what a philosopher *is*, Pythagoras explains to a tyrant how philosophers differ from other people by observing that the life of human beings resembles a marketplace at a Panhellenic festival:

> For just as there [at the festival] some have trained their bodies and seek glory and fame through being crowned victor, others are led by an ambition to buy and sell and make a profit, but there is also a category of people, and this perhaps the most noble, who seek neither applause nor profit, but come for the sake of seeing and to watch studiously what is being done and how; likewise we, as if from some city to a gathering at a marketplace, have in the same way set out into this life from some other life and nature, [and] some of us are slaves to glory, others to money, and those individuals are rare who value all other things at nothing and studiously contemplate the nature of things. These ones call themselves students of wisdom—for that is the meaning of "philosophers."[19]

This kind of schema, focusing on the objects a person most valued and sought, could be used to diagnose one's entire character—in Greek, *ēthos*, and in Latin, *mores*. The tripartite model was often connected implicitly or explicitly to tripartite models of the soul. Often the model is reduced to a simple dichotomy between the practical life (*bios praktikos*) and the contemplative life (*bios theōrētikos*). Sometimes it is added to: Aristotle differentiates the life of contemplation, the life of seeking wealth, and the life of seeking honor, which he treats as the basis of the political life, but also observes that "the majority of people, and the most lowly, ... cherish the life of enjoyment (*bios apolaustikos*) .... They have some reason for their choice given that many people in high places feel the same way as Sardanapallus"—the notoriously luxurious king of Assyria.[20]

A unique but highly effective form of ethical—and social—critique was the literary discourse of satire and the satirization of habits. The best-known surviving Roman satirist is Juvenal (late first/early second century CE), who attacks human error such as our greedy requests to the gods: "Led by the impulse and great blind lust of our minds, we seek a marriage and for our wife to give birth, but [the gods] *know* what our sons will be, what our wife will be like."[21] Juvenal's famous remedy has a systematicity that resembles philosophical doctrine:

> You should pray to have a sound mind in a sound body (*mens sana in corpore sano*).
> Ask for a courageous heart that is not terrified by death,
> that counts a long lifespan among nature's gifts,
> can bear any struggle, knows
> not to get angry, lusts after nothing and believes
> the toils and merciless labors of Hercules are greater
> than sex and banquets and the luxurious pillows of Sardanapallus.[22]

The final phrase here recalls Aristotle (above), but Juvenal's plain language and popular, commonsense reasoning bear a different kind of moral authority than philosophical discourse. Satirists frequently turned their mockery directly against higher learning, as in the scathing *Philosophies for Sale*, a dialogue by Lucian (*c.* 120–180 CE) in which Hermes assists Zeus in selling off, as in a slave-market, "philosophical lives of every kind and of diverse moral persuasion."[23]

We often encounter a "politics of immorality"[24]—*ad hominem* satirization in which minor features of a person's character or conduct are treated as moral symptoms with implications for a person's overall political or social standing. In Roman republican oratory, for example, bodily "softness" (*mollitia*) is a subject of criticism; beyond implying effeminacy, hedonism, or sexual penetration by other men, it is "a vivid metonymy for a generalised and pejorative claim," for purposes of political humiliation.[25] Moralism served as a gatekeeper for elite groups in Roman social discourse, ranging from banquet poses to public gesture to more abstract moral profiles, such as the ideal of "endurance" (*patientia*), which oscillates between fortitude and submission.[26]

ANALYZING MORAL EXPERIENCE

The history of ethics is also the history of how people's social lives came to be narrativized as the products of psychological or cognitive processes. Seneca outlines the three components that Stoics differentiate within the moral part of philosophy, each with its own role to play in accounting for a person's conduct: evaluation; impulse; actions. "For it is important first that you judge what each thing is worth; secondly, that you take up an impulse to those things that is ordered and measured; thirdly, that there is correspondence between the impulse and your action, ensuring that you are in agreement with yourself in all these areas. Any lapse among the three disturbs the others also."[27] Only when this psychological machinery works well is a life "in harmony with itself."[28] Epictetus, Seneca's near contemporary, focuses on the exercise of moral "choice" (*prohairesis*) and emphasizes several other components of Stoic ethics, characterizing moral action as a matter of how one "uses" sensory "impressions" (*phantasiai*), how one follows "natural standards" (*phusika metra*), and the extent to which people "preserve what is appropriate to them as men, as sons, as parents, and the other roles of social relations in turn."[29] These fine-grained characterizations of moral conduct facilitated comparison and contrast between philosophical doctrines, with each school having its own concepts and priorities.

Many ethical prescriptions were couched in terms of evaluation, as noted above, and also in terms of the implications of recognizing what the highest good was—that is, the goal (*telos*) of life, the thing(s) guaranteeing happiness (*eudaimonia*). Aristotle and his

Peripatetic successors followed Socratic and Platonic values in treating the knowledge and practice of moral virtue as the highest good, but they also held that one's state of happiness could be improved by certain material circumstances. Aristotle famously discusses the case of Priam, king of Troy: "No one can call a person happy who underwent such misfortunes and died so wretchedly."[30] For the Stoics, virtue was not simply the highest but also the sole good, sufficient for happiness even without certain "preferred indifferents" such as wealth or well-being. The Cynics made a more strident claim about virtue's sufficiency, as seen with the barrel-dwelling Diogenes or his fellow-Cynic, Antisthenes, who pointed to Heracles as evidence that enduring pain was a good thing.[31] For the Epicureans, in turn, virtue was integral to happiness, but only as a means, or at best an accompaniment, to their ultimate goal of living a life free from bodily pain and mental distress. As a consequence, Epicureans and other philosophical hedonists were vulnerable to satirization as having adopted the life of pleasure understood in terms of sensual excess—a life resembling the life of enjoyment mocked by Aristotle and Juvenal (above).

The analysis and evaluation of a person's moral profile was facilitated by the formal mapping of an open-ended set of cardinal virtues. Plato's Socratic dialogues had informally distinguished a set that included piety (the focus of *Euthyphro*, above), bravery (the focus of *Laches*), and justice (the starting point of the *Republic*). In the course of the *Republic*, Plato has his interlocutors spell out the goodness of the perfect city in terms of four virtues—wisdom (*sophia/phronēsis*), bravery (*andreia*), temperance (*sōphrosunē*), and justice (*dikē*)[32]—and these, sometimes with the addition of piety (*hosiotēs*), were to serve as a standard reference point, translated into Latin with *sapientia/prudentia*, *fortitudo*, *temperantia*, *iustitia*, *pietas*. Aristotle, however, distinguishes between wisdom as an "intellectual" virtue and the others as "moral" virtues, and in the latter category he systematically maps out some common structures—such as the idea that each virtue is usually a middle point between two extremes. He also devotes a separate analysis to virtues concerned with the use of wealth, such as "liberality" (Gk. *eleutheriotēs*; Lat. *liberalitas*), which stands between the extremes of meanness and prodigality, and "magnificence/munificence" (Gk. *megaloprepeia*, *megalopsuchia*; Lat. *magnitudo animi*), which stands between vulgarity and vanity.[33] The virtues, however, were frequently reshuffled or supplemented. In Seneca's *On Clemency* addressed to the young emperor Nero, clemency is not equivalent to mercy or pity,[34] but is a virtue exercised only by a politically more powerful person toward a lower one, and partly for utilitarian reasons—safeguarding the empire and its peoples, safeguarding his monarchy and himself—rather than purely moral ones.

We also see the evolution of a systematic analysis of vices and the experience of emotion and passions. Anger, for example, had been thematized in literature already, notably in Achilles' rage in Homer's *Iliad*. But in Plato's *Republic*, Socrates proposes that poets be excluded from the city, precisely because "when it comes to sex, anger, and all the desires, pains, and pleasures in one's soul," the poets do not help us recover from these, but rather "poetic imitation activates these things in us."[35] A systematic analysis of anger is found in Aristotle, who points out its problematic manifestations but also observes that "we praise someone who becomes angry under the right conditions and at the right people, and also in the right way and at the right time and for the right amount of time."[36] The Stoics viewed the emotions as inconsistent with human rationality. So for Seneca, succumbing to anger is a form of madness and bestiality and is alien to human rationality.[37] Seneca characterizes ancient literature in general—whether the audience is responding to a representation of angry Achilles or menacing Hannibal—as a series of provocations to passion, but while our initial responses to these representations are beyond our control, our considered responses can always be rational.[38] Seneca also presents anger control as conducive to survival for his elite Roman readers confronted by such emperors as Caligula, and his discourse belongs to a broader elite survival project of "restraining rage."[39]

In ancient biography the salient organizing schema is less often the narration of a life in chronological order from start to finish, and more often the analysis of character under rubrics corresponding to particular virtues, vices, or spheres of social conduct. Suetonius (c. 70–130 CE) bookends his biography of Julius Caesar with accounts of Caesar's birth and death and includes sporadic linear narrative, yet many of the chapters are synchronic, covering such topics as sexual restraint (pudicitia), moderation with wine, conduct toward friends, tyrannical deeds and words.[40] In Suetonius the recurrence of the same rubrics in successive biographies (for example, friendship [amicitia]) facilitates the comparison and contrast of good and bad Caesars, just as the parallel lives of Greeks and Romans by Plutarch (c. 45–120 CE) offers broader generalizations about human character types.

SHOWCASING EXAMPLES

We even find encyclopedic collections of moral examples in which types of conduct are illustrated, recommended, or held up as cautionary tales. In his Memorable Deeds and Sayings (c. 27–31 CE), the Roman author Valerius Maximus assembles historical examples of conduct, some from abroad and some from home. Under sexual restraint (pudicitia), his first Roman example is Lucretia, "leader of Roman chastity, whose masculine mind was allotted a woman's body through a cruel error of fortune"; his first foreign example is Hippo, a Greek woman (otherwise unknown) who was captured by enemies but "threw herself into the sea to preserve her chastity."[41] It has been argued that moral examples in a Roman context proceed through "an endless loop of social reproduction" consisting of (1) "an action held to be consequential for the Roman community at large," (2) "an audience of eyewitnesses who observe this action," (3) "commemoration of the deed," and (4) "imitation."[42] Exemplary literature was to become one of the most influential mediums for communicating and reproducing moral ideas into the Middle Ages and Renaissance, from the Christian Golden Legend compiled from classical and early Christian sources to the humanistic collections of exemplary men and women compiled by Petrarch and Boccaccio.

In addition to history, the repertoire for moral exemplification ranges from high literature to the fabric of everyday life. Horace wears his philosophical learning lightly in his Satires and Epistles that concern themselves with robust yet informal analysis of "whether human beings are made happy by wealth or by virtue, what draws us into friendships (utility or right?), and what the nature of the good is, and its perfection."[43] Horace has a flare for providing an apt moral example. Sometimes he extracts it from literature, as when he advises his friend Lollius on how to read the Iliad and Odyssey: "The writer of the Trojan war … tells better and more plainly what is noble, what is disgraceful, what is useful, and what is not."[44] Turning to the world around him, Horace describes Volteius Mena, "an auctioneer of limited income, without reproach, known both for working quickly and for relaxing, for earning and for spending, who took pleasure in humble friends and a house he called his own, the games, and [exercising in] the Campus Martius after his business was complete."[45] The same poet also scrutinizes himself, presenting his own lifestyle as an illustration, as in the famous "diary of a nobody" he pens in one satire, advertising his nonparticipation in the daily greeting routine and thus his freedom from anxiety each morning.[46] This kind of moral exemplification was less likely to be systematized in an encyclopedia, but its potential influence was greater, being predicated on the author's influence and reputation.

The adoption of a given lifestyle and its attendant ethics was often dramatized as a consequential choice between two options. In the Medea plays of Seneca and his Greek predecessor Euripides, the heroine is caught between two conflicting roles—the scorned wife who exacts revenge and the mother who cares for her children (see Figure 3.2).

FIGURE 3.2 Medea and her Children (Jason in background), wall-painting, first century CE, House of the Dioscuri, Pompeii. National Archaeological Museum, Naples. © Prisma Archivo / Alamy Stock Photo.

But where Euripides sets Medea's choice in the moral ambiance of a witnessing chorus of Corinthian women, in Seneca's play her dilemma is played out in solitude as she oscillates between speaking in the voice of the vengeful divorcee and briefly retrieving the voice of the mother. First: "My former children, you must pay the penalty for your father's crimes." But then: "My heart is struck with horror, my limbs freeze, my heart shudders. Anger gives way and the mother returns, the wife totally banished."[47] The most famous fork in the road is the choice of Heracles: Xenophon (430–355 BCE) rehearses a fable ascribed to the sophist Prodicus in which the young Heracles determines his life's path after being confronted by two women, one of simple and pure appearance, the other sumptuously adorned. The latter, known to her adherents and opponents respectively as Happiness and Vice (*Eudaimonia*; *Kakia*), promises Heracles an easy life of pleasures, whereas the former, Virtue (*Aretē*), promises him hard work but moral satisfaction: "If you complete such toils, o Heracles, you child of good parents, it is possible for you to attain the most blessed happiness (*tēn makaristotatēn eudaimonian*)."[48] Such episodes became favorite points of reference for the basic choice between social convention and the moral values of philosophy: Epictetus invokes the example of Medea, quoting Euripides' Medea obeying her "passion" (*thumos*) over her reason, as someone for whom his students should feel pity; he likewise confronts his students with the example of Heracles, taunting: "If Heracles had sat around at home, what would he have amounted to?"[49]

We see an intense and complex mapping of social relations and moral conduct in public spectacle—whether in theatrical genres (see Figure 3.3) or in the Roman amphitheater. A famous letter of Seneca[50] espouses unease with the moral implications of enjoying a noontime spectacle featuring fights to the death between condemned criminals. His unease is due less to the consequences for the fighters than the effect on the captivated audience: "The vices creep into us more easily via pleasure. What do you think I am saying—that I come home more greedy, ambitious, extravagant? Not only this, but I come home more cruel and inhuman, because I have been among human beings."[51] In another work, by contrast, Seneca celebrates the suicide of Cato the Younger as a beautiful image of virtue from which all people can learn, and the god—the Stoic divine personified as Jupiter—can derive pleasure: "Behold, a spectacle worthy of being observed by God as he directs attention to his own work! Behold, a duel worthy of God: a brave man

FIGURE 3.3 Ancient theater, Hierapolis/Pamukkale, Turkey, first–second century CE.
© Isa Özdere / Alamy Stock Photo.

matched with an evil fortune, especially if he actively sought it out."[52] A minor but revealing shift of emphasis is seen when the Christian author Lactantius (*c.* 240–320 CE) modifies Seneca's phrase to characterize God's observation of a martyr: "How pleasant that spectacle was to God."[53]

One of the most spectacular forces in ancient ethics was the rhetoric of moral reasoning, in which words were weaponized to influence the audience's moral experience or choices. A favorite rhetorical exercise was the *suasoria*, in which the speaker was challenged to counsel a figure from myth or history as he or she confronted a difficult choice. Seneca the Elder collects half a dozen *suasoriae*, on topics such as "Agamemnon deliberates whether he should sacrifice Iphigenia" and "Cicero deliberates as to whether he should plead with Antony [for his life]."[54] In the latter case, Seneca recounts, most students of oratory found it easier to argue against this, thereby agreeing that Cicero had in fact done the right thing in standing his ground and being killed by Antony, but at least one student tried reasoning the opposite: that Cicero "had lived long enough for himself, but too short a time for the republic."[55]

Among ancient literary genres there are numerous forms in which we see a given type of social experience connected to specific moral challenges and realizations. In the novel *Metamorphoses* (aka *The Golden Ass*) by Apuleius (second half of second century CE), the protagonist Lucius is transformed into an ass and compares his experience to that of Odysseus, remarking: "I myself give thanks to the ass I was, since he rendered me, if not wise, then certainly knowledgable about many things, by concealing me in his covering and exercising me through diverse fortunes."[56] Apuleius' novel is distinctive for its social realism, as Lucius witnesses such things as the perverse camaraderie of bandits, the labor of slaves and animals in a flour mill, and his own restoration to human form and subsequent conversion to the religion of Isis—all good food for ethical thought.

Contrasting moral norms are a focus in literature devoted to ethnographic comparison, such as the excurses in the *History* of Herodotus (fifth century BCE) and standalone works like *Germania* by Tacitus (*c.* 56–118 CE). Such accounts are usually more about Greece or Rome than about the described culture, the latter serving as a distorted mirror image that either validates or embarrasses the home culture. The figure of Anacharsis the Scythian, the most foreign of the Seven Sages, was to become a hero to the Cynics and a convenient mouthpiece for imagined critical observations on Athenian civic culture. Accompanying the Athenian lawgiver Solon to the assembly, Anacharsis "was surprised that in Greece wise men speak, but fools make the decisions."[57]

It is sometimes observed that the moralizing dimension of ancient historiography is what gives it much in common with tragedy and epic, and indeed at Rome historical events were actually represented in morally loaded forms such as historical drama (the *fabula praetexta*) or epic verse, beginning from Naevius' *Punic War* (third century BCE). Historians from Herodotus onward saw the material of history as profoundly moral or ethical. When Tacitus describes the death of Vitellius, the third of the four emperors proclaimed at Rome in the year 69, the reader must navigate multiple layers of moral evaluation, ranging from a moralistic, "analytic" assessment of Vitellius revealed in his death as a fearful and cruel character to an "audience-based" picture in which the viewpoint of an internal audience "leads us to sympathise with [Vitellius'] fears and pity him."[58] Being mediated through such textualized dramas, the very material of history itself is imbued with conflicting values.

THINKING GLOBALLY

In Greek and Roman tragedy, protagonists do not always choose between right and wrong per se, but frequently their dilemmas involve two value systems, each in its own right ethically coherent and explicit, yet shown to be irreconcilable. Sophocles' character Antigone defends her burial of her brother Polynices, against the strictures of Thebes' ruler Creon, appealing to "as it were unwritten and unfailing decrees of the gods"[59]— which Aristotle famously took up as an example in his discussion of particular laws and general laws.[60] In the context of classical Athens, such dilemmas are often an instantiation of conflict between household (*oikos*) and city (*polis*) in which civic values typically win out over an obsolete ethos, as when the city imposes its system of justice in the *Oresteia*. In *Antigone* the polarities are reversed, at least on the surface, with the divine and natural laws of loyalty to kin superseding the laws imposed by a tyrannical state.

Social relationships both above and below the level of the city were often characterized metaphorically as like the relationships within a city or republic. A classic example is the notion "citizen of the universe" (*kosmou politēs*), first associated with the Cynic Diogenes. Cosmopolitanism was framed by the Stoics through the "community of reason" we share with the divine. It offered a way to respect civic values of law and community *without* necessarily participating in a local city. But we also find the city serving as a model within the household itself, as in Seneca's *Moral Epistles* 47, which advises enslavers not to liberate those they have enslaved, but to treat them better: "Our ancestors removed all resentment from masters and all insult from slaves. ... They allowed them to acquire honors and hold judicial process within the household, and they *judged the household to be a miniature republic*."[61] The idea of the city, then, offers a model for imagining social connections, and moral common ground, far beyond one's immediate peer group—albeit presupposing a free male subject as the privileged focus of ethical considerations (see below).

Moral obligations are often most intensely rejected *or* upheld in ancient literature at moments when agents come into contact in situations beyond the city, such as in international diplomacy and war. The most famous negative instance is the "Melian Dialogue" presented by the historian Thucydides (*c*. 455–400 BCE). Athenian emissaries, urging the leaders of the Spartan colony Melos to capitulate, notoriously observe that "in human reckoning, matters of justice are assessed when there is an equal ability to compel, whereas the stronger do what they can and the weaker fall in line."[62] Conversely, there are moments when the enmities involved in international conflict are undermined, or suspended, to draw attention to a more cogent social relationship. During the battles outside Troy depicted in the *Iliad*, the Greek warrior Diomedes spares the Trojan Glaukos after realizing that he is his "inherited guest-friend" (*xeinos patrōios*).[63] Instead of fighting, the two warriors exchange gifts on the battlefield. That episode taps into the more general international social network of guest-friendship (*xenia*), which persisted as an alternative framework for relationships between elite families of individual Greek cities.

Another manifestation of international ethics, however, distinct from both cosmopolitanism and guest-friendship, was the invention of empire as a network of relationships, whether in the form of the Roman Empire with widely shared Roman citizenship or in the Christian Church that inherited some of the empire's overall structures. Although a global empire found some ideological support in cosmic geopolitics as understood by the Stoics especially,[64] the invention of empire was also facilitated through the construction of relationships and moral networks. The imagining of community, for example, relied upon a notion of *consensus* among rulers and ruled,[65] while we see members of the Julio-Claudian elite involved in "constructing autocracy" through negotiating a workable set of relationships betwen the emperor and themselves. Seneca, for example, counseling Nero in his *On Clemency*, urges the young emperor to think of his role variously as that of a good master or a good father.[66]

Plato's *Republic*, with its analogy between the well-ordered soul and the well-ordered city and its idealistic vision of communitarian society and systematic education of philosopher kings, is simply one of many utopian social worlds. The same author's later dialogue, *Laws*, is no less visionary, though concerned with more pragmatic questions about how to turn ideal into reality. The Stoics also continually explored the "idea of the city"[67] through various imagined societies. Zeno's *Republic*, for instance, appears to have imagined a community centering on the same moral and political ideals imagined by Plato, as well as some of the same policies, such as women held in common, but with greater emphasis on the role of Love (*Erōs*) in ensuring concord.[68] These idealizations can be compared with actual instantiations of philosophical communities, such as the settlements in Magna Graecia in southern Italy associated with Pythagoras (sixth century BCE) and his followers and successors. The Neoplatonist philosopher Plotinus (205–269 CE) supposedly hoped to withdraw from Rome to found a city called "Platonopolis" that would be founded on the principles of Plato's *Laws*.[69] Such notions were clearly influential for Christians, not only in universal or eschatological utopias (e.g., Augustine, *City of God*) but also in the invention of idealizing or ascetic communities, especially in cenobitic monasteries. Saint Benedict (early sixth century CE) begins his *Rule* by differentiating his cenobites, "the type living in a monastery and serving under a rule and abbot," from the hermitic anchorites, the lawless sarabaites, and the wandering gyrovagues.[70] The core of his community involves the shared daily and yearly schedule of prayer and work that all the monks observe together.

MANAGING SOCIAL AND POLITICAL HIERARCHIES

Philosophers often foreground the capacity shared by *all* humans regardless of social identity. We seem to see this, for example, in Musonius Rufus' discourse which finds that women can study philosophy and be virtuous.[71] But when examples of virtuous action by non-free and/or non-male persons are celebrated, the purpose is generally not to militate for equal access and equal rights, or even to ennoble the acts of the socially inferior, but rather to apply moral pressure to the elite actor. Seneca, for example, after recounting the noble acts by which a succession of Roman captives took matters into their own hands and improvised their own deaths before they could be led into the amphitheater, then taunts his friend: "When even lost souls have [the power to] hurt themselves, will this [power] be lacking in those who have schooled themselves for this type of emergency through long meditation and through reason?"[72] He means men like himself and his younger friend, Lucilius.[73]

In most discussions of applied ethics, conditions of social inequality are usually presupposed or even rationalized, as if they have a basis in nature, and indeed are often even forcefully affirmed. In Aristotle's account of women and slaves in the opening chapters of his *Politics*, hierarchy is born from a natural imperative for "the coupling of those who would be incapable without one another, such as the female and male for the sake of procreation ... and the one ruling by nature with the ruled, for the purpose of safety."[74] Seneca, when discussing the question of whether a generous action by a slave that helps the master can be called a "benefit" (*beneficium*), concedes the ethical autonomy of slaves while treating the existence of slavery as an unchanging given.[75]

Greco-Roman expectations about a person's social conduct and capacity are closely dependent on recognizing the particular social roles of the person involved—in terms of status, wealth, gender, ethnicity, occupation, and so on. The Stoic notion of "proper functions" (*kathēkonta*) goes beyond the general notion of virtue to emphasize the various responsibilities that derive from a person's set of social roles. Hence Epictetus' mention (above) of "what is appropriate" to certain men in their role not only as men but also "as sons, as parents, and the other roles of social relations in turn."[76] Attention to social roles will factor into choices about morally significant action. Cicero explains why he did not commit suicide when Cato the Younger did: what was proper for Cato is not necessarily appropriate for Cicero. He appeals to a model described by the Stoic Panaetius, according to which each of us wears four distinct layers of character (*personae*): our common rationality; our individual characteristics given by nature; the constellation of our life circumstances; and our chosen pursuits.[77] Only in the most progressive moments of Roman philosophy do we encounter an explicit sensitivity to the ethics of family life and feminine identity.[78]

One especially influential scenario of moral advising is centered in the household, where we must usually presuppose a subject who is male, married, wealthy, aristocratic, and a slave-owner. In Xenophon's *Oeconomicus* the "fine and good man" (*kalos kagathos*) named Ischomachus describes how he keeps his rural estate in order by supervising his wife's organization of the household and his overseer's management of the daily routine of work.[79] Although Socrates is suspicious of that ideal from a philosophical standpoint, as an idealized image of normative domestic morality grounded in rustic frugality it belongs to a long and influential tradition stretching from Hesiod's *Works and Days* into the various Roman prose works entitled *On Agriculture* (e.g., those by Cato, Varro, and Columella).

In a number of different literary endeavors we encounter temporary suspension of social hierarchies. In one of his *Satires*, Horace gives voice to his slave Davus, as if for an ad hoc Saturnalia (the Roman festival each December in which slaves enjoyed some licentiousness). As an intimate observer of Horace's daily conduct, Davus is able to point out the flaws in Horace's own moralizing: "You praise the life and customs of the people of old, and yet, if some god were suddenly to take you there, you would refuse to go—either because you do not really feel that what you preach is right, or because you are not a strong enough defender of what is right."[80] Such moments are less about interrogating the hypocrisy of the master-slave hierarchy overall than about the *master's* hypocrisy. The slave functions here as an "other self," "a voice in Horace's head—the voice of conscience."[81]

We also see social inequalities integrated into visions of concord. In Suetonius' biographies of the Caesars there is an emerging emphasis on "civility" (*civilitas*), characterizing the emperor's good relations with Romans of every social rank. Vespasian, for example, remained "civil and clement, never seeking to hide his middling origins, and often even touting them."[82] To celebrate civility in an emperor is to recognize him as a kind of paterfamilias of a household—he was, after all, *pater patriae*, father of the fatherland. It also builds upon "concord among ranks" (*concordia ordinum*), an oft-celebrated ideal during the Roman republic. Concord, in Greek *homophrosunē*, is also central to ancient idealizations of the marital relationship. Plutarch's *Advice to Bride and Groom* begins with the author asking Aphrodite and the Muses to supply the same concord for marriage and household that they would supply for a well-tuned lyre.

In numerous ancient political contexts we witness a relatively intimate sphere of ethically significant interaction that serves as a crucible for political flourishing. One such instance is the archaic Greek symposium, in which the minor gestures of convivial interaction were inseparable from political activism and its major consequences. As Alkaios (seventh–sixth century BCE) writes after the death of a tyrant on Lesbos: "Now it is right we get drunk, and drink with all our might, seeing as Myrsilos is dead."[83] The Roman principate was in effect a court society, in which "friendship" (*amicitia*) between elite and princeps was maintained and reproduced through trivial but significant acts such as playful poetic rivalries and daily kisses, along with the daily ritual of *salutatio* (see above). The moralisms found in the poetry of Theognis are couched very much in terms of defining a sociopolitical elite through essentializing terms: "Kyrnos, good men have never yet destroyed a city. Rather, whenever bad men take pleasure in violence, and they corrupt the common people and deliver judgments to unjust men for the sake of private profit and power, you can expect that city will not be without trouble for long."[84]

We often find moral advice targeted at elite subjects facing a political situation in which their traditional sources of power have been undermined. The aspirations of this advice range from self-preservation to self-sublimation, the latter pursued even by succumbing to death. Such was certainly the case among the Roman elite of the early principate under the Julio-Claudian emperors. Seneca's advice on anger control is compatible both with the Stoic extirpation of the passions and with a preference for staying alive. On the other hand, for those members of the Julio-Claudian elite whom scholars once referred to as the "Stoic opposition," Stoic ethics also provided a test of values and the basis for standing one's ground in the face of provocation. Hence a Roman "game of death":[85] the senator Thrasea Paetus, for example, refrained from praising Nero and suffered the consequence, forced suicide, but thereby gained a winning advantage in a battle of reputations. Christian martyrdom was predicated on the possibility of winning by dying, though it possessed its own distinct ethical function for a "suffering self"[86] and the distinct ontology of the Christian afterlife.

Although ancient ethical theorists might reject social convention on the grounds of its misguided, materialist values, they themselves frequently also resorted to the terms and structures by which traditional social hierarchies had been reproduced. Seneca, for example, reinscribes an exclusionary framework that makes philosophy effectively an "aristocracy of virtue,"[87] even as it is presented as a meritocratic contrast to conventional forms of social evaluation. Thus, while dismissing the relevance of conventional markers of aristocratic lineage, such as ancestor masks (*imagines*) displayed in the atrium of one's house, Seneca characterizes the schools of philosophy as households to which we can be admitted: "What happiness and what a fine old age await one who has devoted himself to being a 'client' to these!"[88]

ESCAPING THE SOCIAL WORLD

The goal of enjoying normative social relationships as a participant in a vibrant social world is tested and problematized in circumstances where the ethical theorist counsels withdrawal from public life. The most famous of these is Plato's justification of his own withdrawal from the political life of Athens that he narrates in the opening pages of his *Seventh Letter*. The emergence of cosmopolitan discourse allowed later philosophers to offer a more intentional characterization of withdrawal. In his *On Leisure*, Seneca differentiates between the cosmic republic and one's own local state (e.g., Athens or Carthage), and asserts: "Some men give service to both republics at the same time, the greater and the lesser; some only to the lesser; some only to the greater. This greater republic we can serve even in our leisure—indeed, likely *better* in our leisure."[89]

Ethical theory was often propelled by a need for the writer to accept or even to celebrate the conditions of his ostracism or banishment, overcoming social death through self-sufficiency. Seneca responded to his relegation to Corsica by reassuring his mother Helvia that "two things, which are the most noble, will follow us wherever we remove ourselves to: universal nature and personal virtue."[90] Although a surface reading of Ovid's poetry would lead us to view the poet as reluctantly mapping the indignities of exile as social death in foreign climes, we also see him reasserting some of the foundational moral—and ideological—principles of Roman imperialism and elite community.[91] Favorinus, a Greek philosopher-rhetorician adapting to his (possibly fictitious) banishment from Rome in the early second century CE, further instantiates the "public *dramatizations* of the therapeutic process"[92] seen in consolatory literature, where the author defines the broader cultural and cosmic community to which a person belongs—in his case as a cultivated Greek who can flourish in the Roman Empire.

Philosophical writers on society and ethics are often found prescribing the necessary practices for a person isolated from traditional social contact to survive and even to flourish. Recurring questions include not only whether a person should be involved in public life, but even whether a philosopher should marry or whether he can be happy without friends. Distinct answers are given by the various schools, and in cases where the answer is "Yes," reasons range between the idea that sociality is part of our nature to the idea that it can preserve us from harm. But an utterance ascribed to Scipio Africanus the Elder, that he was "never less alone than when alone,"[93] became a convenient framework within which moralists could carve out a space for quasi-socializing even in the absence of society. The Scipionic ideal is invoked by Cicero after his exclusion from public life in the Roman republic, but it closely informs such works as the *Soliloquies* of Saint Augustine (354–430 CE) and *On the Solitary Life* by Petrarch (1304–74). The life of Saint Anthony described by Athanasius, showcasing his hermit life, is also an heir to this tradition, in which the saint's solitary daily practice enacts an acceptance of everyday mortality and prepares for eternal life.

SEEKING THERAPY IN SELF AND FRIENDS

One of the primary interfaces between a person's private existence and their fuller profile in social situations is the scene of daily self-examination that we see arising in a number of authors where the practice of "philosophy as a way of life"[94] is fully on show, especially in Stoics such as Seneca[95] and Epictetus. In the latter (see Figure 3.4), we read about the kinds of questions that the philosopher could be asking himself each evening, taken from the Pythagorean *Golden Verses* but applied to daily goals: "What is required of you? Rehearse your actions. 'What progress did I make'—in things relevant to a happily flowing life? 'What did I do'—that lacked friendliness, sharing, or thoughtfulness? 'What that I needed to do was not completed'—as regards these goals?"[96] As a contrast, Epictetus mocks what he imagines conventional elite Romans might say to themselves each evening: "'What progress did I make'—in flattery?"[97] For pagan philosophers, the payoff of such daily self-examination appears to be a fine-tuning of the rational machinery by which one's daily

FIGURE 3.4 Epictetus, eighteenth-century book illustration. © Über Bilder / Alamy Stock Photo.

public conduct is controlled. In the rich subsequent tradition of Christian self-examination, as both Hadot and Foucault observed, God's divine authority is enforced by guilt.[98]

While Greco-Roman self-examination is presented primarily as a device for normativizing daily social conduct, we also see terms that originated in social conduct being refined to serve in a primarily moral-psychological sense. The very terms for "virtue" in both Greek and Latin, *aretē* and *virtus*, had applied previously to "excellence" at a community level, especially in military accomplishment, and *virtus* in particular never loses its foundational connection with masculinity (cf. *vir*, "man"). But "virtue" took on an interior life of its own as part of the overall relocation of value. In the Stoic theory of "indifferents," nothing external is good since the only good is virtue—that is, one's perfected "reason" (*logos*), one's "commanding faculty" (*hēgemonikon*), one's "choice" (*prohairesis*). As part of this inward turn, we also see an inventive expansion of one's interior life: Seneca's self-examination (above) has a person conducting a self-observation in which the observer is "judge," "censor," and so forth.

As part of this transposition of terms from external to internal, we see a shift away from the forms of community surveillance and evaluation associated with the idea of a "shame" culture, *not* to a "guilt" culture as such, but to what might better be described as an internalized or self-monitoring shame culture. Seneca aspires to do "nothing for the sake of reputation (*opinio*) and everything for the sake of my own awareness (*conscientia*)," but explains this by saying: "let me believe that whatever I do with myself as the witness is being done with the people watching (*populo spectante*)."[99] So "conscience" here is still characterized in primarily visual and social terms.[100]

When the voice of the moralist is sympathetic rather than hostile, we can discern a subtle art of spiritual direction being applied, often with echoes of medical diagnosis and therapy. When Epictetus is faced with a student who feels humiliated because his Roman social peers pity him for not being wealthy and powerful, he seeks to empower him by suggesting words he can use upon himself. First he might diagnose his problem, admitting: "I am not training (*gumnazō*) or practising (*meletō*) the necessary principles ... with the practice (*meletēn*) that is appropriate for them."[101] Then he might conduct an advance rehearsal (Gk. *meletē*; Lat. *meditatio*) in which so-called misfortunes are confronted: "I am poor, but I have a correct judgment about poverty. So, what do I care (*melei*), if they pity me for poverty? I don't hold office, and others do. But I think what one should think, concerning holding office and not."[102]

One form of therapy centers on systematic meditation, or rehearsal, of future events in which a person is invited to anticipate a series of scenarios that provide exercise in developing an appropriate moral response. In his *Moral Letters* Seneca cycles through the possible threats his friend might face:

> I will become poor.—I will be in company! I will become an exile.—I will imagine that I was born in the place to which I am sent! I will be bound.—So what? Am I unbound *now*? ... I will die.—What you're saying is, I will cease to be able to be sick, I will cease to be able to be bound, I will cease to be able to die.[103]

A supplement to such therapy is the use of proverbial wisdom to transmit moral knowledge or influence behavior, usually drawing upon an influential exhortatory authority. Numerous collections of sayings or advice are preserved, such as the Roman collection of "Catonian Couplets" (*Disticha Catonis*) and the dozens of *Sententiae* of the popular moralist Publilius Syrus: "The sign of a good man is not to know how to do harm." That tradition goes back to the didactic moralisms of Hesiod's *Works and Days* and earlier. A moralist's authority could be deployed through interiorization (above), as when Seneca says to his friend: "Happy the man who can so revere someone [e.g., the Roman ancestor Cato] that he can compose and order himself simply by remembering that person."[104]

Another major story of ancient ethical theory is the development of an ethics of friendship, including the questions of whether a person needs friends, and how friends ought to conduct themselves toward one another.[105] Aristotle devoted two books of his *Nichomachean Ethics* to the concept (*philia*), analyzing how it differs from relations between kin as well as its different kinds and its ethical bases, which include utility and pleasure, though "perfect friendship" is between two persons who "wish good things for one another equally and are good in their own right."[106] The focus is continued in Cicero's essay *On Friendship*, which emphasizes the exceptionality of friendship: "The great power of friendship can best be understood from the fact that out of the infinite association of the human race, which nature herself has convened, [with friendship] things have been tightened and narrowed such that all its affection is joined between two people, or a handful at most."[107] This exceptionality is presented, however, in the form of a dialogue between two famous friends, Scipio and Laelius, an exclusive elite setting with strong implications for the role of friendship in Roman public life, and a model for Cicero's own closest alliances.

RELATING TO DEATH

A person's death was, in ancient ethical reasoning, a privileged setting in which personal values and conduct could be put to the test. Exhibit A, of course, is the death of Socrates. Plato's *Phaedo* answers in detail the question of "what the man said before his death, and how he died,"[108] along with the arguments for the immortality of the soul with which he consoled his tearful friends and did not shed any tears of his own.[109] The other dialogues that belong to the philosopher's "last days," together with the *Apology*, fill out the overall moral exemplarity of his submission to a democratic death decree. The traditions on subsequent philosophical figures, such as Epicurus, Cato the Younger, and Seneca the Younger, all use death as a moral showcase. At least one ancient bust of Seneca posthumously fashioned his role as a moralist on the example of Socrates no doubt due to the similarities of their death scenes (see Figure 3.5).[110] One of the marked dimensions

FIGURE 3.5 Double herm of Seneca (left) and Socrates (right), third century CE. Neues Museum, Berlin. © Album / Alamy Stock Photo.

of these death scenes, beyond the courageous and or tranquil acceptance of death, and the performance of ethical values, is their emphatically social dimension, as the friends bear witness and make of the death a spectacle or an example that can be retold to wider audiences.[111]

In calamities such as exile or death, ethical theory also sought to render therapy to those who survived, in the form of a discourse on consolation, whose ultimate goal was for the addressee to be reintegrated into society as usual. Cicero's famous lost *Consolation to Himself*, for example, was supposedly a failure because of the ways in which it fell short of its reintegrative goal. What was missing, as Cicero makes clear in one letter, was any vestige of the Roman republic that could receive him and console him.[112] Later, Seneca in his consolations accepts this death of the republic, with two consequences: first, given that the heroes of the republic now occupy the afterlife, the deceased has an opportunity to join their ranks, a consoling thought; second, Seneca offers a better account of the contemporary environments into which the survivor can be reintegrated, whether it is a rosy vision of the opportunities offered by the Julio-Claudian principate or a safe path to secure contemplation of nature and the cosmos.[113] The consolation tradition was taken up in turn by early Christian authors, such as Jerome in a letter to the bishop Heliodorus concerning the premature death of a young man.[114] As we have seen with Christian appropriations of other ethical theories and practices considered above, the Christian consoler reworks traditional structures of thought and writing in light of Christian doctrine—in this case, a belief in divine providence, the power of the resurrection, and an afterlife far preferable to the here and now.

CHAPTER FOUR

Politics and Economies

CLIFFORD ANDO

INTRODUCTION

Greek and Roman thought and practice on matters of politics, especially, but also economics long exercised and, indeed, continue to exercise, a great deal of influence in the Western tradition. The nature of this influence has changed profoundly in the modern period. This has come about for reasons that might usefully be considered under three interconnected rubrics. First, the scale of modern states and the nature and reach of their power have changed so fundamentally that ancient theories of politics, oriented as they were to the city-state as norm, have long since ceased to offer useful theories or even heuristics in relation to modern problems. Second, the rise of liberal thought and the rights tradition, alongside concepts of social welfare, have so altered notions of who counts as a political being, of intersubjective relations, and of the mutual duties and obligations of persons to their communities, that ancient notions of membership and participation no longer carry the emancipatory potential they seemed to have upon their "rediscovery" in late medieval and Renaissance Italy. Instead, their primary function in contemporary society is nearly always conservative, urging a retreat from ethical and emancipatory concerns to neo-Aristotelian ones of form. By this I mean the following: contemporary liberal and post-liberal political theory encourages debate on questions of equity and inclusion, both within communities and transnationally. Modern versions of ancient political theory tend to take the *demos* as given; they lack—because antiquity lacked—a vocabulary or theory for international trade and its entailments; and they focus instead, as Aristotle did, on formal analyses of public power.

The third and final rupture between classical antiquity and the modern West concerns economics. The nature of modern economic activity and of modern economic science have advanced in parallel—along with the legal and institutional forms that enable them—in such a way as to appear simply different in kind from the sociological and embedded understandings of economics that prevailed in antiquity. In saying this, I do not claim that modern economics is right to present itself as rational, disinterested, or scientific, or that the disembedding of economic activity from other concerns is either intellectually honest or even useful. Nevertheless, there can be no doubt that ancient and modern economic thought have long since parted ways.[1]

In short, any approach to a cultural history of ideas about politics and economics in antiquity has to have a clear-sighted view of what their politics and economics were, and especially what they were not. This is not a pessimistic statement. Without the very useful anachronism—or even comparison—of alternative visions of what the study of politics and economics can be, we risk accepting the representations of our objects of study as natural. Their boundaries become our boundaries; their interests and blind spots, likewise, ours. To all these issues, I will return in the conclusion.

In what follows, I take up politics first, seeking to set the emergence of ancient normative theory in its historical context, by way of exposing its ambitions as well as its interested nature. Consideration of the political economics of ancient city-states will lead to "their" economics, where the divergence between theory and practice is particularly acute and demands careful and specific explanation.

POLITICS

The City-State: Polis *and* Civitas

Ancient political theory nearly universally took the city-state as its proper context. This fact has a number of consequences of importance for how we read ancient texts. For one thing, it is essential to know that this emphasis on the city-state fails powerfully to accord with the material conditions of social and economic conduct across much of the ancient world, in both time and space, in a number of important ways. For one thing, the historical contingency of the Greek city-state and its powers even in theoretical terms, and the determinate nature of the historical and ecological context of its emergence, are effaced if we take its form for granted and ignore the history of Greek political communities prior to and beyond the *polis*. Homer, Hesiod, and Greek lyric poetry—to say nothing of archaeology and the study of Minoan epigraphy—tell remarkable stories about political economics, institutions of justice, and the social and topographic distribution of political power in the Bronze and early Iron Ages, all of which deserve to be studied in their own right rather than as way-stations on the way to the *polis*.[2] The erasure of these pre-classical forms of politics and economics from "our" history of ideas is a consequence of teleology, of course—namely, our desire to tell a story that ends with a version of ourselves. It also follows upon a strong (if diminishing) tendency among normative political theorists to forgo historical inquiry and a similar unwillingness among historians of political thought to read outside the canon. In short, modern historians of ideas—including ideas about politics and economics—have tended to begin with classical Greece, because the first writers whom we have identified as contributing to "the tradition" of normative political theory dwelt in classical Greece. The necessary next step is simply to acknowledge that this is not the same thing as saying that politics and economics have no history before Plato, and to inquire what ideas drove and were germinated by political and economic conduct in those periods.

The reluctance of historians of political thought to think historically has a complex genealogy. I focus on one issue because it has ancient roots, which is to say, it is part of the cultural history of *their* ideas about politics. This is the tendency of political theorists to think about politics through fictive narratives of the emergence of political societies from nothing rather than to consider how weak, rudimentary, and partial institutions emerge, gradually and non-linearly, from non-juridified social practices.[3] Contractarian political theory of the sort practiced by Hobbes or evidenced in the Roman myth of asylum, which focuses on atomized individuals, or the alternative form visible in Aristotle and Locke, in which the household has an ontology and history prior to politics and states form through the sudden aggregation of households, both operate so as to separate, in the blaze of an instant, the moment of politics from some moment before.[4] In all this literature, fully-fledged political societies, with standardized institutions, similar aspirations to governance and control, and homeomorphic conceptions of public power, emerge instantaneously, as from the head of Zeus, or the actions of a nomothete. The actual history of the emergence of city-state political societies in Greece and Rome—in particular, the transition from something like prejuridical oligarchies that accepted the chieftaincy of kings and lacked ideologies of membership based on descent, to democratic oligarchies with very similar conceptions of ethnic identity and closed membership systems—was thereby deemed by the Greeks themselves to lie beyond the bounds of inquiry.

This ideological occlusion of the emergence of contemporary power structures from past arrangements bears comparison with two literatures that assist in shedding light on its importance.[5] One is precisely early modern theories of sovereignty in the contractarian tradition, by Hobbes or Locke or even Rousseau. By standing outside contemporary events and theorizing the formation of political communities in reference to states of nature, they avoided the hard work of understanding how to manage the distribution of public power across the transition as states emerged from the imperialist landscape of western Europe. Another effect of theorizing political societies as being formed in an instant of union is that it encourages one to imagine all members of society as choosing each other. (Machiavelli by contrast, writing in an earlier age, recognized the necessity of context to politics and wrote with intense familiarity of the contemporary international scene; he also crafted normative theory precisely for conditions of what Hobbes would call sovereignty by acquisition, namely, conquest. More than any discomfort at his realist tendencies, this made him anathema in a world that wished to export European aggression outside the continent and pretend that the age of expansionist empire *within Europe* was over.)

A second literature that sheds light on Greek narratives of the emergence of particular *poleis* is that concerned with what Ronald Gregor Suny calls primordialism. By this, Suny intends the process by which forms of difference and matrices of social and power relations of contemporary salience are narrativized and historicized in a fashion that ascribes to them origins that are both natural and prehistoric.[6] To write in this way amounts to taking an interested view of some aspect of contemporary social relations and placing it beyond question by situating it before history, whether as the way things have always been or, more perniciously, as a state of affairs that ought to be restored. In the ancient world, the emergence of ideologies of descent as a criterion of membership in Greek city-states demanded that the past be rewritten in such a way as to produce an earlier purity continuous with the present that they sought to claim and preserve.[7]

We should also be suspicious of the tendency of ancient political thought to take the city-state as its normative context because the Greek city-state was not a unitary thing, nor was the city-state the only form of political community that Greeks aspired to construct. Not for naught did Aristotle organize the program of his *Politics* around the study of the "constitutions of city-states," both "such as are actually in use as well as those that are propounded by certain thinkers and said to be of merit."[8] (Aristotle famously turns to the *Politics* at the end of the *Nicomachean Ethics,* with the intent "to examine, on the basis of our collection of constitutions, what institutions are preservative and what destructive of city-states in general."[9]) Greek city-states also collaborated in alliances and so built federal states.[10] More importantly, they also aspired to empire and other forms of macro-regional domination and existed within a broader Mediterranean ecology in which empires were an historical constant.[11] The kindred projects of empire and colonialism meant that Greek and Roman city-states came to exist in diverse landscapes whose prior inhabitants had a fundamentally different relationship to the city-state than did the inhabitants of the countrysides of Greek cities in peninsular Greece. For example, Athenian accounts of the emergence of classical Athens qua *polis* assume that members of rural "demes" (i.e., constituent territorial units of population within the city-state) are fully-fledged members of the political community of the Athenians (Figure 4.1).[12] One might compare Roman narratives of the earliest period of Roman conquest, during which defeated neighbors were absorbed not as serfs or subjects but simply assimilated as members.[13] By contrast, by the late classical period, a vast array of Greek cities—soon, a

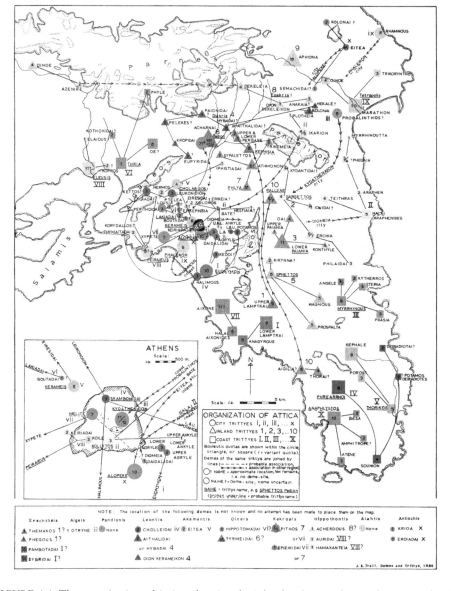

FIGURE 4.1 The organization of Attica, showing the inland, urban, and coastal units. Updated by John Traill from John Traill, Demos and trittys: epigraphical and topographical studies in the organization of Attica (Toronto: Athenians, 1986).

majority of all Greek *poleis* in terms of numbers of citizens—existed outside peninsular Greece, and their relationship to the non-Greek populations in their hinterlands was one of radical exclusion and domination.

The third way in which the focus of theory on the city-state is false to history follows upon the second, and that is that many of the concerns of practical politics in the ancient world were focused precisely on domination, both of empires over city-states and, *within that context*, of city-based elites over the populations in their countrysides. That is to say, at a macro-level, empires needed to instrumentalize cities to garner the money and manpower to sustain themselves. By "instrumentalization" I intend the following: being themselves infrastructurally weak, empires required the collaboration of city-state elites to translate the power that they did have, which was largely military, into the kind of power that they sought, which was fiscal. Hence, as Herodotus informs us, Artapharnes, the regional commander of the Persian Empire, "summoned ambassadors from all the *poleis* [of Ionia] and compelled them to make treaties with each other, so that they would settle their disputes by legal means"; later, Mardonius "put down the tyrants in the Ionian *poleis* and established democracies throughout the city-states."[14] At a micro-level, city-state elites sought to monopolize the provision and enforcement of legal and economic norms to control the incidence of taxation and to diffuse symbolic systems in such a way as to radiate power from the city-state outward to the countryside and to direct economic energy and resources inward, back to the city.[15] Market activity needed to be centralized so as to expose village economies to city-state taxation; legal rules and institutions of dispute resolution had to reinforce a preference for owners of capital in the distribution of risk in agricultural production; the resources of the countryside, in the form of corvée labor of humans and animals, had to be available for work in the city; and so on and so forth.[16] In the long history of the ancient Mediterranean, empires backstopped the power of city-states to effect and sustain such systems. To the extent that modern scholars establish the boundaries of the political in alignment with the ideological commitments of ancient normative thought, with its focus on city-states and their domestic arrangements, these aspects of ancient politics will be rendered invisible.[17]

In short, what we find in ancient normative theory is a model of politics focused on the ethical cultivation of elites and the distribution of power narrowly *within* those deemed members of the city-state.[18] (As importantly, much of ancient political thought is, in Benjamin Straumann's terms, eudaimonistic: it aimed not at the interrogation of power, but at the cultivation of virtuous—and, therefore, happy—citizens.[19]) More importantly, these conversations were conducted via discursive operations and administrative mechanisms that excluded persons and activities outside urban centers from the domain of politics altogether. Even Aristotle proceeded thus: in his words, "a city-state is a composite thing, in the same sense as any other of the things that are wholes but consist of many parts. It is therefore clear that we must first inquire into the nature of the citizen."[20] By citizen, as he goes on to explain, he intends adult males, though he recognizes that women, children, slaves, and foreigners live in cities and contribute to the well-being of citizens and, indeed, may (in the case of male children) grow up to be citizens.[21] This is most visible in Greek in the circularity of its political vocabulary: politics (*to politikon*) is conducted by citizens (*polites*), who do politics (*politeuesthai*) in a political or citizenly way (*politikôs*) in a city-state (*polis*). None of these lexemes or the concepts they signify can easily be transferred to an empire or a village, and once we acknowledge, as we must, that the status of *polis* was subject to rules of recognition, while the status of village was largely ascribed, then the politics of Greek theories of politics become more nakedly apparent. Much the same, *mutatis mutandis*, is true of the focus of Roman theory on autonomous political communities, whether city-states (*civitates*) or municipalities (*municipia*), which have their populations (*populi*) and public things (*res publicae*). To grasp the importance of these claims, one need only pose the question of how different our histories would look if their subject were the ancient city as a whole, and not merely the *polis*.[22] The process by which their gaze, and ours, became so restricted is the subject of the next section.

Citizenship and the Form of Public Power

The primary contributions of Greece and Rome to Western political thought are, first, the conceptualization and preliminary analysis of forms of public power in terms of the ideal-types monarchy, oligarchy, and democracy (whose modern influence derives from their articulation by Aristotle and the neo-Aristotelian tradition[23]); and the juridification of notions of political belonging in the form of citizenship (which is nearly wholly a Roman legacy). To a point, these concepts co-constitute each other in historical development, as will be clear in what follows.

Communities in archaic Greece and central Italy give little to no evidence of policing communal boundaries or having depersonalized mechanisms for adjudicating membership or sustaining membership rolls. Instead, forms of horizontal social mobility were widespread. That is to say, groups of persons moved easily between communities and were accepted into new communities at similar social ranks to those that they had held in their former community. This is most visible in tales of the arrival of aristocratic families, together with their social dependents. (A related phenomenon is the acceptance of strongman rulers from outside, whom Marshall Sahlins calls outsider kings. In such cases, tight-knit oligarchies decline to elevate one among their group in power over the others and instead accept an outsider as preeminent. The position of the outsider-king is then hedged about with institutional safeguards—for example, forms of ceremony or ideas of sacrality—that grant him enormous symbolic power but restrict his access to actual social controls.[24]) On a standard narrative, already visible in antiquity, the emergence of a notion of membership, such that membership entailed a right to a voice in communal affairs, developed alongside the need for communities to call upon members for military service. Lacking the forms of state finance sufficient to pay for soldiers—and in any event lacking access to the excess manpower necessary to the professionalization of soldiering—archaic communities engaged in, and responded to, intercommunal violence and predation by tithing members for military service. Those who could arm themselves came to demand consultation.[25]

Much more might be said of the historical conditions that allowed for the juridification of ideas of membership, including the knowledge technologies that notionally allowed for tracking membership and counting citizens (Figure 4.2). In this context, however, it bears mentioning that early modern theorists draw a strong divide between the premodern and modern worlds precisely along a divide of this kind: the emergence of fiscal regimes and banking systems, as well as demographic conditions, that allowed for the professionalization of military service and the institutionalization of standing armies fundamentally changed the subjective conditions of citizenship, and the relationships of citizens to their states and states to each other.[26] Where the ancient world is concerned, a vector of changes—demographic, having to do with the generation of surplus males; technological, having to do with widespread manufacture and use of coin; and political,

FIGURE 4.2 The so-called altar of Domitius Ahenobarbus, of the late second century BCE. The depiction probably represents the enrolling of citizens for a new colonial project. © Wikimedia Commons (public domain).

being related to the growth of regional powers—did gradually make the use of paid soldiery in the form of mercenaries vastly more common, and the world of ancient politics was never the same again.[27]

Returning to the classical period, what is in any event clear is that classification of forms of public power in terms of monarchy (rule of one person), oligarchy (rule of the few), or democracy (rule by the *dêmos*) was ideal-typical and not empirical in its orientation. That these can scarcely ever have existed in pure form is of course utterly clear: in narrative, Greek kings and tyrants, as well as the kings of Rome, are always aided and sometimes opposed by networks of aristocrats, who are often gathered and whose voice is then institutionalized in a council of some kind. The authority of such councils was often then anchored in the social authority of some domain notionally outside of politics: the council is one of "elders" (it is a *gerousia*) or of "fathers" (the members are *patres*).

Within this tradition of thought, beyond the taxonomy of types of rule according to the number of persons credited with sovereign power lay further considerations of two kinds. On the one hand, it rapidly became common to understand each type of government as having a negative form, such that a bad king was a tyrant (*tyrannis*) and a bad kingship (*basileia*) or rule of one (*monarchia*) was a despotism; a good government by the few was a government of the best (*aristokrateia*), as opposed to one merely of a small number (*oligarchy*). For its part, democracy, once corrupted, devolved into mob rule (*ochlocracy*). Elaborating an argument by Aristotle, the Hellenistic historian Polybius urged that these were not merely analytic types but that they existed in a relation of historical necessity, one succeeding another in a predictable cycle:[28]

> Such is the cycle of political revolution, the course appointed by nature in which constitutions change, are transformed, and finally return to the point from which they started.[29]

Polybius is also responsible for the most sustained argument to survive from the ancient world on behalf of balanced or mixed constitutions, namely, those that incorporated elements from each of the ideal types. On his understanding, the longevity of Rome could be explained by the fact that its consuls exercised a monarchic form of executive power; the Roman senate was an aristocratic element, which controlled foreign policy and the strings of the public purse; finally, the right and power of the people to vote on legislation and elect magistrates amounted to a democratic element.[30]

This analysis of Roman government in Greek terms was immensely influential on the Romans themselves, not least via its reception in Cicero's *On the Republic*—with the caveat that Cicero knows but declines to use the expanded taxonomy of three types and their related perversions, preferring instead a four-fold typology: monarchy, aristocracy, popular government, and the balanced constitution.[31] Cicero also received from Polybius (and Aristotle) a deep-seated suspicion of political-theoretical writings that were wholly divorced from any empirical reality.[32] As a result, when he engages with these Greek traditions in his work *On the Commonwealth*, Cicero enacts a twofold move, one aspect of which was literary, the other normative. As a literary matter, one character, Laelius, accused another, Scipio, of having spoken in the manner of Plato's Socrates, which is to say, he accuses Scipio of having vocalized his own thoughts in the mouth of another.[33] As a normative matter, Laelius avers, Scipio had spoken in a fashion that was false to history, ascribing to a single human agent, Romulus, conditions that in fact came about through chance or necessity. In response, Scipio begins again, and the second book of *On the Commonwealth* therefore recounts the development of the Roman constitution (and Roman state) as the product of historical developments whose causes were multiple, and whose sources of inspiration included Roman borrowing from non-Roman cultures:

> In fact, you will recognize that even more clearly if you watch the commonwealth improving and approaching the ideal condition by a natural route and direction; you will decide that this is itself a reason to praise our ancestors' wisdom, because you will recognize how much better they made the institutions borrowed from other places than they had been in the place of origin from which we adopted them.[34]

Cicero's position in this regard represented the expression in normative political theory of a particular Roman commitment to historicism, which as a related matter declined to freight politics with metaphysical commitments of a Hellenic kind. This attitude, which treated the social as nothing more (or less) than the product of human institution building, and which therefore regarded all social institutions as valuable insofar as they aided in the securing of order in the contexts for which they were developed, is a distinctively Roman tradition within ancient philosophy.[35]

Alas, Cicero's work was lost in late antiquity, until some portion of it was rediscovered on a palimpsest in the second decade of the nineteenth century. This most sustained articulation of a Roman philosophical position on politics was therefore unavailable to several foundational generations of European political thought. The huge influence on the framers of the American constitution of this portrait of the Roman constitution as balanced among powers therefore came not via Roman authors, but through direct reading of the Greek Polybius himself.[36]

Polybius is also a participant in another great theme of ancient literature, one without significant modern reception, analogue, or echo. It consists in the imagining and occasional experience of an end to political societies. (J. G. A. Pocock treats this as a theme in the tradition of republican political thought under the rubric of finitude.[37]) In Polybius, it is the Roman general Scipio, victor over Carthage, who wept as that city burned, remarking to Polybius (who was present) that such a fate awaited Rome too.[38] Annihilation of themselves as a people is the fate that the Trojans expect in despair in Homer's *Iliad*, and which is narrated in Vergil's *Aeneid*. An end to Rome itself was imagined if not achieved in the age of Saint Augustine, in the aftermath of the sack of Rome. His contemporaries, distanced from this classical theme by virtue of the flattery Vergil had paid to Augustus, namely, that Rome would have empire without end, were shocked. Augustine responded by citing the lessons of history: communities, like empires, must have an end. What I would stress is not simply the very different metaphysics of this ancient preoccupation but also its ethics: destruction is something that human societies wreak upon each other, and never cease to do.

Returning to the problematics of public power and speaking now in modern rather than ancient terms, one cannot have a democracy without encountering the democratic boundary problem. By this is meant that the distribution of public power to a collective like the *dêmos* or *populus* demands a resolution to the question of who counts as a member of those groups.[39] This question, and many that are related to it or attendant upon it—most particularly, what was imagined to be the basic unit of social reproduction, and how was it, namely, the household (*oikos*) or family (*familia*), to be regulated—were not resolved quickly, nor were the answers devised by ancient communities terribly stable over time.[40] Nonetheless, it is reasonably clear that notions of communal membership were institutionalized in this context. Three further problems issued from this transformation in the conception of membership, from one of social dependency upon aristocratic houses to one of atomized units in relation to a whole. These were the need to shape, constrain, and direct forms of intersubjective social power among members; the need to develop practices to disguise, ameliorate, or excuse systematic inequalities in the distribution of wealth and political influence; and the accommodation at law of the vast array of communal residents who were not granted membership—resident aliens and slaves above all, but also women and children.

In respect of intersubjective social power within the citizen body, the ancient sources speak primarily of the power of lenders over debtors. Sources in Greek offer relatively little by way of reflection on the structures that produced indebtedness, or the inequalities of wealth and ownership of land that were its conditions of possibility. This is to say, to the extent that classical Greeks worried about wealth inequality and the disparities of power it produced, their solutions were mostly *ex post*, rather than *ex ante* reimaginings of the structures of production.[41] By contrast, Roman sources down to the second century BCE identify conditions of military service as a factor in systematic lower-class indebtedness; indeed, it appears to have been one of increasing political importance across the early years of the late republic.[42] This arose because military campaigns were increasing in complexity and duration, and by virtue of the empire's expansion, in distance from Rome.

In consequence, soldiers in arms were likely to be away from home for longer and longer periods. Because of wealth inequalities, and because—so they said—lower-class families often lived as tenant farmers, the effect of long-term military service on the finances of lower-class households was potentially devastating. Nor, according to representations in ancient sources, was it lost on people that the fruits of empire flowed disproportionately to the Roman elite, neither to the Roman lower-class nor to their Italian allies. The result was contests on multiple fronts about the nature and project of Roman imperialism, and how its fruits were to be distributed.[43]

More broadly, across both Greek and Roman antiquity, the development of ideologies of citizenship connected to public (military) service, together with notions of the community as bounded, enabled the emergence of doctrines that we might variously characterize as equality before the law in respect of rights, or freedom for all from domination by others, or in cases of empire, an equality of some sort among citizens in respect of rights in contradistinction to the dispreferral of those over whom the citizen body as a collective exercised its power (Figure 4.3). Within these contexts, agitation against varied forms of debt servitude *within the citizen body* acquired real power, and we witness, across many legal systems, the imposition of limits on the power of lenders over debtors in default. These arise both out of an anxiety for citizenly dignity in itself, and also to preserve some boundary between free (citizen) and slave. (We will have more to say about slavery, below.) Against a long-term backdrop, involving myriad cultures, in

FIGURE 4.3 Athenian hoplites, from a relief of the early fifth century BCE. © Getty Images.

which indebtedness is figured not simply as a financial failing but also as a moral one, this is a notable moment in the history of debt.

In every ancient society where we can track this information, there is a strong correlation between wealth, social prestige, and political power. In places that operated according to democratic principles for election to office, this was often formalized via wealth qualifications for particular offices. For its part, Rome (like the Persian Empire) sought to cultivate democratic institutions in the juridically constituted communities that were subject to it, with the caveat that it seems to have insisted that access to office should be restricted to the wealthy. For example, the geographer Pausanias recalled that after the sack of Corinth in 146 BCE, Lucius Mummius and the ten senatorial commissioners who were advising him "put an end to rule by the masses and established offices based on property qualifications."[44] One can sense how entrenched wealth was felt to be, as well as the stakes in so conceiving the power it purchased *as* entrenched, in the extraordinary frequency of dyadic formulations of sovereignty. Official acts of the Roman state, for example, are attributed in Roman legal instruments to "The Senate and People of Rome"—the famed *SPQR*.[45] Likewise, many are the Greek communities whose official acts were undertaken by "The Council and the Dêmos of the [name of the people]"[46]— that is to say, political communities represented themselves as speaking with two voices, those of the rich gathered in the Council and the collective voice of all the rest, who were denominated the *dêmos*.[47]

Official responses to the problem of wealth inequality varied. Greek cities often imposed taxes and duties on their richest citizens in the form of so-called liturgies, meaning "work" or "service for the people." The most common liturgies were the duty to fund constituent parts of religious festivals, whether to hire performers, train a chorus, provision a festival delegation, or provide a feast; or, in maritime cities, the obligation to outfit a ship in the fleet. Others included supply of the gymnasium and the keeping of a horse for service in the city's cavalry. It is important to note, however, that already Aristotle understood liturgical systems to be a mechanism to discourage the lower classes from desiring access to office: it was the price that the rich paid for oligarchy.

> The magistrates of the highest rank, which ought to be in the hands of the governing body, should have expensive duties attached to them, and then the people will not desire them and will take no offense at the privileges of their rulers, when they see that they pay a heavy fine for their dignity.[48]

Alongside such tithes on the rich there frequently obtained certain norms against ostentatious displays of wealth.[49] It is essential to observe that these minor gestures at progressive taxation left the structures of economic production and wealth creation, and its legal and institutional supports, intact. We will consider the politics and political economics of a world so ordered further below.

The norms of the Roman republic responded to wealth inequality somewhat differently than did those common to Greek cities of the classical period. Roman public law recognized several different ways of classifying citizens—as patricians or plebeians, which were inherited statuses; or senators, equestrians, and so forth, which were earned and only contingently assigned.[50] In any given period, there must have existed conventional expectations of a correlation between legal rank, social prestige, and political power, even as changing demographic and social conditions regularly placed stress on the system.[51] But what does seem clear is that Romans of the governing class—its elite— understood their society and its institutions in terms of a broad distinction between those who participated in politics through acts of judgment, leadership, and competition for office and honor, on the one hand, and those who participated as auditors in the assembly and soldiers in the military—in other words, those who listened to their betters—on the other.[52] (The normative status of this distinction receives articulation, inter alia, in the insistence by Romans that public policy was only "discussed" in unilateral speech in the assembly, when—in Roman terms—a "lawful guide" selected speakers to address the people, whose role was that of audience.[53]) Although we occasionally hear of laws in Rome against conspicuous consumption, these seem as much as anything to have been directed at regulating intra-elite competition, rather than staving off social unrest consequent upon disparities of wealth.[54] Instead of any interrogation of the systemic sources of inequalities of wealth and power, what we find in Roman theorizing is an imbricated network of bifurcated concepts. For example, liberty, or freedom, if you will, was essential to Roman political thought, but it was of two types: the elite were to be free to exercise virtue; non-elites were free to resist domination. Likewise, elite virtue consisted in defeating their peers in contests for office in order to wage wars of conquest on behalf of their community; the virtue of non-elites consisted in choosing leaders and fighting their wars.

This is not to say that Romans were unaware of the potential for abuse that inhered in the discrepant power to which wealth gave access, but it is in the regular exhortation that the legal system should adhere to its principles and protect the weak against the powerful—and not in legislative action on structural contributors to wealth inequality—that this awareness is visible to us.[55] (That institutions of justice could be corrupted by the rich and powerful is already among the most bitter complaints of Hesiod, at the dawn of classical literature: "Keep watch against this, you princes, and make straight your judgements, you who devour bribes; put crooked judgments altogether aside from your thoughts."[56]) A notable anecdote on this theme features in the miscellany of Aulus Gellius, in a conversation notionally between the sophist Favorinus and the jurist Sextus Caecilius, on the theme of the obsolescence of laws:

> And therefore your friend Labeo also, in the work that he wrote *On the Twelve Tables*, expressing his disapproval of that law, says: "One Lucius Veratius was an exceedingly wicked man and of cruel brutality. He used to amuse himself by striking free men in the face with his open hand. A slave followed him with a purse full of *asses*; as often as he had buffeted anyone, he ordered twenty-five *asses* to be counted out at once, according to the provision of the Twelve Tables. Therefore," he continued, "the praetors afterwards decided that this law was obsolete and invalid and declared that they would appoint arbiters to appraise damages."[57]

To be sure, the story is about the obsolescence of law: a clause of the Twelve Tables, written in the fifth century BCE, remained in force hundreds of years later, by which time the punishment it ordained had become so trivial that it required correction. But the story is also about the failure of the norm that the law sought both to express and inculcate: hence the character at the heart of the tale, Lucius Veratius, abuses the law and his fellow citizens "to amuse himself." His profligacy is thus not measured in the amount of money he wastes in ostentatious disregard of communal norms, but in his exposure of the fact that money can render his disregard of those norms inconsequential. In nearly the same era, a rhetorician and declaimer Calpurnius Flaccus observed of a fictitious opponent in court, "Your riches have elevated you above the standard of citizenly equality."[58]

ECONOMICS

Economic Thought and Economic Activity

The modern study of the ancient economy was long bedeviled by a network of problems that arose from how economics was conceptualized and discussed in literary sources from antiquity.[59] In short, economics was not hived off from other forms of social activity as a domain worthy of analysis in its own right. Instead, many forms of activity that we would denominate economic were treated by them within alternative or, one might say, wider networks of analysis. This includes the management of one's own farm or a network of estates cultivated by tenants (or partially by slaves); the question of what constituted appropriate forms of investment for the wealthy; the social value and prestige of banking, shipping, as wealth-generating activities; and so forth (Figure 4.4). In many cases, ancient writers weigh these questions not simply in light of economic criteria—return on investment, for example, or risk—but explicitly in light of moral and social values. At a theoretical level, scholars view ancient economic thought as embedded within these wider considerations. Substantively, economic historians long classified the ancient economy as primitive because the ancients declined to develop tools to maximize profit and productivity gains, or even to consider these as preeminent variables in weighing choices.

All of this is to say that ancient economic thought—ancient economic ideas—are often discontinuous with our own. This is not to say, however, that their thinking on economic matters is without interest. For one thing, there is a regular interplay in ancient representations of exchange between the framing of such activity in terms of

FIGURE 4.4 Roman mosaic depicting a workman with oxen, late second century CE, Metropolitan Museum. © Alamy Stock Photos.

gift exchange and its framing as organized around a profit motive.[60] In gift exchange, it is the thought that counts, one might say. Or, rather, asymmetries in the economic value of gifts were understood in symbolic terms, which allowed their translation into many other domains of interaction, where the asymmetry might be explained away, or stored, and recompensed in quite different arenas. For another, the ancients often wrote about economic matters in society at large in light of their understanding of the economic activity of households (or farmsteads), so that the economy overall is merely an aggregation of household economies. If they were committed to such a view, this might have hampered—and perhaps did hamper—their efforts to scale up certain activities or modes of production, and perhaps it contributed to the nondevelopment of any literature on macroeconomics or issues of state finance. In any event, their ways of talking about economic activity, which saw economic activity as embedded in a wide array of ethical and aesthetic commitments, might well be more true than our own to the nature of individual decision-making, which is often a value-pluralist enterprise.

Whatever we make of Greek and Roman writing on the economy, it might be more accurate to classify many of their theorizations—particularly those immanent in practice—as contributions to the history of political economy, rather than economics more narrowly. I will turn to this issue in a moment.

The problems of contemporary analysis to which I just referred, namely, the desire to classify the ancient economy as either primitive or modern, or to describe its functioning as autonomous or independent of social and moral considerations or, instead, as embedded in noneconomic forms of social relations, derive in large measure from efforts to understand ancient economic thought, and secondarily from efforts to assess the ancient economy in light of such understandings. But more so than in respect of politics, the gap that looms in economic activity between ancient theory and ancient practice has bedeviled historical study. Even setting aside the limitations of ancient economic thought as derivative from theorizations of the household, there remains the problem that the self-same persons who can be shown to have invested substantially in trade, say, or engaged in agriculture as a business, describe themselves and persons of their class as moral beings first, and their economic activity as directed at culturally approved forms of moral display.[61]

Our ability to assess and understand this gap between ancient discourse and practice has been substantially enhanced in recent years by the massive increase in evidence for economic activity derived from archaeological excavation and the study of documentary texts, on papyrus and other impermanent media in personal use.[62] These records, consisting in letters, accounts, and contracts as well as texts concerned with legal disputes over property and trade, reveal a range of practices with regard to double-entry bookkeeping, risk mitigation, systems of credit and finance as well as simple banking, and strategies in respect of principal-agent issues, about which extant literary sources leave us nearly wholly in the dark. In much the same way, the accounts of large estates in high imperial and late ancient Egypt have been extensively analyzed, in an effort to assess the specifically economic rationality of their owners.[63] To all this might be added the invaluable reconstruction of the operation of state institutions, both in the service of markets (the provision of predictable rules for the enforcement of contract, for one thing; or standardized weights and measures, for another; as well as a remarkable array of efforts at ensuring the supply of markets and control of their prices) and in pursuit of the taxation of their activities. The sophistication of contemporary writings on the ancient economy testify to the bravura use that modern historians have made of this increase in the quantity and variety of evidence, and of course all this human activity was the object of planning and discussion, and humans were and are no less self-interpretive when acting economically than when engaged in other forms of social conduct. Nevertheless, it must be said that no ancient theorization of the economy comes remotely close to capturing the texture or scale of economic activity that modern historical inquiry has revealed, and that is in itself an important fact about their "ideas."

That said, there were moments of wealth transfer that did register widely in social commentary and which received considerable attention in legal sources. Perhaps the most important were testamentary succession and dowry. With good reason, it has been suggested that marriage, and succession to an estate, were the largest economic transactions that most individuals in the ancient world would ever undertake.[64] But these were also preeminently moments when the transfer of wealth was subject to noneconomic principles; indeed, it might be said that at such moments, the transfer of wealth was symbolic of intersubjective commitments as expressed through and interpreted in light of noneconomic norms.[65] How much a father gave to one or another daughter, and the forms of wealth he gave, spoke volumes; as did the distribution of money, objects, legacies, and duties in a will; but those "volumes," as it were, were not "about" the economy.

The legal sources that tell us so much about dowry and succession might also be read so as to tell another, more complicated story about the relationship between politics, political subjectivity, and economic agency. In a remarkable lecture published in 1992, "The ideal of citizenship since classical times," J. G. A. Pocock offered extended characterizations of Greek and Roman citizenship, based in large measure on readings of Aristotle's *Politics* and the *Institutes* of Gaius.[66] (In the Athenian case, he reflected lightly and accurately on the changing context of citizenship from the age of Pericles to the world after Chaeronea; on the Roman side, he stuck close to private law in the age of Republican monarchy, which results in a kind of foreshortened perspective, but this is not the place to critique his work.) In Gaius, he observes, we move from a world of the citizen as political being to a world of the citizen as legal being:

> For the Roman jurist it was altogether different; persons acted upon things, and most of their actions were directed at taking or maintaining possession; it was through these actions, and through the things or possessions which were the subjects of the actions, that they encountered one another and entered into relations [that] might require regulation. The world of things, or *res*, claimed the status of reality; it was the medium in which humans beings lived and through which they formed, regulated and articulated their relations with each other.[67]

This prompts Pocock to reflect on the distance one might be said to have traveled from the citizen in an Aristotelian *polis* to the deracinated citizen of the Roman world empire:

> From being *kata phusin zoon politikon*, the human individual came to be by nature a proprietor or possessor of things; it is in jurisprudence, long before the rise and supremacy of the market, that we should locate the origins of possessive individualism. The individual thus became a citizen—and the word *citizen* increasingly diverged from its Aristotelian significance—through the possession of things and practice of jurisprudence.[68]

In short, intersubjective relations among citizens occur via the mediation of things, and it is those relations that are the subject of legal regulation. (Pocock knowingly sets aside the issue that in reality, and also in metaphor, human beings are among the things of which citizens were proprietors and possessors.) The result is that

> the ideal of citizenship [came] to denote a legal status, which is not quite the same thing as a political status, and which will, in due course, modify the meaning of the term *political* itself.[69]

But to write this history, of course, Pocock did more than cross centuries and cultures, from fourth-century BCE Athens to second-century CE Rome. He also contrasted a work of normative political theory with a handbook on private law. That private law should be felt the domain of ancient thought from which a history of subjectivity might be written is of course an index of the wider set of transformations that Pocock sought to chart.

The Economics of Honor

Assessed in light of post-Ricardian economic science, ancient cultural elites signally failed to develop conceptual apparatus adequate to the scale and complexity of their economic activities. At the same time, despite anxieties about wealth inequality, ancient communities satisfied themselves with the most minimal of tithes on the wealth of economic elites. By this I mean not that the cost of the special contributions requested of elites—so-called liturgies or, in the west, *munera*—was not occasionally high. I emphasize, rather, that public impositions on the wealth of economic elites interfered in no way with the structures of wealth production, and thus posed no threat to the ability of economic elites to reproduce themselves over generations. But this is not the end of the story. For one thing, both comparative and empirical study urges that Mediterranean economies in the classical period produced greater returns on capital than wage labor, with the result that, all else being stable, those controlling the means of production would inevitably have distanced themselves in wealth from their fellow citizens.[70] For another, we have already seen that ancient socioeconomic elites preferred to describe their economic activities as motivated by aesthetic and above all moral concerns, rather than economic ones. In their cultural production, they styled themselves an elite of virtue, and not an elite of wealth. How were these ideological systems actualized in the politics of Greek and Roman city-states?

Although my interest at this juncture lies primarily with how the notionally democratic political structures of the classical Mediterranean city-state sustained inequitable systems for the distribution of wealth and power, one should approach the subject with two factors in mind. First, in the ancient world, neither political nor demographic conditions generally allowed families to reproduce themselves across multiple generations.[71] Second, discrepant norms in respect of succession from culture to culture played an enormous role in sustaining or disintegrating patrimonial wealth. Roman practice in particular favored the distribution of equal shares to all heirs in the first class, with predictable effects on the integrity of intergenerational wealth transfers.[72]

Focusing on discourse and action in the public sphere, the primary mechanism by which wealth inequality was mitigated was through practices and ideologies of public benefaction, which modern scholars term euergetism, from Greek *euergetês* = "benefactor" or "do-gooder."[73] The basic structure of the relevant social action is familiar to all participants in Anglo-American institutional life. (i) Members of an elite of wealth spend private resources on public goods: they donate to a theater or an orchestra, or give to a university. (ii) In the modern world, the goods are often deemed public not simply in politics but also in law, such that the expenditure receives a tax benefit. (iii) The benefactor is publicly thanked for public- or civic-mindedness. (iv) Finally, the public giving of thanks, and the good citizenship of the benefactor, is recorded on a permanent medium in a public space.

On the surface, the thanks conveyed to such benefactors was often a public act, granted by a popular assembly or public council, and so one might view the entire system as a discourse on civic ideals.[74] As an example, consider the following decree of the council of Tergeste (modern Trieste):

> Aspanius Lentulus and [—] Nepos, duoviri with jurisdiction spoke as follows: "Whereas Lucius Fabius Severus, *vir clarissimus*, has already in the past performed great benefactions for our commonwealth, having acted already from a young age in such a way that in aiding his fatherland, he increased his own dignity and eloquence—for he pleaded and conducted and triumphed in many and important public cases before the best of emperors, Antoninus Pius, without any expense to our treasury, in such a way that although he was young, nevertheless, by means of wise and accomplished actions and deeds he bound his fatherland and all of us to him—but now, by means of a benefaction so great and so health-giving and of such permanent utility, he has so aided our commonwealth that he has easily surpassed all his preceding actions, however immense and wonderful they were. In short, the wonderful virtue of this most outstanding man, with respect to which he surpasses himself every day in doing good and in protecting his fatherland—although in proportion to his benefaction we are unequal in giving thanks—nevertheless, he exercises that virtue in regard to time and talent to be of aid [to us]: therefore, the goodwill of this outstanding man must be repaid, not in order to render him more favorable to us—for another such man could not be born—but in order that we should show ourselves grateful to those judging, and worthy of such honor and such protection. Wherefore, what it is pleasing to do, concerning that matter the councilors decreed as follows, with Calpurnius Certus being the first to express his view.[75]

This remarkable but altogether typical preamble is followed by the actual decree of the city council, which includes an account of Fabius Severus' most recent intervention with the emperor, as well as a description of the "thanks" the council voted to him: a gilt equestrian statue, to be erected in the most prominent part of the forum, with the decree of the council inscribed on its base, as a lesson to posterity. A reading of the text within the horizons of its politics suggests that socioeconomic elites such as Fabius Severus, who might have kept their money for themselves, were induced by public honors like equestrian statues and public decrees, to spend money in other-regarding or public-regarding ways, and there is no doubt that this is a legitimate reading of such texts.

That said, one must be clear-sighted about the system, in at least two ways. For one thing, it is essential to imagine how such public goods might otherwise have been funded: political communities might have taxed income or wealth, and their assemblies could have funded public goods, selected by the people themselves, through state appropriations. Structures of this kind operated in many city-states in a minor way; it was not beyond their imagination.

One should also be clear-sighted about the politics of such public thanks, in the system as it actually functioned. Through public benefactions and the thanks and honors that were their regular return, elites of wealth purchased moral esteem, rather than critique, on grounds of justice or economic fairness or mere publicity. What is more, through the operation of civic institutions, which were dominated by their class, members of the elite filled public spaces—they monopolized the public sphere—with memorials like equestrian statues and civic decrees. These celebrated the specific forms of civic virtue that were attainable only by themselves and their peers. One need only study the statue-scape of the public spaces of Greek cities, or survey the records of extant municipal decrees from the Roman west, to see this. In consequence, it was not all citizens who could fulfill the ideals of citizenship and aspire to public honor, but only the rich. In the late classical city and ever after, great personal wealth was preeminent among the conditions of possibility for public honor, with the result that the citizenship of the non-wealthy was, for all intents and purposes, defective in potentiality.[76] We are returned, at last, to the separate virtues of the elite and non-elite in Roman and also Greek political life.

CONCLUSION

Thus far, we have traced the contours of ancient discourse and practices in respect of politics and economics, and performed mostly immanent forms of critique. In closing, I want to suggest some of the constraints we place on historical study when we foreground their terminology and forms of analysis in contemporary research. Let me focus on two populations: slaves and peasants.

Slavery was ubiquitous in the ancient world, so much so that Roman lawyers averred as an empirical matter that no society was known to them that did not practice slavery.[77] The incidence of slavery no doubt differed from region to region, both in populousness and in forms of exploitation. Rome seems to have been unique in its tendency to manumit slaves, not least in that manumission regularly led to citizen status. The result is that slaves—or, rather, ex-slaves, and their stories—are more visible in Roman society and areas governed by Roman legal regimes than elsewhere. That said, modern historians should beware their complicity in ancient representations of politics and the economy. These tended to treat slavery as a moral matter, at best, and therefore neglected the contribution of slaves to ancient economies. It is not farfetched to say that slave labor, alongside transfer payments from empire, were the conditions of possibility of widespread participation in Athenian-style democracy. And yet, the finest modern handbook of the ancient Greek economy devotes nearly as many index entries to oxen as to slaves.[78] Where Rome is concerned, not only is much about slavery revealed by legal sources in themselves, and *ex negativo* in the remarkable evidence for the lives of freedpersons, but also much can be discerned about the form of Roman politics in the mimetic relation of the culture and social relations of the freed in respect of the free.[79] But these acts of historical recuperation are the result of *our* politics, not theirs.

As Greek and Roman culture and law regarded all residents of cities other than adult citizen males as deficient in one or more regards, so it regarded the many populations that lived outside Greek and Roman cities as defective: this is so despite a literature of nostalgia that remembered an age—now emphatically past—when, for example, Roman magistrates had themselves been cultivators of the land, returning to the plough after each period in office. One need only consider Greek and Roman terms for village and "villagey" (which is in fact an English word, though little used): *kômê, kômêtikos, pagus, paganus,* and so forth. The rarity with which anyone claimed in Greek the status of "villagey" for their institutions or culture proves the point, as does the availability of *paganus*, "a rustic"—meaning "a rustic bumpkin"—for the kind of fool that would choose to be non-Christian. This matters because perhaps 85 percent of the population of the ancient Mediterranean world dwelt in the countryside. At a minimum, the absence of their lives from all but the fantasies of most ancient cultural production is a matter of historical and political urgency for modern scholars. Of greater weight is the conjoined operation of systems of political dominance, economic exploitation, and moral disapproval, by which city-state elites—often enjoying equality among themselves—sustained their preeminence.

To illustrate this point, and to bring this chapter to a close at a transformative moment in ancient politics, let me turn to the third edict of the emperor Caracalla contained on the famous papyrus from Giessen that contains the decree by which Caracalla had conferred citizenship on nearly all freeborn residents of the Roman Empire. The third edict sought to expel from Alexandria persons juridically classified as Egyptians:

> All Egyptians in Alexandria, especially country-folk (*agroikoi*), who have fled from other parts and can easily be detected, are by all manner of means to be expelled, with the exception, however, of pig-dealers and river boatmen and the men who bring down reeds for heating the baths. But expel all the others, as by the numbers of their kind and their uselessness they are disturbing the city. I am informed that at the festival of Sarapis and on certain other festal days Egyptians are accustomed to bring down bulls and other animals for sacrifice, or even on other days; they are not to be prohibited from this. The persons who ought to be prohibited are those who flee from their own districts to escape rustic toil, not those, however, who congregate here with the object of viewing the glorious city of Alexandria or come down for the sake of enjoying a more *politikos* life or for incidental business.
>
> A further extract. For genuine Egyptians can easily be recognized among the linen weavers by their speech, which proves them to have assumed the appearance and dress of another class; moreover, in their mode of life their far-from-civilized manners reveal them to be Egyptian country-folk.[80]

To commence the unpacking of the many prejudices and commitments that inform this text, we should first take note of the consistent identification of country-folk (*agroikoi*) with the ethno-legal status of Egyptian. Rusticity and labor fall to some by happenstance; to members of some ethnic groups, it falls by default. Second, while the emperor wants Egyptians who do not belong in Alexandria to be expelled, he allows a number of exceptions: those who are economically or materially useful; those making sacrifices at the temple of Serapis, whether for the festival or some other occasion; and those who want to see the *polis* or enjoy a more *politikos* lifestyle. The end of the text offers instructions about the implementation of the decree: true Egyptians, meaning, perhaps, ethnic Egyptians, can be recognized by their speech, as well as their deportment: they are *agroikoi*, country-folk or rustics, insofar as their behavior is not *politikos*.

But of course, as I have emphasized, life outside a *polis* is by definition not *politikos*: the classification of these people as "uncivilized" was thus overdetermined by prior decisions, made by Greek and Roman officials, to classify communities as cities or villages in public law. In the prejudicial logic of the text, villagers come to the *polis* to admire their betters. In material reality, those who come to the city to sacrifice succumb to an ideology whereby religious commitment requires them to transfer wealth from their communities to the city and to subscribe to a sacred topography in which their own communities are dispreferred. The prejudice in favor of cities and dispreferral of village life is stated as a matter of moral and aesthetic evaluation, and it is assumed that the better among the rustics will share this prejudice. That is why rustics who come to the city for the sake of a "more *politikos*" lifestyle are to be allowed to stay. The simultaneous exclusion and exploitation of such persons by Greco-Roman elites was also a political act, enabled and justified by political ideas, which it is also our duty to recuperate.[81]

CHAPTER FIVE

Nature: Concepts, Origins, and Ambivalences

G. E. R. LLOYD

We may tend to assume that "nature" and "the natural" pick out what is in some sense given, not dependent on human production, intervention, or interpretation. In which case it would be as well to admit the possibility, at the outset, that there is nothing "natural" about the concept of nature itself. There may be a deceptive ease with which we can find what we believe to be good enough equivalents to English "nature" in such other European languages as French, Italian, and German, which all have terms that are similarly derived from Latin "natura," itself regularly taken, by Latin writers as well as by ourselves, as a good enough rendering of Greek *physis*. But if it is indeed the case that the ancient Greeks cast a long shadow over all later ruminations concerning "nature," neither the Greeks' own understandings nor how those understandings came to be used in the convoluted history of European thought down to modern times is in any sense straightforward.

Throughout the account that I shall offer here there is, in particular, a tension between a purely descriptive use of the term and a prescriptive one. Is an entity's nature how it is, or how it ought to be—and who is to decide that? Is "human nature" a matter simply of our common biology—and how do we allow for divergences within what that term covers? Or does that concept of "human nature" mask a raft of value judgments concerning how as humans we should behave? When "nature" is opposed to "culture" or to "nurture" or to "the artificial" or even to the "supernatural," "nature" is in every case the marked term, where the second term in each pair is understood primarily as what "nature" is not. And the very fact that "nature" enters into such a diverse set of binaries further complicates our task for they cannot in any sense be thought of as all synonymous. Doing justice to the complexities of our subject involves deep engagement in the history and philosophy of science, ethics, politics, psychology, aesthetics, social anthropology, and religion. I can do no more than scratch the surface of the problems here, but my aim will be to set down some markers for how the topic is to be approached and to identify some of the pitfalls that should be avoided.

I should begin with some remarks to illustrate and to some extent to justify the claim I have just made that nature is not a robust cross-cultural universal. It is of course regularly used in interpretations of other cultures, but if it is a category that we as commentators employ that does not mean that it corresponds to one that those whom we are commenting on themselves use, an "actors" category, in other words, as well as our "observers" one.

We have a variety of evidence from our literary sources that indicates that initially the Greeks themselves had no overarching category of "nature." To say this about the ancient

Greeks or about any other ancient, early modern, or contemporary culture is not to say that the groups in question had no conception of the regularity in what we call natural phenomena, for example, the risings and settings of the sun and moon, the changes in the seasons, the characteristics and behavior of different types of animals or plants, and so on. But regularity by itself is not enough to imply a category of nature, since many regularities belong rather to the social domain, for instance, the cycles of festivals or the sequences of transformations that may occur as an infant progresses through childhood to adulthood. More importantly it is often assumed that the regularities in the phenomena may be subject to exceptions, some of them rare events that do not conform to a general pattern, but some of those imagined as the direct result of the willful activities of divine or demonic forces. When it is assumed that there may be gods or spirits at work controlling what happens, it implies that the normal regularities may be suspended, which in turn means that there is no notion of a nature or natures that dictates how things must always behave. That point is essential and we shall need to return to it as we proceed.

The claim would be then that while the texts of Homer or Hesiod provide plenty of evidence that illustrates knowledge of what we call natural phenomena, including weather phenomena and the behavior of animals, what is still missing is any overarching concept of nature as such itself. The point can be confirmed by an examination of the one text in Homer that explicitly uses the term *physis*, the standard word for this concept in later writers. In the *Odyssey* 10.302f the god Hermes indicates to Odysseus the *physis* of a special plant, *moly*, which he is to use to counter the charms of Circe who will try to turn him into a pig—as she had already succeeded in transforming his companions (Figure 5.1). But so far from this text being a sign that its author has a concept of "nature,"

FIGURE 5.1 Sir Edward Coley Burne-Jones, *The Wine of Circe*, 1900. *Bibby's Annual* 1917.
© Getty Images.

it is rather evidence that no such concept is in play here. This is a plant that has magical properties that can be used to render powerless the spells a witch calls on to achieve her ends. Her transforming Odysseus' companions into pigs does not belong to the realm of the natural, the normal, the regular. Analogously the antidote that Hermes shows Odysseus also belongs to the domain of witchcraft; however that is imagined, it certainly does not conform to the regularities let alone what we could describe as belonging to the laws of the natural world. The god is not giving Odysseus a tutorial that points toward an empirical, naturalistic investigation of plants. He is revealing knowledge of how to combat the dastardly designs of a witch. When he shows the *physis* of the plant in question, the term is used in its primary sense, derived from the root *phunai*, to grow, the way it grows, therefore, an appreciably more restricted topic than everything that might be included by considering its nature in the botanist's sense.

These warnings about the dangers of assuming too readily that a concept of "nature" is present in early Greek texts are underlined when we turn to evidence that relates to how in fact such a concept came to emerge. Of course, the early so-called Presocratic philosophers are often reported to have been interested in "the inquiry into nature," *peri physeōs historia*, which late sources sometimes tell us was the title of the books they composed on the subject. On the one hand, we do have some evidence and not just from those we label "philosophers" that shows an interest in the natures of certain phenomena where that is contrasted with assumptions that they belong to the realm of the divine— which is where an explicit concept of "nature" begins to emerge. On the other, there are also clear signs indicating the risks of assimilating their uses of the term *physis* with what we consider can be included in "nature." Let me deal with the latter point before illustrating the former.

Caution is certainly needed if we try to answer the question of what might have been contained in those texts that our late sources label as concerned with what they call the inquiry into nature. We have accounts of varying degrees of reliability that discuss the origins of things and how they came to be. Where Homer and Hesiod had dealt primarily with the births of gods and goddesses, Thales is reputed to have claimed that things originate from water, *hydōr*. It may be that he also thought that things are made of water, but in the view I favor, that is less likely than the suggestion that his preoccupation was with cosmogony rather than cosmology.[1] But leaving aside that debate, we have to take stock of the fact that while water is named as such, and not identified with the personal name of a god, it was, for Thales, anything but simply an inert, inanimate, physical substance. At least on the authority of Aristotle we learn that Thales proclaimed that "all things are full of gods."[2] Elsewhere Aristotle suggests that what Thales' successor Anaximander chose as his "principle" (*archē*), namely, the Boundless (*apeiron*), is "immortal and imperishable,"[3] and later, admittedly less reliable sources join the chorus of voices that report that for the early Greek philosophers the items that they considered to be the primary constituents or origins of things are divine—as indeed we can confirm from some direct evidence of quotations of their works.[4]

So quite what would have been included under the rubric "*physis*" in archaic Greek speculative thought is more complicated than might appear from the conventional translation "nature." Heraclitus is a prime exhibit to illustrate the point, for when he said that *physis* loves to hide[5] he certainly appears to be denying that the natural characteristics of things can be read off their surface appearances. Of course, we may agree that to understand the properties of natural substances will involve more than merely superficial observation of their behavior. But Heraclitus clearly advances a cosmology that is anything but "physics" in a sense we would recognize. The "cosmos" (that is world-order) is "the same for all: no one of the gods or humans made it, but it was always and is and will be an ever-living fire, being kindled in measures and extinguished in measures."[6] So what some thought of as a substance, though others as a process, namely, "fire," is instinct with life. Indeed "thunderbolt" (a manifestation of fire) "steers everything."[7] When God is said to be "day and night, winter and summer"[8] we can appreciate that Heraclitus' project is as much an investigation into the concept of the divine as it is into what we consider natural phenomena—and indeed human experiences, since that very same quotation continues after "winter and summer" with "war and peace, satiety and hunger."

As a final witness to the nature of the problem of nature I can cite Gorgias. Here for once we have a substantial text of his, that has a three-fold thesis: that nothing exists, that if it exists it is unknowable, and that if it exists and is knowable it cannot be communicated to others. While Parmenides had claimed that "it is and it cannot not be," Gorgias deploys similar arguments to come to his radically negative conclusion. Yet in one of our main sources[9] there is an alternative or additional title to his work, not just "On what is not," but "On *physis*." The rubric of *physis* was thus broad enough to cover the ultimately skeptical view that there is nothing, which would deny the term has any referent whatsoever.

Having reviewed some of the negative evidence that shows how far many early Greek thinkers were from having formulated a clear and distinct notion of what we would call "nature" it is time to look at the sources that can throw light not just on the positive steps taken in that direction but also at the aims and agenda of those who were responsible. First there are texts that suggest at least a certain ambition to restrict the sphere of influence or the domains where gods had previously been thought to be at work. Xenophanes in the late sixth or early fifth century was certainly no atheist, though he mounted mocking attacks on traditional ideas of gods in the form of humans or of other animals,[10] as well as rejecting stories of their immoral behavior.[11] But in one notable fragment he addresses what we should say about "Iris." That was the word commonly used in Greek for the rainbow, but it was also the name of the divine messenger of the gods—for rainbows were often thought to be ominous phenomena. "The one they call Iris," Xenophanes says, "this too is by nature [*pephyke*] a cloud, purple and red and yellow to behold."[12] Xenophanes does not state that this is *all* that Iris is, but it is pretty clearly implied that to see this as ominous is mistaken.

Similar criticisms of particular traditional notions can be found in many different genres from historiography to drama,[13] but for a more sustained and systematic attack on a group of such we need to turn to the medical writers in the so-called Hippocratic Corpus dating mostly from the fifth or early fourth century BCE. The treatise called *On the Sacred Disease* has attracted particular attention in this regard, for its author lambasts those whom he calls "purifiers," whom he compares to Magoi (Persian priests), charlatans, and quacks. They accepted that the "sacred disease" is indeed "sacred": they claimed that they were able to identify which divine or demonic agent is responsible for the different varieties of the disease and, more than that, that they could counter that agency and cure the disease. The alternative the Hippocratic writer offers is clear. This disease has a nature (*physis*) and a cause (for which he uses the terms *prophasis* and *aitia*) like any other and its treatment proceeds (again like other diseases) not by "purifications," that is ritual, but by control of "regimen" (diet and exercise). It is noteworthy that his claim is not that the sacred disease is in no sense sacred, but rather that it is no more sacred than any other: all are sacred but all are natural, evidently because nature herself is in a sense sacred.[14]

Yet the actual causes the writer invokes (the blocking of the vessels by phlegm) are quite speculative and his own claim that every disease is curable provided one catches it at the right moment is very largely wishful thinking.

The crucial point of difference, however, remains. Whereas the purifiers invoke gods and demons, the Hippocratic author insists that medicine is a matter of diagnosing natural causes and treating them with natural remedies. So on the one hand, there is a clear appeal to an explicit concept of nature and to a domain over which natural causes rule, but on the other hand, the claims of secure knowledge of those causes and how to cure the diseases experienced are extravagant. What is at stake—what animates the controversy here—is the competition between rival styles of healing.

The purifiers are not allowed to speak for themselves in this Hippocratic text, but if we ponder for a moment the massive popularity that the medicine practised in the shrines of Asclepius and Apollo enjoyed—and continued to enjoy long after the attacks of Hippocratic authors and others—we may infer that despite those attacks there were plenty of Greeks, patients and their families from all walks of life, who were prepared to suspend their disbelief and put their trust in the gods (Figure 5.2). This was not just in connection with what were recognized as incurable or otherwise hopeless cases. Temple medicine records successful treatments for ailments and misfortunes of every conceivable kind.[15] Belief in the possibility of divine intervention, if you could get the gods on your side, was in no sense defeated by the rise of a new tradition of naturalistic medicine. The same, for sure, is true today, despite the far greater powers that modern biomedicine deploys. Whatever successes that registers, they have not put healing shrines such as Lourdes out of business.

We shall return shortly to the extensive evidence from other cultures and times concerning the rivalries between different styles of medicine. But for now we should stay with the Greeks to point out further aspects of the ambivalence of the concept of *physis* that by the end of the fifth and into the fourth centuries BCE was playing a key role in controversies over a wide range of subject areas. One fundamental topic of dispute focused on the relationship between *physis* and the term generally taken as its antonym, namely, *nomos*. The latter term covered customs, conventions, and laws, which were widely recognized to vary between different peoples. That recognition tended to undermine anyone who claimed that one particular set of laws had universal validity. Yet we find a variety of authors resisting that objection. They claimed that although over a certain range of provisions laws were indeed culture-specific, there are certain *nomoi* that are universal, unwritten laws (*agrapha nomima*) that underpinned morality in every human society. In Sophocles' *Antigone*, for example, they are what Antigone appeals to in order to justify her behavior in burying her brother even though her uncle, Creon, the king of Thebes had forbidden anyone to do so.[16]

The problem with invoking such an argument was obvious, namely, finding good examples of laws or conventions that *are* universally observed. Herodotus already has Darius point out that the proper way in which to treat the dead varied between India, Persia, and Greece itself.[17] Incest was one frequently cited instance, though that was undermined by the realization that royal intermarriage was practised in ancient Egypt. When in Xenophon's *Memorabilia* Hippias and Socrates are represented debating the issue, honoring one's parents is offered as another example,[18] though again that rule was frequently breached.

Against those who hoped to forge some link between what is just and right on the one hand and what is natural on the other, there were articulate proponents of the view that

FIGURE 5.2 Asclepius, god of healing, and Hygieia, goddess of health. Digitally improved reproduction of an original from the nineteenth century. © Bildagentur-online / Universal Images Group / Getty Images.

the principle that operated everywhere in nature was that might is right. In Plato's *Gorgias* Callicles is made to argue that laws were instituted in a vain attempt by the weak to curb the strong,[19] while in the *Republic* Thrasymachus puts it rather that it is the strong who use the laws as a veneer to cloak their appropriation of power.[20] Callicles even says that it is the *nomos* of nature that the strong should rule, where *nomos* does not pick out a legal institution, of course, but is used to describe what generally applies to "animals" as well as to "humans,"[21] just as in Thucydides the Athenians are made to offer as justification for the invasion and enslavement of the island of Melos an appeal to the idea that "it is a necessity of nature always to rule where one can."[22]

The search for some basis of morality led, then, to a bifurcation. Could morality and notions of what is right and just be founded on some appeal to the regularities apprehended in the natural world? Those who sought to argue that it could faced the more or less insurmountable difficulty of exemplifying where what occurs in "nature" tallies with a human sense of right and wrong. Those who took the opposite view left themselves with a gap. If nature could not be cited to underpin the correctness of particular human social and political arrangements, what alternative was there? The realist or cynical conclusion was that morality indeed had no legitimate basis in "nature."

So while some of the writers we have been dealing with started from a concern to establish how cause and effect were related to one another in the natural world, the forging of a category of "nature" had major consequences in the field of ethics—as of course it still has today. While in antiquity nature could be and was discussed in contexts devoid of any implications for morality it is important not to exaggerate that point. As we noted before, while this vocabulary was often used descriptively, to refer to what is the case, it continued to be used also prescriptively to pick out rather an ideal, what should be the case, in other words, rather than what applies always or for the most part.

Aristotle is our key witness here (Figure 5.3). He was of course responsible for an impressive body of work in the field of zoology in particular, describing the different genera and species of animals, their anatomy, modes of reproduction, behavior, and so on. But his use of the term *physis* is certainly not confined to what we can call "natural science" for it is also prominent in his treatises on ethics and politics. Humans are animals, to be sure, blooded, two-footed, and otherwise characterized by physical features. But they are defined as "by nature" (*physei*) "political animals." On the one hand, they can be compared with other kinds of animals that are gregarious or that live in groups. On the other, humans are distinguishable from other animals in virtue of their rational capacities and in particular their exercise of choice, *proairesis*, crucially in matters of morality. When Aristotle comes to consider different modes of social and political organization he recognizes that not every human being lives in a *polis*, that is a city-state. Many human beings, he acknowledges, belong to *ethnē*, "races," who do not enjoy the benefits of the typical institutions of the Greek city-state. So when he says that humans are "naturally" *politika*, we can distinguish a weaker sense in which this is the case (humans have social capacities that mark them out from other animals) and a stronger one. On the latter reading humans are not just social animals, but ones naturally adapted to living in city-states, where that describes not what is the case, but rather the ideal.

Turning back to those impressive treatises on animals we find that this prescriptive use of "nature" is widespread and influential even when we might have expected Aristotle to be concerned exclusively with factual accounts. What he considers and claims to be "natural" is sometimes pure ideology. It is better, he says, for males to be distinct from females: the latter are natural, for sure, but he believes naturally inferior.[23] When he says that their separation off from males allows the males to develop their superior capacities, he is clearly reflecting common assumptions made in the society in which he happened to live. But he goes further. It is better, he says, for the right side of bodies to be distinguished from the left, as is the case with humans, especially, of whom he says the right side is "most right-sided," for humans are, of all animals, most in accordance with nature.[24] "The starting-point (or principle)," he continues "is honourable, and above is more honourable than below, and front than back, and right than left."[25] He even uses

FIGURE 5.3 Statue of Aristotle at the Athens Academy, Athens. © Prisma / UIG / Getty Images.

this principle to explain the position of the heart in humans, "rather in the upper than in the lower half and more in front than behind." Faced with the difficulty that the heart is on the left rather than the right in humans Aristotle does not deny that fact (as Galen was to do when he said it was in the center of the human body) but explains that this is to "counterbalance the chilliness of the left side."[26]

While Aristotle's observations of many different genera and species of animals are, undeniably, impressively detailed, the influence of his assumption of a hierarchy within natural kinds is pervasive. Humans serve, for him, as a model of what in a sense an animal should be, indeed, more narrowly it is male humans that have that role. Females are essential for reproduction, for sure: they are, as we said, certainly natural in that sense. But the chief physiological characteristic that Aristotle thinks marks them out is an inability: they are unable to concoct the blood to produce semen. He never countenances the possibility of categorizing males by their inability to bear children. The female contribution to reproduction is the menses, which is the material that the male seed has to work on to produce offspring.[27] Females are, then, in his view, naturally subordinate to males, even though he is well aware that in some animal species, for example, the bear and the leopard, females are more spirited and courageous than the males, while in others (he mentions Laconian hounds) they are cleverer.[28]

But beyond discussions of the relations between males and females, the notion of hierarchy surfaces strikingly in Aristotle's talk of the way in which certain animals exhibit what he describes as "deformities"—compared that is with other species higher on the Scale of Nature. The mole, for instance, is said to be deformed in that it has (he believes) no sight, although he does recognize that there are residual eyes beneath the skin.[29] His account of the different ways that animals move makes the point especially clear. Humans alone are properly erect: quadrupeds are said to be "weighed down." When he comes to fish they are "even more stunted" (viz. than the birds) in that they have neither legs nor hands nor wings. He is even prepared to consider the whole group he calls the testacea as "maimed" (*anapēron*). They have their heads pointing downward and so like plants indeed they can be thought of as "upside down."[30] Of course, these other types of living beings all belong to nature, but when judged against the standard provided by humans they all fall short.

One final complication in Aristotle's views remains to be considered. He is very well aware of the disputes that existed on the relationship between *physis* and *nomos*. Indeed in the *Sophistic Refutations* he even claims that exploiting the different standards that those two categories were taken to stand for was a regular source of the paradoxes for which some of the the so-called sophists became notorious.[31] But the boundary he drew between these two domains was not where we might locate it. On the *nomos* side of the binary human conventions and customs were recognized to be variable. But humans themselves belong also to nature, to be sure. We have seen that defined as "by nature" "political" animals humans span both domains. But it is particularly striking that the capacity to rule is not just a matter of human social arrangements and conventions. I have already noted that females are regularly labeled inferior and so subject to rule. Faced with the widespread institution of slavery Aristotle concedes that some who have been enslaved have been denied their freedom artificially, that is, by force. Yet he thinks that there are some human beings who are natural slaves. Indeed his characterization of non-Greek "barbarian" peoples gravitates toward treating most of them as such.

So some purely social institutions (as we could describe them) have, for Aristotle, their justification in natural hierarchies. The cosmos as a whole in his view is hierarchical, arranged according to the capacities that different kinds of beings enjoy. Plants are below animals and other animals below humans. Not that humans are supreme, because we are inferior to the eternal heavenly bodies, whose capacities include not just eternal motion but also thought, since the reason Aristotle gives for their moving is that they do so out of love for the supreme divine being, an Unmoved Mover whose perfection is defined in terms of a capacity for "contemplation." If Aristotle has a very clear idea of nature as the domain of what happens "always or for the most part," it is obvious that his studies of that domain, "physics" in his terms, cannot be separated from his concern for cosmology, theology, and what we call "metaphysics." They underpin, as we said, his whole ideology and his endorsement of the social institutions, including slavery and the subordination of women, which his contemporaries largely took for granted.

The fields we think of as "ethics" and "politics" deal with where human choice and morality are at work, and humans, alone of the animals, have a moral capacity. Yet far more generally, Aristotle would say that final causes are to be found throughout "nature" and the universe as a whole is instinct with values. While for long in the history of European philosophy and science the contrast between issues of fact and issues of value has often been thought to be fundamental, we shall be returning later to the question of whether or how far this marks a radical break between modernity and what it inherited from antiquity.

While the notion of *physis* that was introduced into the center of philosophical and other discourse in ancient Greece was subject to the complexities, ramifications, and ambivalences we have indicated, it is still the case that it served for some to identify a subject matter, even a field of research. Whatever was labeled "natural" was investigable. Its causes and explanations were similarly to be sought in the regular behavior of phenomena, without appeal to what lay outside those regularities—the domain of the "supernatural." The label "contrary to nature" is to be used of what is exceptional or irregular, not of what does not belong to "nature" at all.[32] This ruled out any purported explanation that appealed to the interventions of willful gods or divine beings, thought of as doing whatever they wanted, often for reasons that mere humans were incapable of fathoming, though that was not to prevent some folk claiming (as the purifiers attacked in *On the Sacred Disease* apparently did) that they had special knowledge on that question. But the twin issues we now face are the following: to what extent did any such notion get to be made explicit in other societies, and what can we learn from such cross-cultural comparisons about either the commonality or the exceptionality of Greek views on nature? What lessons are there, indeed, for us today?

We can begin with some of the extensive evidence we have for some other ancient societies. In several, we find competing claims made by rival groups or individuals in the matter of being able to explain and to treat diseases, and given the role such a polemic played in the development of the notion of nature in Greece, this would be a promising area to start from. We have rich documentation for such rivalries in ancient Mesopotamia, for instance, where there is a considerable literature dealing with the interpretation of patients' signs or symptoms and with predictions as to the outcomes of their complaints, whether they will die or recover. Two types of healers are mentioned in our sources, the *āšipu* and the *asû*, where one of our authorities offers "exorcist magician" and "physician" as rough and ready translations of those two terms.[33] Yet the positivist associations of this rendering should be resisted. The possibility of divine or demonic intervention in causing or curing diseases is assumed by healers of all types. Their prominence varies, and so too did their use of different symbolic registers in their discourse about disease. The categories are, in any event, permeable ones, in that as Geller remarks, the same individual may combine roles that carry different titles.[34]

The situation in ancient China is similar. The mostly third-century BCE Mawangdui manuscripts studied by Harper[35] provide us with a glimpse of medical traditions that antedate the great canonical text, the *Huangdi Neijing*, composed some time at the turn of the millennium, though it now exists in the shape of three later recensions. While both those sources often imply criticisms of others' medical ideas and practices, we have more direct evidence of that in the biography of one particular second-century BCE doctor,

Chunyu Yi, preserved in the first great dynastic history, the *Shiji*, put together by Sima Tan and Sima Qian around 90 BCE.[36] Chunyu Yi had been called to account to justify his medical practice and although he does not say that he was always able to produce a cure (unlike the claims made for temple medicine in ancient Greece, for instance) he does insist that his understanding of the diseases he treats, his diagnoses or better prognoses, all proved to be correct. He also explains how he achieves this. Although he reports that he studied pulse diagnosis with his teachers—he refers to a book on the subject and clearly did not invent the method himself—he does imply that in his hands it gave uniformly accurate results.

Chunyu Yi thus certainly illustrates a shift away from more traditional appeals to demons (such as had been common in the Mawangdui texts; see Figure 5.4) to a reliance on direct observation of the patient's physical condition. Yet when, as quite often, Chunyu Yi explains how other healers, some named, some just referred to as the "ordinary doctors," got it wrong, the focus is on their individual mistakes in particular case histories. What makes for his success is the accurate interpretation of the signs provided by the pulse: his rivals and opponents misread them or did not see their relevance at all. The issue is how to use the method correctly, rather than a contrast between radically opposed paradigms, one invoking and the other ruling out appeal to demonic intervention.

Turning back to the Greek evidence now, we can say that what is distinctive in the form the polemic takes there is the appeal to what we may call second-order factors. The purifiers, according to the author of *On the Sacred Disease*, *must* be wrong because they do not appreciate the fundamental point that all diseases have a natural cause. Thus, they do not just make individual errors: their whole approach to medicine is flawed because based on what we might call a category mistake, a failure to recognize that natures alone are in play. Of course the Hippocratic author would have been hard put to it, if he had been challenged to justify what is after all a massive assumption. Yet he is confident at least that he knows the shape that any justification would have to take. That is where an explicit appeal to nature plays such a key role in his rhetoric—a move for which we have no parallel in either Mesopotamia or ancient China.

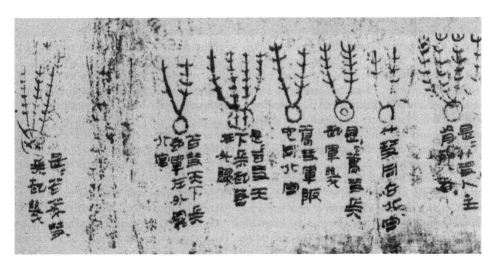

FIGURE 5.4 Mawangdui silk, depicting cometary forms, China, 1754. © Universal History Archive / Getty Images.

If this analysis can be accepted as at least along the right lines, then we can see that the forging of the new category of "nature" in Greek medicine and philosophy can be related to one other feature of Greek intellectual life that becomes prominent in the classical period, namely, a preoccupation with accountability.[37] In a whole range of contexts, political and legal as well as more purely intellectual, those who occupied or claimed positions of particular authority were subject to scrutiny. Candidates for office were subjected to what was called the *dokimasia* to test that they were eligible. At the end of their term of office they were liable to the *euthyna*, the scrutiny of their performance in particular in relation to its financial aspects. According to Herodotus accountability was one of the chief marks of democratic regimes, though it was certainly not confined to them.[38]

Second-order justifications for claims take the form that you must be right and your opponents wrong because you have the right method and understanding of the issues to hand, while they make category mistakes, for example, in muddling nature and the supernatural. But this may in part be seen as the equivalent, in medicine or philosophy or science, of the moves that politicians or orators made when they attempted to undermine their rivals. They may sound plausible, but they fail to appreciate the kind of issue they are dealing with. They are not just mistaken in particular matters: their whole approach is fundamentally flawed. Yet as so many ancient Greeks were aware, this move was itself vulnerable to further challenge. If many claimed their own views could be shown to be not just true, but demonstrably, indisputably true, those claims, no sooner made, were all too often disputed. Incontrovertibility as a goal receded in the face of being repeatedly controverted.

So my argument would be that the development of a concept of "nature" in ancient Greece in the classical period was in many respects distinctive and reflected features of Greek discussion and polemic that had further repercussions in many other contexts of Greek life and experience. However, in other societies we find plenty of terms where standard English translations talk of nature and the natural, so that claim needs further elucidation and justification. Once again the ancient Chinese yield extensive relevant evidence, which I may now attempt to review however summarily.

Classical Chinese certainly possesses a variety of terms that describe the characteristics of certain items where that sometimes corresponds to what we might call their natures. One of these is *xing* often translated as "nature," where there is a notable dispute in the fourth and third centuries BCE between Mencius and Xunzi as to whether the *xing* of humans is good or bad. Mencius taking the first option insists that humans have a moral sense, while Xunzi's focus, in a chapter entitled "human *xing* is bad," is rather on how we need education to behave correctly.[39] But while that looks as if it is talking about what we call "human nature," it is clear that the issue for both is morality, not the physical characteristics that make humans human. That point becomes even clearer if we consider a text in the third-century BCE compendium known as the *Lüshi chunqiu*,[40] which discusses both the *xing* of humans and that of water. In the latter case water's *xing* is said to be "purity," being "clear" (*qing*), and the text continues by identifying the *xing* of humans as "long life" (*shou*). This author is evidently not attempting to define the physical nature of water or of humans, but rather setting out an ideal or an aspiration, the character of the thing at its best.

Other general terms include *li* (pattern), which again, only in particular contexts refers to the regularities of natural phenomena. Meanwhile the cosmos as a whole is referred to using the term *tian* (strictly "heaven") or *tiandi* ("heaven and earth"), though as I shall be mentioning shortly the domain of "heaven" obeys the same rules as are to be found also in human society when it is well ordered and they are even exemplified in the human body. Dealing with the underlying causes of things the Chinese speak of events happening "spontaneously," *ziran* (strictly "self-so") when they occur without human intervention, and so are in our vocabulary "natural" in that sense.

But while, as already noted, all of these and other uses display an implicit appreciation of what we should call the workings of nature, there is no overarching explicit term that treats the problems as all belonging to a single domain, "nature" itself. Yet when we bear in mind the tensions between descriptive and prescriptive uses we found in ancient Greece, there may be a distinct advantage in *not* collapsing all the issues together as if the goal was to run to ground the nature of nature itself. True, close relationships are assumed between the Cosmos, the (sociopolitical) state, and the human body, all of which manifest the same interactions of yin and yang that should ideally be in harmony with one another.[41] But that does not leave the Chinese with a single, multivalent problematic concerning "nature" in all its ambivalence itself.

One upshot of our discussion thus far is to underline the need for extreme caution in making any general assumption that any given society or group will necessarily have clear and explicit notions corresponding to nature and culture or will use that pair as actors' categories. The importance of that lesson can be underlined in light of recent anthropological debates on the underlying issues, and I shall devote this section of my discussion to elaborate some of the fundamental problems this raises. While the contrast between nature and culture had for many years been assumed to provide one and probably the most crucial articulating framework for anthropological fieldwork, that view has recently been not so much questioned as radically undermined. The two scholars who were primarily responsible for this sea-change in the agenda of anthropology were Philippe Descola and Eduardo Viveiros de Castro. But even before they published their pioneering studies challenges had begun to be mounted. Is "culture" a robust cross-cultural universal, that is, does it tally with a domain recognized as such by peoples across the world? The idea that it was, rather, a concept that had to be invented was the chief thesis of a study by Wagner, originally published in 1975.[42] Then in 1980, basing her investigation on fieldwork among Mount Hagen communities in Papua New Guinea Marilyn Strathern published an article attacking both elements in the binary. In "No Nature, No Culture, the Hagen case" she argued that that dichotomy simply did not fit the experience of the Indigenous peoples she studied.[43] If we introduce that contrast in our descriptions of their experience it is bound to distort how they perceive the world, indeed, to distort the world they inhabit.

This in turn led to the fundamental question. Does the study of Indigenous communities give us access not just to different worldviews but also to different worlds? Is it not misleading to suppose that the ontological assumptions in play in different groups are uniform? Both Viveiros de Castro and Descola have focused on the misunderstandings that may arise if we apply our own preconceptions about the nature of reality to the interpretations of others' experience. Descola proposes a four-fold schema of ontologies distinguished by the conceptions of "physicality" and "interiority" that they adopt, the former corresponding to ideas of the stuff or matter that things are made of, while "interiority" picks out ideas of mind, spirit, or selfhood.[44] Focusing on the relationship between humans and other animals, Descola describes as "animist" the assumption that we and they share the same interiority (other animals live in societies like those of humans) while what distinguishes us and them is our physicalities. It is because the jaguar has the body it has that it lives in the world it does. When humans see the jaguar

FIGURE 5.5 The jaguar, native to Central and South America. © Arterra / Universal Images Group/Getty Images.

drink the blood of its prey, the jaguar itself sees itself as drinking beer (Figure 5.5). After a successful hunt it retires to its lair where it lives a social life just like that of humans, with divisions between moieties governing marriage. But while animism presupposes common interiority but divergent physicality the converse of that is what Descola calls "naturalism," the default ontology of Western modernity, where physicality is common (we are all made of the same basic stuff) while what marks out humans from other animals is interiority: we do, but they do not, enjoy cultural relations.

Descola's two further ontologies, labeled "totemism" and "analogism," introduce other possibilities,[45] but to concentrate on the key items of relevance to my discussion here I may add that the broad contrast between "naturalism" and "animism" roughly corresponds to points that Viveiros de Castro has made in relation to what he calls "perspectivism."[46] Again the starting point is the widely reported Indigenous beliefs that humans and other animals share culture, but are distinguished by the bodies we and they possess, which is antithetical to our usual assumption that physical bodies are all composed of the same stuff, while culture is a peculiarly human phenomenon. We moderns may be multiculturalists and mononaturalists: but many Indigenous peoples are monoculturalists and multinaturalists.

To assume that the Indigenous beliefs and practices we are endeavoring to do justice to presuppose some notion of nature or of the natural world is, on this account, a source of radical error. There is no justification for the assumption that our ontological categories apply to their actions and understandings. Yet the problem this poses is obvious. If we are indeed faced with fundamentally different ontologies, how is any understanding of any but our own possible? If the worlds are indeed incommensurable, how is any communication between them possible?

Both Descola and Viveiros de Castro are acutely aware of the problem and cite it to underline the difficulty of the anthropologists' agenda. Yet although the ontological analyses they undertake are their actors' categories, the idea would be that they can serve as a framework within which to describe and begin to interpret otherwise incomprehensible modes of belief and behavior. Whereas in the naturalist regime much of what is reported to be said or done in animist or perspective cosmologies will tend to be held up against the standards of regularity and rationality "we" normally presuppose—held up against them only to be found wanting—the recognition that their Indigenous ontology does not sign up to our assumptions of where the boundaries come between nature and culture, between humans and other animals, between the living and the dead, serves to put us on notice that our task of interpretation is more complex than we had imagined. That recognition does not mean we have secure understandings: it does not yield those understandings on a plate. But it does underline that our interpretations must start further back, examining notions of life, agency, the person, and relations in particular. We cannot assume that the actors we are interested in inhabit a world in which substances are stable entities or that they draw the line between what is capable of agency and what is not where we would locate it. Insofar as the anthropologists' hermeneutic endeavors are successful they help to throw light on such matters as the rationale of sacrifice, the presuppositions of divination, the changing roles of living beings as alternatively predators and prey. "Nature" especially turns out not to be what we can all happily take for granted, a realm of well-ordered entities that may be assumed to behave regularly, obeying "laws of nature" that are accessible to scientists' investigations. Rather, it is the key component in an ontology that is the contingent outcome of the development of Western science.

In a sense, this realization should not come as the shocking surprise that some might suppose it to be. The lesson from anthropology here already tallies with what we can take away from an exploration of ancient societies, which also pose the challenge of how sense can be made of experience *without* an appeal to that key idea that there is a natural world out there for everyone to be attempting to master and explain. So far from that being a universal assumption, I have argued that it was quite exceptional in the ancient world, and when it first began to be formulated in ancient Greece, this was in rather particular circumstances and to serve a certain agenda, as I have endeavored to explain.[47]

Nevertheless, some may still suppose that the developments that began to take place in classical Greco-Roman antiquity were not, or not just, the contingent product of those circumstances, but rather they were the foundation of an altogether more robust understanding of the world. Has the development of what we call "natural science" not transformed both what we can claim to know and how better to order and control the circumstances of our lives? Nature, on that view, would be the label for a positive breakthrough for rationality, not a mere by-product of a particular manner of conducting a polemic between rival claimants to the truth.

To evaluate that view correctly would require, first, an extensive examination of the *fortuna* of *natura*/nature during the crucial periods of its exploitation in late antiquity, through the so-called scientific revolution and early modern period, down to the present day where modernity faces various challenges, including from post-modernity. That is obviously beyond the scope of my discussion here,[48] where I shall limit myself just to two main points that serve to underline some of the complexities, the first to do with those fortunes with the arrival of Christianity and the second with the proper limits of any residual triumphalism that may be associated with where we stand today.

The dominant ancient Greek view, as mentioned, was that nature is the domain over which regular natural causes are at work, which serve to establish what is true "always or for the most part," as Aristotle put it. Natural phenomena were not to be ascribed to willful deities or demons whose behavior is quite unpredictable. But against that it was commonly assumed, in the Greco-Roman world, as it had been also in Mesopotamia, for instance, that the gods are all-powerful. The question that surfaced already in late antiquity, even before Christianity became the official religion of the Roman Empire, was: if God's power is supreme, can he overrule nature? In a telling passage in Galen,[49] he raises the problem and distinguishes his own view from the one he ascribes to Moses. Moses, he says, held that God can do anything, including turning a stone into a human or ash into a horse or cow, breaking, that is, the rules that apply to natural causes and effects. But God, Galen replies, could not have done any such thing, for he always chooses what is best from among the things that are possible, not from what is impossible. The properties of matter are the expression of God's power, in no sense a limitation on it.

Obviously when God is believed to have created the laws or regularities by which the cosmos is governed this could provide a powerful incentive to undertake detailed investigations of nature, as a way of celebrating divine creation.[50] Yet against that, the belief that God—and the saints—can perform miracles, indeed the idea that the creation of the universe itself was the supreme miracle, contrived to suggest that the sway of the laws of nature was subject to limitations or reservations. Indeed, that belief remains a fundamental tenet of the Roman Catholic faith even to this day, insofar as candidates for sainthood have to pass the test of having performed miracles, where the event has to be shown to be beyond all naturalistic explanation.

While one theme that underwent several transformations from classical antiquity onward was the relation between nature and God or the divine, two others were the idea that nature was secretive and the connected notion of the relationship between the natural and the artificial. The former idea already appears, as noted, in Heraclitus, but like the notion that there is order to be found in natural phenomena, it could stimulate the empirical investigation of those phenomena and moreover further the acceptance that some of the findings may be unexpected or counterintuitive. As for the latter topic, a text in the Aristotelian treatise *Mechanics* already quoted the dramatist Antiphon to the effect that "we conquer by art, where by nature we are overcome."[51] While some ancient Greek authors, notably Aristotle himself, considered that art imitates nature,[52] and so nature provides the model that art should follow, this text indicates that nature can in a sense be subordinated to human intervention. The idea of forcing nature to do what we want was a powerful theme in such writers as Bacon, and one that was connected with the relatively new idea that what the investigator has to do, to discover the truth, is to submit nature to experimental tests.[53]

What this amounts to is that so far from "nature" providing a robust universal rubric for talking about what is there for the scientist, any scientist, to explore and discover, we should recognize that this is at best an oversimplification and at worst potentially misleading. First as to the oversimplifications. To talk of nature and the natural sciences tends to gloss over the considerable differences both in the subject matter and in the methods of the disciplines involved, from cosmology to genetics. The problems posed by the Big Bang overlap those of fundamental particle physics, but it is notorious that we are still very far away from resolving those associated with the search for a unifying Grand Universal Theory. When we contemplate the other proliferating disciplines and subdisciplines of science the idea of a Theory of Everything appears increasingly chimerical. To be sure, different inquirers share the ambition to discover the underlying causal factors at work in whatever it is they are investigating. But it is not that the same methods are always appropriate for this end. Direct experimentation is not practical in such areas as cosmology. While model-building is a feature of most inquiries, the character and status of those models are not uniform. As we discover more—as science advances—we learn that there is so much more that we are still unable to comprehend. Nature, on this view, is not so much a single determinate goal as an ever-receding horizon.

Moreover, when we turn back to ancient history and to anthropology we can see the possibly distorting effects of our appeal to some such category as "nature" in our interpretative efforts. This is certainly going to be the case where we hold up the cosmologies or ontologies of the peoples we are studying against the model we assume to be correct, that provided by our own modern natural science. That tactic, as I have argued, can be quite inappropriate, and it has the effect of distracting our attention from a more open-minded appreciation of alternative ways of organizing experience. We do not need to invoke the notion that "they" live in totally different worlds from ours, which some would see as negating the very possibility of our achieving any understanding whatsoever. But we do have to take into account that very different perceptions can legitimately be entertained about where we as humans fit into the cosmos, about our relations with other living creatures, about the kind of upbringing and education that is appropriate for our children, today's future citizens of the world. We respect cultural differences in general, do we not? But within what limits, up to what point? Do we never intervene, never pass judgment? Surely not. But on what basis are we to do this? It will no longer do to say that such and such a practice (say female circumcision or male castration) is wrong because it is not "natural." That will not do, since it is not "natural" either to shave off facial hair, and we would not want to condemn that as immoral. So we need other arguments (as well) on which to base our judgments (something to do with harm, though what counts as harm is still problematic enough even with the possibility of an appeal to the principle of "doing unto others as you would they should do to you"[54]). We need an anthropologically sophisticated moral philosophy, and at present neither the philosophers nor the anthropologists can be said to have much to offer.[55]

Taking a stand on such issues always implicates values. It is not that we should or even can adopt a principle that all such are equally acceptable. But before deciding on whether we do indeed endorse the values adopted by those whom we study, the first task is indeed to endeavor to understand them without prejudging the issues by treating them as botched attempts at approximating to our own preconceptions. For that endeavor it is best to eschew the concept of "nature" or at least be wary of its oversimplifications. What we call the "natural" sciences grow and grow, to be sure, but their relationship with the "social" ones and certainly the very concept of "human nature" itself remain deeply problematic. Given that "nature" is plastic, the elements that are to be assigned to either side of the "nature"/"nurture" or "nature"/"culture" binaries are not so clearly marked off from one another as used to be supposed. Accordingly while "nature" continues to underpin many of the key assumptions of Western modernity, it has been my principal theme that we should pay due attention to its contingent and polemical origins and to its ongoing ambivalences.

CHAPTER SIX

Religion and the Divine

ZSUZSANNA VÁRHELYI

About a decade ago John Coffey and Alister Chapman issued a call for a collaboration among those studying intellectual and religious history, intending to chart a new space for integrating these two fields, especially with regard to the modern and contemporary eras.[1] While fields studying these distinct aspects of the Greco-Roman world may not have developed quite as fully separate disciplinary identities, historians attempting to contribute to an intellectual history of ancient religion, as I am doing here, may still be tempted by narratives that dichotomize the generally secular intellectual developments in understanding the world, on the one hand, and traditional religious practices, superstition, and magic as backward forces, on the other. This temptation is further complicated for classical antiquity because in questioning the rationality of Greco-Roman religious practices we follow in the footsteps of those late antique and later Christian writers who sought (and at times celebrated) those ancient figures who questioned "paganism." Yet it was exactly these Christian authors who transmitted most of what we know about ancient religions.

The primary difficulty in discussing the intellectual history of Greco-Roman religions in the past century has been the long-standing sense that, especially in the inevitable comparison to modern world religions, non-Judeo-Christian, Western antiquity prioritized practice over theology in religion.[2] Although this stark dichotomy of the before, "practice," and the after, "theology," is now disappearing in scholarship—as both the theological interests of the ancients and the practical varieties of modern religions are highlighted—we should still acknowledge that the absence of a strict theology and of an associated specifically theological authority significantly and somewhat uniquely shaped Greco-Roman religions.[3] Religious authority existed, but the focus was primarily on proper religious practice, or lack thereof. The pull of such a practice-oriented religious culture tends to separate scholarly discussion into two distinct areas: first, into a primarily action-oriented engagement with religious practices, bracketing their potential meanings, and, second, into an idea-heavy focus on ancient thinkers who supposedly questioned or challenged the frequently unwritten assumptions that were implied by common religious customs. The problems with each of these approaches on their own are rather obvious: in the first case, the influence of emerging notions constantly changing those practices and their representations can be easily missed; in the second case, the influence of changing social realities and imagery may be underappreciated in shaping those ideas. But my main interest here is in how the bifurcation itself challenges our study of ancient religion in its full richness of practices and ideas by denying the connections among its many theoretical and practical manifestations.

Accordingly, the main goal of this chapter is to engage the possibility of a dynamic study in which ancient Greek and Roman religions are appreciated primarily for their intellectual richness, yet with an eye to the ongoing practices and, to the extent possible, their wider sociohistorical context. Especially when it comes to religion, the mutual influence of discourses and practices on each other is key: representations shape our engagement with what is perceived as the reality of religion. Even if innovative religious ideas might gain their first impetus without being heavily shaped by the lived experience of their creator, the formulation, delivery, and reception of the new notion will be subject to the creator's own times: the language, evolution, variations, and ultimately longevity of the idea will be heavily influenced by the receiving culture. But the reason for an integrated approach is not only theoretical but also inevitable, based on the available evidence. For most of antiquity firm evidence for real religious practices is largely elusive, and we have to rely on the same corpus of texts that we study for intellectual innovation to deduce what those practices most likely were. What we have is primarily textual, and to make things even more complicated, generally literary: as Elizabeth Clark has pointed out, even supposedly historical premodern texts are best seen as driven by generic rules distinct from our own sensibilities, and those representations, in turn, end up shaping human engagement with material and power structures, leading to a "reality" of the world as constructed and experienced by human institutions.[4] My interest here is thus in those innovative religious ideas that are nevertheless shaped by both such generic, largely philosophical, contexts as well as by contemporary historical realities and, to the extent we can tell, in how such ideas may have shaped contemporary religious practices. I will focus on two richly attested periods, late fifth-century Athens and mid-first-century Rome, both BCE, to study intellectual innovations related to religious life, and how those innovations were received by and also shaped religious life in turn. Inevitably, my examinations are neither intended to be complete nor definitive; rather, I hope to highlight the kind of analysis that can be possible without the sort of divisions, between theology and practice, tradition and innovation that have been often shaping the implicit assumptions in some prior work.

ATHENS IN THE LATE FIFTH CENTURY BCE

One reason Athens in the late fifth century BCE is an especially fitting place and time to investigate these questions is the heightened and often politicized tensions around the limits of religion's apparent freedom in what Popper once famously identified as the first open society. Although the political structure of the *polis* did indeed offer one of the most unrestricted public spaces for discussion about some matters in Western history, religious matters did not benefit from the same kind of openness: key festivals such as the Panathenaia visibly connected religious fundamentals with the very essence of belonging to Athenian society. Within the study of ancient Greek religion, recent scholarship nevertheless suggests that it may not be fully sufficient to focus on the *polis* and its structures and on the binary of acceptable versus unacceptable actions and thoughts alone when studying this period; rather, we also need to pay attention to individual actors and to the web of social relations they were embedded in.[5] Intellectual ideas similarly emerged and evolved exactly within such social networks.

These were challenging years for Athenian religion: the Spartans sought the support of Delphic Apollo against Athens in advance of the Peloponnesian War; the fighting led to an overwhelming plague in the city at a time when access to religious aid via Apollo or Asclepius was limited; and finally, seers, key figures in military planning, repeatedly failed in their projections about the outcomes of war actions.[6] One of the great modern debates about this period of Athens has centered on the question of whether and how the entrance of sophistic thought into the *polis* shaped Athenian ideas in general.[7] There is practically no evidence to establish the depth of how far such ideas may have penetrated Athenian society, especially beyond the elite. Yet even those who are skeptical about the reach of sophistic challenges to traditional ideas, whether religious or otherwise, cannot argue with the fact that some of our best evidence for the tensions in Athenian society at this time comes from writings that confirm that individuals with innovative thoughts or actions could be attacked in public, including on the theater stage, and legally, in court, for views that could be considered to be violating rules of some sort about what was not (quite) negotiable about the gods. This negotiability—namely, who was to define and enforce it, how, and what exactly lay outside of such boundaries—was first discussed exactly at this time as matters of religious controversy arose. It was supposedly Pericles who first stated that religious impiety was in the category of "unwritten laws,"[8] possibly in the context of an anti-Periclean political upheaval in the 430s BCE—around the same time when Diopeithes would have introduced a very much written law against those who "did not worship the gods or delivered teachings about the heavens," if the law is indeed historical.[9] The incident certainly had a political aspect to it: its main focus was Anaxagoras of Klazomenai, the first philosopher known to have settled in Athens. Insofar as Anaxagoras did so on the invitation of Pericles himself, Pericles, too, was indirectly assailed. But instead of dismissing the religious content, it is worth looking at this moment as a time when a definition of proper religious behavior came under discussion, at least in part in response to various contemporary intellectual developments.

A keyword of the debate became *nomizô* (νομίζω), which I translated as "worship" above. Although potentially suspicious, as a later term applied by Plutarch some half a millennium later for the Diopeithes decree, it actually occurs as early as 400 BCE in the prosecution speech against Andokides[10] and soon after against Socrates.[11] Debate on the exact meaning of this term has divided modern scholarship, as it is inextricably linked to the charges against and the defense of Socrates: one possibility is that it implies participation in customary worship (Robert Garland and many others since); another is that it indicates something closer to formal belief in the existence of the gods (Hendrick Versnel).[12] More recently, a number of scholars proposed that customary religious practice may have been a sufficient, but not necessarily fully encompassing, meaning of *nomizein*, that is, that it may have had both potential meanings, a notion that comparative and cognitive research also confirms.[13]

In the context of this ambiguity about the exact lexical implications of this word, we may note that the prosecution speech in pseudo-Lysias distinguishes between words and actions against the gods:

> And how far more impious this man (i.e. Andocides) has turned out than Diagoras of Melos; for he was impious in speech (*logos*) with regard to the sacred matters and festivals of a foreign city, but Andocides was impious in deed (*ergon*) with regard to those of his own.[14]

The same distinction between word and deed in religious matters occurs in a variety of fourth-century texts, suggesting an ongoing concern about both improper actions and improper ideas expressed.[15]

The Diagoras mentioned in the above case was in fact a poet, whose crime may have been as simple as revealing something about the Eleusinian mysteries, but the time when he was charged, the year 415, marked another crisis point. The mutilation of "almost all Herms" and the profanation of the Mysteries that occurred at this time were the first instances in which formal prosecution was moved against those who committed acts against public cults in Athens. Unlike the much more celebrated instances of the impiety trials in fifth- and fourth-century BCE Athens, the historicity of which scholars have increasingly questioned over the past three decades, here we know for sure that those found guilty were legally punished, and the language of the punishment, as preserved on the so-called Attic stelai, specifically called them *asebeis*.[16] A particularly religious punishment was developed in the decree of Isotimides, which excluded anyone who confessed to impiety from Athenian sanctuaries.[17] Aside from the question of to what extent such a sentence could actually be enforced, the symbolic significance of such an exclusion, essentially an exclusion from the community itself, confirms that when under attack, Athenian religious traditions could be seen to stand for the very community itself.

Beyond the particular and particularly large-scale scandal of 415 BCE, we have rich evidence that suggests the existence of a number of smaller groups challenging traditional religious notions. The so-called Kakodaimonistai, worshippers of bad luck, met and dined together on days of ill omen in purposeful opposition to those who celebrated the new moon (the Noumeniastai).[18] Demosthenes mentions the Triballoi, who ate food offered after purification to Hecate and the testicles of pigs sacrificed prior to assembly meetings, and who were later supposedly sentenced to death.[19] While we only have hostile sources for these groups, it is striking that the main intellectual move is against traditional forms of sacrifice, shared meals, and festivities, and the context is small, private group meetings. Remarkably, such groups are parallel to the kind of private symposia that Socrates might attend, and during which significant discussions about religion could also take place (Figure 6.1). Although we can only speculate about such matters, it is not at all impossible to imagine that someone might have crossed circles that encompassed what we today may wish to distinguish as Socratic/philosophical and as more generally subversive religious groups. In fact, it is possible, if hard to prove, that such groups were—at least in part—motivated by the new kinds of intellectual discussions taking place around the city; of course, general social subversion could also have played a role in these likely elite gatherings of free males.[20]

It was only in the legislative, juridical, and the theatrical arenas that large-scale discussion about such matters could take place. While the legal perspective of Diopeithes' and other later accusations, with the possible exception of that of Socrates, may not be very clear with regard to what exactly constituted a crime, Athenian theatre offered a much less contested space in which less formal challenges to intellectual innovation could take place. In fact, contrary to the later lists of numerous fifth-century representatives of complete disbelief in the gods (*atheos*), which scholars today are generally skeptical about trusting, theatre has an ongoing record of mocking certain new ideas. Within this line of thought one highly popular topic from the 420s BCE onward was the supposed atheism of those who studied the natural world, in particular the sky: in the second half of the decade Cratinus attacked the philosopher Hippon on this account, and Aristophanes, of course, criticized Socrates along lines that may have been more fitting for Anaxagoras.[21]

The comedies of Aristophanes, most importantly, offer specific insights into perceptions about such figures in Athens. For example, Protagoras' ideas, the contrast between *physis* and *nomos*, nature and tradition, as well as the sophists' rhetorical claim to be able to

FIGURE 6.1 Red-figure kylix depicting a symposium scene from Athens, late fifth century BCE. New York, Metropolitan Museum: 41.162.137 (Beazley 216232). © Artokoloro / Alamy Stock Photo.

make the weaker argument stronger, all seem to be required knowledge to understand what makes Aristophanes' *Clouds* funny.[22] Originally produced in 423, the comedy puts on stage the contest between the traditional and the innovative, and the latter attacks the common acceptance of poetry and mythology. Although the person under attack here is patently Socrates, Protagoras' teachings are very much present: Socrates and the weaker argument specifically challenge the existence of the traditional gods, such as Zeus:

Socrates: What do you mean, Zeus? Do stop driveling. Zeus doesn't even exist!

Given what we know of fifth-century thought in Athens, this passage is most reflective of the famous argument that Protagoras put forth about the gods:

I am not able to know if the gods exist or if they do not, or what they look like. Many are the things that prevent my knowing: the lack of clarity about the gods and that the life of a human being is short.[23]

A subtler reading of this text would note that Protagoras does not deny the existence of the gods, but simply dismisses the possibility of knowledge about them.[24] But it is noteworthy how Aristophanes explicitly collapses this distinction between atheism and agnosticism, and challenges traditional societal norms that required, for example, that one swears oaths by the gods. A further idea also entered the list of potential criticisms in a comedy of Aristophanes a few years later. In 414 BCE, the sophist Prodicus of Keos was mocked on the comic stage for his idea that the gods were originally natural or even human benefactors or inventors, such as the planets or Demeter. This questioning of the very origin of the gods must have been a theme at this time: less than a decade later, even if now far from Athens, Euripides composed his *Bacchae*, in which the seer Tiresias also calls Demeter herself the Earth and the inventor of bread, along with Dionysus, the inventor of wine, in what again foreshadows the later work of Euhemerus.[25] The seer then proceeds to offer a historical rationalization of the myth that Dionysus was born of Zeus' thigh, possibly as another example for the kind of intellectual engagement with religious matters, among others, that sophists were famous for.[26]

In a passage that likely contributed to a later attack on him by Aristophanes for teaching people not to trust whether the gods exist,[27] Euripides himself wrote some of the most famously atheistic lines in his tragedy, *Bellerophon*:[28]

Does anyone say that there are gods in heaven?
There are not, there are not, unless a human wants
to rely on ancient wisdom like a fool.[29]

The argument is notable for questioning the usefulness of trusting ancient wisdom when it comes to the gods, similarly to the idea proposed by Xenophanes. The surviving text continues by offering proof of this absence of influence by gods, namely, that the greedy are rewarded with riches, while the pious often suffer, a frequent *topos* of complaint, that nevertheless suggests popular Athenian engagement with the idea of divine (in)justice in this period. We know well that there were numerous, easily available "let-out clauses" or "blocks to falsifiability" already earlier in the fifth century that allowed the key assumption about divine justice, namely, that an intervention of the gods will punish unjust acts, to remain valid—despite inevitable evidence to the contrary. These included arguments such as that retribution is rarely direct; that the gods do not punish every offence; that the punishment may be delayed; and, finally and simply, that the gods or the divine are not always just.[30] When a character in Euripides' tragedy challenges the existence of the gods with arguments that could be so readily dismissed, and were likely dismissed so by most, we may wonder about the function of presenting characters featuring such a perspective.

One possible but likely less widespread explanation for divine injustice was to suggest that the gods exist, but do not care about humans. This was the view of Aristodemus, an enthusiastic acolyte of Socrates, at least according to his depiction in Xenophon's *Memorabilia*, who employed it to justify his lack of participation in most civic religious activities.[31] Interestingly, this same view is also brought up by Plato, who repeatedly mentions this, along with atheism, as problematic views about the gods in *Republic* 2, *Laws* 10 and 12. On a wider scale, such lack of attention on the part of the gods associated with *polis* worship may have also contributed to the turning by individuals toward cultic activities with more specifically personal dimensions, a change in emphasis characteristic of the years during the Peloponnesian War (such as private funerary commemorations or individual dedications to gods). Yet others connected individualized offerings with the larger benefit of the *polis* (e.g., Nicias on Delos after the purification of the island following the second outbreak of the plague).[32]

A third possibility of problematic views according to Plato concerned the relationship between humans and gods; this would be to think that the gods exist but can be easily persuaded by sacrifices and prayers. Plato's *Republic* in particular takes on those begging priests and seers who promise to influence the gods either by gaining atonement or securing divine punishment.[33] He is especially concerned that these individuals claim that they "have persuaded the gods to act as their servants." While mutuality in social relations was a key value of classical Athens, the hierarchical dynamic implied here, especially with the gods at the lower end of the equation, was not acceptable, as it suggested an inequality in which humans had the upper hand. In addition, there is the element of force implied here, which has important implications about how prayer actually works: as Pulleyn emphasized, the interaction was seen as a request and response, and not as a contractual obligation.[34] This is further shown by the temporal varieties possible in prayer language: *da quia dedi* (based on past gifts by the human), *da quia (non) dedisti* (based on past behavior of the god), and *da quia dabo* (based on future promise by the human).

Ultimately the fault lines seem to have fallen around the issue of challenging traditional religious forms in ways that made participation in public and private rituals, established earlier, untenable. This is why Xenophon in his *Memorabilia* emphasized that Socrates, probably the most famous impiety case of antiquity, participated in public and private sacrifices in Athens.[35] Such participation, according to the evidence of vase paintings, was of increasing importance to the wider public in these decades in Athens, and depictions newly focused on showing scenes of the sacrificial meal (Figure 6.2).[36] Further, innovation, in itself, was not necessarily a problem:[37] these same years saw the establishment of numerous new religious festivals under a variety of public and private arrangements: the markedly barbarian goddess Bendis was introduced from Thrace around 430 BCE, and the healing god Asclepius from Epidauros in 420 BCE. Independently from the public (in the first case) or private (in the latter case) organization of these new cults in the city at first, they both meet *polis* interests and concerns around the war and the plague that occupied Athens in these years.

In sum, it is likely that at least some innovative aspects in the sophists' and philosophers' intellectual challenges to religion were incorporated into the kinds of discussions taking place in fifth-century Athens: divine (in)justice and proper behavior concerning the gods. Much of what survives about these discussions nevertheless comes from the public arena, and it is only rarely that we can get tantalizing insights into the private enterprises that emerged in response to these concerns: Plato's *Republic* mentions *agyrtai* (begging priests) and *manteis* (seers) who knock on doors and offer their services to appease the gods for current or prior misdeeds.[38] In Euripides' *Bacchae*, Pentheus calls Dionysus a *goês epoidos* (singing sorcerer) offering initiations, suggesting that such figures would have been familiar to the Athenian audience (234). In a section of his *Laws* in which he suggests that the best state response to injury by religious means, such as incantations and binding spells, is death, Plato also implies that many who offered such "magical" services may have been easily associated with seers or diviners.[39]

An additional development that relates to notions of critical knowledge concerned the usage of written texts to imply expertise—a tool likely relied upon by a number of these itinerant religious experts.[40] Less directly connected to the intellectual developments, but shaped by expectations of literacy and literary form, Orphic poetry was becoming popular in late fifth-century Athens, engaging concerns with mortality and a desire for knowing more about the divine world. In this and other varied formats, intellectual developments reached a much wider audience than those attending philosophical discussions and opened up new ways for individuals to engage with the divine world.

FIGURE 6.2 Red-figure bell-krater depicting a sacrificial scene from Athens, late fifth century
BCE. New York, Metropolitan Museum: 41.162.4 (Beazley 217473). © Agefotostock / Alamy
Stock Photo.

LATE REPUBLICAN ROME

Turning now to late Republican Rome, in the middle decades of the first century BCE,
we find a society in similar tensions between sociopolitical challenges and intensified
intellectual engagement with religion. In contrast to Athens, many members of the elite
were leading participants, as priests, in the city's traditional religious rituals, and the
whole social order that supported the privileges of this elite was entwined with the
traditions of Roman religion. The period of the late Republic nevertheless saw this social
order challenged, violently, by practically continuous factional fighting from the 80s BCE

on. Against this historical background, elite competition intensified both in traditional religious terms with major figures, from Cicero to Caesar, seeking priestly titles, and also in innovative ways, as many of these same figures sought to make, claim, and challenge connections with divine power.

Significantly, writers of this era were the first generation in Rome for whom a number of antiquarian works from a prior generation were available, providing a powerful historical perspective on contemporary Roman religious practices. The three towering figures of the period were Varro, Nigidius Figulus, and M. Tullius Cicero, all of whom aimed at cataloging and systematizing the widely varied phenomena related to Roman religion. It was Cicero who offered the first categorical definition of *religio*, via the character of the *pontifex* Cotta, as encompassing *sacra* (traditional cults), *auspicia* (divine signs), and predictions from the Sibylline Books and by the haruspices, emphasizing just how much any such definition was caught up in Rome's traditions.[41] However, that tradition was also saturated with often contradictory material left behind by a wide range of practitioners. Rather all too conveniently for all later evaluative attempts, Varro popularized in Latin a not original, but now widely available intellectual division of traditional religion, the so-called *theologia tripertita* (three-part theology)—the "three-fold way of talking about the gods." This classification distinguished among a *theologia naturalis* (the philosophers' way of talking about the gods), *civilis* (the one belonging to states), and *mythica* (the one belonging to poets).

Varro's *Divine Antiquities*, published in the 40s BCE, took the philosophical perspective, but not necessarily a completely critical attitude to the traditions of the increasingly varied religious landscape in the growing empire. In fact, of possible rationalizing or critical expressions in response to mainstream cult practices, his writings, as most other surviving works, suggest a general tendency to try to preserve in writing as much of the traditional material as possible. This antiquarianism was paired with an attempt at making sense of religion, an attempt at creating a distinct body of knowledge, for which the educated elite can serve as a guard.[42] Varro's work can be best seen today as creating a historical model in which an original religion (the *naturalis*) was possibly not anthropomorphic in its very beginnings, and was enhanced by a long line of political leaders who, as philosopher kings, created the gods' names, images, and rituals to appeal to the wider population.[43] In this quasi-historical reconstruction, Varro also made a Greek connection: Rome's second king, and the identified founder of its religious culture, Numa, was claimed to be a student of Pythagoras.

Although Varro himself, rather tantalizingly, sought out a Pythagorean burial for himself, suggesting interest in the possible survival of the soul after death, the best-known Pythagorean of the time was Nigidius Figulus. He gathered a group around him that wanted to be identified as "followers of Pythagoras," but in fact combined philosophical and religious discussions with political concerns as well.[44] A later commentator actually applied the politically threatening word *factio* to the group, while the contemporary invective against Sallust, a presumed member, calls them a "religious brotherhood of sacrilege."[45] Unfortunately, we only get negative portrayals of Pythagorean groups in Rome in Cicero's surviving works, especially in his invective against Vatinius, suggesting that they would conjure the dead, sacrifice children's organs to the gods of the underworld, and defy auspices.[46] In reality, Nigidius does seem to have practiced an unusual range of activities (including collecting Etruscan thunder omens and creating a brontoscopic calendar, eliciting prophecies from young boys, and ultimately forecasting Octavian's rise via a Chaldean horoscope), but probably the most upsetting element, the one that also led to the verbal charges by his opponents, was the political engagement of his divinatory activities.[47] Like many others among his contemporaries Nigidius explored a combination of traditional methods and less usual sources, including Chaldaean astrology and Orphic theology. In reality, philosophical purity was likely a lesser concern for most in the circle than a deep interest in understanding the divine principles of the world. Some of the most creative ideas to emerge from this curiosity included the notion, proposed by Valerius Soranus, that Jupiter was both the male and female begetter of the world, and both a singular god and all gods:[48]

> All-powerful Jupiter, father and mother of kings, of the world, of the gods;
> The god of gods, one and all.

Cosmic and cosmologic connections also flourished, possibly encouraged by the rising popularity of astrology, which many members of the elite sought out.

Despite this diversity of thought, the primary intellectual drive behind most intellectual approaches to contemporary religion came from Greek thinkers. Elite access to and endorsement of these largely philosophical ideas came with significantly fewer restrictions than those we saw in Athens. It may have helped that the same elite was also holding leading priestly positions of the city, and could be seen, in public, as representatives of religious authority (Figure 6.3). Cicero's dialogical works, such as his *On the Nature of the Gods* (*De natura deorum*), allow for the presentation of an elite society in which different speakers represent distinct philosophical perspectives on particular questions; for example, Epicurean, Stoic, and Academic speakers disagree on whether the gods were ultimately anthropomorphic or whether they cared for humankind. In the conclusion of that work, Cicero appears to side with Q. Lucilius Balbus, a Stoic and former student of the famous philosopher Panaetius, likely a popular view among the elite.[49] Nevertheless, one of the most difficult aspects of reading such texts today is to gauge where exactly speakers personally stand once they have elaborated their philosophical position, for example, in the notoriously difficult concluding sections of Cicero's *On Divination*, with regard to a highly contested area of religion and in a dialogue where he himself is depicted as saying:

> I want it precisely understood that with the demolition of superstition, religion is not obliterated. For it is part of wisdom to uphold the institutions of our ancestors by preserving the rites and ceremonies; and, the beauty of the world and the order of celestial phenomena make me confess that there is some superior and eternal element and that it should be respected and admired by humankind. For which reason, just as religion, which is connected to the knowledge of nature, should be extended, thus all kinds of superstition are to be driven out.[50]

This is the closest Cicero appears to come in taking a stand on his sense of philosophical enquiry as the primary way to understand the universe and religion, of the distinction between this and its alternative, superstition (in this context primarily referencing a range of divinatory practices), and of the nevertheless compelling desire to maintain Rome's religious traditions. Any characterization of what constitutes *superstitio* is of course a key element in defining mainstream Roman religion.[51] Unlike other works of his, this dialogue ends with his expressing a commitment to discussing rather than settling these questions, a feature he associates with Socrates and with his own Academic position, skeptical of the possibility of finding a solution to these most fundamental questions. In addition to antiquarian preservation and direct challenge on philosophical grounds, this

FIGURE 6.3 Section from Augustus' Altar of Peace depicting priests in procession, Rome, Italy, 13–9 BCE. © Adam Eastland / Alamy Stock Photo.

intellectual approach to dealing with the apparent inconsistencies in Roman religion—namely, taking a sophisticated position of Academic skepticism—was likely a relatively popular one among members of the educated elite.[52]

In his representations of such philosophical debates, Cicero also included the Epicurean perspective—presented, for example, in his *On the Nature of the Gods*, by a senator, C. Velleius—which was potentially the most subversive toward the traditional Roman religious system. Best and most impressively represented by Lucretius' *On the Nature of Things*, written during Pompey's and Caesar's increasingly violent conflict for individual power, Epicurean thought in its Latin form offered a direct challenge to Roman tradition. Rehearsing key arguments, such as the gods' lack of care or humans' atomic dispersal upon death, Lucretius is passionate about challenging those who "fear" the gods. Not afraid of calling out iconic examples and predecessors from the Latin tradition, such as Ennius' references to the afterlife, the poet challenged those who would associate religion with piety and philosophy with its lack:

I fear in these matters lest you may perhaps think
You would undertake something impious in philosophy and you would
enter on a path of crime. On the contrary, that religion itself
has given birth to deeds both criminal and impious.[53]

Although charged with atheism in times both ancient and modern, Lucretius appears in most recent readings as a sophisticated and engaged intellectual in terms of religious experience; whether that meant engaging contemporary intellectual trends such as allegorical and euhemeric rationalizations of religion or, as it has been also proposed, an understanding of the gods as existing, via visualization, in the "reality" of our own imagination.[54] The epic is still the most unique and innovative combination of the creative freedom of Latin literature and the trend of philosophical inquiry in this age. Yet our best sense of what an actual Epicurean enthusiast may have looked like in this period comes from Herculaneum, where the Villa dei Papiri hosted a large Epicurean library in largely the same period. The collection, which originated with the Epicurean Philodemus of Gadara, was housed in the villa of Lucius Calpurnius Piso Caesoninus (cos. 58 BCE), father-in-law of Julius Caesar. Although the book collection and the surviving wall paintings from the villa, with sacred landscapes (Figure 6.4), may suggest something akin to a religious community with canonical books and godlike authority attributed to figures such as Epicurus, the villa is more likely to be a representation of the increasing desire among elites to be familiar with philosophical teachings and the popularity of Epicurean views among a number of them.[55]

Significantly, most members of the Roman elite showed no anxiety with regard to their theodicy of good fortune, and endorsed the unique benefits bestowed upon them by the religious system.[56] Largely independently from whether they had Epicurean, Stoic, or Academic philosophical interests, as priests, officials, and military commanders, they took on leading roles in representing Roman religious traditions. The fact that members of this elite had a powerful sense of their own agency in matters related to the gods may appear as a form of disillusionment or cynicism toward Roman religion, rather than a

FIGURE 6.4 Fresco from the Villa of the Papyri in Herculaneum, Italy, depicting sacred landscape, first century BCE–first century CE. Museo Archeologico Nazionale, Naples. © Album / Alamy Stock Photo.

philosophical stance. But it need not be so: Varro treated human antiquities prior to the divine because he accepted that Roman religion was bound to its establishing force, the city itself, and argued that the truly religious person does not fear the gods, but rather venerates them as parental figures.[57] Certainly, there was a certain level of comfort with expressing skepticism even toward religious activities one participated in: from Cicero's letters we learn that, among the augurs, App. Claudius Pulcher promoted the ongoing capacity of divination on the part of the priestly college while C. Claudius Marcellus said such capacity never existed.[58] Cicero, himself also an augur, a priestly position he was very proud of, suggested that augury used to be able to predict the future, but could not any more, due to the time that has passed and human neglect. When it was in their interest, senators may have chosen not to pursue becoming a priest: a key priesthood, that of the *flamen Dialis*, which was particularly limiting due to the constraints that the priesthood imposed on its occupants with respect to the aristocratic pursuit of military success, remained unfilled between 87 and 11 BCE.[59]

We can gain further insight into the religious self-conceptions of this elite on a few key occasions when our evidence allows us to observe elite conflicts playing out in religious terms. During Caesar's consulship, in 59 BCE, his fellow consul, M. Calpurnius Bibulus, tried to oppose his legislation, especially concerning the distribution of land to veterans. When Bibulus failed to achieve his political goals and started to be physically attacked by Caesar's followers when trying to go about his public business, he withdrew into his home, and declared that on public meeting days he was observing the heavens.[60] The implications were serious: when Bibulus sent messengers to legislative meetings who reported that he had seen ill omens, it should have, according to traditional rules, led to the suspension of further legislation. As he was not present in person, however, the prevailing view, advanced by Caesar and at least some of his followers, was that these "distant" instances of reports did not count. But in the following year, L. Domitius Ahenobarbus accused Caesar in the Senate of acting against the auspices, a charge that Cicero listed as a typical tool of rhetorical attack, but that had the potential to lead to sanctions.[61] In a striking distinction from ancient Greece, these debates clearly played out primarily on the Senate floor as an exclusive concern of the same elite that might in another context engage in the abovementioned philosophical discussions about the validity of the very system they might ferociously argue to defend when in the Senate. This might also contribute to a clear sense that these kinds of political-cum-religious controversies often remained unresolved in the period, marking ongoing disagreements, especially among members of the elite, concerning the limits of agency individual leaders had in applying and challenging religious actions—very similarly to how the extent of individuals' political powers were debated and fought out in the Senate and ultimately in the battlefields of the empire.[62]

Just such a possibly characteristic religious exchange is preserved in a controversy Cicero found himself in when trying to reclaim one of his houses after the tribune Clodius destroyed it and built a sanctuary to the goddess Liberty on its site (a slight, in addition to the monetary loss). Importantly, Cicero's arguments in trying to recover this prime spot of real estate employ the language of impiety to attack his opponent: what he claims is at stake is which of the two men is the more pious and better interpreters of religious signs.[63] They combine the language of standard rhetorical attack with both political and religious arguments, attesting to how much these spheres could be intertwined even after the evolving specialization of the religious field.[64] Most importantly, the debate gives us unique insight into just how much even such fundamental questions of Roman religion as divination remained an object of ongoing debate and of interpretation within the Roman Senate, and how much the language of impiety might have played a role in such debates.[65] It confirms that the language of *impietas* and of *superstitio*, importantly both words that we inherited from Latin, lacked strict outlines in terms of a set of illicit actions in the way those words are used today to depict a fixed set of practices or beliefs. Rather, these words came to life as contemptuous, rhetorical characterizations that encompassed religious practices as much as someone else's character itself.[66]

The case of Cicero's house also engaged divine signs reported and experienced by the wider public in 57 BCE: strange noises were heard outside of the city, which led to the consultation, upon the Senate's decision to do so, of the Etruscan soothsayers, the *haruspices*. In the year 42, even stranger natural phenomena led to the introduction of the first gladiatorial games at regularly scheduled festivals in Rome.[67] So far, these events still fit the bill of the elite taking on a leadership role in managing religious concerns among the public. But manipulating public emotions by select members of the elite seems to come to the fore in 63 BCE, when the tribune Labienus restored the law that designated the election of priests to the tribal assembly, making these positions of at least supposed religious authority thereby a matter of at least some public contention.[68] We have evidence that Caesar was hissed at upon entering gladiatorial games after he dismissed his fellow consul's religious protestations and that Pompey was ridiculed during the Games of Apollo by Diphilus, an actor.[69] Tribunes such as Clodius were particularly well positioned to elicit negative popular responses to what may have been seen as improper religious actions on the part of the elite or un-Roman cultic activities.[70] There may also be some truth to Plutarch's later assessment of Caesar's experimentations with royal representations: he had a priest place a royal diadem on his head for the first time during the Lupercalia festival of 44 BCE, which clearly engaged and elicited the public's negative response, only to send, subsequently, the diadem to Jupiter Optimus Maximus in the Capitoline Temple.[71]

However, the influence of any public opinion was ultimately limited by political realities, most importantly by the rising power of individual leaders, such as Pompey and Caesar. These profound political changes of the time were felt by most of the writers discussed here, and it reflects these realities that, for example, Varro dedicated his *Divine Antiquities* to Caesar. Caesar clearly chose to engage and embrace at least some of Rome's religious traditions, especially to the extent they were expedient to his ambitions, but he also pushed the limits of these traditions by gathering more religious authority to himself than had ever been done before. He took on priestly positions as both pontifex maximus (since 63 BCE) and augur (since 47 BCE), and widely publicized this extraordinary combination on a newly issued silver denarius with both pontifical imagery (the ritual cup, the *culullus*, and the sprinkler, the *aspergillum*), and the augurs' symbols (a jug and the curved staff, the *lituus*, RRC 467) (Figure 6.5). His Forum featured the temple of Venus Genetrix, the goddess from whom, in another first, he claimed descent.

The change in power dynamics in late Republican Rome made urgent another issue, that was not of much concern in fifth-century Athens yet: claims by powerful individuals to divinity. In his *On the Republic* of 54 BCE, Cicero famously had Scipio endorse the idea that deserving leaders of Rome were to become divine based on their virtues, even if in the face of Caesar's power grab he also stressed that such divinization is posthumous.[72] This was not completely new: over a century earlier, the poet Ennius popularized the ideas of the Greek Euhemerus, who claimed that Zeus (Jupiter) was a human ruler with significant cultural achievements that led to his transmigration into a god upon death. Although engaging with this tradition and with Platonic metaphysics, Cicero especially emphasized the Stoic connection of virtue with divinization, establishing the outlines

FIGURE 6.5 Silver denarius of Julius Caesar with representation of his double priesthood, Rome, Italy, 46 BCE. © Eduardo Estellez / Alamy Stock Photo.

of a common elite perspective for a long time to come: becoming a god has less to do with power, and more with being a deserving leader. The reality was more complicated, as the following bloody decade was to prove. Yet, the evolution of Cicero's thought allows us to appreciate that ultimately in this period the most important source of the transformation of intellectual life, especially in terms of the organization and evolution of religious knowledge, was the transformation of power. This shift has been variably described as a change in kind, that is, a change from the openness of philosophical query to the primarily poetic engagements of the next, Augustan, generation; or, rather, as a change in the social background of those most intensively engaged with such religious ideas, a shift from aristocrats to specialists. In either case, most scholars today agree that the "revolution" at the end of the Republic, both in a political and a religious sense, came due to the grip enforced by the rule of singular emperors as prime benefactors and beneficiaries of Rome's gods.[73]

CHAPTER SEVEN

Language, Poetry, Rhetoric

SEAN GURD

FROM LANGUAGE TO ART

In 427 BCE the city of Corcyra (on the island today called Corfu) descended into internecine war. According to the historian Thucydides, this was the first instance of a kind of civil strife, or *stasis*, that would soon become endemic through the Greek world. One of the earliest casualties of this kind of strife, he thought, was language:[1] the value and hence the names of different actions and behaviors suddenly changed, and things once designated by words with negative connotations were suddenly re-characterized with words of seemingly positive implication ("irrational daring," *tolma alogistos*, for example, became "loyalty and courage," *andreia philetairos*).[2] In effect, the moral polarity of terms had reversed, and a kind of social inversion was the consequence.[3] Plato identified a similar phenomenon. In his account of political revolution in the *Republic*, he imagined the corrosive effects an overly democratic culture could have on language: the young, in particular, risked being exposed to "false and deceptive words and opinions" which caused them to give things the wrong names.[4] Not only in politics but also in intellectual circles, language seemed to have entered a critical phase: sophists like Euthydemus and his brother Dionysodorus exploited homophonies and puns to win arguments with no concern for what might be true. Even Socrates was befuddled (*ekpeplegmenos*) by these linguistic pyrotechnics (or he pretended to be, anyway).[5]

In response, Plato and others found themselves proposing what amounted to a wholesale linguistic reform that included securing the meanings of words in such a way that they could not be manipulated by dishonest intellectuals or perverted by pathological historical situations. Prodicus of Ceos was one of the first to attempt to regulate the "correctness of names" (*orthotes onomaton*); he appeared in Plato's *Protagoras* lending authority to the idea that being and becoming, *einai* and *genesthai*, were two different things.[6] Thucydides was committed to a similar form of linguistic hygiene: his diagnosis of the consequences of *stasis* on language presumed a firm opinion of what the right words for things actually were, and he was bold enough to identify certain uses as politically induced perversions.[7]

To insist that a word should have some stable or enduring meaning implied a critique of earlier intellectual projects, many of which reveled in the malleability of words. Heracleitus of Ephesus exploited homophones (or almost-homophones) in Greek to advocate a theory entailing the unity of opposites—the aphorism in which he claimed that "the bow's name is life, but its work is death," for example, exploited the near-similarity of sound between the word for bow (*bios*) and the word for life (*bios*).[8] Not much later, teachers of rhetoric and members of what would come to be called the "sophistic movement" asserted that language produced persuasion almost as though it were a magical substance.[9] So efficacious was this remarkable linguistic stuff that it could lead people to believe either side of any argument or, in an expression that Aristophanes would make notorious, could "make the weaker argument stronger."[10] As the anonymous *dissoi logoi* claimed, propositions could be convincingly taken as true or false depending on the arguments one used or the point of view one brought to them.[11] Most of our reports of these ideas come from hostile later authors, but it is evident enough that their perspective entailed well-elaborated theoretical positions. Strong countermeasures were needed.

And strong countermeasures were found. At the core of the solution was the idea that words were in some kind of tightly bound relationship with intellectual entities that, though less concrete than the words themselves, were nonetheless more reliable tools for the work of understanding. In the *Cratylus*, Plato had Socrates suggest that the designations of words needed to be abstract and perduring—they needed to be ideas, in brief.[12] For Plato the linguistic argument was closely connected to a radical position on the nature of reality: such ideas were, in fact, far more real than whatever appeared to the senses, and they enjoyed a kind of eternal being, a stable and enduring reality only accessible via the capacity for reason. In other authors the implications were less extreme but no less far reaching. A series of definitions in Aristotle established that spoken words were symbols (*symbola*) of experiences (*pathemata*) in the soul.[13] These, in turn, were related to things (*pragmata*) by natural processes of causation: via the mediation of some sensual capacity, a form (*morphê*) was produced in the soul that had a likeness to the stimulus; that form, which was implanted by sensation in the imagination and then stored in memory, was capable of being attached to a name.[14] Since they did no more than provide tokens for thoughts, words just let us make our ideas public, submitting them to communal scrutiny—but it was the thought that really mattered. Aristotle also specified that truth and falsehood were not to be sought in the relationship between a word and its corresponding mental image, but rather in the combinations of words: "white" could not be assessed for truth or falsehood, but "the man is white" could.[15] This second proposition, which insisted on the primacy of *syntax*, established a close relationship between language theory and the rigorous science of argumentation known, after Aristotle, as dialectics. Whatever else Aristotle's innovations did, they established criteria for the evaluation of all forms of communication: speech was to be dealt with within the gravity field of logic and in terms of its relationship to a signified realm of thoughts assessable as true or false according to a canon of combinatorial rules.

A perspective emphasizing the combination of elements was quite amenable to rhetorical theory. The issue was evident in Plato's work. In the *Phaedrus* one of Socrates' criticisms of Lysias' speech was that it had no rationally determinate order of parts: he compared it to a funerary epigram which made sense no matter what order the lines were inscribed in.[16] Aristotle continued the theme with a theory of rhetorical *taxis*. The *Rhetoric* articulated a position on the parts of a speech that pretended to be extremely parsimonious: a speech needed to name its subject and provide arguments.[17] Other proposals were insensitive, said Aristotle, to the needs of context and genre; demanding a narrative in every speech, he claimed, failed to appreciate that epideictic speeches did not need them, and only the statement (*prothesis*) and the proof (*pistis*) were universally necessary.[18] Rhetoric was for Aristotle a close cousin of dialectics (he tends to describe it as a lax or lazy dialectics, a dialectics for the intellectually slack and easily distractable),[19] and the structure of *prothesis* and *pistis* corresponded precisely to that of problem and

FIGURE 7.1 The Greek rhetor Demosthenes training his voice, etching after a painting by Jean-Jules-Antoine Lecomte du Nouÿ, *circa* late nineteenth century. © Pictore / Getty Images.

syllogism in dialectics.[20] Later theorists turned to the problem of sequencing arguments within the broader architectonics of a speech: Quintilian, most notably, recognized this as an unusually intense difficulty.[21] Seneca the elder recalled a declamator, Haterius, who would constantly lose his place in the heat of delivery.[22] Others flipped the perspective implied here, finding that one could communicate an impression of passion or even of sublimity if one were able to produce artful disorder in one's expression.[23]

In both Latin and Greek the word for rhetoric (*rhetorikê, oratio*) refers to speech, and the art was consistently felt to be a matter of communicating in the medium of language. But the interface between language and poetry was less neat and clean. The Greek words from which our "poetry" derives designate the act of making, and ancient reflections consistently focused on the *act of production* rather than on the function or the materials of communication. Latin terminology—*carmen*, most notably—was equally independent of the idea of language; "song" interfaces with the voice as a site of sonorous power, but not necessarily with language.[24] That is not to say that poetry did not have language in

FIGURE 7.2 Socrates, teaching on the verge of death, engraving from 1876. © Grafissimo / Getty Images.

it, or that ancient habits did not associate it with things made out of language. But just as one does not typically define a guitar as "wood" (or even as "made from wood"), so ancient thinkers did not exhaust their discussions of poetry with the observation that poems had words in them. The linguistic substrate of poetry was a basic fact beyond which interpretive and theoretical arguments rapidly moved.

In an important early definition, the south-Italian rhetorician, teacher, and ambassador Gorgias of Leontini defined poetry as "*logos* [language] with meter" (*logon echon metron*).[25] *Metron* could mean "meter" and "measure" and even, in a pinch, "mean"; the syntax of Gorgias' sentence makes it unclear whether poetry is logos with *metron* or *metron* with logos. That is not a trivial difference: while the first reading implies a subdivision of types of language use (prose, poetry), the second reading, which I suspect most modern *grammatikoi* would dismiss as simply wrong, implies a unity of arts in that all worked with some concept of form or measure: architecture is "measure with stone and wood," music is "measure with tone and time," and poetry is "measure with logos." Gorgias' syntax, with its exquisite ambiguity, suggests that we are not to decide between these readings; rather, we are to contemplate both at once. Not only is poetry language crafted into metrical form; in addition, the meter is a kind of regulatory container: it is, so to speak, what holds language together. (I would be willing to risk exploiting etymology here to claim that *metron* is the *epoche* of language.) Such ideas would have an important role to play in philosophical aesthetics: in the *Philebus* of Plato it was a crucial critique of many so-called arts, for example, that they lacked *metron* and therefore could not be treated on the same level as disciplines such as mathematics.[26] We project Platonic ideas back into the fifth century with great peril, but I think there is good reason to suspect that Gorgias' brief discussion of poetry interfaced with a conception similar to Plato's. Gorgias imagined language to be a physical force that entered the soul and has an inexorable, almost material effect on it.[27] To do so, it would need a shape or a form capable of so affecting souls. A measure that "holds" language, and thanks to which language *has* measure, would be just what was needed. Democritus, exploiting similarities between letters, words, and atoms, might have used the word *rhythm* (*rhysmos*, "form") where Gorgias says *meter*.[28] Gorgias' discussion, in other words, shows signs of an understanding in which poetry is a *perceptual form* rather than a linguistic artifact.

Plato certainly recognized that song contains a linguistic element. Socrates' virtuosic reading of Simonides' epinician for Skopas in the *Protagoras*, for example, depended on a careful application of the principle of "the correctness of names." But mimesis mattered more than language.[29] If a song was a representation of something, it was a copy and thus ontologically inferior to the original, which itself had less value than the intellectual entities or ideas that for Plato were *really* real and the only worthy object of attention. As chess moves go, this is a pretty good one: if one were to argue that songs were not copies of copies, Plato was ready with the riposte that the only alternative was for them to be simply false. Aristotle's answer in the *Poetics* attributed truth value to poetry on the basis of the plot's combination (*synthesis*) of elements: good plots had beginnings, middles, and ends, joined to each other by relations of causality or probability. They could therefore be described as the consequence of serious investigation: tragic plots were "more philosophical" than historical narrative because the latter only told you what happened, while the former told you what was likely to happen.[30] They tended, in other words, to make more universalizable claims. The key to Aristotle's approach lies in the fact that plot is treated as a consequence of combinatorial procedures—it has a syntax comparable to, if not identical with, the syntax of the syllogism. This looks like it "saves" poetry by assimilating it to Aristotle's view of language as a mimetic token of thought. Indeed, the *Poetics* contains a lengthy discussion of language, keyed to detailing ways linguistic considerations could help answer objections to poetic texts; Grinster has shown that both plot and language in Aristotle's account are defined by their essentially syntactical combination of elements.[31] Still, the intimacy linking language and *poiesis* is not as clear-cut as at first appears. In fact, the opening definitions of the *Poetics* make it plain that as an essentially mimetic art, *poiesis* included entirely non-linguistic art forms: harmony and rhythm can occur independently of *logos* in music for aulos and lyre.[32]

An apparently strong focus on language in Alexandrian scholarship had the surprising result of transforming into social or even political considerations. Scholars working within the orbit of the Ptolemaic library sometimes seem to treat language as a storehouse of historical information: the elucidation of texts was accompanied by the compilation of vocabulary lists and glosses.[33] Poetic composition exploited and celebrated the results of this labor (*ponos*) in verbal choices aimed at achieving maximal levels of allusive density.[34] In Rome a movement emerged in the early first century BCE that appears to have adopted the Alexandrian approach. How this worked in Latin letters is harder to judge than with the Greeks because so little of the Roman literary heritage from before this period has survived, but we can at least see how "neo-Alexandrianism" could make a poet such as Catullus appear both to imitate Greek models *and* to have a strongly Roman character: language here is valued as a medium for the storage and recovery of a past. Alexandrian influences are also palpable in Horace's statements on poetry in the second book of *Epistles* and in the *Ars Poetica*, where an emphasis is placed on the poet's mandate to deliberate over words, deriving effect from the selection of unusual words and lending grace to common words by setting them within a euphonious composition.[35] But Horace's development of the theme, well grounded in theory as it may have been, is modulated in such a way as to have clearly social overtones. The poet who revises, exiling some words

FIGURE 7.3 The library of Alexandria, an emblem of empire. © Nastasic / Getty Images.

from his text and welcoming others, is like a censor maintaining the citizen lists that represent the social order.[36] It is not an accident that these issues arise in a poet working at the time of the Augustan consolidation, any more than it was an accident that the first poetic movement to have valued word choice occurred in the Alexandria of the early Ptolemies: these were both moments when imperial power was being established, and these were both powers which used collections—of libraries, of scholars, of words—to create images of empire.

FROM ART TO POETICS

Language, rhetoric, and poetry were treated by many theorists as *technai* (arts). Hippocratic medicine was one of the first locations for the explicit theorization of *technê*; here it was important to carefully delimit the significance of "effectiveness" in art, and the Hippocratics were remarkably subtle on this topic.[37] Fifth-century teachers of rhetoric may have described their model texts, which students were to study and imitate, as *technai*.[38] Aristotle, by contrast, thought *technê* lay not in a text but in the soul: it was one of two productive capacities (*hexeis poietikai*) that could be developed there. The other was experience (*empeiria*). Experience resided in those who could make but could not explain what they made, while *technê*, in Aristotle's view, was reserved for those who could also give an account of their practice. For Aristotle this meant being able to specify the causes or principles (*archai*) of the art.[39] Though Aristotle's distinction between art and experience did not hold for all writers at all times, it did help to facilitate the common belief that arts could be given "theoretical" or "technical" expositions: it overstates only a little to say that there is poetic and rhetorical theory because Aristotle thought artists (*technitai*) should be able to offer explanations.

The practice—well underway in the fifth century BCE—of sending children to a *grammatikos* to learn to read and write[40] eventually became the kernel around which a *technê grammatikê*, or "art of letters," crystallized. Influenced both by Aristotelian and Stoic theories of language, the *technê grammatikê*'s canonical statement, a short work attributed to Dionysius of Thrace, received voluminous commentary by ancient readers, and makes it clear that the *technê grammatikê* was much more than just a matter of literacy: it amounted to a systematic attempt to treat language as an art along the same lines as those of medicine or rhetoric. Dionysius of Thrace calls *grammatikê* "experience (*empeiria*) of what is said by poets and writers" (note that in contradistinction to strict Aristotelian terminology, a *technê* is defined as an *empeiria*).[41] *Grammatikê* is, in other words, far more like what many would today call philology than it is like the modern science of linguistics. But the text of the *Technê* itself deals almost exclusively with linguistic matters; despite the complete curriculum offered at its start, this is an overview of "grammar" in the more constrained sense. The division of the art includes a number of topics that are linguistic, which would become the typical location for later, more systematic treatments of language: after "reading, exegesis, explanation of obscure words," Dionysius of Thrace lists "discovery of etymologies" and "reasoning out analogy" (*etymologias heuresis, analogias eklogismos*). Etymological speculation as we find it in Varro's *De lingua Latina*, and the sophisticated work on syntax by Apollonius Dyscolus are both located, in other words, within the sphere of grammatical studies.

The *technê grammatikê* was different from modern linguistics in one crucial way. While modern linguistics is descriptive, *grammatikê* was normative: it represented a model of how language *should* be, not what it was under natural conditions. Indeed, the Greek it taught amounted to a canonical language, developed out of the written records of historical poetry and prose, and it had diverged from local dialects, as these were actually spoken by the early Hellenistic period. It seems counterintuitive but it is not incorrect to refer to the language of *grammatikê* as "artificial": it was the product of art, instilled in students from a young age, and demonstrative not of human capacities to communicate but of a cultural machinery to which only the most wealthy had reliable access. From the beginning, the study of classical languages was aimed at the production of distinction and the marking off of a cultural "elite," which mapped closely onto the (unequal) distribution of wealth.

Students who followed a complete curriculum stayed with a *grammatikos* until their early teens, at which point they moved to a *rhetorikos*. Though rhetoric had an unmistakable centrality in elite education and produced a large body of theoretical literature, there existed an abiding debate over whether or not it could truly be treated as a *technê*. This was already an issue in Plato's work: the *Gorgias* has Socrates objecting that given the sophist's failure to define basic elements of his practice, it had to be accepted that rhetoric was not a *technê* at all but an *empeiria,* a form of experience or even habit.[42] Henceforth, rhetoric's status as an art was a common theme of disagreement. Figures who denied that rhetoric was an art took Plato's criticism in the *Gorgias* as a methodological first principle: if you wanted to understand rhetoric, such a position claimed, it was crucial to appreciate that it was not a *technê.* Corollaries were that it depended fundamentally on the talent of the orator; that it was ultimately a matter of inspiration, not technique; and that "technical" topics such as *lexis* and rhythm made no meaningful contribution to successful persuasion.[43] The Epicurean philosopher Philodemus reported further objections: it was impossible to clearly define the aims of rhetoric, since its use was so context dependent; it was liable to frequent failure in that people were often not convinced by an argument; if a *technê* was defined, as some Stoics defined it, as having a goal that was useful or beneficial, rhetoric clearly presented difficulties, since it could be used for morally dubious purposes.[44] These arguments, which seem to imply that one could be an orator without being part of an educational or theoretical system, naturally led to no explicit body of doctrine (equally naturally, they are alluded to in our sources only polemically), and all extant writers ultimately assert that rhetoric is, indeed, an art.

Statements about rhetoric are more varied than those about language: we do not have, as we do for *grammatikê,* a single, apparently widely used textbook. Instead major personalities wrote major texts, and each of these inevitably reflected their authors' talents and ambitions. Isocrates, a contemporary of Plato and the operator of a successful school of advanced studies that had persuasive prose at the core of its curriculum, called what he taught not "rhetoric" but rather philosophy.[45] Aristotle treated rhetoric primarily as an art of constructing "proofs" (*pisteis*); his feelings about the whole enterprise were, as we have seen, quite ambivalent. It was style and the orders of style that were at the center of attention for Demetrius of Phaleron and Dionysius of Halicarnassus. Cicero's primary emphases were political and moral: the orator was above all an advocate and a statesman. But in his real or imagined debate with the so-called Atticists, he too relies on a doctrine of styles to mount his argument.[46]

The situation for poetry was, once again, more complex and ambiguous. There are few surviving writings on what we would call poetics after Aristotle; most extant texts treat it through the lens of either *grammatikê* or *rhetorikê.* Poems and their evaluation are, as we have seen, at the center of grammatical study; rhetoricians valued poetry because it exemplified stylistic canons (especially, though not exclusively, the grand style, which rhetoricians could refer to simply as the "poetic" style).[47] What poetic theory did exist seems to have been shaped by the memory of a lingering Aristotelian difficulty: his definitions suggest that the expression *technê poietikê* would be, at best, a pleonasm. As we have seen, a *technê* was a "productive capacity" (*hexis poietikê*) accompanied by the ability to give an account. By this definition, *all technai* were poetic, in a quite precise sense—architecture, instrument making, acting, rhetoric, and painting counted, so long as the artist could give an explanation (otherwise it was just "experience"). But the precision of this definition is not matched by Aristotle's writing as a whole, where we find three divergent ways of talking about *poiesis.* While the *Metaphysics* treats *poiesis* as part of the productive capacity that is *technê,* the *Poetics* treats it as a process of mimesis. And although in the *Poetics* Aristotle argues that simply casting words into metrical lines does not make poetry (it is the logic or syntax of the representation that matters, not the surface features, as it were, of the expression), the *Rhetoric* quite explicitly discusses *poiemata* as forms of expression defined (apparently exclusively) by their having meter.[48]

There is no sign that Aristotle tried to systematize these terms, but in the third century BCE the Peripatetic philosopher Neoptolemus did make such an attempt. According to a highly hostile report in Philodemus, Neoptolemus defined poetics under three aspects (*eidea*): *poiema* (which described the "synthesis of the lexis"[49]); *poiesis* (which designated the poem as signifying [*semantikon*]); and the poet (*poietes*).[50] This tripartite division corresponds with the three kinds or aspects of poetics we find disparately discussed in Aristotle.[51]

ARISTOTLE	NEOPTOLEMUS
poiema	*poiema*
poiesis (mimesis)	*poiesis*
poiesis (hexis poietikê)	*poietes*

It appears (again primarily through the filter of Philodemus' mostly hostile reports) that the triple distinction outlined by Neoptolemus provided the basic matrix from which many Hellenistic discussions emerged. A group of theorists known via Philodemus as "euphonists" defined poetry as "good sound," taking that as "epiphenomenal" to the synthesis of the diction—they appear to have believed, in other words, that what Neoptolemus called *poiesis* (and Aristotle associated with *mimesis*) was, in essence, irrelevant, and that only the *poiema* was what mattered. That euphonist theory emphasized *poiema* at the expense of *poiesis* and *poietes* may be suggested by the work of Pausimachus. According to Richard Janko's reconstruction, Pausimachus denied all relevance to generic or semantic considerations in assessing the value of poetry: a poem was simply recognized as such by the ear, which responded to the good sound that was supervenient upon its composition.[52] He seems to have drawn implications from this for the doctrine of the *poietes*: since a poem was defined by the euphony that emerged from the way its words were put together, the poem would be destroyed if the *lexis* was changed, and as a result one could not "work up" or revise a poem—it just flashed into being with its good sound; further, when one put together texts that were not euphonic, one was not a poet; that flash brought both poem and poet into being simultaneously.[53]

An interest in auditory presence persisted in all the regions covered by this paper—not surprising, given the existence of a willingness to be guided by linguistic sonorities even in the *Odyssey* (think of Penelope working at her loom, *histos*, while Odysseus is tied to his mast, *histos*; this particular pun structures the epic so profoundly that one is tempted to compare Homer with Raymond Roussel).

In the *Cratylus*, Plato developed an extended rhapsody of puns and etymologies that depended on the evidence of the ears. A materialist philosophy lurks in the background of Plato's language games, which relate words to each other on the basis of similarities in the configuration of their elements (sounds or letters). The inspiration may be Democritus, who seems to have explained phenomenal entities as the consequence of configurations of invisible material elements, and illustrated this theory with respect to the way letters were shaped and words were formed.[54] Socrates' explorations assume a gradual transformation of words, so that you can trace current words back to their original forms (and meanings) by modeling the slow alteration of their elements. What he finds at the origin of this history of language is a kind of oral dance, a stomatic choreography.

Odyffeus

FIGURE 7.4 Odysseus tied to his mast while the Sirens sing, wood engraving, published in 1880. © Getty Images.

The original words, he imagines, were created by "name givers" who beheld the world and moved their mouths in imitation of what they beheld (Figure 7.5).[55] The sounds of such words are little more than the consequences of a modulation of the movements of the mouth into another medium: as the tongue rolls, it causes a certain eddy in the stream of the voice that we hear as a "letter." The sound games of the *Cratylus* were meant, in fact, as a kind of joke: Plato was critical of the point of view that would have taken such exercises seriously, and the conclusion of the *Cratylus* raises the possibility of the rigorous semantics we discussed above: surely the only solution to the problem of names, Socrates suggests there, is to accept that they designate ideal entities that are ever and always the same.[56] Later theorists who attended to the sonorous presences of auditory art seem to have been influenced not by Plato but by his successors and rivals—figures such as Xenocrates, who compared the sensation of tone to the line one sees when one paints a dot on a disk and then spins that:[57] just as the line is an appearance that supervenes on a spinning dot, a tone is epiphenomenal to the sequence of impacts that strike the ear, and euphony is epiphenomenal (said the euphonists) to the collocation of words (and letters in words) in a *poiema*. Some euphonists thought the recognition of good sound by the ear was an irrational, intuitive process, while others thought the ear recognized rational principles in successful poems—an idea they might have garnered from the Aristotelian music theorist Aristoxenus.[58]

The difference, of course, between a musical tone and a poem is that words have meaning, and various attempts were made to reconcile sound and sense, *poiema* and *poiesis*. Some claimed that good sound led to the appreciation of content, while others

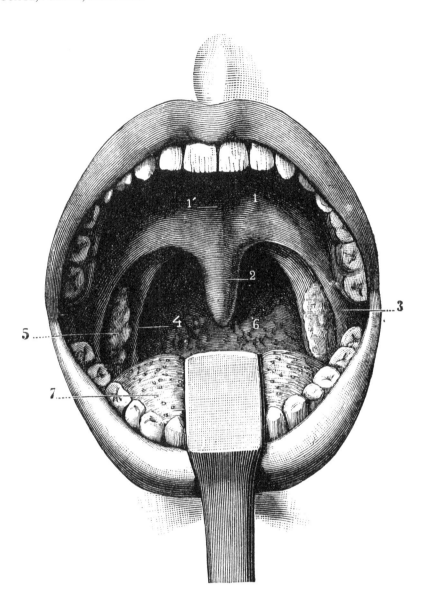

FIGURE 7.5 Anatomy of the mouth, medical scientific image. © Ilbusca / Getty Images.

argued that the key was a relationship of appropriateness between sense and sound.[59] One group of critics of euphony were, literally, critics, *hoi kritikoi*, though this group may have been given *ex post facto* unity by Crates of Mallos, a second-century BCE theorist associated with the library at Pergamon.[60] As Crates saw it, critics were involved in linguistic investigation, but they were also required to possess vast amounts of knowledge about the world. They were, as Sextus Empiricus put it, "experienced in all forms of knowledge."[61] This gives a clue as to why Crates objected to euphonism in its strictest forms: euphonism was too limited in purview. In contrast, he seems to have wanted to attend to *poiesis* (meaning) as well as to *poiema* (*lexis* or its ephiphenomenal euphony). Philodemus, who tells us about Crates, seems to have objected to the very division of poetry into three parts: he thought a poem was defined by its singular and unanalysable combination of words and sense.[62] The least that can be gathered from this is that Aristotelian conceptual unclarity over the status of poetry proved a regulatory factor in Hellenistic debate.

It is possible that the debates over sound and sense in Hellenistic poetry, which revolved around sometimes mind-bogglingly fine distinctions, reached such a state of confusing finesse that many interested parties tuned out. But its insights, or at least ideas cognate to them, did find a home in mainstream rhetorical theory.[63] In Cicero, Dionysius of Halicarnassus, and Quintilian, concerns over word junctures and clausulae can probably be understood as importations from euphonist thought into rhetorical theory.[64] In the tradition that James Porter has identified as "sublime,"[65] practical and theoretical concerns with sound and sonic presence were a constant: we detect the influence of materialist perspectives as well. Gorgias of Leontini, who conceived of language as a physical force that affected the soul on a material level, wrote in a style heavy with sound effects and was widely recognized by later critics to have pioneered a "poetic" approach to rhetorical distinction. Demetrius of Phaleron had his ears wide open, too, in attending to different characters of expression, in particular to the "grand style." Demetrius was sensitive to the way hiatus could reduce the sonority of a style, and he had thought about the way different vowel sounds could contribute to a speech's fabric.[66] But in remarkable contrast to the euphonists, Demetrius sees not *euphonia* but *kakophonia* or *dusphonia* as being important components of the grand style as early as the Homeric epics.[67] Should we hear in Demetrius' praise of cacophony part of a polemic with theorists who valued only the *eu-* in their auditory investigations? Similar ideas are given extensive treatment in Dionysius of Halicarnassus, whose detailed and elaborate theory of stylistic orders incorporated sonic considerations across the whole spectrum of styles. *De Compositione* contains an advanced form of Cratylism, in which different letter sounds are sequenced in a descending scale from best (long alpha) to worst (sigma).[68] Like the poetic euphonists, Dionysius attributes sonic effects to the composition (*synthesis*) of letters in words and words in sentences: he does not espouse, at least not explicitly, a theory of ephiphenomenalism, but he does attribute the recognition of such qualities to the ear (which he calls irrational).[69] Though he does not acknowledge critics or euphonists as predecessors, he clearly depends heavily on music theory, to such an extent that he makes rhetorical style into a kind of musical expression—different stylistic levels are called *harmoniai* (harmonies) and are analyzed in terms of *emmeleia* (melody), *rhythmos* (rhythm), and *metabole* (modulation).

Philodemus objected quite strenuously to Neoptolemus' contention that the *poietes* should be a distinct aspect of the art—rather, presumably, than being the one that "has" the art.[70] But Neoptolemus' position seems to make perfect sense once it is set against the background of Aristotelian distinctions.[71] All Neoptolemus did was acknowledge that the productive capacity was acquired through training and habituation: to have an art was to have subjected oneself to a formative technique. Similar insights were applied to oratory. In truth, there had been a tradition associating rhetorical training with personal development since at least the early fourth century. Isocrates' pedagogy was aimed not only at sharpening his students' argumentative tools but also at giving them the ability to revise their ideas and, more than this, to have the courage to say what needed to be said even in the face of hostile powers.[72] Cicero's *De Oratore* is above all about education, personal praxis, and internal discipline. Indeed, it could well be described as a systematic attempt to treat the ethical side of the rhetorical art. The remarkable portraits of Roman *patroni* (Antonius, Crassus) that he offers here are more than merely acts of piety: they emphasize the crafted self as the site where language, philosophy, and practice are integrated. We may observe a very similar tendency in Quintilian: here the education of the orator is undertaken through a curriculum that begins with learning to read and ends with successfully improvising political speeches on the highest matters of policy. Quintilian is not creating a philosopher, but philosophers would have recognized common concerns, including the centrality of contemplative practices such as the art of memory and the concentrated visualization that leads, says Quintilian, to effective emotional representation. In fact, philosophers *did* recognize that oratorical expression could be connected to personal technique: Seneca the Younger in a particularly well-known epistle argues that a fine ear should be able to discern a writer's moral status through the sounds of his expressive style.[73] The tragedy of rhetoric in the imperial period, according to the young Tacitus of the *De Oratoribus*, was not so much a decline in *linguistic* craft as it was the sidelining of an entire class of political agents, with the result that the inward development lacked an outlet for outward expression. This was an impression, perhaps, that the younger Pliny's self-portraiture was meant to mitigate: the letters detail the minutiae of the life of an orator of the highest status, as though the crafted oratorical person were more valuable as an exemplum than the speeches he might pronounce.

Nobody knows who Horace's *Ars poetica* is supposed to spoof,[74] but it surely sends someone up: here is a sometimes eloquent, not uninformed authority on Hellenistic poetic theory who is also given to undercutting himself with embarrassing admissions ("no matter how hard I work, all I manage to make are tiny little failures")[75] and is, at best, insouciant about the organization of his ideas.[76] This writer, in other words, has some ability at diction (*poiema*) and matter (*poiesis*) but has not crafted himself carefully enough so as to be able to produce a coherent text. The speaker of the *Ars poetica*, in other words, is not a *poietes*.[77] This is, incidentally, just the kind of figure who is so typically Horace's target throughout his hexameter verse. No surprise, then, that when Horace becomes more serious about poetry in the epistles to Florus and Augustus, it is to describe not poetic technique, but rather morals: the poet in these works has a social function, and this function is grounded in a sense of the self as guided above all by personal technique.

This tradition of thought emphasized textual interactions that were focused on explications of a historical or lexicographical nature and on the comparative evaluation of different texts. What we might call higher-order interpretation, but what was certainly much more ambitious in its scope, was practiced in other areas. The so-called Derveni Papyrus, for example, offered elaborate allegorical readings of Orphic poetry; Stoicism read traditional poems and myths as allegorical disclosures of the nature of the universe; Philo of Alexandria, followed by both Neoplatonists and early Christians, took up these approaches with some enthusiasm, reading out of the canon of classical literature detailed descriptions of the cosmos and the position of the soul within it. As Peter Struck has emphasized, such approaches seem to have assumed that words were somehow connected to things by natural links. These hardwired and non-arbitrary connections allowed for bold connections to be made between radically different areas of experience. Equally important, I think, is the social division of labor. Allegorical interpretation was performed not by grammarians or teachers of rhetoric but by philosophers and spiritual leaders, and a different art entirely was being promulgated: that of the good life, however defined.

FROM PERCEPTION TO THE SELF

Closely linked to the question of *technê* was the insight that poetry and rhetoric were *aesthetic*. "Aesthetics," in Anglo-American philosophical circles, has come to be associated with the study of "beauty": this tradition is rooted in Plato's *Philebus* and is a crucial element in post-Renaissance European thinking about art. I mean aesthetic in a more restricted, etymologically more faithful way, as referring to the role and nature of perception (*aisthesis*). From the fourth century BCE on, theorists interested in *technê* recognized the importance of trained perception in the process of artistic making; and in later antiquity perception was increasingly recognized as a crucial element in reception as well. The specific perceptual faculty in question, for both rhetoric and poetry, was the hearing (*akoê*). The idea that hearing could judge artistic experiences appeared in slightly different forms in different authors. As we have seen, Aristotle imagined that repeated perceptions of a class of things could lead to experience (*empeiria*); joined by *logos* this became art (*technê*). Musicians appear to have been particularly important to this interpretation of the senses: in an example given by Speusippus, then repeated by the stoic Diogenes of Babylon and (thence, possibly) Dionysius of Halicarnassus, the idea of an expert ear was supported by the fact that trained musicians could listen to a song and then repeat it with no reflection or hesitation: they have exercised their hearing to such a degree of precision, these authors claim, that it just knows what it is listening to.[78] All these figures insist that such hearing is made, not born: it is a reflection of deep training and long practice and not innate in any way. Dionysius of Halicarnassus insisted that his own ability to recognize certain styles (especially the charming style of Lysias) came from a hard-to-articulate sense whose basis was years of reading and study.[79] Dionysius' validation of highly trained perception was not idiosyncratic: it seems to have become an important component in the self-construction of literary authority. Aulus Gellius tells a story about Probus, who dismissed a student who could not appreciate the differences between two different spellings of the same word in different lines of Vergil. This reflects the belief that a certain amount of acoustic refinement was required to appreciate poetic expression: its absence made one liable to ridicule, which Probus happily delivers.[80]

This is all clearly normative, and even exclusive: theorists up to Dionysius of Halicarnassus are primarily (and often explicitly) interested in the dynamics of expert *aisthesis*. There can be no doubt that this continued to be a central area of concern in the high empire and later; but a new interest in the nature of unlearned responses also emerged. Dionysius of Halicarnassus recognizes that while trained perception was capable of identifying different styles, the *point* of technique was to move even the untrained;[81] he says little more, but the idea becomes central to the work of "Longinus," the author of *On the Sublime*. If for Dionysius the charm of Lysias was evident to him because he had put in the requisite hours of study, Longinus claims that true sublimity is evident to *everyone all the time*.[82] What is remarkable here is that universality is no longer a consequence of art, as it is in Dionysius of Halicarnassus, for whom the refinement and practice characteristic of art leads to a universal appeal, such that if there is art, then there is a kind of mass popularity; in Longinus, by contrast, a universal experience is the *criterion* of the sublime, such that if there is a universal feeling, then the sublime exists in the stimulus text. Given the difficulty of actually *testing* this, however (how could we ever determine that everybody at every time was really carried away by a text?), Longinus proposes an alternative epistemological method. The idea is not to internalize a set of technical assumptions through lore and practice (as in Dionysius of Halicarnassus), but to attend to the less rational parts of one's *own* response, which in effect stands in as proxy for the unknowable universal response.[83] The sublime is hard or even impossible to theorize, but it is also impossible to withstand or forget, so to recognize and then reproduce it one must become aware of one's own extra-theoretical responses. The differences between Dionysius' and Longinus' respective advice to aspiring authors reflect a divergence between Dionysius' emphasis on expert perception and Longinus' on universal affect: Dionysius says, in effect, that the student should read and practice, and assumes in an Aristotelian mode that repeated exposure will lead to expertise, but Longinus recommends a variety of far more demanding exercises. One must emulate the great authors,[84] or use one's capacity for mental images to enter the scene one speaks about.[85] (Some of this material could also be found in Quintilian's instructions to an orator on how to achieve vividness.[86]) These techniques could be summarized, I think, as aimed at building an art out of the phenomenology of untrained response. They could also be described as emphasizing a close identity between the reader and the author: to write, one must first be a highly self-aware reader, even or especially when reading leads one to forget oneself. Indeed, Longinus' idea of the writer as reader is fundamentally different from the image of the "learned reader" that had so much currency in poetic circles from the Alexandrian period on, that reader who through years of labor had acquired a literary fluency that allowed him to produce statements of maximum poetic density by choosing the most loaded, allusive words.[87] Longinus steps outside this mode, questioning the unmastered affects generated by a powerful piece of poetry or rhetoric. And yet despite the significant differences between the tradition emphasizing technical perception and Longinus, even here the distinction between *poiesis*, *poiema*, and *poietes* can be felt to be at work. Longinus insists, for example, that production of that lofty feeling requires attention to ambition of thought, extreme and inspired emotion, correct use of figures, diction, and composition.[88] A little agility permits us to see how these fit with the old post-Aristotelian distinctions: to have great thoughts and to feel emotion strongly provides material to imitate (*poiesis*, concerned above all with *mimesis*); figure, diction, and composition are the traditional materials of *poiema*. The *poietes* is produced by means of that process of study and self-reflection on the powerful emotions that occur when one is overwhelmed by the gust of powerful writing. An accommodation to the fact that Longinus' interest lies outside the enclosure of technical perception may lie in his redefinition of the boundaries of *technê*: here only figures, diction, and composition are treated as technical, while the rest is "self-generated" (*authigenes*). Technique has been limited to language, to that part of the expressive process that can be assimilated to *grammatikê* and the more elementary parts of *rhetorikê*.

Describing sublimity and prescribing methods for creating it, in other words, requires Longinus to engage in relatively profound self-observation: he seeks to understand, articulate, and then reproduce his own most passionate readerly responses. Though its aims are almost diametrically opposed, Plutarch's essay on *How the Young Man Should Study Poetry* recommends a very similar cognitive comportment. Plutarch's concern is very similar to Longinus' interest: poetry is deeply affecting, almost uncontrollably powerful. Plutarch, however, sees this (in a Platonic mode) as a danger: the lures and pleasures of poetry could easily damage an unprepared young reader. But there are also benefits, and so Plutarch sets out a series of theoretical precepts, that, if properly learned, could function as prophylaxis against poetry's worse depredations. The drift of the essay could be rephrased as follows: Plutarch is proposing that the passionate affects a reader of poetry is liable to suffer could be mitigated by means of a constant and rigorous self-surveillance in which literary theory is wielded apotropaically; the result will be that the dangerous stuff is converted into useful pedagogical material. What Plutarch has in common with Longinus—practically all the two have in common—is the self-reflexivity, the insistence on a careful form of self-regard. These tendencies became more pronounced in later antiquity, where among writers both Christian and pagan reading and writing were often intimately and self-consciously intertwined. Aaron Pelttari has shown that when Servius, our authoritative commentator on the work of Virgil, sought to provide detailed factual and stylistic information to assist in the comprehension of Virgil, he provided a theater for other readers to reflect on their own experiences with the text.[89] The second book of Augustine's *De ordine*, similarly, offers a narrative in which reason rises through an educational curriculum entailing grammar, rhetoric, music, and mathematics by means of a process of self-observation: watching itself use words, reason arrives at the arts of grammar and rhetoric; observing the regularities of its utterances it comes to a sense of music (for Augustine, music is treated almost entirely as rhythm); contemplating rhythm it arrives at a concept of number, which leads to the idea of unity.[90] Intimately linked to this is a crucial ambiguity: it is unclear in Augustine's account whether he is talking about individuals' *ratio*, or about *Ratio* in a universal sense. But the idea that self-reflexivity should lead not only to self-understanding but also to a sense of what is true for everyone at all times lines Augustine's thought up, in at least this respect, with the ideas of Longinus.[91] It may be one of the signal developments of literary thought in the centuries after Dionysius of Halicarnassus to have taken an experience that in the Hellenistic period was understood as a matter of passionate and in some degree untrustworthy perception and to have made that into a platform for searching inward investigation.

CHAPTER EIGHT

The Arts

RUTH WEBB

INTRODUCTION

Defining and delimiting the "arts" in ancient thought should be simple: books and articles on ancient art are devoted to painting on vases, walls, and panels; to sculpture, large and small, relief and in the round; and occasionally, to architecture. But, as has often been noted, no single ancient term corresponds satisfactorily to the modern category. There are certainly words in the Greek and Latin languages that can be translated as "art"—technê and "ars" respectively—but their range of meaning encompasses techniques, crafts, skills, military stratagems, even treachery and deceit.[1] More precisely, they implied the existence of a body of knowledge, including practical skills, that could be communicated and transmitted through teaching,[2] hence the "arts" of grammar, rhetoric, medicine, and gymnastics and, in Latin poetry, Ovid's *Ars amatoria*, the art of seduction. The scope of this chapter represents a compromise between this ancient, expansive, idea of *technê* and the modern understanding of "the arts" and will focus on painting, sculpture, and drama, not forgetting the complex of music, dance, and song. That some affinities or similarities were felt to exist between these is suggested by the existence of a network of comparisons between them, within which poetry and rhetoric, the subject of another chapter in this volume, also figure. Despite their differences in medium and form, these arts also have in common their mimetic character and this will be explored in this chapter.

The period covered by this volume creates a particular challenge encompassing as it does over a thousand years and covering an immense geographical area occupied by a multiplicity of shifting cultural, political, and religious systems. This volume takes in the small communities of Archaic Greece, the cultural and political rise and fall of Athens, the spread of Greek culture throughout the Eastern Mediterranean and as far as North India in the Hellenistic period, Rome's rise to the center of an empire and the spread of Christianity across that empire in late antiquity. Across these times and places, what we might call the arts played an immense variety of public roles: creating cohesion through participative performances or through mass spectatorship; displaying civic or individual identity and wealth; expressing political domination through the transfer of objects, as in the wholesale importation of Greek artifacts to Rome from the late third century BCE onward with its complex ethical and political implications; honoring and remembering individuals through the dedication of monuments, not to mention the role and function of images, particularly statuary, in religious contexts.

The contexts of production and display varied enormously too, from the agonistic festivals of the Greek world where musicians, poets, orators, and occasionally visual artists competed, often alongside athletes, to the collections of paintings and sculptures in Hellenistic cities, private Roman villas, or late antique bath complexes and palaces.[3] Collections of precious dedications housed in temples remind us of the entanglement of art and religion, through subject matter, function, and in the case of theatre and music, performance context. The status of practitioners of the arts differed: some arts—like choral dance and song, and Attic tragedy at its beginnings—involved community participation, others were the work of professionals who might be respected (like the star painters and sculptors of classical Greece recorded by Pliny and others) or reviled as manual laborers or worse, like actors in Rome.[4] The artists themselves would no doubt have had different views that are not easily accessible to us.

DEFINING "THE ARTS" IN ANTIQUITY

As Paul Oskar Kristeller pointed out in a pair of articles (1951 and 1952) it is difficult to project the modern conception of "the arts" onto antiquity, but there are many caveats to be added. The lack of autonomy that he ascribed to artistic practices in antiquity, in contrast to his vision of eighteenth-century Europe, was not as total as he suggests. The arts in antiquity were without a doubt firmly embedded in religious, political, and social life as reflected in the constant concern about their ethical impact. This embeddedness enriches and informs ancient ideas without entailing a total lack of autonomy:[5] the festivals that provided the contexts for music, drama, poetry, and sometimes the visual arts throughout antiquity were political and religious events, but they also served to frame a time and space distinct from the quotidian.[6] In the Greek context, the competitive nature of public performances of drama and music encouraged the development of shared aesthetic criteria[7] and it is noticeable that Aristotle's analysis of tragedy says nothing about the religious context of its performance.[8] The practice of reviving classical dramas in Athens from 386 BCE contributed to the constitution of corpora and a sense of a living theatrical history that existed alongside the project to preserve and study the scripts of plays.[9] In the case of paintings and sculptures, the constitution of collections removed them from any direct religious context and encouraged viewers to compare techniques and styles and to make connections between the narrative scenes portrayed.[10]

However, it is only at the very end of our period that we find attempts to articulate explicit boundaries between the products of the various arts and their religious contexts, as the spread of Christianity prompted a wholesale renegotiation and reconceptualization of traditional practices including the production and reception of the visual and performing arts. In the case of architecture and architectural decoration, an edict from the 340s CE specifies that pagan temples associated with public entertainment should be protected from destruction while others protect those images within pagan buildings that are considered significant for the "value of their art" (*pretium artis*) rather than for their religious significance (*divinitas*).[11] The new needs and concerns of an empire in the process of Christianization made it necessary to clarify boundaries and the polemics surrounding theatrical performance in late antiquity reveal the intense debates and negotiations involved.[12] As this suggests, both the conception and the function of the arts in antiquity were constantly reshaped in relation to their changing cultural contexts.

IDEAS OF "THE ARTS" IN ANTIQUITY

Ideas about the arts are to be found in a wide variety of sources. Alongside the philosophical discussions in Plato, Aristotle, and others, poetry, laws, anecdotes, myths, and even the works of art themselves convey ideas. First of all, from the earliest moments of Greek literature it is possible to discern a network of comparisons between different arts. These comparisons may rest on their representational function as in the well-known claim by the lyric poet Simonides that "painting is silent poetry while poetry is painting that speaks" quoted by Plutarch in the late first or early second century CE within a discussion of *enargeia*, or the quality of vividness that appeals to the mind's eye, in historiography.[13] This is echoed, with a different emphasis, by Horace's list of similarities between the effect on the audience of different styles of poetry and of painting that forms the context for the aphorism "ut pictura poiesis" in his *Ars poetica*, 361.[14] In addition, Greek and Latin poets lay claim to the status of sculptors and architects when they compare the memorializing function of poetry to that of statues or architecture and attribute the permanence of stone to poetry.[15] Rhetoric and the visual arts are often compared explicitly by authors seeking to characterize rhetorical style[16] or implicitly in claims that rhetorical discourse, like poetry or historiography, can "make visible" its subject matter.[17]

The modern system of the arts identified by Kristeller as the norm against which to measure antiquity places painting and sculpture at the heart of "the arts," leaving theatre, and particularly dance, in a marginal position. It is true that, for modern students of antiquity, the evaluation of these arts is made particularly difficult by the evanescent nature of performance which has left us few direct traces. But these arts played a central role in ancient culture and dance, in particular, was woven into the web of parallels and comparisons. The mimetic pantomime dance of the Roman period, with its mythological narratives, was also compared with poetry, sometimes in terms identical to the comparison between poetry and painting.[18] Moreover, Plutarch, in the same passage, uses analogies with the visual arts to express the way in which pantomime dancers would stop and take up a pose (*schema*) "as if in a painting" (*graphikos*). The comparison may tell us something about the dancers' technique, but most importantly it implies a more profound connection and that audiences could use the same body of knowledge to interpret the fluid and rhythmic movements of dance and the postures depicted in the visual arts.[19]

This network of comparisons suggests that a complex web of interrelationships was perceived to exist between the visual, verbal, and corporeal arts. This impression is reinforced by the use of shared critical vocabulary such as *rhuthmos* and *summetria* for dance, poetry, rhetoric, and the visual arts, as well as architecture, a usage that, rather than being a sign of an impoverished lexicon, implies a perceived affinity between the arts as experienced.[20] In some cases these terms do not simply pull dance into the orbit of the other arts but derive first and foremost from there, reminding us of its centrality within ancient culture and its deep entanglement with sung poetry. So, where Kristeller reflects the modern usage of the term "arts" by granting pride of place to practices productive of static objects that persist over time in their singularity (paintings, sculptures, buildings), the oldest conceptions of the arts in antiquity attribute great, if not the greatest, importance to the evanescent arts of song, rhythm, and movement and to the arts as performances, actualized in front of an audience.

FIGURE 8.1 Sarcophagus with reliefs of Muses, mid-second century CE. Louvre. © Araldo de Luca / Corbis / Getty Images.

Synaesthetic unity also underlies the conception of the Muses in archaic and classical Greece.[21] The attribution of particular arts to each of the nine Muses, as on this Roman sarcophagus, was a postclassical phenomenon (Figure 8.1). In their archaic and classical form, their number varied and they represented a synaesthetic nexus of music, sung poetry, and dance (the Greek *mousikê*), linked to the celebration of the past through their mother, Mnemosyne (Memory).[22]

The names given to them by Hesiod—Kleio, Euterpe, Thaleia, Melpomene, Terpsichore, Erato, Polymnia, Ourania, and Kalliope—evoke singing (*melpo*), beauty (*kallos*), the voice (*ops*), and dance (*choreia*), along with the emotions that they evoke— desire (*eros*) and pleasure (*terpsis*)—and the function of song in spreading fame (*kleos*) and ensuring the flourishing (*thallo*) memory of a person in addition to their therapeutic role (see Sissa in this volume).[23] And, as Habinek shows, this applies as much in the Roman context as in archaic Greece (see also Gurd in this volume).[24]

The Muses' names also direct our attention toward the impact of the arts on the listener or viewer. They can, it is implied, inspire desire (*eros*) and create a feeling of delight (*terpsis*), the feeling evoked by aesthetic experiences in the Homeric poems: Achilles feels terpsis as he handles and looks at the weapons made for him by Hephaistos[25] as do the audiences for song and dance[26] and the the participants in games[27] or in the pleasures of food and sex.[28] In the *Laws*, Plato's suggestion that "joy" (*chara*) is the etymological root of participatory choral song and dance breaks down the boundary between producers and receivers pointing to the embodied nature of that response.[29]

However, Hesiod's Muses are also unsettlingly ambiguous, announcing their ability to tell lies as well as true things (*a-lêthea*—the absence of forgetting) in the poet's account of his meeting with them on Helicon.[30] The tricky, deceptive nature of artistic creation is also evident in Hesiod's accounts of the creation of Pandora from clay and her beautification at the hands of the gods.[31] Although the written sources are later (from the early fifth century onward), the stories about Daidalos similarly portray the artisan's skills as a source of danger and destruction. The shell of a cow he builds for Pasiphae succeeds in tricking the bull but gives rise to a deadly hybrid while his attempt to enable his son to imitate a bird ends in tragedy.[32]

MIMESIS

One concept that helps to unify various practices that we might call "arts" is *mimesis*.[33] Though it does not account for every instance of artistic creation and has the disadvantage of deflecting attention from the arts' materiality, it does provide an avenue of approach to the creation and reception of the visual and performing arts and to their ontological status. In the introduction to his *Poetics*, Aristotle treats *mimesis* as a unifying principle, bringing together painting, music, dance, prose drama, and dialogue as well as poetry and later on referring to the "mimetic [arts]" (*tais mimetikais*).[34] The inclusion of painting, in which the viewer interacts with the product in the absence of the artist, reflects painters' rise in importance in Athens during the fifth century.[35]

As Halliwell points out, Aristotle's treatment of *mimesis* played an important, if often hidden, role in the constitution of the modern category of "the arts."[36] However, it also serves to highlight a fundamental difference. The continued centrality of performing arts in Aristotle's list serves as a reminder of the core sense of *mimesis* as an active copying, "acting like" the object of *mimesis*, meaning that the production of a simulacrum, separate from both the artist and the object of *mimesis* (as a painting or a sculpture is), was not central to the ancient idea.[37] In addition to drama and some forms of dance, *mimesis* encompasses all cases of copying actions, as in the process of socialization or technical training where the result is ontologically identical to the model: in copying adults, the child grows into a fully acculturated member of her society, just as in copying his master, the apprentice shoemaker will achieve the same—or equivalent—state.[38] In this model, there are no sharp boundaries between imitator, prototype, or when this is the human body, medium. "Imitation," with its pejorative connotations of secondariness and lack, is therefore an unsatisfactory translation for *mimesis* whose meaning is sometimes close to "representation" (when the imitator uses paint, stone, music, or words) and at others to "acting like" (when the imitator works with her own body).[39]

This active conception of *mimesis* underlines the porosity of the boundaries between "the arts" and processes of socialization, acculturation, and appropriation.[40] At the same time, not all ancient art was mimetic in any sense of the word as is illustrated by an anecdote from Pliny: finding that the artist Protogenes was not at home, Apelles drew a line on a blank panel to serve as a calling card; Protogenes then responded by drawing an even finer line over the first only to be defeated when Apelles drew an even finer one.[41] Here, art is celebrated as the sensuously perceptible result of technical skill, in this case the trace of a gesture standing for the physical presence of the artist.[42]

So, although *mimesis* is not coextensive with either "art" or "the arts" it is a fruitful starting point that allows us to consider together various visual, poetic, and performing arts.[43] One unifying characteristic of artistic, as opposed to social or educational *mimesis* is the difference—the ontological and/or qualitative gap—between the prototype and the mimetic artifact, whether the stylized words and gestures that distinguish the tragic actor's *mimesis* from words and actions in the real world, or the distinction between stone and flesh, or that between the painted surface and the fictive space that is represented by illusionistic painting.[44] Two further Plinian anecdotes, this time about the classical painter Zeuxis, emphasize these gaps. In the story of the women of Kroton (or Akragas) he is said to have drawn on a plurality of models for his painting of Helen, selecting the best feature of each and creating an exact likeness of none.[45] The other is his spontaneous contest with Parrhasios which shows him asking for a painted curtain to be swept aside. The impossibility of the act serves to underline the difference between this painted cloth and its model.[46]

MIMESIS IN ARISTOTLE

I will treat Aristotle before Plato because of the range of arts he considers under the heading of *mimesis* and for his direct interest in those arts and their role in the city. His discussion of mimesis in the *Poetics* begins with a list of the types of poetry that are mimetic: epic, comedy, and tragedy, dithyramb as well as most music for the *aulos* (pipes) and all *kithara* (lyre) music.[47] Where these differ, in Aristotle's analysis, is in their media, objects, and modes of *mimesis*, a point he illustrates by analogy with painting in which *mimeseis* are produced with colors and shapes, while others use the voice, and different combinations of rhythm, language, and melody (*harmonia*). Danced *mimesis* uses rhythm alone without melody to produce *mimeseis* of characters or states of mind (*êthê*), emotions (*pathê*), and actions (*praxeis*) through what Aristotle calls "figured rhythms."[48] The list is subordinated to Aristotle's immediate interests in the *Poetics* but points to an understanding of *mimesis* as encompassing a wide range of phenomena, from the visual artist's rendering of appearances in two dimensions (sculpture is not discussed) to the actor's performance on stage of the words and actions of a character. It also includes narrative poetry in which the performer spoke the characters' words[49] or recounted their actions. Beyond their engagement in *mimesis*, all these arts have in common, in Aristotle's analysis, human (including heroic and divine) activity and characters as their subjects.[50]

   In the case of drama, dance, and painting there is a visible and/or audible analogy between the mimetic version and the real or imaginary original, but the case of music is far more puzzling at first sight. Aristotle's thought on this is clarified in the *Politics* where he explains that music imitates the emotions or states of mind (*êthê*) themselves rather than their external signs embodied in a human figure as painting does (smiling lips or frowning eyebrows).[51] These signs are distinguished from the "likenesses" or "equivalents"[52] (*homoiomata*) of *êthos* contained within music. Moreover, he goes on to attribute to music the power to produce these emotions or states in the listener.[53] This discussion—a further reminder of the centrality of music—shows that *mimesis* is not reduceable to the reproduction of physical appearances: it can also produce an experience of the object of the *mimesis* in the audience and is not purely reproductive but has the potential to transform the viewer or listener. The *Poetics*, with its pronounced lack of interest in tragedy as multisensorial performance, gives prominence to the plot in the treatment of pity and fear and of the *katharsis* that results;[54] but, in the *Politics*, it is music that brings about *katharsis*.[55]

PLATO'S *REPUBLIC* 3: MIMETIC CONTAGION

Plato's treatments of the arts are largely subordinated to the surrounding discussions of metaphysical, educational, and political questions and reflect a range of attitudes.[56] The most influential passages are those on poetry and painting in the *Republic*, which are highly critical of both. Socrates first excludes traditional poetry from the education of the Guardians of his ideal city in *Republic* 2 and 3 because of the false or inappropriate stories about the gods and heroes in epic and tragedy and their potential for misleading readers, particularly the young. But he soon moves on to a more fundamental concern about the role play that is central to the conception of *mimesis*: the famous contrast between *mimesis* (direct speech) and *diegesis* (narrative) treats the inclusion of speeches by characters in epic as a form of deception in which the poet tries to pretend that he is the character.[57] This assimilation of the poet with his characters relies on a conception of

Homer as bard, giving a live performance, even implying that Homer, the dissimulating poet, is present each and every time the epics are recited.[58] Further on, however, Socrates identifies the real danger as the mimetic assimilation to the character that occurs when the student reads these speeches aloud: "*mimeseis*, if they are allowed to continue from a young age, establish themselves in the character (*êthos*) and nature (*phusis*) of the person's body, voice, and mind."[59]

This conception of reading poetry in an educational context as a type of actorly role play is striking for the modern reader but Plato is working with a model of reading-as-performance that allows him to cast the epic poet as scriptwriter and the reader as actor (a variant on the poet-performer amalgam he started from). Socrates thus moves from condemning poetry as a bad example presenting untruths to its audience to seeing it as a means of shaping the very being of the reader-aloud. The root sense of *mimesis* as "acting like" is very much alive here and the claim that the active imitator—particularly when young—runs the risk of becoming assimilated to the model depends on the absence of clear linguistic and conceptual boundaries between artistic *mimesis*, carried out within a framed context and in a ludic manner, and the serious business of educative *mimesis* that shapes the youngster into an adult member of society. It is an ambiguity that follows artistic *mimesis* of all types and attributes to the arts the power not just to reflect the world but to shape it.

PLATO, *REPUBLIC* 10: THE DECEPTIVE IMAGE

If the discussion in book three leaves space open for an acceptable form of purely narrative poetry, the discussion of poetic and painterly *mimesis* in book ten of the *Republic* raises different problems.[60] The focus remains on epic and tragedy and their role in the city, but the intervening books have introduced the theory of Forms (books 5–7) and the division of the human soul into rational and irrational parts (books 4, 8, and 9) and the second discussion of the arts takes place against this background. Painting, in particular, is introduced as the prime example of *mimesis*, understood as the mere reproduction of external appearance, requiring no specialist knowledge of the thing represented, in contrast to other crafts.[61] The example of the painting of a bed, existing at two removes from the ideal Form of the bed, enables Plato, through Socrates, to condemn all *mimesis* as false and secondary. As Nehamas and others have pointed out, the choice of painting here as the paradigmatic example of *mimesis* is unusual in that the most obvious example for Plato's contemporaries would surely have been acting.[62] But this choice, and particularly the unusual subject matter of the hypothetical work, allows Plato to place *mimesis* as a whole on the side of the derivative and the deceptive. He is here responding to contemporary practices in painting and sculpture that created an illusion of depth through the play of color and light and shade (*skiagraphia*) and perspective (*skenographia*), which took account of the position of the viewer.[63] These "distorted" likenesses are then associated with the basest, non-rational part of the soul with which they entertain a quasi-erotic relationship.[64] By analogy, the intense emotions depicted in and aroused by tragedy and epic involve the basest part of the soul.

Plato's treatment of the arts in the *Republic* is extreme and is not taken up by other ancient commentators, except in the case of early Christian opponents of the theater, discussed below (p. 148). However, concern about the ethical impact of the arts, combined with a conception of the individual as vulnerable to the effects of perception entering the body is widespread in both Greek and Roman culture, as is the exploration in many modes of the gaps between appearance and reality, and between the objects of *mimesis* and the media used to represent them in the arts. This lack of complete equivalence gives rise to different evaluations. It can be seen as a deficiency, as in Plato's treatment of painting in *Republic* 10, or as a positive characteristic as is suggested by Aristotle's claim at *Poetics* 9 that poetry, unlike history, treats what could happen and not just what has happened and is therefore closer to philosophy.[65]

MIMESIS BEYOND PLATO

One consequence of placing performance at the center of *mimesis* is to bring out the potential of the mimetic work to transform the viewer. As in the case of music in Aristotle, the impact on the audience can be understood as temporary (the process of *katharsis* or the mood induced by a particular musical mode) or deeply transformative (as in Plato's model of the students irrevocably transformed by their repeated performances of epic). Ideas of mimetic influence and contagion—viewers being acted upon by paintings, sculptures, or drama and responding to the representation as if it were real or assimilating themselves to it—recur in ancient discourse about the arts and represent an area where "artistic," "religious," and "magical" practices overlap.[66] Most problematic of all though is the art of acting in which the human body is at once the object of the imitation and the material and which threatens the very identity not only of the actor but also of the audience.

The dangers involved in theatrical mimesis are the subject of intense debate at the end of antiquity in which Plato's ideas, adopted and adapted by Christian thinkers, loom large. In his own context, however, his was one of several voices as the contrast with Aristotle's views of *mimesis* as pleasurable suggests. Ischomachus, the Athenian householder in Xenophon's *Economicus*, does equate painting—particularly the illusionistic rendering of flesh by the painter Zeuxis—with appearance (*doxa*), defined in opposition to both truth and nature and functioning as a form of deceit (*apate*).[67] As in Plato, the example of painting serves to condemn another practice: the use of cosmetics by his wife to alter the appearance of her own skin. Another work by Xenophon (*Memorabilia*) gives a very different impression of Socrates' views of art and artists, showing him discussing the problem of representation with the painter Parrhasius and then with the sculptor Kleiton.[68] He leads both artists to accept that, although character (*êthos*) in itself is not visible, it is made apparent through the expressions, postures, and movements of the human body, which can be represented in painting and sculpture. Xenophon's Socrates, free from Plato's metaphysical preoccupations, thus acknowledges that painting and, to a somewhat lesser degree, sculpture can represent the invisible (*êthos*) through the visible and distill into one represented body the signs of a particular *êthos*, as Lysippos famously did in his portrait of Alexander (Figure 8.2).[69]

Direct responses to Plato's *Republic* are found in the later philosophical tradition. The incompatibility between art and the reality represented by the Forms was challenged by Neoplatonic philosophers, particularly Plotinus in the third century CE. As part of his argument that beauty (*kallos*) exists in the perceptible world he cites the example of the forms (*eidê*) created in the artist's mind and realized through human art (*technê*) in sculpture.[70] This beauty derives not from the material, the stone, but from the preexisting form (*eidos*) in the mind of the one who conceived it (*ennoeô*). His specific example is Phidias' chryselephantine statue of Zeus at Olympia created, he claims, through an

FIGURE 8.2 Detail from the Alexander Mosaic showing Alexander the Great in battle against Persian King Darius III, Roman copy of a Hellenistic painting, original *c.* 310 BCE, copy *c.* 100 BCE. © Universal History Archive / Universal Images Group / Getty Images.

intellectual understanding of how Zeus would look if he chose to reveal himself. This view was adumbrated in Dio Chrysostom's *Olympian Oration* (*Or.* 12) (late first century CE) which identifies Phidias' Zeus as comparable to, or in rivalry with, (*paraballomai*) the famous description of Zeus nodding his assent to Thetis at *Iliad* 1.528–30.[71] Later in the speech though, the apparently equal status of sculpture and poetry is complicated as Dio places painting and sculpture among the sources of human conceptions of the divine but makes the visual arts posterior to and dependent on poetic representations of the gods.[72]

So, for Dio here, the artists of the classical past gained a place among intellectuals, but at the price of minimizing the materiality and sensuality of their works, just as Plotinus excises the physical labor of the sculptor in favor of a purely intellectual conception of the divine.

These responses to Plato argue that the visual arts, rather than being imperfect simulacra, can reveal more than direct sense perception is able to and can make visible the invisible.[73] In a further example, from Philostratus' *Life of Apollonius of Tyana*, the sage claims that *mimesis* represents what it has seen while *phantasia* is able to represent "what it has not seen" on the basis of what it has seen.[74] This qualification indicates that Philostratus' *phantasia* is not as revolutionary or as distant from traditional definitions of *mimesis* (like Zeuxis' composite Helen) as it might seem.[75] What it does show is an acknowledgment of the possibility that the visual arts can represent and provide access to entities beyond what is ordinarily accessible to the bodily senses.[76]

PRESENCE AND ILLUSION

A recurring theme in discussions of mimetic arts in all media is the tension between presence and absence. The idea that the subject of the *mimesis* is made available to the spectators' and/or listeners' senses and can affect them in similar ways to the prototype, is in constant tension with the audience's awareness of the medium and of the work's ontological status, as Verity Platt has brought out with particular clarity in the case of representations of the gods in the visual arts in Greece and Rome.[77] These discussions take place against the background of the absence of a clearly articulated and culturally accepted concept of fiction as a "likeness to truth" to which the audience can react in full knowledge that it is not true. As Halliwell points out, this concept is not completely lacking in these fourth-century discussions, but it is neither fully defined nor placed center stage.[78] The closest parallels are to be found in the first and second Sophistics. One is Gorgias' claim for the greater "justice" or "appropriateness" of those who engage in deception (*apatê*).[79] The other is the Younger Philostratos' defense of viewing paintings and "responding to things that are not present as if they were present" as a harmless activity.[80]

In what follows I will look in turn at some of the questions raised by painting, sculpture, and theatrical *mimesis*. All of these arts have in common the fact that they are primarily perceived through the sense of sight, so ancient theories of vision are also relevant.[81] The details of these theories varied widely but two important characteristics are the lack of sharp distinction between viewer and viewed, and the related idea that seeing involves a form of physical touching (*hapsis*). These ideas are found in Plato's *Timaeus* in the form of the fiery rays sent out from the eyes that merge with the light outside the viewer's body, as well as in Stoic models of vision, which used the analogy of the stick, feeling the environment around the viewer and were widespread in Greek and Roman culture.[82] Viewer and viewed thus merge and sight can be conceived of—even experienced—as a form of touch.[83]

PAINTING AND SCULPTURE

Ancient anecdotes about the visual arts frequently present claims that seeing a sculpted or painted image provokes the same—or similar—response as seeing the subject of the image itself. Such reactions are often mentioned as proof of the artist's particular skill as in the stories in poetry and prose of humans and animals responding to painted—or more usually sculpted—figures as if they were the real thing: Pliny's birds pecking Zeuxis' grapes,[84] or the many epigrams on Myron's sculpted heifer that play on the possibility that other animals or humans might respond to it as a living being thanks to the sculptor's deceptive *technê*.[85] Similar responses to graphic art are to be found in Hellenistic poetry, where they are attributed to female viewers. Herodas' 4th *Mimiamb*—a poem that itself imitates a theatrical *mimesis* of everyday life—takes the form of a dialogue between two women visiting the temple of Asklepios on the island of Cos. In front of a painting by Apelles they exclaim about the lifelikeness (*zoê*) of the figures and one, Kokkale, remarks on the painted boy's flesh, speculating that if she scratched it, it would bleed.[86] The tactile nature of this hypothetical response reflects the notion of the haptic gaze as well as pointing to the capacity of painting to suggest depth beyond the colored surface and to the importance of the depiction of flesh (*chros*) in color (*chroma*) in ancient discussions of illusionistic painting.[87]

There is no need to assume that Herodas is using Kokkale to express a typically "popular" attitude, to be contrasted with the type of erudite response reflected in other Hellenistic epigrams on art objects that talk the viewer through the interpretation of rebus-like representations.[88] As Michael Squire points out, the epigrams on Myron's cow contrast the deceived human and animal viewers with the knowing author and reader, both fully aware of the illusion.[89] The more expansive *Imagines* of Philostratus from the early third century CE allow the erudite describer of the paintings displayed in an elegant villa to alternate between the two postures, interspersing learned explanations of the paintings' narrative content and of the technical virtuosity of the unnamed artists with exclamations, addresses to the characters, and invitations to respond emotionally and even corporeally to the characters depicted.[90] Like the authors of the epigrams, Philostratus himself plays with the tension between seeing the painting as an artifact made of wood, pigment, and wax and responding *as if* the object of the painted *mimesis* were present and available to all the senses.

In other sources, we can see a distinction between the presence-making capacity of free-standing sculpture, which exists palpably within the same space as the viewer, and that of painting, which creates the illusion of palpability (as in Herodas' 4th *Mimiamb*) and of the existence of a fictive dimension beyond the physical surface of the painting (illustrated in the anecdote of the painted curtain that Zeuxis tried to draw aside to see what was behind).[91] Several Pompeian wall paintings, for example, create an illusion of depth beyond the physical barrier of the wall while simultaneously marking this plane by representing low parapets, votive reliefs, or masks, as if to remind viewers that the painted dimension is on a different ontological level, even as they invite them to project themselves into it (Figure 8.3).[92]

Accordingly, anecdotes often associate the strongest responses with freestanding sculptures. In Xenophon's *Memorabilia*, Socrates attributes the ability to represent the signs of character and passion to the posture of the sculpted body.[93] This may imply that the viewer engages in an intellectual act of decoding but, if we bear in mind the familiarity of ancient audiences with dance as spectators and practitioners, it allows for an embodied understanding of the emotional and ethical meaning of these postures leading to a similarly embodied response.[94] Examples of such responses to both paintings and sculptures are found in the portrayals of viewers impelled to interact with the sculpture as if it were flesh and blood, as in the case of Myron's cow, or like Herodas' Kokkale, to touch the painted body.

FIGURE 8.3 Fresco of a garden from the House of the Golden Bracelet, first century CE.
Museo Archeologico Nazionale di Napoli. © Fine Art Images / Heritage Images / Getty Images.

The most dramatic response is that evoked by Praxiteles' statue of a naked Aphrodite
on Knidos (*c.* 350 BCE), standing as if caught by surprise by the viewer (Figure 8.4).[95]

Though the surviving copies are in white marble, the original would have been painted
to look like flesh.[96] Pliny and a text attributed to Lucian tell the story of how the sight of
this statue worked such an overwhelming impact on one young man that he attempted to
have sex with the statue and left an indelible mark on the marble.[97] The viewer and the
statue are thus both drawn into a nexus of action and reaction that leaves both physically
affected.[98] It is interesting to compare this story with that of Zeuxis pulling back the
painted curtain. Both involve gestures provoked by an image, but the hand remains at
the surface of the painting, attempting but failing to remove an obstacle to sight, while
the three-dimensional statue provokes a bodily interaction. The anecdotes about this
incident are ironic and ludic commentaries whose impact once again derives from the
contrast between the reader's awareness that the illusion is the result of art and the
fictional viewer's response. They also interrogate the gap between what is represented—
the naked female form caught in a moment of vulnerability—and the matter and mode of
representation (impenetrable marble imitating the appearance of soft flesh).[99]

This anecdote also draws our attention to the function of cult statues such as the
Aphrodite of Knidos that make present the divinity's power in the sanctuary: the young
man in the story is subject to the influence of the goddess of sexual desire. More clearly
than any other story, this one reveals how cult statues could be thought of simultaneously
as the divinity and (as in Phidias' statue of Zeus at Olympia) an individual artist's
appropriate and effective representation of that divinity.[100]

While some ancient authors, for instance, Dio and Plotinus, speak of the intellectual
knowledge of the gods conveyed by statues,[101] the Emperor Julian, writing in the fourth
century CE, points to the importance of embodied responses to cult statues, arguing that
seeing a representation of god in human form helped the human devotee to perform the
necessary rites.[102] As Elsner points out, interaction with a cult statue involved an array

FIGURE 8.4 The Colonna Venus, Roman copy in marble of Aphrodite of Cnidus by Praxiteles, lost. Vatican Museums. © DeAgostini / Getty Images.

of ritual choreographies in which the body of the viewer interacted with the statue and other objects within the physical context of the shrine. The behavior of the young man on Knidos is thus a heightened example of what seems to have been common ritual practice of physically interacting with the statue: combing the hair, bathing it as if it had human needs.[103] These rites are known to us through Christian texts that sought to ridicule pagan practices precisely by contrasting the material qualities of the statue with its representational function, but some Christians at least appear to have understood that statues of the gods *were* potentially animated and needed to be disabled just like a living human body through decapitation, mutilations targeting the feet, and dismemberment.[104]

Ideas about the relationship between paintings or sculptures and their models thus cover a wide spectrum running from condemnation of their inadequacy as representations to an identification that endows them with qualities of the prototype. As we have seen, many poetic and rhetorical responses to works of art play upon the tensions between these different attitudes. In terms of their reception, works of art may bring about an intellectual pleasure in the act of recognition, as suggested by Aristotle in the *Poetics*, and may also serve to make visible entities or qualities that are not available to normal human perception (like the appearance of the gods).[105] Alongside these cognitive aspects of reception, painting and sculpture, like music, could also be held to affect viewers' behavior, as dramatized in the stories about the Knidian Aphrodite. Style and technique are far less frequently discussed in our surviving texts, although a critical vocabulary was developed in the Hellenistic period, as reflected in Pliny's *Natural History*.[106] Roman copies show that the contrast between archaic and classical styles in Greek sculpture and painting was recognized and used.[107]

THEATRE AND DANCE

If sculpture and, to some extent, painting were thought to work a physical impact on the viewer, it was the theatre that evoked the strongest anxieties throughout antiquity. This was partly due to the public, collective, and therefore political nature of the experience and partly due to the physical presence of the performer whose material was his or her own body. Xenophon's account of the mimetic dance of the meeting of Dionysos and Ariadne at the end of his *Symposium* sums up the problems: at some points the language expresses ideas of likeness and notes the technical gestures (*schemata*) used by the two artists, at others the narrator speaks as if the characters themselves were interacting before the audience's eyes.[108] What is more, the couple's performance is said to inspire an erotic desire in its male audience, sending the married men home to find their wives and to act out what they have seen. Despite the differences in the form and context of drama, questions of the identity of the actor or actress and of his or her effect on the spectator can be found throughout antiquity from classical Athens to the late antique polemics about the theatre, particularly the danced pantomime, which merged the moving body with the potentially overwhelming influence of music.[109] In the classical period, the question of the actor's identity is posed with the greatest clarity by another work of art, the Pronomos Vase made around 400 BCE showing a flute player surrounded by actors, some in full costume while others hold their masks as if off-stage (Figure 8.5).[110] What is remarkable is the way in which the actors playing satyrs are depicted as fully satyr the moment they don their mask, implying a complete identification between actor and role. The impact of theatrical mimesis on the *playwright* is raised by the depiction of Agathon in Aristophanes' *Thesmophoriazousai*, produced in 411, several decades before Plato composed his *Republic*. The cross-dressing Agathon is shown playing the woman's role in life in order to write female characters, merging playwright, actor, and character into a whole in an act of *mimesis* that spills out of its frame from art into (fictional) life.[111] Plato focuses on the intensity of the emotions aroused by tragedy and, to a lesser extent, comedy but their fictitious nature is not his prime concern.[112] Later on, though, theatrical fiction became a useful phenomenon to think with, as in the Stoic Seneca's use of the

FIGURE 8.5 The Pronomos Vase, *c.* 400 BCE. Museo Archeologico Nazionale di Napoli.
© Fine Art Images / Heritage Images / Getty Images.

emotions aroused at seeing staged shipwrecks (the language implies the comic mime) as an example of the involuntary first reactions that precede reflexion and are not to be considered as real passions.[113]

We see the most acute anxieties about the ontological status of the actor and the impact of the spectacle on the audience in the responses to pantomime dancing in the Roman Empire. These debates were shaped by the nature of the pantomime: the silent art that conveyed stories, characters, and emotions through gesture, posture, and movement against a musical background. The principal accusation against these dancers, mostly men who played both male and female roles, was that they themselves were made effeminate by their actions. This accusation is visible in the stereotypical representation of pantomime dancers in elite texts in a return to Plato's warnings about mimetic contagion in *Republic* 3. But what mattered most was the risk of this mimetic effeminacy being transmitted to their audiences.[114] These debates emerge with the greatest clarity and urgency in early Christian authors writing in both Greek and Latin such as Tatian, John Chrysostom, Lactantius, Cyprian, and Augustine, and the fact that they pay far more attention to the mimetic aspects of the dance than to the pagan subject matter suggests both that theatrical mimesis itself is the problem, not the particular subject, and that their polemics draw on a long tradition. The underlying ideas are old ones: that music and physical gestures have an impact on the inner *êthos* of the performer and that the sight of a gesture can encourage a transformative mimetic response in the spectator.[115]

A key element of these anti-theatrical positions is the denial of *technê*—transmissible skill—to the dancers through the claim that their art is simply a matter of personal inclination. Here we do have some glimpses of artists' responses, for example, in the inscriptions recording their victories in competitions and on epitaphs that mention their *technê*, their "precision" (*akribeia*), and their "excellence" (*aretê* or *virtus*).[116] The polemics also record traces of counterarguments against the harmful nature of the shows including claims that any impact was temporary and confined to the time and place of the performance. Such moves placed the drama into a separate, autonomous domain, independent of everyday life and free from judgment by moral criteria.[117]

The end of antiquity, as we have already seen in the case of the laws protecting monuments for the "value of their art" (p. 134), thus saw attempts to remove the visual and performing arts from the religious domain. The meaning and value of famous cult statues—including both Praxiteles' Aphrodite and Phidias' Zeus from Olympia— were also adapted by their removal from their contexts to be displayed in fifth-century Constantinople.[118] It would be too simple to take these developments as a step toward a Kristellerian conception of "the arts," particularly in the light of late antique and medieval uses of religious images. Rather, they can be seen as attempts to delimit a domain that was neither "Christian" nor "pagan" in response to the radical redefinition of culture and society brought about by the process of Christianization, to contain the potentially dangerous and destabilizing impact of artistic productions of all kinds on viewers, and to create a new space for Christian representations.

CHAPTER NINE

History

LUCAS HERCHENROEDER AND CLIFFORD ANDO

This chapter examines the history of historical thought in the ancient Mediterranean. It is a commonplace in histories of historical writing to urge that the writing of history commences in ancient Greece. What is intended by this is often quite ill-defined, such as that Herodotus and Thucydides are the first authors whom we recognize as ancestors to the modern historian, or whose texts participate in a genre intended to recount and explain past events within a rationalized worldview. To place in view a properly cultural understanding of the history of historical thought, one should perhaps seek to unpack what is generally unspoken in such claims. What seems required to sustain a strong version of this claim is the operation in a given context of a number of conditions: a social awareness of the past as past, namely, the possibility of knowledge of past events beyond the memory of the individual; the existence of models of causation that seek to explain past events, not least in their connection to, or their impinging upon, the present; and an incipient understanding of society, which is to say, an awareness of human existence as operative within matrices of collective practices and institutions. The continuity of these practices and institutions—within some pattern of sameness, change, and rupture—from past to present to future is what ancient historical writing assumes as context (and what much modern historical writing takes as its object of explanation).[1] So understood, historical thinking can be seen as operative across a vast array of cultural production, from genealogy to legislation, in forms of public and popular memory far beyond the literary genres that make up ancient historiography. It is the object of this chapter to bring this wider world into view.

This multiplicity of contexts of historical thinking draws attention to two further issues that will form important themes in what follows. The first theme concerns evidence. Historians in the ancient world drew on a remarkable array of evidence in their research: not simply earlier narratives and oral testimony, but documentary records on both permanent and impermanent media, imaginative texts in poetry and prose, the material remains of cities and battles, art historical data, and more besides. The list is as long as the interests of ancient historical inquiry, which included everything from religious practices, to painting, to colonization, to language change, to war. A second important theme concerns the relationship among this multiplicity of forms of memory—from influence, to succession, mimesis, and rivalry—as well as the contests for authority to which this multiplicity gave rise.

GENEALOGY AND ITS KIN

The early development of a concept of history in Greece is immediately visible in developments in the practice of genealogy, connected with the appearance of written works on the subject around the end of the sixth century.[2] This is a fitting place to begin: the idea that a substantive link with the past might be grounded in precise claims of genealogical ancestry forms about as basic a condition for memory as one tends to find in traditional societies. Abundant evidence survives from early Greece for works of narrative poetry concerned with the family relationships of gods and heroes, in texts such as the Hesiodic *Theogony* and *Catalogue of Women*, as well as genealogical works in epinician and sympotic contexts.[3] Such works demonstrate the weight of genealogical thought in late archaic memory and its importance in contexts of civic festival and other venues of poetic performance.[4] The turn to fix this material in writing, as opposed to continuing its transmission via an unstable performance culture, reflects efforts to seek new grounding for knowledge in light of literate technologies that were then coming into use. It also suggests new ways of thinking about descent as a means of access to the past. Evidence for this activity is now scarce in the extreme: we possess the fragments of works of *Genealogies* attributed to Hecataeus of Miletus and to Acusilaus of Argos (the title *Histories* also is attested for the former); and similar treatises are ascribed to Pherecydes of Athens and Hellanicus of Lesbos.[5]

What seems clear from the evidence that we do possess is that such writers operated out of a sense of need, namely, that one should put in order the scattered, local traditions of memory circulating in the Aegean. The context of these works was thus not simply "late archaic Greece," or even "late archaic performance culture," but the dispersed world of late archaic colonization. That dispersal had established the conditions of possibility for late archaic cultural production, through its deep contacts with symbolic and mythopoetic traditions in Anatolia and the Near East. It also called out for the systematization of knowledges of the past, eliminating contradiction and reconciling inconsistencies wherever possible, to produce a past that could serve a present that demanded coherence. The same processes of encounter, recognition, and assimilation between disparate cultures in the wider Mediterranean world account for the invention of synchronisms. By this is intended more than the preparation of chronological tables by which to make multiple pasts visible to one another. The term refers, instead, to the recrafting of local historical traditions so as to bring the pasts and presents of particular cultures into potential alignment. The claim by late Republican Romans that they overthrew their monarchy and established a democratic republic in the same year as the Cleisthenic reforms at Athens is only the most famous case in point.[6] These maneuvers expose to view the utility of history to processes of renewal and revision in (ancient) cultural self-understanding. The heterogeneity of the Mediterranean's pasts, and the superabundance of evidence for them, enabled this work to a baroque and splendid degree.

In the emergence of written works of genealogy, what is noteworthy within a cultural history of ideas is how these works contributed to redefine many traditional institutions of culture. That written works of genealogy might dislodge fixtures of local, civic memory, transmitted in contexts of poetic performance, signaled a rupture in existing systems of authority. Formerly authoritative means for the routine transmission of knowledge of the past came now to be seen as, or at least could be figured as, the source of a problem. Outward expressions of this include the derision of Hecataeus for the laughable inconsistencies of "the stories of the Greeks," as we find in the prologue to his *Genealogies*, in reference to the "correction" of poetic sources of genealogy.[7] This triumph in culture of one technology over another—in which written, rationalized knowledge simultaneously used poetry for its data but also damned it with withering criticism—operated by alienating local poetic traditions from their primary contexts of production and performance, only to juxtapose them to a mode of culture that set itself beyond them.

Beyond its transmission of genealogical knowledge, hexametric poetry of the archaic period also put on display two other means of engaging and activating the past that we may contrast with historical thinking as described in the normative definition offered at the outset of this chapter. These are, first, the typological narratives of aristocratic encounter that populate the Homeric poems: two heroes meet on the battlefield, and it is revealed in courteous exchange that their encounter repeats an earlier one by near ancestors of the present parties. The second form of knowledge of the past on display in hexametric poetry that might be contrasted with "properly" historical thinking is the object biography: the respectful recitation within the poem of the origin of an artifact or work of art, as well as its history of ownership, transmission, and exchange.[8] These forms are sometimes conjoined; a particularly famous instance is the encounter between Glaukos son of Hippolochos and Diomedes son of Tydeus in *Iliad* book six.[9] It commences when the etiquette of martial encounter demands mutual recognition:

> Now Glaukos, sprung of Hippolochos, and the son of Tydeus
> came together in the space between the two armies, battle-bent.
> Now as these advancing came to one place and encountered,
> first to speak was Diomedes of the great war cry:
> "Who among mortal men are you, good friend?"

The reply of Glaukos runs for more than sixty lines, narrating the origin and story of his family; it opens and closes with lines that function as colophons to his excursus:

> High-hearted son of Tydeus, why ask of my generation?
> ...
> But Hippolochos begot me, and I claim that he is my father;
> he sent me to Troy, and urged upon me repeated injunctions,
> to be always among the bravest, and hold my head above others,
> not always shaming the generation of my fathers, who were
> the greatest men in Ephyre and again in wide Lykia.
> Such is my generation and the blood I claim to be born from.

The information shifts the direction of their meeting: Diomedes recalls aloud an earlier encounter between their grandparents, and the gifts exchanged on that occasion. In consequence, they too are friends in civilian contexts, and the power of the past is respected through repetition and renewal:

> See now, you are my guest friend from far in the time of our fathers.
> Brilliant Oineus once was host to Bellerophontes
> the blameless in his halls, and twenty days he detained him,
> and these two gave to each other fine gifts in token of friendship.
> Oineus gave his guest a war belt bright with the red dye ...
> ... Therefore I am your friend and host in the heart of Argos;

you are mine in Lykia, when I come to your country.
...
But let us exchange our armour, so that these others may know
how we claim to be guests and friends from the days of our fathers.

It merits observation that these poetic subgenres generally do not affirm the pastness of the past. It is not simply that the events they describe are comparatively recent—narratives rarely exceed two generations and so rely, for all their grandeur, on living memory. In addition, within the world the poems describe, it is the structural similarity of past to present that endows the past with normative power: men who meet on the battlefield do no more (and no less) than repeat the encounters of their parents.

The distinctiveness of the object-biographies in archaic epic emerges with particular clarity when contrasted with the rationalized and historicized view in the emergent field of the history of art, whose development we can trace from the third century BCE to late first century CE in Rome.[10] The earliest histories of painting and sculpture are attributed to Xenocrates of Sicyon and a writer known as Antigonus (possibly identifiable with the philosopher of Carystus), both of whom appear to have concerned themselves with technical questions and details of artists' biography.[11] Both are said by Pliny the Elder to have described the painter Parrhasius' achievements in mastering proportion and depicting elements of facial appearance;[12] other identifiable fragments of Xenocrates in Pliny ascribe the invention of foreshortened images to the early painter Cimon[13] or trace the progressive development of techniques of bronzework dealing with problems of proportion and bodily detail from Pheidias onward.[14] These works belong to a late classical and Hellenistic scholastic culture that exhibited a powerful interest in the history of intellectual and creative disciplines, organized around the search for origins and the identification of agents of change in practice. Roman-era works such as Pliny's *Natural History* and Pausanias' *Description of Greece* preserve vital indications of this tradition, albeit in new form, organized as they often are so as to record the fate of specific objects in the contexts of collection and display in an imperial context that felt itself belated.

Art history may thus be contrasted with the archaic object biography in ways that align with the contrast between systematized works of genealogy, on the one hand, and the mythic and aristocratic genealogies of hexametric poetry, on the other. In both cases, subgenres of poetic knowledge were confronted by new genres, whose authors transformed the earlier material (and genres) into "evidence" before surmounting them. More than this, the disembedding of historical information from some original or primary context, where it had worked to sustain local systems of prestige, and the re-situating of this information in new genres and contexts, operated in a twofold way to transform culture itself. On the one hand, it effected what Ventralla calls an "interruption" of symbolic function: objects that had lives and were endowed with meaning become, instead, luxury items that have provenance and were appraised for value.[15] On the other hand, the moves performed in these genres operated, in aggregate, so as to endow "culture" with a past.

HISTORIA AND HISTORICAL PROSE

Late archaic Greece was thus a world in which not simply knowledge of the past, but ways of knowing the past, were becoming increasingly differentiated and contested. This is the landscape in which systematizing prose works of genealogy claimed authority for themselves through critique of poetic license, as when Xenophanes of Colophon railed against "fictions from the past."[16] The social authority granted to hexametric poetry is visible more broadly in the extent to which new, specialized domains of intellectual life, which rapidly consolidated into "traditions," formed themselves via imbricated processes of acceptance and critique of epic poetry.[17] This is also the context for the emergence of new sciences of the human world, including ethnography, geography, medicine, and of course history.[18]

Modern "history" derives from the Greek concrete *histôr* ("judge," "arbiter"). The context of the abstract noun *historia* was thus a framework of knowledge conceived on the model of a judge's function in resolving disputes.[19] The sixth and fifth centuries BCE witnessed a remarkable expansion in the domains where knowledge might be produced from such processes of inquiry and critique, including philosophy[20] and medicine,[21] and much more besides. Strong, exclusionary association of the term with inquiry into, and literary description of, past events would come in the fourth century, typically in the context of denoting the *contents* of a historiographical work (often in the plural, *historiai*) or even with the sense of a distinctive literary genre. What matters at the outset is not the division of historiography into named genres, but rather the cultural work implicit in the varied operations of selection, synthesis, and critique prompted by the perceived multiplicity of the field of knowledge.

An emphatic claim on behalf of inquiry and judgment as necessary to knowledge of the past in just this language opens the seminal work of prose historiography in the classical tradition, at once staking a claim for itself and establishing the conditions of its genre.

> These are the researches of Herodotus of Halicarnassus, which he publishes, in the hope of thereby preserving from decay the memory of what men have done.[22]

For Herodotus, *historia* designates the great gathering of knowledge he performed about the world's diverse memory traditions, and the peoples and places that lay behind the work.[23] The immediate reference of his expanded language, namely, "the great and wonderful actions of the Greeks and barbarians," is to the effects on world history wrought by the great civilizations of the past. At the same time, the scope of what is memory worthy includes physical reminders of greatness left behind in things like monuments and spectacular building projects, as well as strange and wondrous phenomena.[24] It is at the intersection of the narration of deeds, on the one hand, and marvelous description, on the other, that one finds the distinctive register of the work, which assimilates the distant in time and space.[25] It is, furthermore, through the comparative gestures at the present and past of other cultures, and the historical consideration of his own, that Herodotus achieves his remarkable sense of the contingency of culture writ large.

A full account of Herodotus' methods exceeds what can be done here, but it is notable that a concept of method of any kind can be claimed of the work (Figure 9.1).[26] The idea that the early history of Lydia, for instance, should be rehearsed with due regard for the credibility of one's sources—as opposed to, say, simply repeating what one was told—marks itself an innovation. Nothing of the kind is found in epic, for instance, in which the narration of deeds is imagined as flowing from divine sources of inspiration.[27] By contrast, Herodotus stresses the human voice as the arbiter and source of narrative. By questioning and comparing his sources of information, and discussing the deferral of judgment, Herodotus constructs a distinctive authorial persona, the effect of which is to raise and accentuate problems of veracity while also creating distance from the historian's sources. Regular use of attributive statements ("they say," "it is said") and tracts in indirect discourse create a sense that sources speak for themselves. The result is a form of narrative conceived not so much in terms of closed description of events and places, but rather as a series of incitements to a reader (or audience) to engage actively in the interpretation of the text. For our purposes, the contribution of the work is to be understood in terms of this cultivated distance from the sources of memory in the historian's approach.

In the ensuing generation, Thucydides' *History of the Peloponnesian War* offers an interesting case for comparison, in part for the reason that the work is presented so strongly

FIGURE 9.1 Herodotus, in a nineteenth-century representation outside the Austrian parliament.

in opposition to Herodotus (Figure 9.2).[28] Part and parcel of this program is the omission of the language of *historia*; in its place one finds, for example, that of "composition," "interrogation," and "investigation." Thucydides also signals via criticism his rivals as authorities of memory: they include "the poets and logographers" as well as prose writers such as Hellanicus of Lesbos and Antiochus of Syracuse. Ways of handling the past in contexts of state business especially seem to have attracted Thucydides' attention, with which he saw himself in direct competition as a writer on political affairs.[29] Yet what is interesting is how the work is situated among these conventional sources of memory, as we might call them, by the historian's strong concept of method. In key passages in book one, Thucydides describes "painstaking" efforts to which he has gone in obtaining and verifying the right kinds of evidence and the difficulties of working with informants, as well as his method of composing historical speeches.[30] The result is a more restrictive sense of what one can know of the past and, indeed, how one knows what one knows than anything else seen in the period. The scope of the work is narrow in comparison with Herodotus, focusing on contemporary events almost exclusively and with minimal digression. Sources are drawn from eyewitness accounts chiefly or direct involvement in the events described. The way sources are rarely disclosed or their problems of reliability and interpretation rarely raised suggests a conception of the text as closed, final, and authoritative, asking little of the reader; on the contrary the narration is led by strong statements of interpretation expressed in claims of the probable and constructions of the ideal reader.

The concept of method formulated by the historian has special implications for treatment of the remote past and, by implication, for the contest of authority between formal history writing and other sources of memory in the wider culture. The distinction drawn between the events of the archaic past and those of the Peloponnesian conflict denotes, in Thucydides' argument, a boundary of theme, but also a wider, evidentiary concern. He focuses on the Peloponnesian war because of its intrinsic interest, and for the important lessons one might draw from it. But it is also the case, he avers, that the record of the past found in the poets and logographers is simply inadequate to the kinds of verification or "clarity" achievable with recent or contemporary affairs.[31] By implication, the sort of knowledge of the past that those writers—and genres—can convey is unsuitable as the foundation for practical knowledge going forward.[32]

Thucydides' statements on method thus invite his readers to engage with him in a broader reconsideration of varied forms of cultural production as sources of knowledge. Apart from Homer, to whose poetry special consideration is given as a "sufficient" account for events otherwise lost,[33] Thucydides raises these issues in particular via criticism of the methods of other writers. Hecataeus, who presented things merely "as they seemed," is a case in point. But the topic is most richly pursued in Thucydides' rivalry with Herodotus and his sources. For Herodotus, the local informant occupied a privileged point of access to other cultures. Thucydides by contrast strongly denigrates reliance on the eyewitness: they are prone to bias and distortions of memory, which can only be corrected by the skilled hand of the expert.[34] He condenses this polemical strand in his contrast between the concepts of *ergon*, namely, that which is factual, and *logos*, or that which is merely reported.[35] By this means, varied forms of epic and poetic memory were reconfigured as merely the starting points of knowledge. Thucydides performs a similar transformation in the evidence value of monuments and the built environment of human cultures. An illustration is the remarkable passage in book one in which Thucydides imagines the great pains at which the future visitor to Athens and Sparta

FIGURE 9.2 A double bust of Herodotus and Thucydides. Naples Archeological Museum.

would be in comprehending the relative strengths of the two cities in Thucydides' own day from inspection of their physical remnants alone.[36] Apart from the striking instance of projection of the historian's function into the future, which suggests a capacity for abstraction unlike anything seen in the prior tradition, the force of the passage lies in the challenge made to the premise of monumentality so integral to previous notions of memory, and in particular Herodotus.

The combination of capacious gathering of information, and a critical stance in respect of that information, that we find in Thucydides is carried forward and made explicit by Aristotle and his students. This occurs across the full range of their inquiries, which they termed *historia*.[37] The vast researches carried out by the philosopher and his pupils in the latter part of the fourth and early third centuries, reaching from zoology to politics to meteorology and beyond, proceeded from the distinction, at the level of method, between the preliminary collection and classification of knowledge in a given domain, on the one hand, and its analysis and explanation in the subsequent, theoretical stage of inquiry, on the other.[38] "Historical" research in the Peripatetic sense of the term referred especially to this preliminary collection of particulars, and assumed a capacious view of the scope of observation, encompassing the opinions expressed on a subject—or simply "the things said"—as much as observed phenomena.[39] One therefore drew upon the reports of hunters and fishermen in zoology, or the testimony of statesmen and others connected to the affairs of state, in the study of politics, the result of which is to produce the great store of "facts," on which the subsequent work of theorization and explanation would be based. (A conventional formulation distinguished between "knowledge that" and "knowledge why."[40])

Where our topic is concerned, one implication of the sweeping collection of data was a vast expansion in the topics appropriate to an archaeology of the past, in Aristotle's school and beyond. At the level of evidence, "inquiry" was now directed not simply to literary texts but also coinage, inscriptions, weights and measures, topography, and more. Thematically, the past practices of human societies subjected to research and explanation—"history" in our sense of the term—now included everything from cult practice, athletics, and material culture to dining, dramatic festivals, and money.[41] Works like the *Homeric Questions* explained elements of ancient custom and material culture found in the epics, and exemplary works by Aristotle's pupils include Dicaearchus' *On Musical Contests* and *Greek Way of Life*.

HISTORY IN THE AGE OF THE LIBRARY: BELATEDNESS AND ERUDITION

The ensuing period saw wide transformation of the Mediterranean political landscape, with the transition to macro-regional Macedonian empires in its eastern portions first, and the furthering of Hellenism in much of the area affected; and later, in the long sequence of hegemonic wars that culminated in the rise of Rome. With political change came change in intellectual life as well, as contests for hegemony played themselves out at the level of culture in the expansion of systems of royal patronage and creation of the great library facilities of the Hellenistic world.[42] Vastly heightened degrees of political unification—at least from the Greek perspective—did more than make basic cultural data from diverse sources widely available; it also raised the stakes in the systematizing and rationalizing of this surfeit of information. The (political) unity of the world produced an expectation that its multiple pasts be intelligible in light of one another.

The practice of history also would undergo change as the increased availability of texts for interrogation of the past—and the creation of a scholarly culture devoted to their preservation and interpretation—encouraged new ways of thinking about the historian's sources and function. While it would be a mistake to speak of categorical change, as the study of texts had formed part of historical inquiry since its earliest stages, in its scale and diversity of usage, the turn to textual knowledge about the past was unprecedented in the period. This occurred not least because of the sheer weight of such material, which the institution of the library contributed to make visible: one senses in the second century BCE, and in a recurring way thereafter, real attention on the sheer volume of the past and belatedness of the present. In short, the late classical world threatened always already to be postclassical. This section will consider ways the idea of history changes in light of these dynamics.

Historical (and scientific) research on the model of the Peripatetics continued, naturally, and was greatly aided by the concentration of resources and exchange of persons and ideas made possible by the library.[43] The range of research enabled by the use of library resources is telling. Scholars continued to compose accounts of genealogy and colonial foundations, and to describe the migrations of early peoples in the Mediterranean; early customs and laws were compiled and cataloged, along with early political institutions and notable inventions in the history of culture; detailed histories of creative and intellectual disciplines were produced, and lists of notable historical figures and events produced and organized. The library supplied the basis for the maturation of specific disciplines with special relationships to history. Geography and chronography, which benefited greatly from the concentration in a unified institutional space of spatial and calendrical knowledge, occupy pride of place among these. It also fostered wholly new disciplines, not least *grammatikê* (philology), the quintessential Alexandrian discipline in its consolidation of the great literary inheritance of Hellenism.[44]

A new genre within this wider Hellenic world consolidated around histories of sites of particular prominence in archaic and classical cultural production. The periegete Polemon of Ilium, for example, produced a description of the treasuries of Delphi, as well as guides to the sites of Ilium and Athens. Though the texts were known for drawing on local sources of knowledge, their audience was outside those locales, and interested because of the prestige of those sites in the cultural imaginary of Hellenism.[45] The commentary on the Iliadic catalog of the Trojans produced by Demetrius of Scepsis similarly relied upon the author's close acquaintance with peoples and places in the Troad to explicate a text now threatened with obscurity, but assumed also the stature of Troy as a vital site of memory in contemporary Hellenism.[46] Indications that the (apparently now vexed) question of whether Troy could be identified with contemporary Ilium was revisited in the work are especially suggestive of the way that local tradition, and lived experience of place, could be mediated by scholastic interest.[47]

At Rome, a culture of antiquarian learning is seen from the second century BCE, fostered there, too, by the inflow of persons and materials accompanying the gains of empire, and taking shape especially during successive stages of social crisis.[48] Orderly study of the city's early institutions and customs, its calendar and topography, the history of Latin, and similar topics provided a valued link with the past in times of uncertainty. The work of recovery and preservation of cultural patrimony regularly went hand in hand with normative argument, as seen in works such as the *Tripertita* of Sextus Aelius Paetus (*c.* 190 BCE), which provided a text and commentary for the Twelve Tables and guidance to contemporary legal procedure, or in separate works examining the traditional powers of magistracies by M. Iunius Gracchanus (*De potestatibus*) and M. Iunius Tuditanus (*De magistratibus*) (both mid-second century BCE).[49] There also abided, throughout the long history of Roman learning, an essential connection between historical, geographic, and scientific inquiry, on the one hand, and empire, on the other, in works as diverse in form, intent, and time as Cato's *Origines* and Pliny's *Natural History*.[50]

The potent urge for knowledge of a more ordered past during times of political crisis and social disorder reached a peak in the last decades of the Roman Republic, and found its most powerful exponent in Marcus Terentius Varro. In the testimony of Cicero, Varro's learning was so deep and the range of his inquiry so capacious that his works reacquainted the Romans with their city when it had become obscure to them:

> For we were wandering and straying about like visitors in our own city, and your books led us, so to speak, right home, and enabled us at last to realize who and where we were. You have revealed the age of our native city, the chronology of its history, the laws of its religion and its priesthoods, its civil and its military institutions, the topography of its districts and its sites, the terminology, classification and moral and rational basis of all our religious and secular institutions.[51]

Cicero delineates the topics covered in Varro's *Human and Divine Antiquities*, which gathered together in forty-one books available knowledge of early Roman rites and institutions.[52] The work's division into *res humanae* and *res divinae*, which was traditional, and subdivision of people, places, times, and actions for each reflected the totalizing ambitions of the project. Its mode of presentation was largely expository and descriptive, as far as can be told: how old was Rome? Whence were names of the hills of Rome derived?[53] By what route did Aeneas arrive in Italy?[54] Such questions assumed the loss of important cultural knowledge, and hence the sense of distance that animated the project, but the form of the work Varro produced in response assumed a framework for past knowledge that suggests a common understanding of how such knowledge was to be mapped. In other works, Varro engaged in bravura experiments in literary form, but the totalizing instinct on display in the *Antiquities* underlies a wide range of conservative gestures over the centuries, works that asserted their own authority—and the stability of their object of knowledge—by means of technocratic form: catalogs, lexica, corpora, and above all, the list.[55]

NARRATIVE AND ITS KIN

Alongside the proliferation of forms and topics in historical research, interest in narrative history continued unabated and, indeed, produced its own experiments in form. The distinctive form of such works—accounts of *praxeis* ("deeds") in Greek, *res gestae* in Latin—was temporal and linear; they described events in sequence or grouped them in a well-defined period. Often composed by men of politics, usually with direct experience of the events described even, such works typified the way history was imagined as the appropriate domain of such men.[56] The cultural work of such historical prose was thus not limited to the transmission of memory; they also did important ideological labor, in affirming a view of who acted, and should act, on the stage of history. Concern for political affairs formed an important impetus for the development of historical writing at Rome, commencing with Fabius Pictor's account of the Hannibalic War (written in Greek), though works in Latin by Cato the Censor and numerous successors would provide the contours of a lasting tradition focused on the deeds of the Roman state and political life of the city of Rome.[57]

The expansion of the Greek world during and after the conquests of Alexander produced both opportunities and challenges for narrative historical writing. The period is especially identified with dramatic enlargement of the scope of historiography, as seen in the many works of so-called universal history that appeared, commencing in the later fourth century BCE. In some cases these extended to dozens of volumes and concerned themselves with events taking place in a space identifiable with the known world and reaching backward to the earliest times.[58] But such efforts to understand the whole, as it were, were subtended by new efforts of "local" history, focused not simply on the city-state but the region or ethnic group. These included descriptions of Sicilian and Italian affairs (*Sikelika, Italika*), modeled to an extent on regional histories of Greece and the Aegean world (*Hellenika*) that had appeared in the fourth century. To the same category roughly belong histories of the Persian world (*Persika*) and Babylonian and Egyptian political and cultural histories (*Babyloniaca, Aegyptiaca*) produced by members of the priestly classes and bureaucracies of the great eastern kingdoms.[59] Finally, there were of course the specialist histories of wars, in which histories of the conquests of Alexander the Great occupy a special position, uniting as they did the narratives of Europe and Asia.

Utility arguments, to the effect that knowledge of the past could be identified closely with aims of political leadership, had a long pedigree in Greek letters, familiar since Thucydides' claim to have produced a "possession for all time" for the student of human affairs.[60] The idea that past events had practical value in providing instruction for the statesman would become a commonplace of the fourth century, in part through the influence of Isocrates, who cultivated a strong understanding of the role of exemplary deeds in framing moral action, but also in the way moral didacticism was embraced by historians themselves—Xenophon is a case in point.[61] Such claims were repeated and elaborated in Greek historiography's new context under Rome. Polybius' concept of *pragmatikē historia*, presented in key sections of the writer's *Histories*, is among the most substantial of any on historical method to survive from antiquity. They present a model for composing a record of action, based on an understanding of what is useful in historical description: this includes articulating causal relationships among events[62] and adhering to a high standard of truthfulness,[63] as well as drawing upon political and military experience in imparting all of it.[64] But the concept also assumed a restrictive understanding of the historian's appropriate subject, dividing the serious history of *pragmata*, that is political and military affairs, from accounts of genealogies and colonial foundations that were popular in less serious forms of historical writing, at least as Polybius saw them.[65] The point may be obvious but deserves stress nonetheless, that such homologies between cultural production and contemporary politics worked strongly to sustain elitist and patriarchal conceptions narrowly of citizenship but also broadly of human dignity.

These associations of history with the actions in politics of elite males were then reinforced by the increasing formalization of rhetorical training. The evolving curriculum of exercises in declamation and composition engaged students in reflection on specific well-known episodes and exemplary situations from the historical tradition, as well as the texts responsible for their transmission.[66] On one level, this mode of education introduced students to particular ways of thinking narrowly about history and broadly about human affairs. On another, it worked subtly to affirm as canonical both a narrow selection from among the forms of historical prose, and further a narrow group from among writers of narrative. In so doing, the educational system unsurprisingly endorsed the experience of men in politics as preeminent among topics for public speech, for prepared writing, and for ethical consideration.

INSTITUTIONAL AND PUBLIC MEMORY UNDER THE EMPIRE

The forms of historical memory that we have considered thus far—whatever their original performance context, and whatever their relation of rivalry and co-constitution with one another—have in common their authorship by named individuals. Their reception in generations after composition was surely also predominantly private and individual. But collective and institutional forms of memory also flourished in antiquity, and these operated in fascinating patterns of recursive influence with the historiographic enterprises of high culture. This last section surveys three examples from this landscape.

We might begin with the list.[67] At Rome under the Republic, for example, the dating of public events—public memory broadly construed—was organized around the succession of pairs of magistrates to the annual office of consul, and the validity of the community's memory of itself was affirmed through the gradual production and public inscription of an authoritative list of such magistrates, from the foundation of the Republic to the Augustan era. (The organization of many systems of historical memory around named magistrates is part of what made the production of trans-regional and so-called universal histories difficult, and it likewise may have inspired the first use of the "table" as a graphic for organizing knowledge.) Related lists recorded series of events by type, of which at Rome the most significant were the *fasti*—the chronological list—of individuals who had been granted the right to hold a triumphal parade; the entries in the list also recorded the name of the defeated community (Figure 9.3). The list of magistrates was a genre of profound conservatism: it suggested immense continuity at the level of institutional operations, by suggesting that the only thing of significance that had changed about Rome was the identity of the consuls. For their part, beyond offering a mapping of a kind of outward motion of Roman arms, the triumphal *fasti* urged a continuity of culture: generations of Romans had dedicated themselves to the pursuit of virtue in arms, and conspired to direct their lust for domination outward, in support of empire. The prestige of such public lists then became foundational for the list as a literary genre, which received an ironic twist in late antiquity when, in a text that purported to relate the origins of the Roman people, the author announced his intent to describe: "The origin of the Roman people from its founders Janus and Saturn through the kings succeeding one another until the tenth consulate of Constantius."[68] As the list advertised and required institutional continuity as the condition of its coherence, so an author writing under monarchs was forced to rewrite the history of Rome from its original kings to his own day as if the Republic had never existed: "the kings succeeding one another," it was always kings—and not ever consuls—all the way down.

FIGURE 9.3 A fragment of the Fasti Capitolini as reconstructed in Musei Capitolini, Rome.

A related portrait of historical continuity, even in contexts of difference, was offered by varied forms of public epigraphy, which frequently situated documents of a particular genre in relation to one another, whether the so-called Athenian tribute lists or records of grants of citizenship (in the case of Rome). In the Roman case, the copies that survive to us are frequently those that were made for the recipient of the grant, but these nearly universally make reference to archives of such records at Rome, such that individual memory, and individual identity in a provincial context, is grounded in the superior resources of memory at the metropole. A case in point is offered by the protocols of a tablet discovered at Banasa in Mauretania, deriving from the reign of Commodus. The documents it contained, the text avers, had been:

> Copied and verified from the record of those granted Roman citizenship by the divine Augustus and Tiberius Caesar Augustus and Gaius Caesar and the divine Claudius and Nero and Galba and the divine Augusti Vespasian and Titus and Domitian Caesar and the divine Augusti Nerva and Trajan Parthicus and Trajan Hadrian and Hadrian Antoninus Pius and Verus Germanicus Medicus Parthicus Maximus and Imperator Caesar Marcus Aurelius Antoninus Augustus Germanicus Sarmaticus and Imperator Caesar Lucius Aurelius Commodus Augustus Germanicus Sarmaticus, which file Asclepiodotus the freedman produced, that which is written below.[69]

The single document, the list, and the archives that the document referenced operated in concert to present a picture of institutional stability, and to affirm the accuracy of the knowledge each contained. Such archives made similar, strong claims for the importance of the past to the present when, as at Aphrodisias in Asia Minor, earlier documents were collected and reinscribed as an archive in the late high empire (Figure 9.4); and the origin of documents in the past was underlined when, as at the colony of Urso in Spain, its charter from the age of Caesar was reinscribed in the Flavian period, but using the spellings of words that were current at its date of composition.

A final example brings together government and church and carries us into the high and late empires.[70] Commencing in the second century BCE, the Romans developed a

FIGURE 9.4 Aphrodisias archive wall. © NYU-Aphrodisias Excavations.

set of tools and genres for recording the processes and decisions of deliberative bodies. The genres included the rationalized paraphrase of adversarial argumentation, which the Romans included by way of justifying decrees of the Roman Senate, as well as the stenographic transcript of hearings, the so-called record of proceedings. These purportedly verbatim transcripts were made possible through the use of shorthand, varieties of which begin to be known to us in the Roman period. Standardized protocols signalled the status of such texts as products of the operation of government institutions: declarations of location, date, presiding magistrate, as well as formal flags within the text announcing the identity and status of the speaker.

The profound importance of these varied systems of public memory is revealed to us above all in the records of the institutionalized communities of the Christian church. This is perhaps most true of texts of the third and early fourth centuries CE, when the reliance of Christians on Roman institutions for the validation of their past stood in ideological tensions with their legal status vis-à-vis the state. In this period, in so-called martyr acts and related genres, Christians crafted their own genres of historical writing in mimetic reduplication of Roman ones. In this way, certain practices of Roman government came to function as cultural archetypes for the recording of public memory, while the Christians, for their part, acknowledged the legitimacy and reliability of the Roman government's procedures, if not its acts.

So, for example, in the *Acts of Apollonius*, when Apollonius is summoned before a senatorial court, the first stage of the hearing consisted in the recitation of the transcript of the earlier interrogation, the one conducted by Perennes.[71] Likewise, in the *Acts of Pionius*, when Pionius is summoned before the proconsular governor, the text observes that minutes were kept of the hearing.[72] In both cases, the truth claim of the Christian texts gestures toward conditions of possibility that were established by the system of their adversaries. Later Christians demonstrated similar faith in the ability of Roman technologies to discover and record social truths when they cited as reliable the fact-findings and statement-recordings of Roman courts. So, for example, the ecclesiastical historian Eusebius cites Apollonius of Ephesus as railing against the Montanist Alexander on the grounds of his lowness of character. This may be known from the fact that Alexander was convicted for banditry by the provincial governor, and any who wish to confirm this are invited to consult the public archives of the province of Asia.[73]

THE VARIETIES OF HISTORY

A proper cultural history of historical thinking reveals a world of information, exploration, and cultural production vastly expanded beyond the genres of prose narrative that modern scholars long recognized as ancestral to themselves. In this larger world, hexametric poetry, family trees, and even the ruins of cities contributed to an awareness—gradually codified, systematized, and always contested—of the many pasts of human societies. In so doing, the many forms of historical research and writing in antiquity did more than contribute essentially to the sense of self that made the ancient Greek and Roman worlds classical; they also contributed foundationally to the emergence of a concept of culture itself.

NOTES

Introduction

1 For wide-ranging studies on the archaic period see M. L. West, *The East Face of Helicon: West Asiatic Elements in Greek Poetry and Myth* (Oxford: Oxford University Press); and Carolina Lopez Ruiz, *When the Gods Were Born: Greek Cosmogonies and the Near East* (Cambridge, MA: Harvard University Press, 2010); for detailed studies of cultural exchange in the Hellenistic period see Ludwig Koenen, "The Ptolemaic King as a Religious Figure," in *Images and Ideologies: Self-Definition in the Hellenistic World*, eds. Anthony Bulloch, Erich S. Gruen, A. A. Long, and Andrew Stewart, 25–115 (Berkeley: University of California Press, 1993); and Susan A. Stephens, *Seeing Double: Intercultural Poetics in Ptolemaic Alexandria* (Berkeley: University of California Press, 2003).

2 Mary Beard, "A Complex of Times: No More Sheep on Romulus' Birthday," *Proceedings of the Cambridge Philosophical Society* 33 (1987): 1–15.

3 Reviel Netz, *Scale, Space and Canon in Ancient Literary Culture* (Cambridge: Cambridge University Press, 2020).

4 Michel Foucault, *L'Archéologie du savoir* (Paris: Gallimard, [1969] 2008).

5 Claude Lévi-Strauss, "Introduction à l'œuvre de Marcel Mauss," in Marcel Mauss, *Sociologie et anthropologie* (Paris: Presses universitaires de France, [1950] 2013), IX–LII.

6 Philippe Descola, *Beyond Nature and Culture*. Translated by Janet Lloyd (Chicago: University of Chicago Press, [2005] 2013); Eduardo Viveiros de Castro, *Cannibal Metaphysics* (Minneapolis, MN: Univocal, 2014).

Chapter 1

1 For example, when Odysseus' men discourage him from investigating the Kyklopes' island further, he demurs, hoping for gifts: "But I would not listen to them, it would have been better their way, not until I could see him, see if he would give me presents" (Homer, *The Odyssey of Homer*. Translated with an introduction by Richmond Lattimore [New York: Harper & Row, 1977], 9.228–9). Likewise, when contemplating the exploration of Circe's island, Odysseus asks his men: "Hear my words, my companions, in spite of your heart's sufferings. Dear friends, for we do not know where the darkness is nor the sunrise, nor where the sun who shines on people rises, nor where he sets, then let us hasten our minds and think whether there is any course left open to us. But I think there is none" (Homer, *Odyssey*, 10.189–94).

2 On microecologies see Peregrine Horden and Nicholas Purcell, *The Corrupting Sea: A Study of Mediterranean History* (Malden, MA: Blackwell Publishers, 2000), 53–80.

3 *Iliad* 2.485–6.

4 Hesiod, *Theogony* 27–8.

5 On the meaning of *alethea* see Marcel Detienne, *The Masters of Truth in Archaic Greece*, trans. J. Lloyd (New York: Zone Books, 1999); on *etymos* see Alexander J. Beecroft, "'This Is Not a True Story': Stesichorus' Palinode and the Revenge of the Epichoric," *Transactions*

of the American Philological Association 136, no. 1 (2006): 47–70. The relationship between *pseudea* and *alethea* is also clear in Hesiod's description of Nereus, old man of the sea: he does not mislead and he does not overlook (Hesiod, *Theogony* 233 with discussion by Detienne, *The Masters of Truth in Archaic Greece*). The lexicographer Hesychius says *alethea* are "things that do not fall into oblivion" (Hesychius, s.v. *alētheia* = α 2921). Thomas Cole ("Archaic Truth," *Quarderni Urbinati di Cultura Classica* 13 [1983]: 17–28) and J. H. Lesher ("Archaic Knowledge," in *Logos and Mythos*, ed. William Wians [New York: State University of New York Press, 2009], 13–28) discuss the terminology of knowledge in archaic Greek literature.

6 Hesiod, *Theogony* 887–9.

7 See the forthcoming discussion by Russell Pascatore, "Zeus' Plan in Early Greek Poetry's Construction of Political and Social Identity" (PhD dissertation, University of Southern California, in progress). On human evolutionary need to insulate against deceit see Roy Rappaport, *Ritual and Religion in the Making of Humanity* (Cambridge: Cambridge University Press, 1999); on religion as a means of addressing lack of strategic information see Pascal Boyer, *Religion Explained: The Evolutionary Origins of Religious Thought* (New York: Basic Books, 2001).

8 Hesiod, *Works and Days* 58–9.

9 Ibid., 266.

10 Ibid., 281–3.

11 Ibid., 293–7.

12 Homer, *Iliad* 20.203–5.

13 Homer, *Odyssey* 1.3–4.

14 Ibid., 9.187.

15 Ibid., 9.174.

16 Ibid., 9.213.

17 Ibid., 12.184–200.

18 Ibid., 19.380–1 and 467–8.

19 F 6.3 = Graham 23.3; references to presocratic texts are drawn from Daniel Graham, *The Texts of Early Greek Philosophy: The Complete Fragments and Selected Testimonies of the Major Presocratics*, Part 1 (Cambridge: Cambridge University Press, 2010), and follow Graham's numeration.

20 F 4.13–14 = Graham 21.13–14.

21 On event recognition and binding see B. Stafford, *Echo Objects: The Cognitive Work of Images* (Chicago: University of Chicago Press, 2007).

22 [Editor: The following material limns the material that Habinek sketched for this note.] *Histōr* is sometimes translated as arbiter, but this does not fit either Iliadic context. At *Iliad* 18.501 it is clear that others beside the *histōr* will perform the actual judgment, and at Iliad 23.486 the *histōr* is present to make sure that the participants in a bet on the outcome of a race do not change their predictions once the outcome is evident. Compare A. Bergren, *The Etymology and Usage of Peirar in Early Greek Poetry: A Study in the Interrelationship of Metrics, Linguistics, and Poetics* (Philadelphia: American Philological Association, 1975) on the term *peirar*, "boundary": in the first instance, we need someone to grasp the limit of something, not to render judgment but to set the limits of the dispute, which will then be judged by others.

23 F 13 = Graham 22.

24 Herodotus, *Histories* 1.1.

25 Thucydides, *History of the Peloponnesian War* 2.48.3.

26 Rosalind Thomas, "Thucydides and his Intellectual Milieu," in *The Oxford Handbook of Thucydides*, ed. S. Forsdyke, E. Foster, and R. Balot, 567–86 (Oxford: Oxford University Press, 2017).

27 Hippocrates, *Art* 2.

28 Hippocrates, *Ancient Medicine,* 2.1–2, following the analysis of Mark Schiefsky, *Hippocrates: On Ancient Medicine* (Leiden: Brill Academic Publishers, 2005), 148–50.

29 Jaap Mansfeld, *"Techne*: A New Fragment of Chrysippus," *Greek Roman and Byzantine Studies* 24, no. 1 (1983): 57–65.

30 Ruth Webb, *Ekphrasis, Imagination and Persuasion in Ancient Rhetorical Theory and Practice* (Burlington, VT: Ashgate Publishing, 2009).

31 [Editor: Habinek suggested a reference to Aristotle, *Posterior Analytics.* In context, it seems probable that he intended a reference to Aristotle's argument for the contribution of passive sense-perception to one's understanding of first principles at *Posterior Analytics* bk. 2, 99b.15–100b.17.]

32 F 24 = Graham 27.

33 *Iliad* 1.70; Homer, *The Iliad of Homer*, trans. with an introduction by Richmond Lattimore (Chicago: University of Chicago Press, 1976).

34 Hippocrates, *Ancient Medicine* 2.

35 P. N. Singer, "Galen," *The Stanford Encyclopedia of Philosophy*, ed. Edward N. Zalta, Winter 2016 Edition. Available online: https://plato.stanford.edu/archives/win2016/entries/galen/ (accessed January 9, 2022).

36 Peter Struck, *Birth of the Symbol: Ancient Readers at the Limits of their Texts* (Princeton, NJ: Princeton University Press, 2004); Ilaria Ramelli, "The Philosophical Stance of Allegory in Stoicism and its Reception in Platonism, Pagan and Christian: Origen in Dialogue with the Stoics and Plato," *International Journal of the Classical Tradition* 18, no. 3 (2011): 335–71; Mikolaj Domaradzki, "Theological Etymologizing in the Early Stoa," *Kernos* 25 (2012): 125–48.

37 Jerry Toner, *Popular Culture in Ancient Rome* (Cambridge, UK: Polity Press, 2009), 48. See also E. Eidinow, *Oracles, Curses, and Risk Among the Ancient Greeks* (Oxford: Oxford University Press, 2007), who sees risk as socially constructed as opposed to risk management of objective dangers.

38 Peter Struck, *Divination and Human Nature: A Cognitive History of Intuition in Classical Antiquity* (Princeton, NJ: Princeton University Press, 2016), 11.

39 Hesiod, *Theogony* 233. For detailed discussion see Detienne, *The Masters of Truth in Archaic Greece*, 53–67, 158–60.

40 Hesiod, *Theogony* 236.

41 Ibid., 80–7.

42 Ursula Klima, *Untersuchungen zu dem Begriff Sapientia: von der republikanischen Zeit bis Tacitus*, Habelts Dissertationsdrucke, Reihe klassische Philologie, 10 (Bonn: Rudolf Habelt, 1971); Thomas Habinek, "The Wisdom of Ennius," *Arethusa* 39, no. 3 (2006): 471–88.

43 Richard Martin, "The Seven Sages as Performers of Wisdom," in *Cultural Poetics of Archaic Greece: Cult, Performance, Politics*, eds. Carol Dougherty and Leslie Kurke, 108–30 (Cambridge: Cambridge University Press, 1993).

44 Carl Huffmann, *Archytas of Tarentum: Pythagorean, Philosopher, and Mathematician King* (Cambridge: Cambridge University Press, 2005); Philip Sydney Horky, *Plato and Pythagoreanism* (Oxford: Oxford University Press, 2013).

45 D. R. Dudley ("Blossius of Cumae," *Journal of Roman Studies* 31 [1941]: 94–9), is doubtful, but presents the relevant evidence; see also Adrienne Mayor, *The Poison King: The Life and*

Legend of Mithradates, Rome's Deadliest Enemy (Princeton, NJ: Princeton University Press, 2010), 59–61.

46 [Habinek intended a note on this topic. See David S. Potter, *Prophets & Emperors: Human and Divine Authority from Augustus to Theodosius* (Cambridge, MA: Harvard University Press, 1994).]

47 Miranda Anderson, Douglas Cairns, and Mark Spevak, eds., *History of Distributed Cognition in Antiquity* (Edinburgh: Edinburgh University Press, 2018).

48 F 2 = Graham 8.

49 F 18 = Graham 31. Note that *phronimos* is later used to describe a quality of the good statesman, perhaps to be translated "prudent."

50 A1 = Diog. Laertius 9.2 = Graham 1, F 16 = Graham 26, F 98 = Graham 143.

51 A16 = Graham 171 = Sextus Empiricus, *Against the Professors* 7.134; trans. Graham.

52 *nomos, ananke*: F 271 = Graham 402.

53 *eupeitheos*, F 1.29 = Graham 10.29.

54 Graham 35 = Plato, *Philebus* 58a7–b2.

55 F 10.11 = Graham 49.11, trans. Graham.

56 cf. F 10. 8 = Graham 49.8.

57 Aristotle, *Rhetoric* 1.4.

58 Thomas Habinek and Hector Reyes, "Distributed Cognition and its Discontents: A Dialogue across History and Genre," in *History of Distributed Cognition* in Antiquity, eds. Miranda Anderson, Douglas Cairns, and Mark Spevak (Edinburgh: Edinburgh University Press, 2018).

59 [Editor: regarding the history of certainty and etymology of Latin *certum*, Habinek made a general reference to Charles Joseph McNamara, "Quintilian's Theory of Certainty and Its Afterlife in Early Modern Italy" (PhD dissertation, Columbia University, 2016). He was particularly interested in the possibility that it derives from *consto*, to agree, rather than *cerno*, to perceive.]

60 For the application of Condorcet's theorem to democratic theory, see Josiah Ober, *Democracy and Knowledge: Innovation and Learning in Classical Athens* (Princeton, NJ: Princeton University Press, 2008), 108–14.

61 Ober, *Democracy and Knowledge*, xiii, 2.

62 Arthur Eckstein, *Mediterranean Anarchy, Interstate War, and the Rise of Rome* (Berkeley: University of California Press, 2006).

63 On Scipio Africanus see Cicero, *On Duties* 3.1.1–4; on the passage and the world it describes see Enrica Sciarrino, *Cato the Censor and the Beginnings of Latin Prose: From Poetic Translation to Elite Transcription* (Columbus: Ohio State University Press, 2011), 179–87.

64 Reinhard Neudecker, "Archives, Books and Sacred Space in Rome," in *Ancient Libraries*, eds. Jason König, Katarina Oikonomopoulou, and Greg Woolf, 312–31 (Cambridge: Cambridge University Press, 2013).

65 Jason König, Katarina Oikonomopoulou, and Greg Woolf, eds., *Ancient Libraries* (Cambridge: Cambridge University Press, 2013), 7.

66 Xenophon *Memorabilia* 1.6.14; cf. the critique offered by Socrates of Euthydemus's passion for book-collecting at *Mem.* 4.2.8–39.

67 [Editor: Habinek left a note to himself only to investigate the literature on Eratosthenes further. Klaus Geus (*Eratosthenes von Kyrene, Studien zur hellenistischen Kultur- und Wissenschaftsgeschichte*, Münchener Beiträge zur Papyrusforschung und antiken Rechtsgeschichte, 92 [Munich: C. H. Beck, 2002]) was the first and remains the only monographic treatment, and offers exceptionally full access to earlier bibliography.]

68 Cicero, *Academica* 1.9.

69 Amy Richlin, "Pliny's Brassiere," in *Sexuality and Gender in the Classical World: Readings and Sources*, ed. Laura K. McClure (Oxford: Blackwell Publishers, 2002).

70 Lloyd Gerson, *Ancient Epistemology* (Cambridge: Cambridge University Press, 2009).

71 Jacques Brunschwig, "Epistemology," in *Greek Thought: A Guide to Classical Knowledge*, eds. Jacques Brunschwig and Geoffrey E. R. Lloyd, 72–93 (Cambridge, MA: Harvard University Press, 2000), 74.

72 F 1.29–30 = Graham 10.29–30; cf. F 17.50–2 = Graham 17.50–2.

73 Plato, *Republic* 7.533e–534a.

74 See, e.g., Plato, *Republic* 6.508b–c, although here he is also talking about sunlight as intermediary.

75 *histores*, F 19 = Graham 32.

76 Sophie Grace Chappell, "Plato on Knowledge in the *Theaetetus*," *The Stanford Encyclopedia of Philosophy*, ed. Edward N. Zalta, Winter 2013. Available online: https://plato.stanford.edu/archives/win2013/entries/plato-theaetetus/ (accessed January 9, 2022).

77 Plato, *Theaetetus* 145e5.

78 Plato, *Theaetetus* 179c1–183c2.

79 [Editor: Habinek intended a note on the concepts of *nous, noēsis*, and *epistēmē* in Aristotle, and their relationship to *epistēmē* in Plato. On Aristotle on knowledge—on the themes of interest to Habinek—beyond the survey of ancient epistemology in Gerson, *Ancient Epistemology*, see Terence H. Irwin, *Aristotle's First Principles* (New York: Oxford University Press, 1988), ch. 7, §73–4; Murat Aydede, "Aristotle on Episteme and Nous: The Posterior Analytics," *Southern Journal of Philosophy* 36, no. 1 (1998): 15–46; and Zeev Perelmutter, "'Nous' and two kinds of 'epistēmē' in Aristotle's *Posterior Analytics*," *Phronesis* 55 (2010): 228–54.]

80 Aristotle, *Metaphysics* A 981a5–7; the translation derives from Gerson, *Ancient Epistemology*, 69. See also Aristotle, *Posterior Analytics* bk. 2, 100a1–13.

81 Aristotle, *Posterior Analytics* bk. 2, 90b23–32.

82 Edward Hussey, "Aristotle and Mathematics," in *Science and Mathematics in Ancient Greek Culture*, eds. C. J. Tuplin and T. E. Rihll, 217–29 (Oxford: Oxford University Press, 2002), 221–3.

83 Following the interpretation of Hussey, "Aristotle and Mathematics."

84 Aristotle, *On the Soul* bk. 3, 430a17–18, trans. Gerson, *Ancient Epistemology*, 85.

85 Anthony A. Long and David N. Sedley, *The Hellenistic Philosophers*, 2 volumes (Cambridge: Cambridge University Press, 1987), 1:89.

86 Thomas Habinek, "Tentacular Mind: Stoicism, Neuroscience, and the Configurations of Physical Reality," in *A Field Guide to a New Meta-Field: Bridging the Humanities-Neuroscience Divide*, ed. Barbara Stafford, 64–83 (Chicago: University of Chicago Press, 2011).

87 Sextus Empiricus, *Against the Professors* 7.247–52, translated in Long and Sedley, *The Hellenistic Philosophers*, 1:243; see also Diogenes Laertius 7.46 = Long and Sedley, *The Hellenistic Philosophers*, 1:242.

88 Sextus Empiricus, *Against the Professors* 7.151, translated by Long and Sedley, *The Hellenistic Philosophers*, 1:254, modified.

89 Long and Sedley, *The Hellenistic Philosophers*, 1:249.

90 The concept of strategic information has been particularly influential in and through the work of Pascal Boyer ("Functional Origins of Religious Concepts: Ontological and Strategic Selection in Evolved Minds," *Journal of the Royal Anthropological Institute* 6 [2000]: 195–214); see, e.g., Benjamin G. Purzycki, Daniel N. Finkel, John Shaver, Nathan Wales, Adam B. Cohen, and Richard Sosis, "What Does God Know? Supernatural Agents' Access to Socially Strategic and Non-Strategic Information," *Cognitive Science* 36 (2012): 846–69.

91 Claude Imbert, "Stoic Logic and Alexandrian Poetics," in *Doubt and Dogmatism: Studies in Hellenistic Epistemology*, eds. Malcolm Schofield, Myles Burnyeat, and Jonathan Barnes, 182–216 (Oxford: Oxford University Press, 1980); Simon Goldhill, "The Naïve and Knowing Eye: Ekphrasis and the Culture of Viewing in the Hellenistic World," in *Art and Text in Ancient Greek Culture*, eds. Simon Goldhill and Robin Osborne, 197–223 (Cambridge: Cambridge University Press, 1994); Simon Goldhill, "Refracting Classical Vision: Changing Cultures of Viewing," in *Vision in Context: Historical and Contemporary Perspectives on Sight*, eds. Teresa Brennan and Martin Jay, 15–29 (New York: Routledge, 1996); Thomas Habinek, "Rhetoric, Music, and the Arts," in *The Oxford Handbook of Rhetorical Studie*s, ed. Michael J. McDonald, 289–300 (Oxford: Oxford University Press, 2017); Thomas Habinek and Hector Reyes, *Methodical Fire: The Physics of Art and Art Theory from Zeno to Baudelaire* (forthcoming).

92 Stephen Menn, "Plotinus on the Identity of Knowledge with its Object," *Apeiron* 34, no. 3 (2001): 233–46.

93 Plotinus, *Ennead* IV.4.24; Plotinus, *Plotinus*, trans. Stephen Mackenna (London: P. L. Warner, Publisher to the Medici Society, 1921).

94 Plotinus, *Ennead* V.3.8.

95 M. Mendelson, "Saint Augustine," *The Stanford Encyclopedia of Philosophy*, ed. Edward N. Zalta. Winter 2016. Available online: https://plato.stanford.edu/archives/win2016/entries/augustine (accessed January 9, 2022), section 6.

96 Mendelson, "Saint Augustine."

97 Gregory of Nyssa, *De opificio hominis* 8.4.

98 For example, Gregory of Nazianzen, *Second Theological Oration* 22–30.

99 The most influential expression of this view is a qualified one, that of Augustine regarding the social and ethical utility of human institutions, by which an earthly and temporary peace is achieved: Augustine, *City of God* 19.13–14, 17; see also *Against the Academics* bk. 3, *On the Trinity* bk. 10. However, see also *Ep.* 189 to Count Boniface, where Augustine allows that the need to act in the world on the basis of purely human knowledge will inevitably present ethical difficulties.

100 Panayiota Vassilopoulou, "Introduction," in *Late Antique Epistemology: Other Ways to Truth*, eds. Panayiota Vassilopoulou and Stephen R. L. Clark, 1–17 (London: Palgrave Macmillan, 2009), 7.

101 Joachim Lacrosse, "Plotinus, Porphyry, and India: A Re-Examination," in *Late Antique Epistemology: Other Ways to Truth*, eds. Panayiota Vassilopoulou and Stephen R. L. Clark, 103–17 (London: Palgrave Macmillan, 2009).

Chapter 2

1 Johann Gottfried Herder, "Das Kind der Sorge" (1787), in *Johann Gottfried von Herder. Volkslieder, Übertragungen, Dichtungen*, Bibliothek deutscher Klassiker 60, ed. Ulrich Gaier, 743–4 (Frankfurt: Deutscher Klassiker-Verlag, 1990).

2 Hesiod, *Works and Days* 49, 95. This and all Hesiod's citations hereafter are from Hesiod, *Hesiodi Theogonia. Opera et dies. Scutum. Fragmenta selecta*, eds. Friedrich Solmsen, Reinhold Merkelbach, and Martin L. West (Oxford: Clarendon Press, 1990).

3 Hesiod, *Theogony* 585. Trans. Evelyn-White 1914. For this myth see Hes. *Theog.* 535–602 and *WD* 59–105.

4 Hes., *WD* 91–2. Trans. Evelyn-White 1914.

5 Hes., *WD* 94.

6 Hes., *WD* 93.

7 Hes., *WD* 95.

8 Hes., *WD* 47–9.

9 Hes., *WD* 112–13.

10 Hes., *WD* 115.

11 Hes., *WD* 116–18.

12 Hes., *WD* 118–19.

13 Hes., *WD* 120.

14 Hes., *WD* 140–78.

15 Hes., *WD* 112.

16 Hes., *WD* 114–15.

17 Hes., *WD* 177.

18 Hes., *WD* 178.

19 Hes., *WD* 135–6.

20 Hes., *WD* 145–6.

21 Hes., *WD* 160.

22 Hes., *WD* 170.

23 Hes., *WD* 178.

24 Hes., *WD* 200.

25 Hes., *WD* 49, 90–5.

26 Hes., *WD* 103, 118.

27 For a problematization of nature, see Lloyd in this volume.

28 Hes., *WD* 363.

29 Hes., *WD* 366–7.

30 Hes., *WD* 364.

31 Hes., *WD* 367.

32 Hes., *WD* 412.

33 Hes., *WD* 49, 95.

34 Hes., *WD* 112.

35 Hes., *Theog.* 61.

36 Hes., *Theog.* 37, 51.

37 Hes., *Theog.* 55.

38 Hes. *Theog.* 97–103.

39 Plato will also focus on the chromatic, and at the same time aural, vocal, and musical aspect of poetry. What the poets say, "stripped bare of the colors of music" (*epei gymnôthenta ge tôn tês musikês chrômatôn*, Plato, *Republic* 10, 601b 2) is not beautiful (*kalôn de mê*, Pl. *Resp.* 10, 601b 7). This and all *Republic*'s citations hereafter are from Plato, *Platonis Rempublicam: Recognovit brevique adnotatione critica instruxit*, ed. S[imon]. R. Slings (Oxford: Clarendon Press, 2003). On poetry and its effects, see Webb and Gurd in this volume.

40 Hes., *Theog.* 61.

41 The anxiolytic nature of pleasure agrees with the synesthetic sensuality inherent in the idiom of sweetness. On this language, see Rana Saadi Liebert, *Tragic Pleasure from Homer to Plato* (Cambridge: Cambridge University Press, 2017).

42 Hes., *WD* 82.

43 Hes., *Theog.* 585.

44 Hes., *WD* 66.

45 Hes., *Theog.* 100–1.

46 Pietro Pucci, *Hesiod and the Language of Poetry* (Baltimore: Johns Hopkins University Press, 1977), 8–44.

47 Andrew Ford, *Homer: The Poetry of the Past* (Ithaca, NY: Cornell University Press, 1992), 53; see also Detienne, *The Masters of Truth in Archaic Greece.*

48 Hes., *Theog.* 97.

49 Hes., *Theog.* 98.

50 Whenever other people matter to us, and only if they do, the representation of their predicaments can affect us. This is what Aristotle will call "pity" (*eleos*), the proper enjoyment of tragedy. Pity involves fear, namely, the apprehension that something similar to what befell the characters could, hypothetically, happen to us. Pity and fear are forms of concern. See Aristotle, *Rhetoric* 2.

51 This and all *Odyssey*'s citations hereafter are from Homer, *Homeri Opera. Recognovit adnotatione critica instruxit Thomas W. Allen. Tomus III: Odysseae Libros I–XII continens. Tomus IV: Odysseae Libros XIII–XXIV continens. Editio altera* (Oxford: Clarendon Press, 1917).

52 Homer, *Odyssey* 7.208–10.

53 Hom., *Od.* 7.212–13.

54 Hom., *Od.* 7.215. See also Hom., *Od.* 19.509–17, where Penelope invites Odysseus to sleep, notwithstanding his being *kêdomenos*, before mentioning her own distress, more to the point her "sharp cares" (*oxeiai meledônai*, Hom., *Od.* 19.517).

55 Hom., *Od.* 7.241–3.

56 Hom., *Od.* 5.5.

57 Hom., *Od.* 11.369, 376.

58 Hom., *Od.* 11.465–6.

59 Hom., *Od.* 11.333–4. Homer, *The Odyssey: Volume I: Books 1–12*, Loeb Classical Library, trans. August T. Murray and revised by George E. Dimock (Cambridge, MA: Harvard University Press, 1919). On this passage and the aesthetic experience as silence and fascination, see Anastasia-Erasmia Peponi, *Frontiers of Pleasure. Models of Aesthetic Response in Archaic and Classical Greek Thought* (New York: Oxford University Press, 2012).

60 Hom., *Od.* 8.75.

61 Hom., *Od.* 8.91–2.

62 Hom., *Od.* 8.149: Odysseus is challenged to engage in the games, and to abandon his cares (*kêdea*); 8.154: Odysseus replies that cannot enjoy the games on account of his *kêdea*.

63 Hom., *Od.* 8.368–9.

64 Hom., *Od.* 8.485–520.

65 Hom., *Od.* 8.521–46. Alcinous says that all should enjoy the song, the hosts and the guest (Hom., *Od.* 8.639–43).

66 Mary Scott, "Some Greek Terms in Homer Suggesting Non-Competitive Attitudes," *Acta Classica* 24 (1981): 1–15.

67 Hes., *Theog.* 98.

68 Plato, *Statesman* 261d 5–6. This and all *Statesman*'s citations hereafter are from Plato, *Platonis Opera. Recognoverunt brevique adnotatione critica instruxerunt Elizabeth A. Duke, W. F. Hicken, W. S. M. Nicoll, D. B. Robinson, J. C. G. Strachan. Tomus I: Tetralogias I–II continens* (Oxford: Clarendon Press, 1995).

69 Pl., *Stat.* 276b 8.

70 Pl., *Stat.* 276c–d.

71 Pl., *Stat.* 276e 12–14.

72 Pl., *Rep.* 3, 415d 3.

73 Pl., *Rep.* 8, 543c 2–3.

74 Pl., *Rep.* 3, 412c 11.

75 Pl., *Rep.* 2, 375a–376a.

76 Pl., *Rep.* 3., 412c 14.

77 Pl., *Rep.* 3, 412e 1.

78 Hes., *WD* 123–26.

79 Pl., *Rep.* X, 606 a–b.

80 Giulia Sissa, "Caregivers of the Polis, Partygoers and Lotus-Eaters. Politics of Pleasure and Care in Plato's Republic," in *Philosophie für die Polis. Akten des 5. Kongresses der Gesellschaft für antike Philosophie 2016*, Beiträge zur Altertumskunde 380, ed. Christoph Riedweg, 175–201 (Berlin: De Gruyter, 2019).

81 Giulia Sissa, "Le Peuple philosophe. Le souci du bien dans la République de Platon et chez les Athéniens," *Chôra. Revue d' études anciennes et médiévales* 15/16 (2017/2018): 203–18.

82 This and all *Fabulae*'s citations hereafter are from Hyginus, *Fabulae*, ed. Peter K. Marshall, 2nd revised edition, Bibliotheca scriptorum Graecorum et Romanorum Teubneriana (Munich: K. G. Saur, 2002).

83 Hyginus, *Fabulae*, 220.

84 Hyg., *Fab.* 220.1.

85 Hyg., *Fab.* 220.1.

86 Hyg., *Fab.* 220.3.

87 Seneca's *Epistles to Lucilius* 124. This and all Seneca's citations hereafter are from Seneca, *L. Annaei Senecae. Ad Lucilium epistulae morales. Tomus II: Libri XIV–XX*, ed. L. D. Reynolds (Oxford: Clarendon Press, 1965).

88 Seneca (the Younger), *Epistles to Lucilius* 124.14.23–4.

89 Sen., *Ep.* 124.12.8; Seneca, *Epistles. Volume III: Epistles 93–124*, Loeb Classical Library, trans. Richard M. Gummere (Cambridge, MA: Harvard University Press, 1925).

90 Sen., *Ep.* 124.23.23.

91 Martin Heidegger, *Being and Time*, trans. John Macquarrie and Edward Robinson (Oxford: Blackwell, 1962) (= Sein und Zeit. In Edmund Husserl, ed., *Jahrbuch für Philosophie und phänomologische Forschung*, vol. 8, 1–438. Halle a. d. S.: Max Niemeyer, 1927), 241–4.

92 Heidegger, *Being and Time*, 244.

93 Heidegger, *Being and Time*, 243.

94 Heidegger, *Being and Time*, 243.

95 Johann Wolfgang von Goethe, *Goethe' Werke: Vollständige Ausgabe letzter Hand. Ein und Vierzigster Band. Faust, Der Tragödie zweyter Theil in fünf Acten (Vollendet im Sommer 1831)* (Stuttgart: J. G. Cotta'schen Buchhandlung,1832), *Faust* Part II, Act 5, Scene 5, 10384–11498; Herder, "Das Kind der Sorge."

96 Drew A. Hyland, "Caring for Myth: Heidegger, Plato, and the Myth of Cura," *Research in Phenomenology* 27 (1997): 90–102; Annie Larivée and Alexandra Leduc, "Le souci de soi dans Être et Temps. L'accentuation radicale d'une tradition antique?" *Revue Philosophique de Louvain*, quatrième série, 100, no. 4 (2002): 723–41; Jesus A. Escudero, "Heidegger: Being and Time and the Care for the Self," *Open Journal of Philosophy* 3, no. 2 (2013): 302–7.

97 Hyland has argued that the categorization of a myth as "pre-ontological" is highly debatable, in Heidegger's own terms. He also draws a parallel between Heidegger's use of Hyginus' *fabula* and Plato's appeal to narratives, such as Aristophanes' anthropogony and Diotima's biography of Eros, in the *Symposium*. Heidegger's *Cura*, Hyland argues, plays a role analogous to that of Plato's *erôs*, since they both act in the genealogical account of human

finitude (Hyland, "Caring for Myth"). For a connection of Heidegger's notion of a care for the self with the Platonic tradition of *epimeleia heautou*, see Larivée and Leduc, "Le souci de soi dans Être et Temps"; Escudero, "Heidegger."

98 Konrad Burdach, "Faust und die Sorge," *Deutsche Vierteljahrsschrift für Literaturwissenschaft und Geistesgeschichte* 1 (1923): 1–60; Warren T. Reich, "History of the Notion of Care," in *Encyclopedia of Bioethics*, revised edition, ed. Warren T. Reich, 319–31 (New York: Simon and Schuster Macmillan, 1995). For a predictably abrasive critique of Heidegger's language of *Sorge*, see Pierre Bourdieu, "L'ontologie politique de Martin Heidegger," *Actes de la Recherche en Sciences Sociales* 1, nos. 5–6 (1975): 109–56.

99 Goethe, *Goethe' Werke*, *Faust*, Part II, Act 5, Scene 5, 10384–1498. On the dialogue between Sorge and Faust, as a source of influence for Heidegger's vocabulary not only of *Sorge*, but also of *dasein*, see Ellis Dye, "Sorge in Heidegger and in Goethe's Faust," *Goethe Yearbook* 16 (2009): 207–18. On the complex relations of Heidegger and Goethe, beyond *Sorge*, see Jean Lacoste, "'L'oeil clairement ouvert sur la nature': Heidegger et Goethe," *Littérature* 120 (2000): 105–27. For a semantic history of care, see John T. Hamilton, *Security: Politics, Humanity, and the Philology of Care* (Princeton, NJ: Princeton University Press, 2013).

100 Johann Wolfgang von Goethe, *Faust: Eine Tragödie* (Tübingen: J. G. Cotta'schen Buchhandlung, 1808), Part I, Act 1, Scene 1 (Night), 644–51; Johann Wolfgang von Goethe, *Goethe, Faust, Parts 1 & 2*, trans. Anthony S. Kline (= *Faust: Eine Tragödie* [Tübingen: J. G. Cotta'schen Buchhandlung, 1808] and *Faust: Der Tragödie zweyter Theil in fünf Acten* [Stuttgart, 1832]). Available online: http://goethe.holtof.com/faust/FaustIScenesItoIII.htm (accessed September 22, 2019).

101 Goethe, *Faust: Eine Tragödie*, Part I, Act 1, Scene 1 (Night), 629.

102 Goethe, *Goethe' Werke*, *Faust*, Part II, Act 5, Scene 5 (Midnight), 11495–8.

103 Martin Heidegger, "What Is Metaphysics? (1929)," trans. David Farrell Krell, in *Martin Heidegger: Pathmarks*, ed. William McNeill, 82–96 (Cambridge: Cambridge University Press, 2010) (= "Was ist Metaphysik?" in *Martin Heidegger: Gesamtausgabe: Band 9, Wegmarken*, ed. Friedrich-Wilhelm von Herrmann [Frankfurt: Klostermann, 2004]), 93, 113. See also Régis Jolivet, *Les doctrines existentialistes de Kierkegaard à J.-P. Sartre* (Abbaye Saint-Wandrille: Editions de Fontenelles, 1948), 109: "L'exister est un fait primitif: au moment où je m'interroge sur lui, j'existe déjà, avec tout ce que cela implique pour moi de nécessité de me projeter en avant de moi-même, c'est-à-dire d'être 'souci de'. Le souci comme anticipation de soi n'est donc pas une conduite particulière et contingente du Dasein par rapport à lui-même: il définit adéquatement, dans leur unité foncière, toutes les déterminations de l'être. Je n'ai pas du souci, ou si j'ai du souci, *si je veux, désire, si je suis incliné et poussé, c'est à titre de conséquence: je suis souci*, en tant même que je suis."

104 *Im Leben gehört es der Sorge* (Herder, "Das Kind der Sorge," 35).

105 Michel Foucault, *Histoire de la sexualité, Volume 3: Le Souci de soi* (Paris: Gallimard, 1984). On Stoic moral philosophy, see James Ker in this volume.

106 Pierre Hadot, "Réflexions sur la notion de 'culture de soi,'" in *Michel Foucault philosophe: rencontre international, Paris, 9, 10, Il janvier 1988*, ed. the Association pour le Centre Michel Foucault, 261–70 (Paris: Seuil, 1989).

107 On Heidegger's and Foucault's take on care, see Peter Sloterdijk, *You Must Change Your Life: On Anthropotechnics*, trans. Wieland Hoban (Cambridge, UK: Polity, 2013); Jussi Backman, "Self-Care and Total Care: The Twofold Return of Care in Twentieth-Century Thought," *International Journal of Philosophy and Theology* 81, no. 3 (2020): 275–91.

108 Hes., *Theog.* 103.

109 Cicero, *Nature of the Gods* 1.2–4.

110 Hom., *Il.* 1.196; 209. This and all *Iliad*'s citations hereafter are from Homer, *Homeri Opera. Recognoverunt brevique adnotatione critica instruxerunt David B. Munro et Thomas W. Allen. Tomus I: Iliadis Libros I–XII continens. Tomus II: Iliadis Libros XIII–XXIV continens. Editio tertia* (Oxford: Clarendon Press, 1920).

111 Hom., *Il.* 24.104–5.

112 Giulia Sissa and Marcel Detienne, *The Daily Life of the Greek Gods*, trans. Janet Lloyd (Stanford, CA: Stanford University Press, 2000) (= *La vie quotidienne des dieux grecs* [Paris: Hachette, 1989]).

Chapter 3

1 In my focus on social practices, I aspire, however imperfectly, to follow the example of Thomas Habinek. I am grateful to Tom for the encouragements and provocations he gave me since my student days. My thanks also to Cliff Ando for his insightful comments.

2 Translations from Greek and Latin texts are mine.

3 Seneca the Younger, *On Tranquillity of Mind* 2.

4 Hesiod, *Works and Days* 38.

5 Hes., *WD* 27–9.

6 Horace, *Epistles* 2.1.103–7.

7 Martial, *Epigrams* 8.44.3–5.

8 See Cicero, *Tusculan Disputations* 1.74.

9 Aristotle, *Politics* 1.1–2.

10 Arist., *Pol.* 1.2.

11 Long and Sedley, *The Hellenistic Philosophers*, 1:54.

12 Seneca the Younger, *Moral Letters* 121.16, 108.8.

13 Seneca the Younger, *Natural Questions* 1.17.4.

14 See Andrea Nightingale, *Genres in Dialogue: Plato and the Construct of Philosophy* (Cambridge: Cambridge University Press, 1995).

15 Plato, *Euthyphro* 4e.

16 Plato, *Apology* 18bc.

17 Diogenes Laertius, *Lives of the Eminent Philosophers* 1.20.

18 See Anthony A. Long, *Epictetus: A Stoic and Socratic Guide to Life* (Oxford: Oxford University Press, 2002).

19 Cicero, *Tusculan Disputations* 5.9.

20 Aristotle, *Nicomachean Ethics* 1.5.

21 Juvenal, *Satires* 10.350–3; my emphasis.

22 Juv., *Sat.* 10.356–62.

23 Lucian, *Biōn prasis* 1.

24 Catharine Edwards, *The Politics of Immorality in Ancient Rome* (Cambridge: Cambridge University Press, 1993).

25 Edwards, *The Politics of Immorality in Ancient Rome*, 68.

26 See Robert Kaster, "The Taxonomy of Patience, or, When Is 'Patientia' Not a Virtue?" *Classical Philology* 97 (2002): 133–44.

27 Seneca, *Moral Letters* 89.14.

28 Sen., *Moral Letters* 89.15.

29 Epictetus, *Discourses* 4.6.25–6.

30 Aristotle, *Nicomachean Ethics* 1.9.

31 Diogenes Laertius, *Lives of the Eminent Philosophers* 6.2.

32 Plato, *Republic* 427e.

33 Arist., *Eth. Nic.* 4.1–2.

34 See Seneca the Younger, *On Clemency* 2.4.

35 Pl., *Resp.* 10, 606d.

36 Arist., *Eth. Nic.* 4.5.

37 Seneca the Younger, *On Anger* 1.3.

38 Sen., *On Anger* 2.1.

39 William V. Harris, *Restraining Rage: The Ideology of Anger Control in Classical Antiquity* (Cambridge, MA: Harvard University Press, 2001).

40 Suetonius, *Deified Julius* 49–52, 53–4, 72, 76–7.

41 Valerius Maximus, *Memorable Deeds and Sayings* 6.1.

42 Matthew B. Roller, "Exemplarity in Roman Culture: The Cases of Horatius Cocles and Cloelia," *Classical Philology* 99 (2004): 4–6; emphasis in the original.

43 Horace, *Satires* 2.6.73–6.

44 Hor., *Epist.* 1.2.1–4.

45 Hor., *Epist.* 1.7.56–9.

46 Hor., *Sat.* 1.6.119–20.

47 Seneca the Younger, *Medea* 924–8.

48 Xenophon, *Memorabilia* 2.1.21–34.

49 Epictetus, *Discourses* 2.17.44.

50 Sen., *Moral Letters* 7.

51 Sen., *Moral Letters* 7.2.

52 Seneca the Younger, *On Providence* 2.9.

53 Lactantius, *On the Deaths of the Persecuted* 16.6–7; see James Ker, *The Deaths of Seneca* (New York: Oxford University Press, 2009), 184.

54 Seneca the Elder, *Suasoriae* 6.

55 Sen., *Suas.* 6.13.

56 Apuleius, *Metamorphoses* 9.13.

57 Plutarch, *Life of Solon* 5.

58 David S. Levene, "Pity, Fear and the Historical Audience: Tacitus on the Fall of Vitellius," in *The Passions in Roman Thought*, eds. Susanna Braund and Christopher Gill (Cambridge: Cambridge University Press, 1997), 148.

59 Sophocles, *Antigone* 454–5.

60 Aristotle, *Rhetoric* 1.13.2.

61 Seneca the Younger, *Epistles* 47.4; my emphasis.

62 Thucydides, *History of the Peloponnesian War* 5.89.

63 Homer, *Iliad* 6.215.

64 Brent D. Shaw, "The Divine Economy: Stoicism as Ideology," *Latomus* 64 (1985): 16–54.

65 Clifford Ando, *Imperial Ideology and Provincial Loyalty in the Roman Empire* (Berkeley: University of California Press, 2000).

66 Matthew B. Roller, *Constructing Autocracy: Aristocrats and Emperors in Julio-Claudian Rome* (Princeton, NJ: Princeton University Press, 2001), 213–87.

67 Malcolm Schofield, *The Stoic Idea of the City* (Cambridge: Cambridge University Press, 1991).

68 Schofield, *The Stoic Idea of the City*, 22–56.

69 Porphyry, *Life of Plotinus* 12.

70 Saint Benedict, *Rule of Benedict* 1.

71 Musonius Rufus, fr. 3.

72 Sen., *Ep.* 70.27.

73 Ker, *The Deaths of Seneca*, 61–2.

74 Aristotle, *Politics* 1.2, 1252a26–31.

75 Seneca the Younger, *On Benefits* 3.18–28.

76 Epictetus, *Discourses* 4.6.26.

77 Cicero, *On Duties* 1.107–16; see P. A. Brunt, "Stoicism and the Principate," *Papers of the British School at Rome* 43 (1975): 7–35.

78 Gretchen Reydams-Schils, *The Roman Stoics: Self, Responsibility, and Affection* (Chicago: University of Chicago Press, 2005); Alex Dressler, *Personification and the Feminine in Roman Philosophy* (Cambridge: Cambridge University Press, 2016).

79 Xenophon, *Oeconomicus* 7–21.

80 Hor., *Sat.* 2.7.22–6.

81 William Fitzgerald, *Slavery and the Roman Literary Imagination* (Cambridge: Cambridge University Press, 2000), 20.

82 Suetonius, *Life of Vespasian* 11–12.

83 Alkaios, fr. 332.

84 Theognis, lines 43–7.

85 Paul Plass, *The Game of Death in Ancient Rome* (Madison: University of Wisconsin Press, 1995).

86 Judith Perkins, *The Suffering Self: Pain and Narrative Representation in the Early Christian Era* (New York: Routledge, 1995).

87 Thomas N. Habinek, *The Politics of Latin Literature: Writing, Identity, and Empire in Ancient Rome* (Princeton, NJ: Princeton University Press, 1998), 137–50.

88 Seneca the Younger, *On the Brevity of Life* 15.2.

89 Seneca the Younger, *On Leisure* 4.1–2.

90 Seneca the Younger, *Consolation to Helvia* 8.2.

91 See Habinek, *The Politics of Latin Literature*, 151–69.

92 Tim Whitmarsh, *Greek Literature and the Roman Empire: The Politics of Imitation* (Oxford: Oxford University Press, 2001), 140; emphasis in the original.

93 Cicero, *On Duties* 3.1.

94 Pierre Hadot, *Philosophy as a Way of Life: Spiritual Exercises from Socrates to Foucault*, trans. Michael Chase (Oxford: Oxford University Press, 1995).

95 Sen., *On Anger* 3.36.

96 Epictetus, *Discourses* 4.6.35.

97 Epictetus, *Discourses* 4.6.34.

98 Hadot, *Philosophy as a Way of Life*; Michel Foucault, *Technologies of the Self: A Seminar with Michel Foucault*, eds. Luther Martin, Huck Gutman, and Patrick Hutton (Amherst: University of Massachusetts Press, 1988).

99 Seneca the Younger, *On the Happy Life* 20.4.

100 See Roller, *Constructing Autocracy*, 82–8; Catharine Edwards, "Self-Scrutiny and Self-Transformation in Seneca's Letters," *Greece & Rome* 44 (1997): 23–38.

101 Epictetus, *Discourses* 4.6.16.

102 Epictetus, *Discourses* 4.6.22–3.

103 Sen., *Moral Letters* 24.17; my emphasis.

104 Sen., *Moral Letters* 11.9.

105 David Konstan, *Friendship in the Classical World* (Cambridge: Cambridge University Press, 1997).

106 Arist., *Eth. Nic.* 8.3.

107 Cicero, *On Friendship* 20.

108 Plato, *Phaedo* 57a.

109 See Emily Wilson, *The Death of Socrates* (Cambridge, MA: Harvard University Press, 2007).

110 Ker, *The Deaths of Seneca*, 182–3.

111 See Catharine Edwards, *Death in Ancient Rome* (New Haven, CT: Yale University Press, 2007).

112 Cicero, *Letters to his Friends* 4.5.

113 See Ker, *The Deaths of Seneca*, 89–92.

114 Jerome, *Letter 60*; see David H. Scourfield, *Consoling Heliodorus: A Commentary on Jerome Letter 60* (Oxford: Oxford University Press, 1993).

Chapter 4

1 David Grewal, "The Invention of the Economy: A History of Economic Thought" (PhD dissertation, Harvard University, 2010); see also Jonathan Schlefer, *The Assumptions Economists Make* (Cambridge, MA: The Belknap Press of Harvard University Press, 2012); Peter Spiegler, *Behind the Model: a Constructive Critique of Economic Modeling* (Cambridge: Cambridge University Press, 2015).

2 Moses I. Finley, *The World of Odysseus* (New York: Viking Press, 1965); Anthony Snodgrass, *Archaic Greece: the Age of Experiment* (London: J. M. Dent, 1980).

3 To elaborate, it might help to imagine the world of Ithaka in the Odyssey. There was no class of persons—there were no "Ithakans"—whose relationship to the "state" was legal, and which entitled them to demands on the community at large, which itself did not exist, whether in theory or in institutional life. "Ithaka" was aggregated out of aristocratic houses, and everyone in Ithaka was related to one or another house via kinship or some relation of social dependency. Life outside those structures—as an individual!—would have been precarious indeed.

4 Ann Cudd and Seena Eftekhari, "Contractarianism," in *The Stanford Encyclopedia of Philosophy*, ed. Edward N. Zalta. Summer 2018 Edition. Available online: https://plato.stanford.edu/archives/sum2018/entries/contractarianism/ (accessed January 10, 2022).

5 Hent Kalmo and Quentin Skinner, eds., *Sovereignty in Fragments: The Past, Present and Future of a Contested Concept* (Cambridge: Cambridge University Press, 2010); Richard Tuck, *The Sleeping Sovereign: The Invention of Modern Democracy* (Cambridge: Cambridge University Press, 2015); John L. Brooke, Julia C. Strauss, and Greg Anderson, eds., *State Formations. Global Histories and Cultures of Statehood* (Cambridge: Cambridge University Press, 2018).

6 Ronald Grigor Suny, "Constructing Primordialism: Old Histories for New Nations," *Journal of Modern History* 72 (2001): 862–96; see also Thomas Sizgorich, *Violence and Belief in Late Antiquity: Militant Devotion in Christianity and Islam* (Philadelphia: University of Pennsylvania Press, 2009), 66–70.

7 Nicole Loraux, *The Invention of Athens: The Funeral Oration in the Classical City*, trans. Alan Sheridan (Cambridge, MA: Harvard University Press, 1986); Nicole Loraux, *Born of the Earth: Myth and Politics in Athens*, trans. Selina Stewart (Ithaca, NY: Cornell University Press, 2000).

8 Aristotle, *Politics* bk. 2.1, 1260b27ff. (trans. after Rackham).

9 Aristotle, *Nicomachean Ethics* bk. 10.9, 1181b13–22 (trans. after Rackham). In the catalog of Aristotle's works preserved by Diogenes Laertius are listed "Constitutions of 158 *poleis*, in general and in particular, whether ruled by the *demos*, the few, the best, or a tyrant" (Diogenes Laertius, *Lives of the Eminent Philosophers* 5.27).

10 Hans Beck and Peter Funke, eds., *Federalism in Greek Antiquity* (Cambridge: Cambridge University Press, 2015).

11 Clifford Ando, "Colonialism, Colonization: Roman Perspectives," in *The Oxford Handbook of Literatures of the Roman Empire*, eds. Daniel L. Selden and Phiroze Vasunia (Oxford: Oxford University Press, 2016).

12 Aristotle, *Constitution of the Athenians* 21.4.

13 Clifford Ando, "Making Romans: Democracy and Social Differentiation Under Rome," in *Cosmopolitanism and Empire. Universal Rulers, Local Elites and Cultural Integration in the Ancient Near East and Mediterranean*, eds. Myles Lavan, Richard E. Payne, and John Weisweiler, 169–85 (Oxford: Oxford University Press, 2016).

14 Herodotus 6.42–3 (trans. after Godolphin).

15 Robin Osborne, *Demos: The Discovery of Classical Attika* (Cambridge: Cambridge University Press, 1985).

16 Clifford Ando, "City, Village, Sacrifice: The Political Economy of Religion in the Early Roman Empire," in *Mass and Elite in the Greek and Roman World from Sparta to Late Antiquity*, ed. Richard Evans, 118–36 (New York: Routledge, 2017).

17 Clifford Ando, "The Political Economy of the Hellenistic Polis: Comparative and Modern Perspectives," in *The Polis in the Hellenistic World*, eds. Henning Börm and Nino Luraghi, 9–26 (Stuttgart: Franz Steiner, 2018); Clifford Ando, "Race and Citizenship in Roman Law and Administration," in *Xenofobia y Racismo en el Mundo Antiguo*, eds. Francisco Marco Simón, Francisco Pina Polo, and J. Remesal Rodríguez, 175–88 (Barcelona: Edicions de la Universitat de Barcelona, 2019).

18 J. G. A. Pocock, "The Ideal of Citizenship since Classical Times," *Queen's Quarterly* 99 (1992): 33–55; see also J. G. A. Pocock, *Barbarism and Religion, Volume 3: The First Decline and Fall* (Cambridge: Cambridge University Press, 2003), 203–35.

19 Benjamin Straumann, *Crisis and Constitutionalism: Roman Political Thought from the Fall of the Republic to the Age of Revolution* (New York: Oxford University Press, 2016).

20 Aristotle, *Politics* 1274b38–40.

21 Aristotle, *Politics* bk. 3.1, 1274b38–1275a2 (trans. Rackham); see also *Politics* bk. 1, 1260b12ff., where he allows that the education of women matters because they make up half the population, while their male children will grow up to take part in government.

22 Ando, "The Political Economy of the Hellenistic Polis."

23 The first surviving rehearsal of this typology is found in Herodotus 3.80–2.

24 David Graeber and Marshall Sahlins, *On Kings* (Chicago: HAU Books/University of Chicago Press, 2017).

25 This kind of argument is visible in fragments in antiquity: see Aristotle, *Politics* bk. 4.3.13–14, 1291a20–34 and bk. 6.4.4–6, 1321a15–43; see also Aristotle, *Constitution of the Athenians* 23–4. Modern confidence in this narrative was shaken to a remarkable and enduring degree by A. M. Snodgrass, "The Hoplite Reform and History," *Journal of Hellenic Studies* 85 (1965): 110–22; but cf. John Salmon, "Political Hoplites?," *Journal of Hellenic Studies* 97 (1977): 84–101.

26 Charles Tilly, *Coercion, Capital, and European States: AD 990–1990* (Cambridge, MA: Blackwell, 1990) represents a watershed in this tradition.

27 For a broad analysis of the relationship of technologies of money and currency to state power see David Graeber, *Debt: The First 5,000 Years* (Brooklyn, NY: Melville House, 2011); on mercenaries in ancient Greece, see Matthew Trundle, *Greek Mercenaries: From the Late Archaic Period to Alexander* (London: Routledge, 2004).

28 On the nature and limits of Polybius' debt to Aristotle see Thomas Cole, "The Sources and Composition of Polybius VI," *Historia: Zeitschrift für Alte Geschichte* 13 (1964): 440–86.

29 Polybius 6.9.10 (trans. Paton, revised by Walbank and Habicht).

30 Polybius 6.11–18.

31 Cicero, *On the Commonwealth* 1.41–5.

32 Polybius 6.47.7–8; Cicero, *On the Commonwealth* 2.21: "That great man, the greatest of all writers, chose his own territory on which to build a state to suit his own ideas. It may be a noble state, but it is totally alien to human life and customs" (trans. Zetzel).

33 Cicero, *On the Commonwealth* 2.22.

34 Cicero, *On the Commonwealth* 2.30 (trans. Zetzel).

35 Clifford Ando, *Roman Social Imaginaries: Language and Thought in Contexts of Empire* (Toronto: University of Toronto Press, 2015), 53–86.

36 Mortimer N. S. Sellers, *American Republicanism: Roman Ideology in the United States Constitution* (New York: New York University Press, 1994); see also Charles Howard McIlwain, *Constitutionalism Ancient and Modern* (Ithaca, NY: Cornell University Press, 1940); J. G. A. Pocock, *The Machiavellian Moment: Florentine Political Thought and the Atlantic Republican Tradition* (Princeton, NJ: Princeton University Press, 1975).

37 Pocock, *The Machiavellian Moment*; see also Pocock, *Barbarism and Religion*.

38 Appian, *Libyan War* 628–30.

39 F. G. Whelan, "Democratic Theory and the Boundary Problem," *Nomos* 25 (1983): 13–47.

40 For an exemplary exploration of these issues in an ancient context see Susan Lape, "Solon and the Institution of the 'Democratic' Family Form," *Classical Journal* 98 (2002–2003), 117–39; see also Susan Lape, "Racializing Democracy: The Politics of Sexual Reproduction in Classical Athens," *Parallax* 9 (2003): 52–63.

41 David Asheri, "Leggi greche sul problema dei debiti," *Studi classici e orientali* 18 (1969): 5–122; M. I. Finley, *Economy and Society in Ancient Greece*, ed. with an introduction by Brent D. Shaw and Richard P. Saller (London: Chatto & Windus, 1981), 150–66.

42 P. A. Brunt, *Social Conflicts in the Roman Republic* (London: Chatto & Windus, 1971) is an exceptionally powerful study of these issues. For treatments with full scholarly apparatus see P. A. Brunt, *The Fall of the Roman Republic and Related Essays* (Oxford: Clarendon Press, 1988), 1–92, 240–80.

43 Fergus Millar, *Rome, the Greek World, and the East, Volume 1: The Roman Republic and the Augustan Revolution*, eds. Hannah M. Cotton and Guy M. Rogers (Chapel Hill: University of North Carolina Press, 2002), 143–61.

44 Pausanias 7.16.9.

45 Perhaps the earliest attestation is *Inscriptiones Latinae Selectae* no. 15.

46 The data may be rapidly consulted in Peter J. Rhodes and David M. Lewis, *The Decrees of the Greek States* (Oxford: Clarendon Press, 1997).

47 Daniela Cammack, "The Dêmos in Dêmokratia," *Classical Quarterly* 69, no. 1 (2019): 42–61.

48 Aristotle, *Politics* bk. 6.7, 1321a30–5.

49 Ryan K. Balot, *Greed and Injustice in Classical Athens* (Princeton, NJ: Princeton University Press, 2001).

50 Claude Nicolet, *The World of the Citizen in Republican Rome*, trans. P. S. Falla (Berkeley: University of California Press, 1980), 49–88.

51 Karl-Joachim Hölkeskamp, *Die Entstehung der Nobilität: Studien zur sozialen und politischen Geschichte der Römischen Republik im 4. Jhdt. v. Chr.* (Stuttgart: Steiner, 1987); see also Karl-Joachim Hölkeskamp, *Reconstructing the Roman Republic: An Ancient Political Culture and Modern Research*, trans. Henry Heitmann-Gordon (Princeton, NJ: Princeton University Press, 2010).

52 Cf. Pocock, *Barbarism and Religion*, 203–35.

53 Peter O'Neill, "Going Round in Circles: Popular Speech in Ancient Rome," *Classical Antiquity* 22 (2003): 135–66.

54 Andrew Wallace-Hadrill, *Rome's Cultural Revolution* (Cambridge: Cambridge University Press, 2008), 315–55.

55 Thomas A. J. McGinn, "*Cui bono?* The True Beneficiaries of Roman Private Law," in *Ancient Law, Ancient Society*, eds. Dennis P. Kehoe and Thomas A. J. McGinn, 133–66 (Ann Arbor: University of Michigan Press, 2017).

56 Hesiod, *Works and Days* 263–4 (trans. Evelyn-White, modified).

57 Gellius, *Attic Nights* 21.1.13 (trans. Rolfe) = Labeo frag. 25 Huschke-Seckel-Kübler.

58 Calpurnius Flaccus 6.

59 The entire debate can be studied around reactions to Moses Finley, *The Ancient Economy*, 2nd edition (Berkeley: University of California Press, 1985); see also Alain Bresson, *The Making of the Ancient Greek Economy: Institutions, Markets, and Growth in the City-States*, trans. Steven Rendall (Princeton, NJ: Princeton University Press, 2016), 1–15.

60 Neil Coffee, *Gift and Gain: How Money Transformed Ancient Rome* (New York: Oxford University Press, 2017).

61 See, e.g., John H. D'Arms, "Republican Senators' Involvement in Commerce in the Late Republic: Some Ciceronian Evidence," in *The Seaborne Commerce of Ancient Rome: Studies in Archaeology and History*, eds. John H. D'Arms and E. C. Kopff, 77–89 (Rome: American Academy in Rome, 1980), on Cicero.

62 David Jones, *The Bankers of Puteoli: Finance, Trade and Industry in the Roman World* (Stroud: Tempus, 2006).

63 Todd M. Hickey, *Wine, Wealth, and the State in Late Antique Egypt: The House of Apion at Oxyrhynchus* (Ann Arbor: University of Michigan Press, 2012); see also Dennis Kehoe, *The Economics of Agriculture on Roman Imperial Estates in North Africa* (Göttingen: Vandenhoeck & Ruprecht, 1988); Dennis Kehoe, *Management and Investment on Estates in Roman Egypt during the Early Empire* (Bonn: R. Habelt, 1992); and Dennis Kehoe, *Law and the Rural Economy in the Roman Empire* (Ann Arbor: University of Michigan Press, 2007).

64 Michael Leese, "An Economic Perspective on Marriage Alliances in Ancient Greece," in *Ancient Law, Ancient Society*, eds. Dennis P. Kehoe and Thomas A. J. McGinn, 32–45 (Ann Arbor: University of Michigan Press, 2017).

65 Edward Champlin, *Final Judgments: Duty and Emotion in Roman Wills, 200 B.C.–A.D. 250* (Berkeley: University of California Press, 1991).

66 Pocock, "The Ideal of Citizenship Since Classical Times."

67 Ibid., 39–40.

68 Ibid., 40.

69 Ibid., 41; italics in the original.

70 Thomas Piketty, *Capital in the Twenty-First Century*, trans. Arthur Goldhammer (Cambridge, MA: The Belknap Press of Harvard University Press, 2014) provides the model for this analysis.

71 Keith Hopkins, *Death and Renewal* (Cambridge: Cambridge University Press, 1983).

72 Eva Jakab, "Inheritance," in *The Oxford Handbook of Roman Law and Society*, eds. Paul Du Plessis, Clifford Ando, and Kaius Tuori, 498–509 (Oxford: Oxford University Press, 2016) provides a guide.

73 Paul Veyne, *Le pain et le cirque: sociologie historique d'un pluralisme politique* (Paris: Seuil, 1976).

74 John Ma, *Statues and Cities: Honorific Portraits and Civic Identity in the Hellenistic World* (Oxford: Oxford University Press, 2013).

75 *Inscriptiones Latinae Selectae* no. 6680.

76 Clifford Ando, Review of John Ma, *Statues and Cities. Honorific Portraits and Civic Identity in the Hellenistic World* (Oxford: Oxford University Press, 2013), *Bryn Mawr Classical Review* (2014). Available online: http://bmcr.brynmawr.edu/2014/2014-02-21.html (accessed August 2, 2018).

77 Ulpian, *Institutes* bk. 1 frag. 1912 Lenel = *Dig.* 1.1.4.

78 Bresson, *The Making of the Ancient Greek Economy*.

79 Henrik Mouritsen, *The Freedman in the Roman World* (Cambridge: Cambridge University Press, 2011); Rose MacLean, *Freed Slaves and Roman Imperial Culture. Social Integration and the Transformation of Values* (Cambridge: Cambridge University Press, 2018).

80 *P.Giss.* 40, col. 2, lines 17–30; translation from *Sel. Pap.* no. 215.

81 My remarks at this juncture are indebted to Clifford Ando, "City, Village, Sacrifice: The Political Economy of Religion in the Early Roman Empire," in *Mass and Elite in the Greek and Roman World from Sparta to Late Antiquity*, ed. Richard Evans, 118–36 (New York: Routledge, 2017). Ari Z. Bryen, "Reading the Citizenship Papyrus (P.Giss. 40)," in *Citizenship and Empire in Europe, 200–1900: The Antonine Constitution After 1800 Years*, ed. Clifford Ando, 29–43 (Stuttgart: Steiner, 2016) offers a splendid study of this text.

Chapter 5

1 The point is controversial: see, for example, W. K. C. Guthrie, *A History of Greek Philosophy, volume 1* (Cambridge: Cambridge University Press, 1962), 64–7; G. E. R. Lloyd, *Early Greek Science: Thales to Aristotle* (New York: Norton, 1970); *Early Greek Philosophy 2: Beginnings and Early Ionian Thinkers, Part I*, ed. and trans. Andre Laks and Glenn M. Most (Cambridge, MA: Harvard University Press, 2016).

2 Aristotle, *de Anima* 411a8. This dictum is also cited by Plato, at *Laws* 899b, where, however, no mention of its author or authors is made.

3 Aristotle, *Physics* 203b13ff.

4 The point can be confirmed for Xenophanes, Heraclitus (as I shall illustrate shortly), and Empedocles.

5 Fr. 123, quoted by Themistius. (Presocratic fragments are from H. Diels and W. Kranz, eds., *Die Fragmente der Vorsokratiker*, 6th edn., Berlin: Weidmann, 1951; hereafter D-K.) Themistius is a late commentator who has his particular agenda in selecting citations from earlier authorities, as indeed has Hippolytus, responsible for Frr. 64 and 67 quoted below, as demonstrated most notably by Catherine Osborne, *Rethinking Early Greek Philosophy* (Ithaca, NY: Cornell University Press, 1987). By late antiquity ancient authorities are often cited pro and contra Christian theological positions.

6 Fr. 30, D-K.

7 Fr. 64, D-K.

8 Fr. 67, D-K.

9 Sextus Empiricus, *Adversus mathematicos* 7.65.

10 The one true god is "unlike mortals in form or in thought" (Fr. 23). Mortals have thought the gods are born and have clothes, voice, and form like their own (Fr. 14). Each race, Ethiopians and Thracians, makes their gods like themselves (Fr. 16).

11 Fr. 11, D-K, singles out Homer and Hesiod for ascribing to the gods everything that is shameful among men: thieving, adultery and deceiving one another.

12 Fr. 32, D-K.

13 See G. E. R. Lloyd, *Magic, Reason and Experience* (Cambridge: Cambridge University Press, 1979), 29–32 on Herodotus and 17 n. 41 on Sophocles and Aristophanes.

14 The literature on the ongoing acceptance of traditional views of the sacred in Hippocratic writers is considerable. The extent to which the author of *On the Sacred Disease* signs up to traditional religious views is controversial. See P. Van der Eijk, "The 'Theology' of the Hippocratic Treatise *On the Sacred Disease*," *Apeiron* 23 (1990): 87–119.

15 The inscriptions set up at the shrine of Asclepius at Epidauros all record successful outcomes when individuals came to consult not just about diseases but about such misfortunes as a lost child or lost treasure. See Lynn R. LiDonnici, *The Epidaurian Miracle Inscriptions: Text, Translation and Commentary* (Atlanta, GA: Scholars Press, 1995); G. E. R. Lloyd, *In the Grip of Disease: Studies in the Greek Imagination* (Oxford: Oxford University Press, 2003), ch. 3.

16 Sophocles, *Antigone* 453ff.

17 Herodotus, *Histories* 3.38. Conversely at 7.136, Xerxes is made to claim that the rule that heralds are to be respected holds for all humans.

18 Xenophon, *Memorabilia* 4.4.18ff.

19 Plato, *Gorgias* 483b–c, cf. 492c.

20 Plato, *Republic* 338e.

21 Pl., *Grg.* 483d–e.

22 Thucydides, *History of the Peloponnesian War* 5.105.

23 Aristotle, *Generation of Animals* 731b18ff.

24 Aristotle, *Progression of Animals* 706a19ff.

25 Aristotle, *Progression of Animals* 706b12f.

26 Aristotle, *Parts of Animals* 666b6ff.

27 Although Aristotle states that the male contribution to reproduction is to supply the form and the moving cause, while the female provides the matter, this should not be overinterpreted. Sophia E. Connell, *Aristotle on Female Animals* (Cambridge: Cambridge University Press, 2016) examines in detail the images and vocabulary that Aristotle uses that suggest that the matter the female supplies has positive characteristics, implying that the female is anything but a passive partner in reproduction as if her matter were merely inert. We gather this notably when the male and female contributions are described as interacting with one another like eddying currents.

28 *History of Animals* 608a21ff.

29 *History of Animals* 533a2ff. and other texts cited in G. E. R. Lloyd, *Science, Folklore and Ideology: Studies in the Life Sciences in Ancient Greece* (Cambridge: Cambridge University Press, 1983), 40 n. 154.

30 Full documentation of these points is to be found in Lloyd, *Science, Folklore and Ideology*, 41 and nn. 158–64.

31 Aristotle, *Sophistic Refutations* 173a7ff. (cf. already Pl., *Grg.* 483d).

32 cf. Lloyd, *Magic, Reason and Experience*, 36 n. 129.

33 Simo Parpola, *Letters from Assyrian and Babylonian Scholars*, State Archives of Assyria, 10 (Helsinki: Helsinki University Press, 1993).

34 Markham J. Geller, *Ancient Babylonian Medicine: Theory and Practice* (Chichester, UK: Wiley-Blackwell, 2010).

35 Donald Harper, *Early Chinese Medical Literature: The Mawangdui Medical Manuscripts* (London: Kegan Paul International, 1998).

36 Elisabeth Hsu, *Pulse Diagnosis in Early Chinese Medicine: The Telling Touch*, University of Cambridge Oriental Publications 68 (Cambridge: Cambridge University Press, 2010).

37 Detailed documentation for each of the points made here can be found in Lloyd, *Magic, Reason and Experience*, 252–7.

38 Herodotus, *Histories* 3.80.

39 Jingyi Jenny Zhao, *Aristotle and Xunzi on Shame, Moral Education and the Good Life* (Oxford: Oxford University Press, forthcoming).

40 *Lüshi chunqiu* (1/2/2).

41 G. E. R. Lloyd and Nathan Sivin, *The Way and the Word: Science and Medicine in Early China and Greece* (New Haven, CT: Yale University Press, 2002).

42 Roy Wagner, *The Invention of Culture*, 2nd edition (Chicago: University of Chicago Press, [1975] 2016).

43 Marilyn Strathern, "No Nature, No Culture: The Hagen Case," in *Nature, Culture and Gender*, eds. Carol MacCormack and Marilyn Strathern, 174–222 (Cambridge: Cambridge University Press, 1980).

44 Philippe Descola, *Beyond Nature and Culture*, translated by Janet Lloyd (Chicago: University of Chicago Press, 2013).

45 For critiques of the four-fold schema see G. E. R. Lloyd, *Being, Humanity and Understanding: Studies in Ancient and Modern Societies* (Oxford: Oxford University Press, 2012), cf. William Matthews, "Ontology with Chinese Characteristics," *HAU: Journal of Ethnographic Theory* 7, no. 1 (2017): 265–85.

46 Eduardo Viveiros de Castro, "Cosmological Deixis and Amerindian Perspectivism," *Journal of the Royal Anthropological Institute*, n.s., 4 (1998): 469–88; Eduardo Viveiros de Castro, *Cannibal Metaphysics*, ed. and trans. Peter Skafish (Minneapolis: Univocal, 2014).

47 Descola himself (*Beyond Nature and Culture*) treats ancient Greece as representative of an "analogist" regime as indeed is ancient China in his view. But that, I would argue, is to underestimate the extent to which various Greek writers anticipated the key tenets of "naturalism," notably the idea that everything is made of the same stuff, and that the difference between humans and other animals lies in our possessing culture and morality. See further Lloyd, *Being, Humanity and Understanding*, 69–70. For confirmation that ancient Mesopotamian investigations of heaven and earth, for instance, do not presuppose a concept of "nature," see Francesca Rochberg, *Before Nature: Cuneiform Knowledge and the History of Science* (Chicago: University of Chicago Press, 2016).

48 In particular I cannot here do justice to how Latin authors take over but in subtle respects go beyond Greek models, other than to note the obvious point that Latin *natura*, like Greek *physis*, continues to serve as the key framework for studies in cosmology (Lucretius, *De Rerum Natura*), in theology (Cicero, *De Natura Deorum*), and in "natural history" (Pliny, *Naturalis Historia*). In each case indebtedness to Greek authors is explicit, even while each of those Latin authors evidently takes pains to gear his work to what he considers an educated Roman public needs and will benefit from.

49 Galen, *On the Use of Parts* XI ch. 14 K 3 905.15–911.2. Elsewhere he polemicises against Christians in particular (several passages, including some that come from treatises that are only extant in Arabic or Syriac versions, are collected at Richard Walzer, *Galen on Jews and Christians* (London: Oxford University Press, 1949), 14–16.

50 The idea is foreshadowed already in Aristotle who even quotes Heraclitus in support, *On the Parts of Animals* I ch. 5, 645a17ff. Cf also Ptolemy's account of the contributions that the study of the heavens can make not just to human understanding but to human moral development: *Syntaxis* 1 1.

51 *Mechanica* 847a20. The classic study of the "mechanical hypothesis" in ancient Greek thought is Sylvia Berryman, *The Mechanical Hypothesis in Ancient Greek Natural Philosophy* (Cambridge: Cambridge University Press, 2009).

52 The theme is a recurrent one and not just in the zoological treatises of Aristotle.

53 However, the idea that the Greeks totally failed to appreciate the importance of the experimental method has been subject to much exaggeration. For the expression of some cautions in that regard see G. E. R. Lloyd, *Methods and Problems in Greek Science* (Cambridge: Cambridge University Press, 1991), ch. 4.

54 Some such principle, the "Golden Rule," can be exemplified in ancient China (Confucius), in the Old Testament, in some Buddhist texts, and in ancient Greece.

55 The problem takes on particular urgency in relation to human interventions on the environment. We have been modifying plant and animal species ever since the agricultural revolution: it is just that there are now much more powerful, precise, and effective means of doing so—and again no sense of where we should stop, with other species and with humans. Appeals to nature do not help the problems of morality or even of policy, but merely obfuscate them. Control of values and of education was where most of the heat of the ancient debate was generated: to that we have now to add control of those interventions.

Chapter 6

1 John Coffey and Alister Chapman, "Introduction," in *Seeing Things Their Way: Intellectual History and the Return of Religion*, eds. Alister Chapman, John Coffey, and Brad S. Gregory, 1–23 (Notre Dame: Notre Dame University Press, 2009).

2 For the practice/belief dichotomy now see Thomas Harrison, "Belief vs. Practice," in *The Oxford Handbook of Ancient Greek Religion*, eds. Esther Eidinow and Julia Kindt, 21–8 (Oxford: Oxford University Press, 2015), with earlier literature and some original suggestions.

3 Esther Eidinow, Julia Kindt, and Robin Osborne, eds., *Theologies of Ancient Greek Religion* (Cambridge: Cambridge University Press, 2016), in particular in the editors' introduction, discuss both the plurality of theologies *and* the lack of formal theological authority for the Greek world. The main advocate for a practice-focus within Roman religion has been Scheid (cf. John Scheid, "Polytheism Impossible; or, the Empty Gods: Reasons Behind a Void in the History of Roman Religion," *History and Anthropology* 3, no. 1 [1987]: 303–25), now best read with the critical comments of Clifford Ando, "Evidence and Orthopraxy," *Journal of Roman Studies* 99 (2009): 171–81.

4 Elizabeth A. Clark, *History, Theory, Text: Historians and the Linguistic Turn* (Cambridge, MA: Harvard University Press, 2009), ch. 8, with the comments of Denis Feeney, *Literature and Religion at Rome: Cultures, Contexts, and Beliefs* (Cambridge: Cambridge University Press, 1998), 1–2.

5 Hugh Bowden, "Impiety," in *The Oxford Handbook of Ancient Greek Religion*, eds. Esther Eidinow and Julia Kindt, 328–38 (Oxford: Oxford University Press, 2015).

6 For a good recent discussion see Michael Flower, *The Seer in Ancient Greece* (Berkeley: University of California Press, 2008).

7 See most recently Alexander Rubel and Michael Vickers, *Fear and Loathing in Ancient Athens: Religion and Politics During the Peloponnesian War* (London: Routledge, 2014).

8 Lysias 6.10.

9 Plutarch *Life of Pericles* 32.1. For a discussion of the historicity of this law see David Cohen, *Law, Sexuality, and Society: The Enforcement of Morals in Classical Athens* (Cambridge: Cambridge University Press, 1994), ch. 8.

10 Lysias 6.19.

11 Xen., *Memorabilia* 1.1.1.

12 Robert Garland, *Introducing New Gods: The Politics of Athenian Religion* (Ithaca, NY: Cornell University Press, 1992); H. S. Versnel, *Coping with the Gods: Wayward Readings in Greek Theology* (Leiden: Brill, 2011), 539–59.

13 Alexandre Jakubiec, "Rites and Religious Beliefs of Socrates according to Xenophon (Apology of Socrates 11 and Memorabilia 1.1.2)," *Classical Quarterly* 67, no. 1 (2017): 291–3, for the first suggestion and Harrison, "Belief vs. Practice," for the second.

14 Lysias 6.17.

15 Plato, *Laws* 885b, Hyperides, fr. 14.

16 On the stelai see most recently Aurian Delli Pizzi, "Impiety in Epigraphic Evidence," *Kernos. Revue internationale et pluridisciplinaire de religion grecque antique* 24 (2011): 59–76.

17 Andocides 1.71.

18 Lysias frag. 53 Thalheim / 195 Carey.

19 Demosthenes 54.39.

20 Cf. Tim Whitmarsh, "Atheism as a Group Identity in Ancient Greece," *Religion in the Roman Empire* 3, no. 1 (2017): 50–65, on impiety as a possible source of group identity.

21 Jan N. Bremmer, "Atheism in Antiquity," in *The Cambridge Companion to Atheism*, ed. Michael Martin, 11–26 (Cambridge: Cambridge University Press, 2006); David Konstan, "Socrates in Aristophanes' *Clouds*," in *The Cambridge Companion to Socrates*, ed. Sara Abel-Rappe and Rachana Kamtekar, 75–90 (Cambridge: Cambridge University Press, 2011).

22 On this most recently see Nikolaos Papageorgiou, "Prodicus and the Agon of the 'Logoi' in Aristophanes' 'Clouds,'" *Quaderni urbinati di cultura classica* 78, no. 3 (2004): 1000–9.

23 *Clouds* 367. Protagoras, fr. 80 B4, *Die Fragmente der Vorsokratiker*.

24 On contemporary agnosticism see also Melissus of Samos, from the Eleatic School, who positively dismissed any "knowledge" (γνῶσις) of the gods (30 A 1, *Die Fragmente der Vorsokratiker* = Diogenes Laertius 9.24) in distinction from appearances.

25 Euripides, *Bacchae* 274–85.

26 Greta Hawes, *Rationalizing Myth in Antiquity* (Oxford: Oxford University Press, 2014), 14.

27 Aristophanes, *Thesmophoriazusae* 450–1.

28 For a full discussion with earlier literature see Dustin W. Dixon, "Reconsidering Euripides' Bellerophon," *Classical Quarterly* 64, no. 2 (2014): 493–506.

29 Euripides, fr. 286, 1–3, Bruno Snell, Richard Kannicht, and S. L. Radt, eds., *Tragicorum Graecorum Fragmenta* (Göttingen: Vandenhoeck & Ruprecht, 1971–2004).

30 Thomas Harrison, "Greek Religion and Literature," in *A Companion to Greek Religion*, ed. Daniel Ogden, 371–84 (Oxford: Wiley-Blackwell, 2010), 376–80.

31 Xenophon's *Memorabilia* 1.4.10.

32 Flower, *The Seer in Ancient Greece*, 7.

33 Plato, *Republic* 2.364E.

34 Simon Pulleyn, *Prayer in Greek Religion* (Oxford: Oxford University Press, 1997), 16–38.

35 Xenophon, *Memorabilia* 1.2–3.

36 Sheramy D. Bundrick, "Selling Sacrifice on Classical Athenian Vases," *Hesperia: The Journal of the American School of Classical Studies at Athens* 83 (2014): 653–708.

37 See the useful discussion in Rubel and Vickers, *Fear and Loathing in Ancient Athens*, ch. 6.

38 Pl., *Resp.* 364b.

39 Plato, *Laws* 11 933E.

40 Matthew W. Dickie, *Magic and Magicians in the Greco-Roman World* (London: Routledge, 2001), 68–75.

41 *De natura deorum* 3.5; cf. Jörg Rüpke, *Religion in Republican Rome: Rationalization and Ritual Change* (Philadelphia: University of Pennsylvania Press, 2012), chs. 10–13 for how such definitions could serve as part of a process of rationalizing inherited Roman traditions.

42 Jörg Rüpke, *Religious Deviance in the Roman World: Superstition Or Individuality?* (Cambridge: Cambridge University Press, 2016), makes the case that these writers intended to maintain elite control over religion in this transformed, "knowledge"-based form as well.

43 Peter van Nuffelen, "Varro's Divine Antiquities: Roman Religion as an Image of Truth," *Classical Philology* 105, no. 2 (2010): 162–88.

44 *Scholia Bobiensia*; Cicero *Against Vatinius* 14.

45 A "sodalicium sacrilegi," Ps.-Cicero, *In Sallustium invectiva* 5.14. Note though the important critique of this reading of the passage by Federico Santangelo, "Whose Sacrilege?: A Note on Sal. 5.14," *Classical World* 104, no. 3 (2011): 333–8, citing other, earlier critical literature.

46 Cicero, *Against Vatinius* 14.

47 Suetonius, *Augustus* 94; Apuleius, *De magia* 42; cf. Katharina Volk, "Signs, Seers and Senators: Divinatory Expertise in Cicero and Nigidius Figulus," in *Authority and Expertise in Ancient Scientific Culture*, eds. Jason König and Greg Woolf, 329–47 (New York: Cambridge University Press, 2017), although I find such use of divination in this period is less unusual than she implies.

48 Augustine, *City of God* 7.9; hexameter verses preserved via Varro.

49 Cf. Keimpe Algra, "Stoic Philosophical Theology and Graeco-Roman Religion," in *God and Cosmos in Stoicism*, ed. Richard Salles, 224–51 (Oxford: Oxford University Press, 2009), on how Stoic views were more easily reconcilable with common Roman religious practices, and how this played out in philosophical debates with the Epicureans.

50 Cicero, *De divinatione* 2.148–9. For two seminal contributions to our understanding of this text see Mary Beard, "Cicero and Divination: The Formation of a Latin Discourse," *Journal of Roman Studies* 76 (1986): 33–46; and Malcolm Schofield, "Cicero For and Against Divination," *Journal of Roman Studies* 76 (1986): 47–65.

51 On these issues see Richard Gordon, "Superstitio, Superstition and Religious Repression in the Late Roman Republic and Principate (100 BCE–300 CE)," *Past and Present* 199 (suppl. 3) (2008): 72–94; and Federico Santangelo, *Divination, Prediction and the End of the Roman Republic* (Cambridge: Cambridge University Press, 2013), 10–47.

52 For a discussion of this learned hesitation to take the final position among other writers, see also Trevor Murphy, "Privileged Knowledge: Valerius Soranus and the Secret Name of Rome," in *Rituals in Ink: A Conference on Religion and Literary Production in Ancient Rome Held at Stanford University in February 2002*, eds. Alessandro Barchiesi, Jörg Rüpke, and Susan Stephens, 127–37 (Stuttgart: Franz Steiner Verlag, 2004).

53 Lucretius, *On the Nature of Things* 1.80–3.

54 For the former view, see Monica R. Gale, *Myth and Poetry in Lucretius* (Cambridge: Cambridge University Press, 1994); for the latter, Chris Eckerman, "Lucretius on the Divine: DRN 3.17–30, 5.1161–93, and 6.68–79," *Mnemosyne* 72, no. 2 (2019): 284–99.

55 Dirk Obbink, "Craft, Cult, and Canon in the Books from Herculaneum," in *Philodemus and the New Testament World*, eds. John Fitzgerald, Dirk Obbink, and Glenn Holland, 73–84 (Leiden: Brill, 2004); and David Sedley, "Epicureanism in the Roman Republic," in *The Cambridge Companion to Epicureanism*, ed. James Warren, 29–45 (Cambridge: Cambridge University Press, 2009).

56 Gordon, "Superstitio, Superstition and Religious Repression."

57 Clifford Ando, *The Matter of the Gods: Religion and the Roman Empire* (Berkeley: University of California Press, 2008), 15–17. Cf. Augustine, *City of God* 6.4; 6.9.

58 Cicero, *De legibus* 2.32–3; *De divinatione* 2.75. Cicero had access to Claudius Pulcher's work on the subject, cf. *Epistulae ad familiares* III.4.1.

59 Tacitus, *Annales* 3.58; Cassius Dio 54.36.1.

60 The best concise discussion of this controversy is Mary Beard, John North, and Simon Price, *Religions of Rome, Volume 1: A History* (Cambridge: Cambridge University Press, 1998), 1.126–29.

61 See Lindsay G. Driediger-Murphy, "Falsifying the Auspices in Republican Politics," in *Institutions and Ideology in Republican Rome: Speech, Audience and Decision*, eds. Henriette van der Blom, Christa Gray, and Catherine Steel, 183–202 (Cambridge: Cambridge University Press, 2018), for a careful analysis of how this played out in the conflict between M. Licinius Crassus and the tribune C. Ateius Capito with regard to the former's disastrous campaign in the East.

62 For an earlier instance, see Zsuzsanna Várhelyi, "Political Murder and Sacrifice," in *Ancient Mediterranean Sacrifice*, eds. Jennifer Wright Knust and Zsuzsanna Várhelyi, 125–41 (Oxford: Oxford University Press, 2011).

63 Anthony Corbeill, "The Function of a Divinely Inspired Text in Cicero's De haruspicum responsis," in *Form and Function in Roman Oratory*, eds. D. H. Berry and Andrew Erskine, 139–54 (Cambridge: Cambridge University Press, 2010).

64 For a good discussion of Cicero's speech now see Ingo Gildenhard, *Creative Eloquence: The Construction of Reality in Cicero's Speeches* (Oxford: Oxford University Press, 2011), especially his useful chart on page 305.

65 Mary Beard, "Cicero's 'Response of the Haruspices' and the Voice of the Gods," *Journal of Roman Studies* 102 (2012): 20–39, examining recent scholarly debates on this subject.

66 Gordon, "Superstitio, Superstition and Religious Repression." Cf. his point about the limited use of *superstitio* for non-Romans in this period, although human sacrifice now came to be seen as a particularly barbarian ritual.

67 Cassius Dio 47.40.

68 Cassius Dio 37.37; cf. also Cicero, *De lege agraria* 2.17–19.

69 Cicero, *Epistulae ad Atticum* 2.19.3.

70 Cf. Eric Orlin, *Foreign Cults in Rome: Creating a Roman Empire* (Oxford: Oxford University Press, 2010), ch. 7 with a subtle reading of Clodius' connections to the cult of Isis and possible reactions against Magna Mater.

71 Plutarch, *Life of Caesar* 61.3–4; J. A. North, "Caesar at the Lupercalia," *Journal of Roman Studies* 98 (2008): 144–60, suggests that the connection Caesar sought was with Romulus, another divinized former leader.

72 For a careful reading of the evolution of Cicero's thinking on the subject, now see Spenser Cole, *Cicero and the Rise of Deification at Rome* (Cambridge: Cambridge University Press, 2014).

73 Arnaldo Momigliano, "The Theological Efforts of the Roman Upper Classes in the First Century BC," *Classical Philology* 79, no. 3 (1984): 199–211; and Wallace-Hadrill, *Rome's Cultural Revolution*.

Chapter 7

1   Thucydides 3.82.1–5.

2   See Nicole Loraux, "Thucydide et la sédition dans les mots," *Quaderni di storia* 12 (1986): 95–134; June W. Allison, *Word and Concept in Thucydides* (Atlanta, GA: Scholars Press,

1997); Jonathan J. Price, *Thucydides and Internal War* (Cambridge: Cambridge University Press, 2001).

3 So the valuable discussion of Allison, *Word and Concept in Thucydides*, 164–72.

4 Plato, *Republic* 560c–e.

5 Plato, *Euthydemus* 275d; *Protagoras* 339e.

6 Plato, *Prt.* 339e5–340d. Relevant here as well are *Phaedrus* 267c4–6, 267b10. See William Fortenbaugh, *Theophrastus of Eresus, Volume 8: Commentary* (Leiden: Brill, 2005), 227–8. On Prodicus, see David Corey, "Prodicus: Diplomat, Sophist and Teacher of Socrates," *History of Political Thought* 29 (2008): 1–26; *Prodicus the Sophist: Text, Translation, and Commentary*, ed. Robert Mayhew (Oxford: Oxford University Press, 2012).

7 The tyrannicide committed by Harmodius and Aristogeiton, for example, was not a heroic act (as it was celebrated in Athens) but the result of irrational daring (*alogistos tolma*) provoked by erotic passion (*di' erotiken lupen*). Thuc. 6.94. Discussed by Allison, *Word and Concept in Thucydides*, 183–4.

8 They differ in the placement of the pitch accent. Heraclitus fr. 66B. See extensive discussion in Heraclitus, *The Cosmic Fragments*, trans. with an intro. by G. S. Kirk (Cambridge: Cambridge University Press, 1962), 116–22; Carol Poster, "The Task of the Bow: Heraclitus' Rhetorical Critique of Epic Language," *Philosophy and Rhetoric* 39 (2006): 1–21. (Presocratic fragments are from *Die Fragmente der Vorsokratiker*, eds. H. Diels and W. Kranz, 6th edn. [Berlin: Weidmann, 1951]; hereafter D-K).

9 Gorgias B11.8 D-K, with Charles P. Segal, "Gorgias and the Psychology of the Logos," *Harvard Studies in Classical Philology* 66 (1962): 99–155; James I. Porter, *The Origins of Aesthetic Thought in Ancient Greece: Matter, Sensation and Experience* (Cambridge: Cambridge University Press, 2010), 298–308. See also Philip Sydney Horky, "The Imprint of the Soul: Psychosomatic Affection in Plato, Gorgias and the 'Orphic' Gold Tablets," *Mouseion* 6 (2006): 371–86; J. A. E. Bons, "Gorgias the Sophist and Early Rhetoric," in *A Companion to Greek Rhetoric*, ed. Ian Worthington, 37–46 (Oxford: Wiley-Blackwell, 2007); E. E. Bieda, "Persuasion and Perception in Gorgias' 'Encomium to Helen': About the Powers and Limits of λόγος," in *Parmenides, Venerable and Awesome. Plato, Theaetetus 183e: Proceedings of the International Symposium*, ed. Néstor-Luis Cordera, 311–17 (Las Vegas: Parmenides Publications, 2011). Similar ideas were prevalent in fifth-century discussions of song: musical structures such as tunings and rhythms were thought to affect certain moods or states of soul (*ethê*) in their hearers. See Warren D. Anderson, *Ethos and Education in Greek Music: The Evidence of Poetry and Philosophy* (Cambridge, MA: Harvard University Press, 1966); Carnes Lord, "Damon and Music Education," *Hermes* 106 (1978): 32–43; Eleonora Rocconi, "La dottrina aristossenica dell' 'ethos' musicale nel 'de musica' dello Ps.-Plutarco," *Seminari romani di cultura greca* 8 (2005): 291–7; Robert W. Wallace, *Reconstructing Damon: Music, Wisdom Teaching, and Politics in Perikles' Athens* (Oxford: Oxford University Press, 2015).

10 Gorgias B11.11 D-K; Aristophanes, *Nubes*, esp. 890–1104; Aristophanes, *Clouds*, ed. K. J. Dover (Oxford: Clarendon Press, 1968), lvii–lxvi; Plato, *Apology* 17b.

11 See section 90, D-K, on Dissoi Logoi.

12 See especially Plato, *Cratylus* 437a–440e.

13 Aristotle, *On Interpretation* 16a4–9.

14 Aristotle covers the basic elements of his position at *On the Soul* 416b32–417b26 (on the causes of perception) and 427a18–433a9 (on the conversion of sensation into cognition); he sums it up almost aphoristically at *Posterior Analytics* 100a3–100b5.

15 Aristotle, *On Interpretation* 16a15–19.

16 Pl., *Phdr.* 264b–266b.

17 Aristotle, *Rhetoric* 1414a.

18 Arist., *Rh.* 1414b.

19 Arist., *Rh.* 1415b.

20 Arist., *Rh.* 1415b; 1414b; *Topica* 100a. There is a good discussion of the word *problema* in Aristotle, *Aristotele Organon*, ed. M. Migliori (Milan: Bompiani, 2016), 2184–6.

21 Quintilian, *Institutio oratoria* 10.3.33; see Sean Alexander Gurd, *Work in Progress: Literary Revision as Social Performance in Ancient Rome* (New York: Oxford University Press, 2012), 40.

22 Seneca, *Controversiae* 4 *praef.* 7–9.

23 Longinus, *On the Sublime* 22.

24 See Thomas Habinek, *The World of Roman Song: From Ritualized Speech to Social Order* (Baltimore: Johns Hopkins University Press, 2005); Maurizio Bettini, "Authority as 'Resultant Voice': Towards a Stylistic and Musical Anthropology of Effective Speech in Archaic Rome," *Greek and Roman Musical Studies* 1, no. 1 (2013): 175–94.

25 Gorgias B11.9 D-K.

26 Plato, *Philebus* 55e–56d (and what follows).

27 Gorgias B11.8 D-K.

28 Democritus B 5, 15c, 266; A 38, 44, 125 D-K.

29 Pl., *Resp.* 3.392d–298b (where "mimesis" means primarily the performative imitation of character) and *Resp.* 10.595a–608b, where it is associated with ontological degradation down and away from ideality and "really being."

30 Aristotle, *Poetics* 1450a5, with 1450b21–1451a35.

31 Nikolay P. Grintser, "Grammar of Poetry (Aristotle and Beyond)," in *Grammatical Theory and Philosophy of Language in Antiquity*, eds. Pierre Swiggers and Alfons Wouters, 71–99 (Leuven: Peeters, 2002). Grintser also saw that the *Poetics* was a distant influence on the syntax-theory of Apollonius Dyscolus.

32 Arist., *Poet.* 1447a20–5; Gurd, *Work in Progress*, 80–7.

33 Rudolph Pfeiffer, *History of Classical Scholarship from the Beginnings to the End of the Hellenistic Age* (Oxford: Clarendon, 1968), 79, 90, 123–51, 228; Rudolf Blum, *Kallimachos: The Alexandrian Library and the Origins of Bibliography*, trans. Hans H. Wellisch (Madison: University of Wisconsin Press, 1991); Peter Bing, "The Unruly Tongue: Philitas of Cos as Scholar and Poet," *Classical Philology* 98 (2003): 330–48.

34 See Gurd, *Work in Progress*, 80–7.

35 Hor., *Ars P.* 70–3, 46–8.

36 Horace, *Epistles* 2.2.109–19. See Gurd, *Work in Progress*, 95–103.

37 See especially Hippocrates, *De vetere medicina*.

38 On "practice and demonstration texts," see Thomas Cole, *The Origins of Rhetoric in Ancient Greece* (Baltimore: Johns Hopkins University Press, 1991), 81.

39 Aristotle, *Nicomachean Ethics* 1140a9; *Metaphysics* 981a10–981b7; *Posterior Analytics* 100a3–100b5.

40 Henri-Irénée Marrou, *Histoire de l'éducation dans l'antiquité* (Paris: Éditions du Seuil, 1965); Raffaela Cribiore, *Gymnastics of the Mind: Greek Education in Hellenistic and Roman Egypt* (Princeton, NJ: Princeton University Press, 2001).

41 Dionysius Thrax 1. See Robert Henry Robins, "The Initial Section of the Tékhnê grammatikê," in *Ancient Grammar: Content and Context*, ed. Pierre Swiggers and Alfons Wouters, 3–15 (Leuven: Peeters, 1996).

42 Plato, *Gorgias* 463a.

43 Quint., *Inst.* 2.11.4; 10.3.15; Hor., *Ars P.* 453–76; Dionysius of Halicarnassus, *On Literary Composition* 25 (Usher), *Demosthenes* 49–50.

44 David Blank, "Philodemus and the Technicity of Rhetoric," in *Philodemus and Poetry*, ed. Dirk Obbink, 178–88 (Oxford: Oxford University Press, 1995); Philodemus, *On Rhetoric, Books 1 and 2: Translation and Exegetical Essays*, trans. Clive Chandler (New York: Routledge, 2006), 59–104.

45 See especially Isocrates, *Against the Sophists*.

46 Cicero, *Brutus*, especially. See John Dugan, "Preventing Ciceronianism: C. Licinius Calvus' Regimens for Sexual and Oratorical Self-Mastery," *Classical Philology* 96 (2001): 400–28, 412–13.

47 See Dionysius of Halicarnassus, *On Literary Composition* throughout, as well as Longinus, *On the Sublime*.

48 Arist., *Rh.* 1408b.

49 Philodemus, *On Poems* 5, col xv.1–17. (Filodemo, *La Poesia V*, ed. C. Mangoni [Naples: La scuola di Epicuro, 1993]). See the remarkable discussion in James I. Porter, "Content and Form in Philodemus: The History of an Illusion," in *Philodemus and Poetry: Poetic Theory and Practice in Lucretius, Philodemus, and Horace*, ed. Dirk Obbink, 97–147 (Oxford: Oxford University Press, 1995), esp. 104–5.

50 C. O. Brink, *Horace on Poetry* (Cambridge: Cambridge University Press, 1963); Porter, "Content and Form in Philodemus," 143–152.

51 See Nathan A. Greenberg, "The Use of Poiema and Poiesis," *Harvard Studies in Classical Philology* 65 (1961): 263–89; G. B. Walsh, "Philodemus on the Terminology of Neoptolemus," *Mnemosyne* 40 (1987): 56–68; Elizabeth Asmis, "Crates on Poetic Criticism," *Phoenix* 46 (1992): 138–69. Elizabeth Asmis ("Neoptolemus and the Classification of Poetry," *Classical Philology* 87 [1992]: 206–31) identifies a conceptual triad similar to the one we are concerned with here in the area of oratorical theory, and speculated that that might be the source of Neoptolemus' distinctions. I emphasize the ultimate font of this tradition in Aristotelian unclarity about the nature of *technê*. It may indeed be, as Asmis suggests, that the Academy played a role in mediating and giving coherency to insights that, in our extant Aristotelian writings, remained unreconciled.

52 Philodemus, *On Poems. Book One*, ed. and trans. Richard Janko (Oxford: Oxford University Press, 2000), 165–89.

53 Philodemus, *On Poems*, 167–8, 237.

54 Arist., *Metaph.* 985b4 = 67 A6 D-K.

55 Pl., *Cra.* 411b–c.

56 Pl., *Cra.* 437a–440e.

57 Xenocrates, in Porphyry, *Commentary on Ptolemy's Harmonics* 30.27–31.26 (=F9 in *Xenokrates: Darstellung der Lehre und Sammlung der Fragmente*, ed. Richard Heinze [Hildesheim: Olms, 1965]).

58 Philodemus, *On Poems*, 121.

59 Asmis, "Crates on Poetic Criticism," contains an excellent overview here.

60 Asmis, "Crates on Poetic Criticism"; David Blank, "Diogenes of Babylon and the κριτικοί in Philodemus: A Preliminary Suggestion," *Chronache Ercolanesi* 24 (1994): 55–62; Philodemus, *On Poems*, 125–7.

61 Sextus Empiricus, *Adversus mathematicos* 1.79; discussion in Asmis, "Crates on Poetic Criticism."

62 This is one takeaway from his objection to euphonist uses of metathesis: when you change the order of words, says Philodemus, you also inevitably change the meaning as well. See, from

the Herculaneum Papyri, P. Herc. 1676 *Tractatus tertius* col. V.26–vi.27, p. 251 Sbordone, with David Armstrong, "The Impossibility of Metathesis: Philodemus and Lucretius on Form and Content in Poetry," in *Philodemus and Poetry: Poetic Theory and Practice in Lucretius, Philodemus, and Horace*, 210–32 (Oxford: Oxford University Press, 1995), esp. 220.

63 Discussed (with further bibliography) in Philodemus, *On Poems*, 173.

64 Cicero, *Orator* 81; Hor., *Ars P.* 47–8; Dionysius of Halicarnassus, *On Literary Composition* passim; compare Demetr., *Eloc.* 183–6.

65 James I. Porter, *The Sublime in Antiquity* (Cambridge: Cambridge University Press, 2016).

66 Demetrius, *On Style* 74, 176.

67 Demetrius, *On Style* 40, 105, 219, 255.

68 Demetrius, *On Style* 82, 96, 114.

69 See, for example, Dionysius of Halicarnassus, *Lysias* 11.

70 Philodemus, *On Poems* 5 col. xvi.5–11 (Mangoni), with Porter, "Content and Form in Philodemus," 105–7.

71 As Asmis ("Neoptolemus and the Classification of Poetry") saw.

72 Gurd, *Work in Progress*, 28–32. See also David Depew and Takis Poulakos, eds., *Isocrates and Civic Education* (Austin: University of Texas Press, 2004).

73 Seneca, *Epistles* 114.

74 But see David Armstrong, "The Addressees of the Ars Poetica: Herculaneum, the Pisones and Epicurean Protreptic," *Materiali e discussioni per l'analisi dei testi classici* 31 (1993): 185–230.

75 Hor., *Ars P.* 139.

76 Brink, *Horace on Poetry*, 1.3–42.

77 There is, to put this another way, a powerful and generative irony linking the persona of the poem and the subject of *Ars Poetica* 295–476. See Michael Wigodsky, "Horace and (Not Necessarily) Neoptolemus: The Ars poetica and Hellenistic Controversies," *Cronache Ercolanesi* 39 (2009): 8, and the excellent interpretation offered by Péter Hajdu, "The Mad Poet in Horace's Ars Poetica," *Canadian Review of Comparative Literature/Revue Canadienne de Littérature Comparée* 41 (2014): 28–42.

78 Speusippus: Sextus Empiricus, *Adversus mathematicos* VII.145–6 (fr. 75 ed. Taran). Diogenes of Babylon: Philodemus, *On Music* (ed. Delattre), col. 34.6–15. Dionysius of Halicarnassus, *On Literary Composition* 25.241–6.

79 Dionysius of Halicarnassus, *Lysias* 11.

80 Aulus Gellius, *Attic Nights* 13.21.

81 Dionysius of Halicarnassus, *Lysias* 11; *Thucydides* 51, with Cynthia Damon, "Aesthetic Response and Technical Analysis in the Rhetorical Writings of Dionysius of Halicarnassus," *Museum Helveticum* 48 (1991): 46–9.

82 Longinus, *On the Sublime* 7.3.

83 Longinus, *On the Sublime* 7.3.

84 Longinus, *Subl.* 14–15.

85 Longinus, *Subl.* 15.

86 Quintilian, *Institutio oratoria* 10.7.9–14.

87 Sen., *Ep.* 84.

88 Longinus, *Subl.* 8.

89 Aaron Pelttari, *The Space that Remains: Reading Latin Poetry in Late Antiquity* (Ithaca, NY: Cornell University Press, 2014), 8.

90 Augustine, *De ordine* 2.12.35–19.51.

91 Brian Stock, *Augustine the Reader: Meditation, Self-Knowledge, and the Ethics of Interpretation* (Cambridge, MA: Harvard University Press, 1996), 130–8.

Chapter 8

1   Michael Squire, "Conceptualizing the (Visual) 'Arts,'" in *A Companion to Ancient Aesthetics*, ed. Pierre Destrée and Penelope Murray, 307–26 (Oxford: Blackwell, 2015), 308–10, notes the difficulties and chooses to focus on painting and sculpture (and their parallel to verbal media). See also Jerry J. Pollitt, *The Ancient View of Greek Art: Criticism, History, and Terminology* (New Haven, CT: Yale University Press, 1974), 32–7; Pierre Destrée and Penelope Murray, "Introduction," in *A Companion to Ancient Aesthetics*, eds. Pierre Destrée and Penelope Murray, 1–13 (Oxford: Blackwell, 2015).

2   Stephen Halliwell, *The Poetics of Aristotle: Translation and Commentary* (Chapel Hill: University of North Carolina Press, 1987), 70: "A *technê* can be roughly defined as a productive skill or activity, which matches rational and knowledgeable means to the achievement of predetermined ends."

3   The *Imagines* of Philostratus (third century CE) claims to describe a collection of paintings in a villa near Naples while the poems of Christodorus of Coptus describe statues in the baths of Zeuxippus at Constantinople. On the collection of statues in the palace of Lausus see p. 148. On competitions in painting see Jeffrey M. Hurwit, *Artists and Signatures in Ancient Greece* (Cambridge: Cambridge University Press, 2015), 154–6. On collections see Jeremy Tanner, *The Invention of Art History in Ancient Greece: Religion, Society and Artistic Rationalisation* (Cambridge: Cambridge University Press, 2006), 21–9; Evelyne Prioux, *Petits Musées en vers: Epigramme et discours sur les collections antiques* (Paris: CTHS-INHA, 2008), 9–24; Agnès Rouveret, "Painting and Private Art Collections in Rome," in *A Companion to Ancient Aesthetics*, ed. Pierre Destrée and Penelope Murray, 109–27 (Oxford: Blackwell, 2015).

4   Aristotle's comments on musicians show that the professional pursuit could be considered unfit for a "free" man while the art itself could be acceptable within certain boundaries. See Pierre Destrée, "Aristotle on Music for Leisure," in *Music, Text and Culture in Ancient Greece*, eds. Tom Phillips and Armand D'Angour, 183–202 (Oxford: Oxford University Press, 2018).

5   As James I. Porter argues in "Why Art has Never been Autonomous" (*Arethusa* 43 [2010]: 165–80), the assumption that arts in the modern world are or were autonomous is itself questionable.

6   Kristeller's dating of the invention of aesthetics as a discipline to the eighteenth century has also raised challenges, most notably from Porter (*The Origins of Aesthetic Thought*) in a study that shifts the focus from aesthetic objects to aesthetic experience and its articulation. See also the contributions to Destrée and Murray, *A Companion to Ancient Aesthetics*.

7   In this respect, Andrew Ford (*The Origins of Criticism: Literary Culture and Poetic Theory in Classical Greece* [Princeton, NJ: Princeton University Press, 2002], 272–93) sees Plato and Aristotle as representing a new departure. On theater audiences in classical Athens see Martin Revermann, "The Competence of Theatre Audiences in Fifth- and Fourth-century Athens," *Journal of Hellenic Studies* 126 (2006): 99–124. The fact that so many Athenian men would have participated in choruses suggests that this expertise was technical. We can compare Aristotle's advice on music in his *Politics*, 1340b20–5: learning to play music as a child is useful for developing critical capacities in later life (for the male member of the leisured class). See Destrée, "Aristotle on Music for Leisure." For similar comments on drawing see Aristotle, *Politics* 1338a30–4.

8   On the *Poetics* see Halliwell, *The Poetics of Aristotle*, 12.

9   See Johanna Hanink, "Archives, Repertoires, Bodies, and Bones: Thoughts on Reperformance for Classicists," in *Imagining Reperformance in Ancient Culture: Studies in the Tradition*

of Drama and Lyric, eds. Richard Hunter and Anna Uhlig, 21–41 (Cambridge: Cambridge University Press, 2017).

10 See the remarks in Jeremy Tanner, "Aesthetics and Art History Writing in Comparative Historical Perspective," *Arethusa* 43 (2010): 274; Thea Ravisi, "Displaying Sculpture in Rome," in *A Companion to Ancient Aesthetics*, eds. Pierre Destrée and Penelope Murray, 248–61 (Oxford: Blackwell, 2015); and Rouveret, "Painting and Private Art Collections in Rome." The closest surviving examples are the rooms in Pompeiian villas with several paintings. On the potential interconnections between these see Jaś Elsner and Michael Squire, "Sight and Memory: The Visual Art of Roman Mnemonics," in *Sight and the Ancient Senses*, ed. Michael Squire, 180–204 (London: Routledge, 2016).

11 *Theodosian Code* 16.10.3; 16.10.8 (382 CE).

12 See Ruth Webb, *Demons and Dancers: Performance in Late Antiquity* (Cambridge, MA: Harvard University Press, 2008), 139–223.

13 Plutarch, *On the Fame of the Athenians* 3 = *Moralia* 346f.

14 Wesley Trimpi, "The Meaning of Horace's Ut Pictura Poiesis," *Journal of the Warburg and Courtauld Institutes* 36 (1973): 1–34. See also the Elder Philostratos, *Imagines, Proem*, 1: "both [painting and poetry] are equally concerned with the deeds and appearance of heroes."

15 Deborah Steiner, *Images in Mind: Statues in Archaic and Classical Greek Literature and Thought* (Princeton, NJ: Princeton University Press, 2003), 281–94; Porter, *The Origins of Aesthetic Thought*, 453–94.

16 Quintilian, *Institutio oratoria* 12.10.1–10. See Jerry J. Pollitt, *The Art of Ancient Greece: Sources and Documents*, 2nd edition (Cambridge: Cambridge University Press, 1990), 221–6; Habinek, "Rhetoric, Music, and the Arts."

17 Webb, *Ekphrasis*.

18 Plutarch, *Table-Talk*, 9.15 = *Mor.* 748 A; see Karin Schlapbach, *The Anatomy of Dance Discourse: Literary and Philosophical Approaches to Dance in the Later Graeco-Roman World* (Oxford: Oxford University Press, 2018), 75–7.

19 As suggested by Michael Baxandall, *Painting and Experience in Fifteenth Century Italy* (Oxford: Oxford University Press, 1974) for the Renaissance and Tanner, *The Invention of Art History in Ancient Greece*, 25, for classical Greek statues.

20 See Agnès Rouveret, *Histoire et imaginaire de la peinture ancienne (Ve siècle av. J.-C.–Ier siècle ap. J.-C.)* (Rome: Ecole Française de Rome, 1989), 438 and 444; Steiner, *Images in Mind*, 40; Porter, *The Origins of Aesthetic Thought*, 59–66, 440–4. On *summetria* see Pollitt, *The Ancient View of Greek Art*, 256–8, on *rhuthmos* see 169–81 and 218–28.

21 Paul Oskar Kristeller's conclusion ("The Modern System of the Arts: A Study in the History of Aesthetics (I)," *Journal of the History of Ideas* 12 [1951]: 506) that there is no systematic ancient thought about "the arts" follows directly on from his discussion of the Muses in which he notes the lack of a Muse of painting.

22 Penelope Murray, "The Muses and their Arts," in *Music and Muses: The Culture of "Mousikê" in the Classical Athenian City*, eds. Penelope Murray and Peter Wilson, 365–89 (Oxford: Oxford University Press, 2004); Murray, "The Muses in Antiquity," in *The Muses and their Afterlife in Postclassical Europe*, eds. Kathleen Christian, Clare Guest, and Claudia Wedepohl, 13–32 (London: The Warburg Institute, 2014); and James I. Porter, "Why are there Nine Muses?" in *Synaesthesia and the Ancient Senses*, eds. Shane Butler and Alex Purves, 9–26 (Durham, UK: Acumen, 2013).

23 Hesiod, *Theogony*, 63–73.

24 Habinek, *The World of Roman Song*.

25 Homer, *Iliad* 19.18–19.

26 See, for example, Homer, *Odyssey* 17.385.

27 Homer, *Odyssey* 1.107.

28 See, for example, Hom., *Il.* 24.3 and 3.441.

29 Anastasia-Erasmia Peponi, "Choral Anti-Aesthetics," in *Performance and Culture in Plato's Laws*, ed. Anastasia-Erasmia Peponi, 212–40 (Cambridge: Cambridge University Press, 2013), 217.

30 Hes., *Theog.* 22–34. In Homer, this aspect of the Muses is attributed to their deadly sisters, the Sirens. See Lillian Doherty, "Sirens, Muses and Female Narrators in the Odyssey," in *The Distaff Side: Representing the Female in Homer's Odyssey*, ed. Beth Cohen, 81–92 (Oxford: Oxford University Press, 1995).

31 Steiner, *Images in Mind*, 24–6.

32 Françoise Frontisi-Ducroux, *Dédale: Mythologie de l'artisan en Grèce ancienne* (Paris: François Maspero, 1975).

33 Stephen Halliwell, "Aristotelian Mimesis between Theory and Practice," in *Rethinking Mimesis: Concepts and Practices of Literary Representation*, eds. Saija Isomaa, Pirjo Lyytikäinen, Sanna Nyqvist, Merja Polvinen, and Riikka Rossi, 1–22 (Newcastle upon Tyne: Cambridge Scholars Publishing, 2012), 10.

34 Stephen Halliwell, *The Aesthetics of Mimesis: Ancient Texts and Modern Problems* (Princeton, NJ: Princeton University Press, 2002), 151–64, and "Aristotelian Mimesis between Theory and Practice."

35 Rouveret, *Histoire et imaginaire de la peinture ancienne*, 118.

36 Halliwell, "Aristotelian Mimesis between Theory and Practice," 10.

37 See Alexander Nehamas, "Plato on Imitation and Poetry in Republic 10," in *Plato on Beauty, Wisdom, and the Arts*, eds. Julius Moravcsik and Philip Temko, 47–78 (Lanham, MD: Rowman and Littlefield, 1982), 56–7.

38 See Halliwell, *The Aesthetics of Mimesis*, 352, on the *mimesis* of nature in Aristotle's *Physics* which does not imply any conscious intention.

39 On the meanings of the term see Göran Sörbom, *Mimesis and Art* (Stockholm: Svenska Bokförlaget, 1966).

40 On cultural *mimesis*, as in the Roman copying of Greek art, as a means of appropriating the power of the original see Feeney, *Literature and Religion at Rome*, 67–8.

41 Pliny, *Natural History* 35.81–3.

42 Porter, *The Origins of Aesthetics*, 248–51. On aniconism in ancient art see Milette Gaifman, *Aniconism in Greek Antiquity* (Oxford: Oxford University Press, 2012).

43 Paul Woodruff, "Mimesis," in *A Companion to Ancient Aesthetics*, eds. Pierre Destrée and Penelope Murray, 329–40 (Oxford: Blackwell, 2015), 338.

44 cf. Plato, *Cratylus* 432d. See Stephen Halliwell, "Beyond the Mirror of Nature: Plato's Ethics of Visual Form," in *Plato on Art and Beauty*, ed. Alison Denham, 173–204 (New York: Palgrave Macmillan, 2012), on the limits of the mirror analogy for painting in Plato's *Republic* 10.

45 Zeuxis and the women of a Sicilian city identified as Kroton or Akragas in Pliny, *Natural History* 35.64; Cicero, *On Invention* 2.1.1 (Pollitt, *The Art of Ancient Greece*, 150–1), and Dionysius of Halicarnassus, *On Imitation* 9.1.4. The same principle underlies Lucian's *Imagines*.

46 Plin., *HN* 35.65.

47 As Andrea Rotstein ("Mousikoi agones and the Conceptualisation of Genre in Ancient Greece," *Classical Antiquity* 31 [2012]: 92–127) has pointed out, his selection is at least partly shaped by the presence of all these arts in Athenian competitions, showing the impact of practice on ideas.

48 Aristotle, *Poetics* 1447 a26–8. On this definition of dance see Anastasia-Erasmia Peponi, "Aristotle's Definition of Dance," in *Choreutika: Performing and Theorising Dance in Ancient Greece*, ed. Laura Gianvittorio, 215–43 (Pisa: Fabrizio Serra, 2017).

49 These cases of direct speech in epic and drama were defined as *mimesis* and contrasted with *diegesis* (narration) by Socrates in Plato's *Republic* 392d5–394c5.

50 Arist., *Poet.* 1448 a1–18.

51 Aristotle, *Politics* 1340a18–b10; see discussion in Göran Sörbom, "Aristotle on Music as Representation," *Journal of Aesthetics and Art Criticism* 52 (1994): 37–46; Halliwell, *The Aesthetics of Mimesis*, 239–49. Also, cf. Xenophon, *Memorabilia* 3.10.1 discussed on p. 140.

52 "Likeness" is the translation proposed by Halliwell, *The Aesthetics of Mimesis*, 240; Mary-Anne Zagdoun, *L'esthétique d'Aristote* (Paris: CNRS Editions, 2011), 200, proposes "équivalence," which brings out more clearly the fact that the Greek term does not necessarily imply a relationship of copy to original.

53 Cf. Pl., *Resp.* 398 b6–401d, referring to the theories of Damon on the impact of different melodies, rhythms, and modes on the state of mind of the listener (400 b1) and *Laws* 656b4–7 on the invasive impact of music.

54 Arist., *Poet.* 1453a; *katharsis* mentioned in passing at Arist., *Poet.* 1449b28.

55 Malcolm Heath, "Aristotle and the Value of Tragedy," *British Journal of Aesthetics* 54 (2014): 111–23; Andrew Ford, "Catharsis: The Power of Music in Aristotle's *Politics*," in *Music and Muses: The Culture of "Mousikê" in the Classical Athenian City*, eds. Penelope Murray and Peter Wilson, 309–36 (Oxford: Oxford University Press, 2004).

56 In the *Sophist* 235b–236c, as in the *Republic*, painting is the prime example of beguiling and misleading appearances (Rouveret, *Histoire et imaginaire de la peinture ancienne*, 27–31; Steiner, *Images in Mind*, 63–70). The discussion in the *Cratylus*, 432a–d, however, seems to hint at the possibility that a visual representation can convey general information about a class of beings and in Plato's *Laws* 797–802 music and dance are admitted into the city albeit with restrictions and supervision. Elsewhere in the *Republic*, the philosopher is compared to an artist: *Republic* 472d4–7 and 484c, see Stephen Halliwell, *Plato, Republic 10: Translation and Commentary* (Warminster: Aris & Phillips, 1988), 8.

57 Pl., *Resp.* 393a3–b2.

58 See Porter, *The Origins of Aesthetics*, 334–5, on recitation as means of reviving the voice of the past. See also the portrayal of Agathon in Aristophanes, *Thesmophoriazousai* (p. 146).

59 Pl., *Resp.* 395d1–3.

60 Among the vast bibliography see Nehamas, "Plato on Imitation and Poetry in Republic 10"; Halliwell, *Plato, Republic 10*; and Judith Moss, "What is Imitative Poetry and Why is it Bad?" in *The Cambridge Companion to Plato's Republic*, ed. G. R. F. Ferrari, 414–44 (Cambridge: Cambridge University Press, 2007).

61 The same concerns are expressed in the distinction between eicastic representations, which respect the proportions of the original, and phantastic painting that produces an illusion through the use of distortions (such as perspective) in the *Sophist*. See Halliwell, *The Aesthetics of Mimesis*, 62–7; and Rouveret, *Histoire et imaginaire de la peinture ancienne*, 27–39.

62 Nehamas, "Plato on Imitation and Poetry in Republic 10," 56.

63 Rouveret, *Histoire et imaginaire de la peinture ancienne*, 13–127; and Jeremy Tanner, "Sight and Painting: Optical Theory and Pictorial Poetics in Classical Greek Art," in *Sight and the Ancient Senses*, ed. Michael Squire, 107–22 (London: Routledge, 2016). Rouveret argues for the theatrical origin for these techniques of trompe l'oeil painting.

64 Pl., *Resp.* 603 a1–b2. See Halliwell, *Plato, Republic 10*, 135 on the erotic connotations of the language used here.

65 Arist., *Poet.* 1451b5–7. See Halliwell, *The Aesthetics of Mimesis*, 193–9, on the interpretation of this difficult passage.

66 Christopher A. Faraone, "Binding and Burying the Forces of Evil: The Defensive Use of 'Voodoo Dolls' in Ancient Greece," *Classical Antiquity* 10, no. 2 (1991): 165–220; and Troels Myrup Kristensen, "Embodied Images: Christian Response and Destruction in Late Antique Egypt," *Journal of Late Antiquity* 2 (2009): 224–50.

67 Xenophon, *Economicus* 10.5. See Laurence Villard, "L'essor du chromatisme au IVe siècle: quelques témoignages contemporains," in *Couleurs et matières dans l'Antiquité: textes, techniques et pratiques*, eds. Agnès Rouveret, Sandrine Dubel, and Valérie Naas, 43–53 (Paris: Editions rue d'Ulm, 2006), 48–9.

68 Xenophon, *Memorabilia* 3.10.1–8.

69 See Plutarch, *Life of Alexander* 4.1, and on Xenophon, Halliwell, *The Aesthetics of Mimesis*, 122–4; Rouveret, *Histoire et imaginaire de la peinture ancienne*, 133–61.

70 Plotinus, "On Intelligible Beauty," *Ennead* 5.8.1, lines 6–40. See Plotinus, *Plotin. Traité 31: sur la beauté intelligible*, trans. and commentary by Anne-Lise Darras-Worms (Paris: Vrin, 2018); Halliwell, *The Aesthetics of Mimesis*, 313–23. Cicero, *Orator* 2.8–9 also speaks of the internal image in the artist's mind.

71 Dio Chrysostom, *Orationes* 12.25–6.

72 Dio Chrys., *Or.* 12.44–6.

73 See Rouveret, *Histoire et imaginaire de la peinture ancienne*, 133–5; Verity Platt, *Facing the Gods: Epiphany and Representation in Graeco-Roman Art, Literature and Religion* (Cambridge: Cambridge University Press, 2011) and Platt, "Sight and the Gods," in *Sight and the Ancient Senses*, ed. Michael Squire, 161–79 (London: Routledge, 2016).

74 Philostratus, *Life of Apollonius of Tyana* 6.19.

75 Halliwell, *The Aesthetics of Mimesis*, 308–10.

76 See Rouveret, *Histoire et imaginaire de la peinture ancienne*, 383–5.

77 Platt, *Facing the Gods*.

78 Stephen Halliwell, "Fiction," in *A Companion to Ancient Aesthetics*, eds. Pierre Destrée and Penelope Murray, 341–53 (Oxford: Blackwell, 2015).

79 Quoted by Plutarch, *On the Fame of the Athenians 5 = Moralia* 348c.

80 The Younger Philostratus, *Imagines*, Proem 4.

81 See Gérard Simon, *Le regard, l'être et l'apparence dans l'optique de l'antiquité* (Paris: Seuil, 1988), 21–41, and the essays in Michael Squire, *Sight and the Ancient Senses* (London: Routledge, 2016).

82 Plato, *Timaeus* 45 b–e. See also the use of the verb *ephaptomai* in Pl., *Ti.* 45d.

83 Both of these ideas are present in the conversation between Socrates and the courtesan Theodote in Xenophon, *Memorabilia* 3.11 that follows almost immediately on from his visits to the painter and sculptor at 3.10. See Simon Goldhill, "The Seductions of the Gaze: Socrates and His Girlfriends," in *Kosmos: Essays on Order, Conflict and Community in Classical Athens*, eds. Paul Cartledge, Paul Millett, and Sitta Von Reden, 105–24 (Cambridge: Cambridge University Press, 1998).

84 Plin., *HN* 35.65.

85 *Greek Anthology* 9.713–42; see Michael Squire, "Making Myron's Cow Moo? Ecphrastic Epigram and the Poetics of Simulation," *American Journal of Philology* 131 (2010): 589–634. Other animals: *Greek Anthology* 9.721, 730, 733–5, 739; humans: 9.715, 724–5, 731, 737, 739, 741.

86 Herodas, *Mimes* 4.59–65. Lifelikeness, at line 68; flesh liable to bleed, at lines 59–62. Text and commentary in Graham Zanker, *Herodas: Mimiambs* (Oxford: Aris and Phillips, 2009). On Herodas' engagement with Hellenistic art theory see Kathryn Gutzwiller, "Apelles and the Painting of Language," *Revue de Philologie, de Littérature et d'Histoire anciennes* 83 (2009): 39–63.

87 See also Xenophon, *Economicus* 10.5 (p. 140) and Villard, "L'essor du chromatisme au IVe siècle."

88 Goldhill, "The Naïve and Knowing Eye."

89 Squire, "Making Myron's Cow Moo?"

90 Zara Newby, "Absorption and Erudition in Philostratus' Imagines," in *Philostratus*, eds. Ewen Bowie and Jaś Elsner, 322–42 (Oxford: Oxford University Press, 2009).

91 The contrast is not sharp as we see in Valerius Maximus, *Memorabilia* 8.11. ext 4, who discusses Myron's cow and Praxiteles' Aphrodite alongside paintings that deceive viewers. See Stijn Bussels, *The Animated Image: Roman Theory on Naturalism, Vividness and Divine Power* (Leiden: Leiden University Press; Berlin: Akademie Verlag, 2012), 162–70.

92 On these effects in Roman painting as a form of art theory in practice see Nathaniel B. Jones, *Painting, Ethics, and Aesthetics in Rome* (Cambridge: Cambridge University Press, 2019), 47–70.

93 Xenophon, *Memorabilia* 3.10.6–8.

94 Cf. Tanner, *The Invention of Art History in Ancient Greece*, 83–4.

95 On the implied viewer see Jean-Marc Luce, "L'observateur implicite dans l'art de l'Antiquité," *Pallas* 105 (2017): 133–4.

96 Christine Mitchell Havelock, *The Aphrodite of Knidos and her Successors* (Ann Arbor: University of Michigan Press, 1995), 13–15.

97 Plin., *HN* 36.20, and pseudo-Lucian, *Amores* 15–16, both in Pollitt, *The Art of Ancient Greece*, 84–6.

98 This ambiguity is dramatized in the pseudo-Lucianic version of the Knidian Aphrodite where the goddess herself is said to have "suffered" (*epathen*) the assault.

99 Rosemary Barrow, "The Body, Human and Divine in Greek Sculpture," in *A Companion to Ancient Aesthetics*, eds. Pierre Destrée and Penelope Murray, 94–108 (Oxford: Blackwell, 2015), 98–100.

100 Jaś Elsner, "Between Mimesis and Divine Power: Visuality in the Greco-Roman World," in *Visuality Before and Beyond the Renaissance: Seeing as Others Saw*, ed. Robert S. Nelson, 45–69 (Cambridge: Cambridge University Press, 2000), 62. As Richard Gordon ("The Real and the Imaginary: Production and Religion in the Greco-Roman World," *Art History* 2 [1979]: 7) has noted, ancient authors often refer to statues by the name of the god making it difficult to know whether a mention of "Artemis" or "Athena" refers to the statue or to the divinity herself. See also Steiner, *Images in Mind*, 134, on the actions of Athena or her statue at *Iliad* 6.311. As Platt, *Facing the Gods*, 31 notes, depictions of divine images within the visual arts also play on the ambiguity.

101 See, for example, Dio Chrysostom, *Orationes* 12.47, and Porphyry fr. 316–18 Sm. See Sarah Iles Johnston, "Animating Statues: A Case Study in Ritual," *Arethusa* 41 (2008): 463–5.

102 Julian, *Letter* 89b ed. Bidez. See Johnston, "Animating Statues," 464; and Giorgios Deligiannakis, "Religious Viewing of Sculptural Images of Gods in the World of Late Antiquity: From Dio Chrysostom to Damaskios," *Journal of Late Antiquity* 8 (2015): 168–94.

103 See Steiner, *Images in Mind*, 156–68. Peter Stewart, "Gell's Idols and Roman Cult," in *Art's Agency and Art History*, eds. Robin Osborne and Jeremy Tanner, 158–78 (Oxford: Blackwell,

2007), points out that these actions on the part of devotees were themselves clearly understood as *mimeseis* in that they could take place at a distance from it.

104 Kristensen, "Embodied Images."

105 Arist., *Poet.* 1448b4–24.

106 Pollitt, *The Ancient View of Greek Art*.

107 Elsner, "Between Mimesis and Divine Power."

108 Xenophon, *Symposium* 9.1–7, *schemata* at 9.5.

109 Ismene Lada-Richards, *Silent Eloquence: Lucian and Pantomime Dancing* (London: Duckworth, 2007); Webb, *Demons and Dancers*.

110 Rosie Wyles, "The Tragic Costumes," in *The Pronomos Vase and Its Context*, ed. Oliver Taplin and Rosie Wyles, 231–53 (Oxford: Oxford University Press, 2010).

111 See Rossella Saetta Cottone, "Agathon, Euripide et le thème de la mimèsis dramatique dans les Thesmophories d'Aristophane," *Revue des études grecques* 116, no. 2 (2003): 445–69. On the meta-theatrical implications of cross-dressing in tragedy see Froma Zeitlin, *Playing the Other: Gender and Society in Classical Greek Literature* (Chicago: University of Chicago Press, 1996).

112 Pl., *Resp.* 10.603c4–606d7. Aristotle's focus is on tragedy as plot rather than as performance.

113 Seneca, *De Ira* 2.2.5. See Brad Inwood, *Reading Seneca: Stoic Philosophy at Rome* (Oxford: Oxford University Press, 2005), 57–9.

114 See Lada-Richards, *Silent Eloquence*; Webb, *Demons and Dancers*.

115 On the potential corporeal impact of the dance on its spectators see Ruth Webb, "Reperformance and Embodied Knowledge in Roman Pantomime," in *Imagining Reperformance in Ancient Culture: Studies in the Tradition of Drama and Lyric*, eds. Richard Hunter and Anna Uhlig, 262–80 (Cambridge: Cambridge University Press, 2017).

116 See, for example, the epitaph for the dancer Vincentius from Timgad (Algeria) in Marie-Hélène Garelli, *Danser le mythe: La pantomime et sa réception dans la culture antique* (Louvain: Peeters, 2007), 429–33, and the honorific inscriptions for Tiberios Ioulios Apolaustos (*Fouilles de Delphes, III. Épigraphie [Paris 1929-]* III.1.551 and I. Eph. 2070 and 1071) in Garelli, *Danser le mythe*, 444–7.

117 For examples see Webb, *Demons and Dancers*, 194–6.

118 Cyril Mango, Michael Vickers, and E. D. Francis ("The Palace of Lausus at Constantinople and its Collection of Ancient Statues," *Journal of the History of Collections* 4 [1992]: 89–98) discuss the later textual evidence. The exact location of the collection is still debated.

Chapter 9

1 J. G. A. Pocock, "The Origins of the Study of the Past: A Comparative Approach," *Comparative Studies of Society and History* 4 (1962): 209–46; J. G. A. Pocock, "Classical and Civil History: The Transformation of Humanism," *Cromohs* 1 (1996): 1–34.

2 Felix Jacoby, "On the Development of Greek Historiography and the Plan for the New Collection of the Fragments of the Greek Historians. The 1956 text with the editorial additions of Herbert Bloch," trans. M. Chambers and S. Schorn, *Histos* Supplement 3 (Newcastle upon Tyne, 2015), 6–8.

3 For example, M. L. West, *The Hesiodic Catalogue of Women: Its Nature, Structure and Origins* (Oxford: Clarendon Press, 1985); cf. Robert Fowler, "Genealogical Thinking, Hesiod's Catalogue, and the Creation of the Hellenes," *Proceedings of the Cambridge Philological Society* 44 (1998): 1–19; L. Bertelli, "Hecataeus: From Genealogy to Historiography," in *The Historian's Craft in the Age of Herodotus*, ed. N. Luraghi, 67–94 (Oxford: Oxford University Press, 2001), 73–6.

4 Generally on traditions of genealogical memory in early Greece and its function in expressions of civic life in archaic performance culture, see Rosalind Thomas, *Oral Tradition and the Written Record in Classical Athens* (Cambridge: Cambridge University Press, 1989), 173–5; Fowler, "Genealogical Thinking"; see also Elias J. Bickerman, "Origines Gentium," *Classical Philology* 47 (1952): 65–81.

5 Fragments of the early genealogists are collected in Felix Jacoby, *Fragmente der griechischen Historiker* (Leiden: Brill, 2013), 1–4 (hereafter *FGH*). Additional sources include texts by Simonides of Ceos (*FGH* 8); Polus of Acragas, *Genealogy of the Greeks and Barbarians who fought at Troy* (*FGH* 7 T1), possibly confused with Damastes of Sigeum's *On the fathers and ancestors of those who fought at Troy* (*FGH* 5 T1); and Anaximander, *Heroologia* (*FGH* 9 F1). On the history of early genealogical literature, see Felix Jacoby, "Hekataios," (1912) RE 7.2, coll. 2667–750; Thomas, *Oral Tradition and the Written Record*, 155–95; Jonathan M. Hall, *Ethnic Identity in Greek Antiquity* (Cambridge: Cambridge University Press, 1997), 40–65; Fowler, "Genealogical Thinking"; Bertelli, "Hecataeus."

6 David Asheri, "The Art of Synchronization in Greek Historiography: The Case of Timaeus of Tauromenium," *Scripta Classica Israelica* 11 (1991– 1992): 52–89; Denis Feeney, *Caesar's Calendar: Ancient Time and the Beginnings of History* (Berkeley: University of California Press, 2007), 7–42.

7 *FGH* 1 F1a. Concise discussion of this fragment in Bertelli, "Hecataeus," 76–89.

8 Jonas Grethlein, "Memory and Material Objects in the *Iliad* and the *Odyssey*," *Journal of Hellenic Studies* 128 (2008): 27–51.

9 Homer, *Iliad* 6.119–236; trans. Lattimore.

10 Pollitt, *The Ancient View of Greek Art*; Tanner, *The Invention of Art History in Ancient Greece*, 205–302.

11 To these may be added works on painting and painters by Duris of Samos (BNJ 76 F31–2). A concise overview of these writers, with excellent bibliography, may be found in Tanner, *The Invention of Art History in Ancient Greece*, 212–14.

12 Pliny, *Naturalis Historia* 35.67–8.

13 Plin., *HN* 35.56.

14 Plin., *HN* 34.59–71.

15 Francesco Ventrella, "Art and Aesthetics," in *A Companion to Intellectual History*, eds. Richard Whatmore and Brian Young, 358–76 (Oxford: Wiley Blackwell, 2015), 362–5.

16 Xenophanes in *Die Fragmente der Vorsokratiker*, ed. H. Diels and W. Kranz, 6th edition (Berlin: Weidmann, 1951) (hereafter D-K) 21 B1, 19–22. We should not forget, of course, that the hexametric tradition had its own means to voice concern about the reliability of information even in authoritative genres of human speech: hence Hesiod's remark concerning the "false things" known by the Muses (*Theogony* 27), on which see the chapter by Thomas Habinek in this volume.

17 On Anaxagoran moral philosophy see D-K 59 A1; for criticism of Homer and Hesiod in the cosmology of Heraclitus see D-K 22 A22, B57.

18 A further context is the revolution in the capacities of memory effected by writing. For important insights on the response of the early historians to the capacities of writing, see Virginia J. Hunter, *Past and Process in Herodotus and Thucydides* (Princeton, NJ: Princeton University Press, 1982), 286–96; with Eric Havelock, *Prologue to Greek Literacy* (Cincinnati: University of Cincinnati, 1971), 53–4, 60; and Cole, *The Origins of Rhetoric in Ancient Greece*, 104–12.

19 W. R. Connor, "The *histor* in History," in *Nomodeiktes: Greek Studies in Honor of Martin Ostwald*, eds. Ralph M. Rosen and Joseph Farrell, 3–15 (Ann Arbor: University of Michigan Press, 1993); Rosalind Thomas, *Herodotus in Context* (Cambridge: Cambridge University Press, 2000), 161–67; R. L. Fowler, "Herodotus and his Prose Predecessors," in

The Cambridge Companion to Herodotus, eds. Carolyn Dewald and John Marincola, 29–45 (Cambridge: Cambridge University Press, 2006), 29–33.

20 Heraclitus, D-K 22 B129.

21 Hippocratic corpus, *De vetere medicina* 20, *de Arte* 1.1.

22 Herodotus, *Histories*, preface; trans. Godolphin.

23 Egbert J. Bakker, "The Making of History: Herodotus' 'historiês apodexis'," in *Brill's Companion to Herodotus*, eds. Egbert J. Bakker, Irene J. F. De Jong, and Hans Van Wees, 3–32 (Leiden: Brill, 2002).

24 H. R. Immerwahr, "*Ergon*: History as a Monument in Herodotus and Thucydides," *American Journal of Philology* 81 (1960): 261–90.

25 On Herodotus's own statements on method see David Asheri, Allen B. Lloyd, and A. Corcella, *A Commentary on Herodotus, Books I–IV*, eds. O. Murray and A. Moreno, with a contribution by M. Brosius (Oxford: Oxford University Press, 2007), 288–32.

26 Valuable introductions include Donald Lateiner, *The Historical Method of Herodotus* (Toronto: University of Toronto Press, 1989); Rosalind Thomas, "Herodotus' 'Histories' and the Floating Gap," in *The Historian's Craft in the Age of Herodotus*, ed. Nino Luraghi, 198–210 (Oxford: Oxford University Press, 2001); Nino Luraghi, "Meta-'historiē': Method and Genre in the 'Histories'," in *The Cambridge Companion to Herodotus*, eds. Carolyn Dewald and John Marincola, 76–91 (Cambridge: Cambridge University Press, 2006).

27 See the chapter of Thomas Habinek.

28 S. Hornblower, *Thucydides* (Baltimore: Johns Hopkins University Press, 1987), 13–33; J. L. Moles, "Truth and Untruth in Herodotus and Thucydides," in *Lies and Fiction in the Ancient World*, eds. C. Gill and T. P. Wiseman, 88–121 (Exeter: University of Exeter Press, 1993).

29 For example, Thucydides, *History of the Peloponnesian War* 1.20, 97, 6.54–5.

30 Thuc. 1.22–3.

31 Thuc. 1.21.1–2.

32 The division between remote and recent past was conventional, familiar since Herodotus (e.g., *Histories* 1.5.3). Some caution is appropriate. Thucydides does not deny all possibility of knowledge of the remote past, describing, for example, the testimony of Homer or the physical remains of a Chian burial site as "tokens" or "signs" of a long-ago past (e.g., Thuc. 1.1.3, 3.3, 20.1, with Hornblower, *Thucydides*, 96–109.

33 Thuc. 1.21.1; see also 1.9.4 and 1.10.3.

34 Thuc. 1.22.3.

35 Thucydides, *The Peloponnesian War, Book II*, ed. J. S. Rusten (Cambridge: Cambridge University Press, 1989), 7–9.

36 Thuc. 1.10.3.

37 For more on this, see the article by Lloyd in this volume.

38 For example, Aristotle, *Historia animalium* 491a7–14.

39 Christopher P. Long, "Saving '*ta legomena*': Aristotle and the History of Philosophy," *Review of Metaphysics* 60 (2006): 247–67.

40 Aristotle, *De incessu animalium* 704b9; see also *Hist. an.* 491a7–14, *De partibus animalium* 646a8–12.

41 Raymond Weil, *Aristote et l'histoire: Essai sur la "Politique"* (Paris: Klincksieck, 1960); Leonid Zhmud, *The Origin of the History of Science in Classical Antiquity*, trans. A. Chernoglazov (Berlin: De Gruyter, 2006).

42 Pfeiffer, *History of Classical Scholarship*, esp. 87–251; König, Oikonomopoulou, and Woolf, *Ancient Libraries*; S. Johnstone, "A New History of Libraries and Books in the Hellenistic Period," *Classical Antiquity* 33 (2014): 347–93.

43 Arnaldo Momigliano, *The Classical Foundations of Modern Historiography*, with a foreword by R. Di Donato (Berkeley: University of California Press, 1990), esp. ch. 3.

44 Chronography: Feeney, *Caesar's Calendar*, 68–107; grammar and literary criticism: Pfeiffer, *History of Classical Scholarship*, 87–251; Francesca Schironi, *The Best of the Grammarians: Aristarchus of Samothrace on the Iliad* (Ann Arbor: University of Michigan Press, 2018); and Gurd in this volume.

45 Mariachiara Angelucci, "Polemon's Contribution to the Periegetic Literature of the II Century B.C.," ὅρμος - *Richerche di Storia Antica* 3 (2011): 326–41.

46 Alexandra Trachsel, "Démétrios de Scepsis et son Τρωικὸς διάκοσμος, ou comment ordonner le passé mythologique de la Troade au IIe siècle av. J.-C.," *Polymnia* 3 (2017): 1–25.

47 *Die Fragmente der griechischen Historiker*, 2013 F26.

48 Elizabeth Rawson, *Intellectual Life in the Late Roman Republic* (Baltimore: Johns Hopkins University Press, 1985), 58–101; Claudia Moatti, *The Birth of Critical Thinking in Republican Rome*, trans. Janet Lloyd, with the collaboration of G. Rowe, J. Prim, and J. Harris (Cambridge: Cambridge University Press, 2015), esp. ch. 1, 3.

49 On Paetus see Moatti, *The Birth of Critical Thinking*, 96–7; on Gracchanus and Tuditanus, see Moatti, *The Birth of Critical Thinking*, 111–12.

50 See Gurd in this volume.

51 Cicero, *Academica Posteriora* 1.9; trans. Rackham.

52 Human Antiquities: Varro, *De M. Terenti Varronis Antiquitatum rerum humanarum libris XXV*, ed. and commentary by Paullus Mirsch (Leipzig: J. B. Hirschfeld, 1882); Divine Antiquities: M. *Terentius Varro, Antiquitates rerum divinarum*, ed. B. Cardauns (Mainz: Akademie der Wissenschaften und der Literatur, 1976). For overviews of Varro's work see A. Drummond, "M. Terentius Varro," in *The Fragments of the Roman Historians*, ed. Tim J. Cornell, 412–23 (Oxford: Oxford University Press, 2013); R. A. Kaster, "Terentius Varro, Marcus," Oxford Classical Dictionary online, https://doi.org/10.1093/acrefore/9780199381135.013.6699.

53 Varro, *Antiquities* 8.1, 4.

54 Varro, *Antiquities* 2.8–10.

55 On lists, see Marie Ledentu and Romain Loriol, eds., *Penser en listes dans les mondes grec et romain* (Bordeaux: Ausonius, 2020).

56 Our most explicit sources for this are found in Polybius, *Histories*; e.g., 12.28.2–5; with F. W. Walbank, *Polybius* (Berkeley: University of California Press, 1972), 66–96; see further below p. 160. Figures such as Callisthenes of Olynthus, Hieronymus of Cardia, and Demetrius of Phaleron all wrote histories from the perspective of close acquaintance with political and military affairs, as did Fabius Pictor, Cato, Postumius Albinus, and many others in the Roman tradition; concise discussion, with sources, in John Marincola, *Authority and Tradition in Ancient Historiography* (Cambridge: Cambridge University Press, 1997), 133–48; cf. the useful qualifications of C. W. Fornara, *The Nature of History in Ancient Greece and Rome* (Berkeley: University of California Press, 1983), 50–6.

57 Tim J. Cornell, ed., *The Fragments of the Roman Historians* (Oxford: Oxford University Press, 2013); Christina Shuttleworth Kraus, "The Language of Latin Historiography," in *A Companion to the Latin Language*, ed. James Clackson, 408–25 (Malden, MA: Wiley-Blackwell, 2011).

58 Peter Liddel and Andrew T. Fear, *"Historiae mundi": Studies in Universal History* (London: Duckworth, 2010).

59 John Dillery, *Clio's Other Sons: Berossus and Manetho, with an Afterword on Demetrius* (Ann Arbor: University of Michigan Press, 2015).

60 Thuc. 1.22. For sources and discussion of the opposition of usefulness and enjoyment, see, e.g., F. W. Walbank, "Profit or Amusement: Some Thoughts on the Motives of Hellenistic Historians," in *Purposes of History: Studies in Greek Historiography from the 4th to the 2nd Centuries B.C.: Proceedings of the International Colloquium Leuven, 24–26 May 1988*, eds. H. Verdin, G. Schepens, and E. de Keyser, 253–66 (Leuven: Katholieke Universiteit, 1990); cf. sources cited by Marincola, *Authority and Tradition in Ancient Historiography*, 43 n. 28. See especially the strong opposition of ψυχαγωγία ("entertainment") and ὠφέλεια ("benefit") in Dionysius of Halicarnassus' assessment of Theopompus (*ad Pomp.* 6.4 [= *FGH* 115 F 20]; cf. 5.56.1, 11.1.3–4). On curiosity as a category for historiographical classification: e.g., Polyb. 9.1–2; Diod. Sic. 1.37.4; Dion. Hal., *Thuc. 5*; cf. sources and discussion in Moatti, *The Birth of Critical Thinking*, 152–4.

61 Xenophon, *Hellenica* 5.1.4, 3.7.

62 For example, Polyb. 3.7.5–7l; 11.19a.1–3, 12.25b.2.

63 For example, Polyb. 1.14.1–6, 12.12.1–3.

64 Polyb. 12.25e.1–7, 25g.1–4.

65 Polyb. 9.1.1–5.

66 See Ker in this volume.

67 Clifford Ando, "Mythistory: the pre-Roman past in Latin Late Antiquity," in *Antike Mythologie in christlichen Kontexte der Spätantike – Bilde, Räume, Texte*, ed. H. Leppin, 205–18 (Berlin: De Gruyter, 2015), with bibliography; Ledentu and Loriol, *Penser en listes dans les mondes grec et romain*.

68 *Origo gentis Romanae*, preface; on this and related texts see Ando, "Mythistory."

69 *Inscriptions antiques du Maroc*, 2 vols., eds. Lionel Galand, James G. Février, Georges Vajda, Maurice Euzennat, Jean Marion, and Nadine Labory (Paris: Editions du Centre national de la recherche scientifique, 1966–2003), 94, lines 22–9.

70 Clifford Ando, "The Certainty of Documents: Records of Proceedings as Guarantors of Memory in Political and Legal Argument," in *The Discovery of the Fact*, eds. Clifford Ando and William P. Sullivan, 155–74 (Ann Arbor: University of Michigan Press, 2020).

71 *Acta Apollonii* 11.

72 *Acta Pionii* 19.1–2.

73 Eusebius, *Historia ecclesiastica* 5.18.9.

BIBLIOGRAPHY

PRIMARY AND COMMENTARIES

Aristophanes. *Clouds*. Edited by K. J. Dover. Oxford: Clarendon Press, 1968.

Aristotle. *Aristotele Organon*. Edited by M. Migliori. Milan: Bompiani, 2016.

Asheri, David, Alan B. Lloyd, and A. Corcella. *A Commentary on Herodotus, Books I–IV*. Edited by O. Murray and A. Moreno, with a contribution by M. Brosius. Oxford: Oxford University Press, 2007.

Early Greek Philosophy 2: Beginnings and Early Ionian Thinkers, Part I. Edited and translated by Andre Laks and Glenn M. Most. Cambridge, MA: Harvard University Press, 2016.

Filodemo. *La Poesia V*. Edited by C. Mangoni. Naples: La scuola di Epicuro, 1993.

Die Fragmente der Vorsokratiker. Edited by H. Diels and W. Kranz. 6th edition. Berlin: Weidmann, 1951.

The Hellenistic Philosophers. Edited by Anthony A. Long and David N. Sedley. 2 volumes. Cambridge: Cambridge University Press, 1987.

Heraclitus. *The Cosmic Fragments*. Translated with an introduction by G. S. Kirk. Cambridge: Cambridge University Press, 1962.

Hesiod. *The Homeric Hymns and Homerica*. Loeb Classical Library. Translated by Hugh G. Evelyn-White. London: H. Heinemann; Cambridge, MA; Harvard University Press, [1936] 1964.

Hesiod. *Hesiodi Theogonia. Opera et dies. Scutum. Fragmenta selecta*. Edited by Friedrich Solmsen, Reinhold Merkelbach, and Martin L. West. Oxford: Clarendon Press, 1990.

Homer. *Homeri Opera. Recognovit adnotatione critica instruxit Thomas W. Allen. Tomus III: Odysseae Libros I–XII continens. Tomus IV: Odysseae Libros XIII–XXIV continens. Editio altera*. Oxford: Clarendon Press, 1917.

Homer. *The Odyssey: Volume I: Books 1–12*. Loeb Classical Library. Translated by August T. Murray and revised by George E. Dimock. Cambridge, MA: Harvard University Press, 1919.

Homer. *Homeri Opera. Recognoverunt brevique andnotatione critica instruxerunt David B. Munro et Thomas W. Allen. Tomus I: Iliadis Libros I–XII continens. Tomus II: Iliadis Libros XIII–XXIV continens. Editio tertia*. Oxford: Clarendon Press, 1920.

Homer. *The Iliad of Homer*. Translated with an introduction by Richmond Lattimore. Chicago: University of Chicago Press, 1976.

Homer. *The Odyssey of Homer*. Translated with an introduction by Richmond Lattimore. New York: Harper & Row, 1977.

Hyginus. *Fabulae*. Edited by Peter K. Marshall. Editio altera. Bibliotheca scriptorum Graecorum et Romanorum Teubneriana. Munich: K. G. Saur, 2002.

Inscriptions antiques du Maroc, 2 vols. Edited by Lionel Galand, James G. Février, Georges Vajda, Maurice Euzennat, Jean Marion, and Nadine Labory. Paris: Editions du Centre national de la recherche scientifique, 1966–2003.

Philodemus. *On Poems. Book One*. Edited and translated by Richard Janko. Oxford: Oxford University Press, 2000.

Philodemus. *On Rhetoric, Books 1 and 2: Translation and Exegetical Essays*. Translated by Clive Chandler. New York: Routledge, 2006.

Plato. *Platonis Opera. Recognoverunt brevique adnotatione critica instruxerunt Elizabeth A. Duke, W. F. Hicken, W. S. M. Nicoll, D. B. Robinson, J. C. G. Strachan. Tomus I: Tetralogias I–II continens*. Oxford: Clarendon Press, 1995.

Plato. *Platonis Rempublicam. Recognovit brevique adnotatione critica instruxit*. Edited by S[imon]. R. Slings. Oxford: Clarendon Press, 2003.

Plotinus. *Plotinus*. Translated by Stephen Mackenna. London: P. L. Warner, publisher to the Medici Society, 1921.

Plotinus. *Plotin. Traité 31: sur la beauté intelligible*. Translation and commentary by Anne-Lise Darras-Worms. Paris: Vrin, 2018.

Prodicus the Sophist: Text, Translation, and Commentary. Edited by Robert Mayhew. Oxford: Oxford University Press, 2012.

Seneca. *Epistles. Volume III: Epistles 93–124*. Loeb Classical Library. Translated by Richard M. Gummere. Cambridge, MA: Harvard University Press, 1925.

Seneca. *L. Annaei Senecae. Ad Lucilium epistulae morales. Tomus II: Libri XIV–XX*, edited by L. D. Reynolds. Oxford: Clarendon Press, 1965.

M. Terentius Varro, Antiquitates rerum divinarum. Edited and commentary by B. Cardauns. Mainz: Akademie der Wissenschaften und der Literatur, 1976.

Thucydides. *The Peloponnesian War, Book II*. Edited by J. S. Rusten. Cambridge: Cambridge University Press, 1989.

Varro. *De M. Terenti Varronis Antiquitatum rerum humanarum libris XXV*. Edited by Paullus Mirsch. Leipzig: J. B. Hirschfeld, 1882.

Xenokrates: Darstellung der Lehre und Sammlung der Fragmente. Edited by Richard Heinze. Hildesheim: Olms, 1965.

SECONDARY

Algra, Keimpe. "Stoic Philosophical Theology and Graeco-Roman Religion." In *God and Cosmos in Stoicism*, edited by Richard Salles, 224–51. Oxford: Oxford University Press, 2009.

Allison, June W. *Word and Concept in Thucydides*. Atlanta, GA: Scholars Press, 1997.

Anderson, Miranda, Douglas Cairns, and Mark Spevak, eds. *History of Distributed Cognition in Antiquity*. Edinburgh: Edinburgh University Press, 2018.

Anderson, Warren D. *Ethos and Education in Greek Music: The Evidence of Poetry and Philosophy*. Cambridge, MA: Harvard University Press, 1966.

Ando, Clifford. *Imperial Ideology and Provincial Loyalty in the Roman Empire*. Berkeley: University of California Press, 2000.

Ando, Clifford. *The Matter of the Gods: Religion and the Roman Empire*. Berkeley: University of California Press, 2008.

Ando, Clifford. "Evidence and Orthopraxy." *Journal of Roman Studies* 99 (2009): 171–81.

Ando, Clifford. *Roman Social Imaginaries*. Language and Thought in Contexts of Empire. Toronto: University of Toronto Press, 2015.

Ando, Clifford. "Mythistory: the Pre-Roman Past in Latin Late Antiquity." In *Antike Mythologie in christlichen Kontexte der Spätantike – Bilde, Räume, Texte*, edited by H. Leppin, 205–18. Berlin: De Gruyter, 2015.

Ando, Clifford. "Colonialism, Colonization: Roman Perspectives." In *The Oxford Handbook of Literatures of the Roman Empire*, edited by Daniel L. Selden and Phiroze Vasunia. Oxford: Oxford University Press, 2016.

Ando, Clifford. "Making Romans: Democracy and Social Differentiation under Rome." In *Cosmopolitanism and Empire: Universal Rulers, Local Elites and Cultural Integration in the Ancient Near East and Mediterranean*, edited by Myles Lavan, Richard E. Payne, and John Weisweiler, 169–85. Oxford: Oxford University Press, 2016.

Ando, Clifford. "City, Village, Sacrifice: The Political Economy of Religion in the Early Roman Empire." In *Mass and Elite in the Greek and Roman World from Sparta to Late Antiquity*, edited by Richard Evans, 118–36. New York: Routledge, 2017.

Ando, Clifford. "Review of John Ma, *Statues and Cities*." *Bryn Mawr Classical Review* (2014). Available online: http://bmcr.brynmawr.edu/2014/2014-02-21.html (accessed August 2, 2018).

Ando, Clifford. "The Political Economy of the Hellenistic Polis: Comparative and Modern Perspectives." In *The Polis in the Hellenistic World*, edited by Henning Börm and Nino Luraghi, 9–26. Stuttgart: Franz Steiner, 2018.

Ando, Clifford. "Race and Citizenship in Roman Law and Administration." In *Xenofobia y Racismo en el Mundo Antiguo*, edited by Francisco Marco Simón, Francisco Pina Polo, and J. Remesal Rodríguez, 175–88. Barcelona: Edicions de la Universitat de Barcelona, 2019.

Ando, Clifford. "The Certainty of Documents: Records of Proceedings as Guarantors of Memory in Political and Legal Argument." In *The Discovery of the Fact*, edited by Clifford Ando and William P. Sullivan, 155–74. Ann Arbor: University of Michigan Press, 2020.

Angelucci, Mariachiara. "Polemon's Contribution to the Periegetic Literature of the II Century B.C." ὅρμος - *Richerche di Storia Antica* 3 (2011): 326–41.

Armstrong, David. "The Addressees of the Ars Poetica: Herculaneum, the Pisones and Epicurean Protreptic." *Materiali e discussioni per l'analisi dei testi classici* 31 (1993): 185–230.

Armstrong, David. "The Impossibility of Metathesis: Philodemus and Lucretius on Form and Content in Poetry." In *Philodemus and Poetry: Poetic Theory and Practice in Lucretius, Philodemus, and Horace*, edited by Dirk Obbink, 210–32. Oxford: Oxford University Press, 1995.

Asheri, David. "Leggi greche sul problema dei debiti." *Studi classici e orientali* 18 (1969): 5–122.

Asheri, David. "The Art of Synchronization in Greek Historiography: The Case of Timaeus of Tauromenium." *Scripta Classica Israelica* 11 (1991–1992): 52–89.

Asmis, Elizabeth. "Crates on Poetic Criticism." *Phoenix* 46 (1992): 138–69.

Asmis, Elizabeth. "Neoptolemus and the Classification of Poetry." *Classical Philology* 87 (1992): 206–31.

Aydede, Murat. "Aristotle on *Epistêmê* and *Nous*: The Posterior Analytics." *Southern Journal of Philosophy* 36, no. 1 (1998): 15–46.

Backman, Jussi. "Self-Care and Total Care: The Twofold Return of Care in Twentieth-Century Thought." *International Journal of Philosophy and Theology* 81, no. 3 (2020): 275–91.

Balot, Ryan K. *Greed and Injustice in Classical Athens*. Princeton, NJ: Princeton University Press, 2001.

Bakker, Egbert J. "The Making of History: Herodotus' *historiês apodexis*'." In *Brill's Companion to Herodotus*, edited by Egbert J. Bakker, Irene J. F. De Jong, and Hans Van Wees, 3–32. Leiden: Brill, 2002.

Barrow, Rosemary. "The Body, Human and Divine in Greek Sculpture." In *A Companion to Ancient Aesthetics*, edited by Pierre Destrée and Penelope Murray, 94–108. Oxford: Blackwell, 2015.

Baxandall, Michael. *Painting and Experience in Fifteenth Century Italy*. Oxford: Oxford University Press, 1974.

Beard, Mary. "Cicero and Divination: The Formation of a Latin Discourse." *Journal of Roman Studies* 76 (1986): 33–46.

Beard, Mary. "A Complex of Times: No More Sheep on Romulus' Birthday." *Proceedings of the Cambridge Philosophical Society* 33 (1987): 1–15.

Beard, Mary. "Cicero's 'Response of the Haruspices' and the Voice of the Gods." *Journal of Roman Studies* 102 (2012): 20–39.

Beard, Mary, John North, and Simon Price. *Religions of Rome, Volume 1: A History*. Cambridge: Cambridge University Press, 1998.

Beck, Hans, and Peter Funke, eds. *Federalism in Greek Antiquity*. Cambridge: Cambridge University Press, 2015.

Beecroft, Alexander J. "'This is Not a True Story': Stesichorus' Palinode and the Revenge of the Epichoric." *Transactions of the American Philological Association* 136, no. 1 (2006): 47–70.

Bergren, Ann. *The Etymology and Usage of Peirar in Early Greek Poetry: A Study in the Interrelationship of Metrics, Linguistics, and Poetics*. Philadelphia: American Philological Association, 1975.

Berryman, Sylvia. *The Mechanical Hypothesis in Ancient Greek Natural Philosophy*. Cambridge: Cambridge University Press, 2009.

Bertelli, L. "Hecataeus: From Genealogy to Historiography." In *The Historian's Craft in the Age of Herodotus*, edited by N. Luraghi, 67–94. Oxford: Oxford University Press, 2001.

Bettini, Maurizio. "Authority as 'Resultant Voice': Towards a Stylistic and Musical Anthropology of Effective Speech in Archaic Rome." *Greek and Roman Musical Studies* 1, no. 1 (2013): 175–94.

Bickerman, Elias J. "Origines Gentium." *Classical Philology* 47 (1952): 65–81.

Bieda, E. E. "Persuasion and Perception in Gorgias' 'Encomium to Helen': About the Powers and Limits of λόγος." In *Parmenides, Venerable and Awesome. Plato, Theaetetus 183e: Proceedings of the International Symposium*, edited by Néstor-Luis Cordera, 311–17. Las Vegas: Parmenides Publications, 2011.

Bing, Peter. "The Unruly Tongue: Philitas of Cos as Scholar and Poet." *Classical Philology* 98 (2003): 330–48.

Blank, David. "Diogenes of Babylon and the κριτικοί in Philodemus: A Preliminary Suggestion." *Chronache Ercolanesi* 24 (1994): 55–62.

Blank, David. "Philodemus and the Technicity of Rhetoric." In *Philodemus and Poetry*, edited by Dirk Obbink, 178–88. Oxford: Oxford University Press, 1995.

Blum, Rudolf. *Kallimachos: The Alexandrian Library and the Origins of Bibliography*. Translated by Hans H. Wellisch. Madison: University of Wisconsin Press, 1991.

Bons, J. A. E. "Gorgias the Sophist and Early Rhetoric." In *A Companion to Greek Rhetoric*, edited by Ian Worthington, 37–46. Oxford: Wiley-Blackwell, 2007.

Bourdieu, Pierre. "L'ontologie politique de Martin Heidegger." *Actes de la Recherche en Sciences Sociales* 1, nos. 5–6 (1975): 109–56.

Bowden, Hugh. "Impiety." In *The Oxford Handbook of Ancient Greek Religion*, edited by Esther Eidinow and Julia Kindt, 328–38. Oxford: Oxford University Press, 2015.

Boyer, Pascal. "Functional Origins of Religious Concepts: Ontological and Strategic Selection in Evolved Minds." *Journal of the Royal Anthropological Institute* 6 (2000): 195–214.

Boyer, Pascal. *Religion Explained: The Evolutionary Origins of Religious Thought*. New York: Basic Books, 2001.

Bremmer, Jan N. "Atheism in Antiquity." In *The Cambridge Companion to Atheism*, edited by Michael Martin, 11–26. Cambridge: Cambridge University Press, 2006.

Bresson, Alain. *The Making of the Ancient Greek Economy: Institutions, Markets, and Growth in the City-States*. Translated by Steven Rendall. Princeton, NJ: Princeton University Press, 2016.

Brink, C. O. *Horace on Poetry*. Cambridge: Cambridge University Press, 1963.

Brooke, John L., Julia C. Strauss, and Greg Anderson, eds. *State Formations: Global Histories and Cultures of Statehood*. Cambridge: Cambridge University Press, 2018.

Brunschwig, Jacques. "Epistemology." In *Greek Thought: A Guide to Classical Knowledge*, edited by J. Brunschwig and G. Lloyd, 72–93. Cambridge, MA: Harvard University Press, 2000.

Brunschwig, Jacques, and Geoffrey E. R. Lloyd, eds. *Greek Thought: A Guide to Classical Knowledge*. Cambridge, MA: Harvard University Press, 2000.

Brunt, P. A. *Social Conflicts in the Roman Republic*. London: Chatto & Windus, 1971.

Brunt, P. A. "Stoicism and the Principate." *Papers of the British School at Rome* 43 (1975): 7–35.

Brunt, P. A. *The Fall of the Roman Republic and Related Essays*. Oxford: Clarendon Press, 1988.

Bryen, Ari Z. "Reading the Citizenship Papyrus (P.Giss. 40)." In *Citizenship and Empire in Europe, 200–1900. The Antonine Constitution After 1800 Years*, edited by Clifford Ando, 29–43. Stuttgart: Steiner, 2016.

Bundrick, Sheramy D. "Selling Sacrifice on Classical Athenian Vases." *Hesperia: The Journal of the American School of Classical Studies at Athens* 83 (2014): 653–708.

Burdach, Konrad. "Faust und die Sorge." *Deutsche Vierteljahrsschrift für Literaturwissenschaft und Geistesgeschichte* 1 (1923): 1–60.

Bussels, Stijn. *The Animated Image: Roman Theory on Naturalism, Vividness and Divine Power*. Leiden: Leiden University Press; Berlin: Akademie Verlag, 2012.

Cammack, Daniela. "The Dêmos in Dêmokratia." *Classical Quarterly* 69, no. 1 (2019): 42–61.

Champlin, Edward. *Final Judgments: Duty and Emotion in Roman Wills, 200 B.C.–A.D. 250*. Berkeley: University of California Press, 1991.

Chappell, Sophie-Grace. "Plato on Knowledge in the Theaetetus." *The Stanford Encyclopedia of Philosophy*, edited by Edward N. Zalta. Winter 2013. Available online: https://plato.stanford.edu/archives/win2013/entries/plato-theaetetus/ (accessed January 9, 2022).

Clark, Elizabeth A. *History, Theory, Text: Historians and the Linguistic Turn*. Cambridge, MA: Harvard University Press, 2009.

Coffee, Neil. *Gift and Gain: How Money Transformed Ancient Rome*. New York: Oxford University Press, 2017.

Coffey, John, and Alister Chapman. "Introduction." In *Seeing Things Their Way: Intellectual History and the Return of Religion*, edited by Alister Chapman, John Coffey, and Brad S. Gregory, 1–23. Notre Dame: Notre Dame University Press, 2009.

Cohen, David. *Law, Sexuality, and Society: The Enforcement of Morals in Classical Athens*. Cambridge: Cambridge University Press, 1994.

Cole, Spenser. *Cicero and the Rise of Deification at Rome*. Cambridge: Cambridge University Press, 2014.

Cole, Thomas. "The Sources and Composition of Polybius VI." *Historia: Zeitschrift für Alte Geschichte* 13 (1964): 440–86.

Cole, Thomas. "Archaic Truth." *Quaderni Urbinati di Cultura Classica* 13 (1983): 17–28.

Cole, Thomas. *The Origins of Rhetoric in Ancient Greece*. Baltimore: Johns Hopkins University Press, 1991.

Connell, Sophia M. *Aristotle on Female Animals: A Study on the Generation of Animals*. Cambridge: Cambridge University Press, 2016.

Connor, W. R. "The *histor* in History." In *Nomodeiktes: Greek Studies in Honor of Martin Ostwald*, edited by Ralph M. Rosen and Joseph Farrell, 3–15. Ann Arbor: University of Michigan Press, 1993.

Corbeill, Anthony. "The Function of a Divinely Inspired Text in Cicero's *De haruspicum responsis*." In *Form and Function in Roman Oratory*, edited by D. H. Berry and Andrew Erskine, 139–54. Cambridge: Cambridge University Press, 2010.

Corey, David. "Prodicus: Diplomat, Sophist and Teacher of Socrates." *History of Political Thought* 29 (2008): 1–26.

Cornell, Tim J., ed. *The Fragments of the Roman Historians*. Oxford: Oxford University Press, 2013.

Cribiore, Raffaela. *Gymnastics of the Mind: Greek Education in Hellenistic and Roman Egypt*. Princeton, NJ: Princeton University Press, 2001.

Cudd, Ann, and Seena Eftekhari. "Contractarianism." In *The Stanford Encyclopedia of Philosophy*, edited by Edward N. Zalta. Summer 2018. Available online: https://plato.stanford.edu/archives/sum2018/entries/contractarianism/ (accessed January 10, 2022).

Damon, Cynthia. "Aesthetic Response and Technical Analysis in the Rhetorical Writings of Dionysius of Halicarnassus." *Museum Helveticum* 48 (1991): 33–58.

D'Arms, John H. "Republican Senators' Involvement in Commerce in the Late Republic: Some Ciceronian Evidence." In *The Seaborne Commerce of Ancient Rome: Studies in Archaeology and History*, edited by John H. D'Arms and E. Christian Kopff, 77–89. Rome: American Academy in Rome, 1980.

Deligiannakis, Giorgios. "Religious Viewing of Sculptural Images of Gods in the World of Late Antiquity: From Dio Chrysostom to Damaskios." *Journal of Late Antiquity* 8 (2015): 168–94.

Depew, David, and Takis Poulakos, eds. *Isocrates and Civic Education*. Austin: University of Texas Press, 2004.

Descola, Philippe. *Beyond Nature and Culture*. Translated by Janet Lloyd. Chicago: University of Chicago Press, [2005] 2013.

Destrée, Pierre. "Aristotle on Music for Leisure." In *Music, Text and Culture in Ancient Greece*, edited by Tom Phillips and Armand D'Angour, 183–202. Oxford: Oxford University Press, 2018.

Destrée, Pierre, and Penelope Murray. "Introduction." In *A Companion to Ancient Aesthetics*, edited by P. Destrée and P. Murray, 1–13. Oxford: Blackwell, 2015.

Detienne, Marcel. *The Masters of Truth in Archaic Greece*. Translated by Janet Lloyd. New York: Zone Books, [1967] 1999.

Dickie, Matthew W. *Magic and Magicians in the Greco-Roman World*. London: Routledge, 2001.

Dillery, John. *Clio's Other Sons: Berossus and Manetho, with an Afterword on Demetrius*. Ann Arbor: University of Michigan Press, 2015.

Dixon, Dustin W. "Reconsidering Euripides' *Bellerophon*." *Classical Quarterly* 64, no. 2 (2014): 493–506.

Doherty, Lillian. "Sirens, Muses and Female Narrators in the Odyssey." In *The Distaff Side: Representing the Female in Homer's Odyssey*, edited by Beth Cohen, 81–92. Oxford: Oxford University Press, 1995.

Domaradzki, Mikolaj. "Theological Etymologizing in the Early Stoa." *Kernos* 25 (2012): 125–48.

Dressler, Alex. *Personification and the Feminine in Roman Philosophy*. Cambridge: Cambridge University Press, 2016.

Driediger-Murphy, Lindsay G. "Falsifying the Auspices in Republican Politics." In *Institutions and Ideology in Republican Rome: Speech, Audience and Decision*, edited by Henriette van der Blom, Christa Gray, and Catherine Steel, 183–202. Cambridge: Cambridge University Press, 2018.

Drummond, A. "M. Terentius Varro." In *The Fragments of the Roman Historians*, edited by T. J. Cornell, vol. 1, 412–23. Oxford: Oxford University Press, 2013.

Dudley, D. R. "Blossius of Cumae." *Journal of Roman Studies* 31 (1941): 94–9.

Dugan, John. "Preventing Ciceronianism: C. Licinius Calvus' Regimens for Sexual and Oratorical Self-Mastery." *Classical Philology* 96 (2001): 400–28.

Dye, Ellis. "Sorge in Heidegger and in Goethe's Faust." *Goethe Yearbook* 16 (2009): 207–18.

Eckerman, Chris. "Lucretius on the Divine: *DRN* 3.17-30, 5.1161-93, and 6.68-79." *Mnemosyne* 72, no. 2 (2019): 284–99.

Eckstein, Arthur. *Mediterranean Anarchy, Interstate War, and the Rise of Rome*. Berkeley: University of California Press, 2006.

Edwards, Catharine. *The Politics of Immorality in Ancient Rome*. Cambridge: Cambridge University Press, 1993.

Edwards, Catharine. "Self-Scrutiny and Self-Transformation in Seneca's Letters." *Greece & Rome* 44 (1997): 23–38.

Edwards, Catharine. *Death in Ancient Rome*. New Haven, CT: Yale University Press, 2007.

Eidinow, Esther. *Oracles, Curses, and Risk Among the Ancient Greeks*. Oxford: Oxford University Press, 2007.

Eidinow, Esther, Julia Kindt, and Robin Osborne, eds. *Theologies of Ancient Greek Religion*. Cambridge: Cambridge University Press, 2016.

Elsner, Jaś. "Between Mimesis and Divine Power: Visuality in the Greco-Roman World." In *Visuality Before and Beyond the Renaissance: Seeing as Others Saw*, edited by Robert S. Nelson, 45–69. Cambridge: Cambridge University Press, 2000.

Elsner, Jaś, and Michael Squire. "Sight and Memory: The Visual Art of Roman Mnemonics." In *Sight and the Ancient Senses*, edited by Michael Squire, 180–204. London: Routledge, 2016.

Escudero, Jesus A. "Heidegger: Being and Time and the Care for the Self." *Open Journal of Philosophy* 3, no. 2 (2013): 302–7.

Faraone, Christopher A. "Binding and Burying the Forces of Evil: The Defensive Use of 'Voodoo Dolls' in Ancient Greece." *Classical Antiquity* 10, no. 2 (1991): 165–220.

Feeney, Denis. *Literature and Religion at Rome: Cultures, Contexts, and Beliefs*. Cambridge: Cambridge University Press, 1998.

Feeney, Denis. *Caesar's Calendar: Ancient Time and the Beginnings of History*. Berkeley: University of California Press, 2007.

Finley, M. I. *The World of Odysseus*. New York: Viking Press, 1965.

Finley, M. I. *Economy and Society in Ancient Greece*. Edited and with an introduction by Brent D. Shaw and Richard P. Saller. London: Chatto & Windus, 1981.

Finley, M. I. *The Ancient Economy*. 2nd edition. Berkeley: University of California Press, 1985.

Fitzgerald, William. *Slavery and the Roman Literary Imagination*. Cambridge: Cambridge University Press, 2000.

Flower, Michael. *The Seer in Ancient Greece*. Berkeley: University of California Press, 2008.

Ford, Andrew. *Homer: The Poetry of the Past*. Ithaca, NY: Cornell University Press, 1992.

Ford, Andrew. "Catharsis: The Power of Music in Aristotle's Politics." In *Music and Muses: The Culture of "Mousikê" in the Classical Athenian City*, edited by Penelope Murray and Peter Wilson, 309–36. Oxford: Oxford University Press, 2004.

Ford, Andrew. *The Origins of Criticism: Literary Culture and Poetic Theory in Classical Greece*. Princeton, NJ: Princeton University Press, 2002.

Fornara, C. W. *The Nature of History in Ancient Greece and Rome*. Berkeley: University of California Press, 1983.

Fortenbaugh, William. *Theophrastus of Eresus, Volume 8: Commentary*. Leiden: Brill, 2005.

Foucault, Michel. *Histoire de la sexualité, Volume 3: Le Souci de soi*. Paris: Gallimard, 1984.

Foucault, Michel. *Technologies of the Self: A Seminar with Michel Foucault*. Edited by Luther Martin, Huck Gutman, and Patrick Hutton. Amherst: University of Massachusetts Press, 1988.

Foucault, Michel. *L'Archéologie du savoir*. Paris: Gallimard, [1969] 2008.

Fowler, Robert. "Genealogical Thinking, Hesiod's Catalogue, and the Creation of the Hellenes." *Proceedings of the Cambridge Philological Society* 44 (1998): 1–19.

Fowler, R. L. "Herodotus and his Prose Predecessors." In *The Cambridge Companion to Herodotus*, edited by Carolyn Dewald and John Marincola, 29–45. Cambridge: Cambridge University Press, 2006.

Frontisi-Ducroux, Françoise. *Dédale: Mythologie de l'artisan en Grèce ancienne*. Paris: François Maspero, 1975.

Gaifman, Milette. *Aniconism in Greek Antiquity*. Oxford: Oxford University Press, 2012.

Gale, Monica R. *Myth and Poetry in Lucretius*. Cambridge: Cambridge University Press, 1994.

Garelli, Marie-Hélène. *Danser le mythe: La pantomime et sa réception dans la culture antique*. Louvain: Peeters, 2007.

Garland, Robert. *Introducing New Gods: The Politics of Athenian Religion*. Ithaca, NY: Cornell University Press, 1992.

Geller, Markham J. *Ancient Babylonian Medicine: Theory and Practice*. Chichester, UK: Wiley-Blackwell, 2010.

Gerson, Lloyd. *Ancient Epistemology*. Cambridge: Cambridge University Press, 2009.

Geus, Klaus. *Eratosthenes von Kyrene*. Studien zur hellenistischen Kultur- und Wissenschaftsgeschichte. Münchener Beiträge zur Papyrusforschung und antiken Rechtsgeschichte, 92. Munich: C. H. Beck, 2002.

Gildenhard, Ingo. *Creative Eloquence: The Construction of Reality in Cicero's Speeches*. Oxford: Oxford University Press, 2011.

Goethe, Johann Wolfgang von. *Faust: Eine Tragödie*. Tübingen: J. G. Cotta'schen Buchhandlung, 1808.

Goethe, Johann Wolfgang von. *Goethe, Faust, Parts 1 & 2*. Translated by Anthony S. Kline (= *Faust: Eine Tragödie*, Tübingen: J. G. Cotta'schen Buchhandlung, 1808 and *Faust: Der Tragödie zweyter Theil in fünf Acten*, Stuttgart, 1832). Available online: http://goethe.holtof.com/faust/FaustIScenesItoIII.htm (accessed September 22, 2019).

Goethe, Johann Wolfgang von. *Goethe' Werke: Vollständige Ausgabe letzter Hand. Ein und Vierzigster Band. Faust, Der Tragödie zweyter Theil in fünf Acten (Vollendet im Sommer 1831)*. Stuttgart: J. G. Cotta'schen Buchhandlung, 1832.

Goldhill, Simon. "The Naïve and Knowing Eye: Ekphrasis and the Culture of Viewing in the Hellenistic World." In *Art and Text in Ancient Greek Culture*, edited by Simon Goldhill and Robin Osborne, 197–223. Cambridge: Cambridge University Press, 1994.

Goldhill, Simon. "Refracting Classical Vision: Changing Cultures of Viewing." In *Vision in Context: Historical and Contemporary Perspectives on Sight*, edited by Teresa Brennan and Martin Jay, 15–29. New York: Routledge, 1996.

Goldhill, Simon. "The Seductions of the Gaze: Socrates and His Girlfriends." In *Kosmos: Essays on Order, Conflict and Community in Classical Athens*, edited by Paul Cartledge, Paul Millett, and Sitta Von Reden, 105–24. Cambridge: Cambridge University Press, 1998.

Gordon, Richard. "The Real and the Imaginary: Production and Religion in the Greco-Roman World." *Art History* 2 (1979): 5–34.

Gordon, Richard. "*Superstitio*, Superstition and Religious Repression in the Late Roman Republic and Principate (100 BCE–300 CE)." *Past and Present* 199 (suppl. 3) (2008): 72–94.

Graeber, David. *Debt: The First 5,000 Years*. Brooklyn, NY: Melville House, 2011.

Graeber, David, and Marshall Sahlins. *On Kings*. Chicago: HAU Books/University of Chicago Press, 2017.

Graham, Daniel. *The Texts of Early Greek Philosophy: The Complete Fragments and Selected Testimonies of the Major Presocratics*, Part 1. Cambridge: Cambridge University Press, 2010.

Greenberg, Nathan A. "The Use of Poiema and Poiesis." *Harvard Studies in Classical Philology* 65 (1961): 263–89.

Grethlein, Jonas. "Memory and Material Objects in the Iliad and the Odyssey." *Journal of Hellenic Studies* 128 (2008): 27–51.

Grewal, David. "The Invention of the Economy: A History of Economic Thought." PhD dissertation, Harvard University, 2010.

Grintser, Nikolay P. "Grammar of Poetry (Aristotle and Beyond)." In *Grammatical Theory and Philosophy of Language in Antiquity*, edited by Pierre Swiggers and Alfons Wouters, 71–99. Leuven: Peeters, 2002.

Gurd, Sean Alexander. *Work in Progress: Literary Revision as Social Performance in Ancient Rome*. New York: Oxford University Press, 2012.

Guthrie, W. K. C. *A History of Greek Philosophy, volume 1*. Cambridge: Cambridge University Press, 1962.

Gutzwiller, Kathryn. "Apelles and the Painting of Language." *Revue de Philologie, de Littérature et d'Histoire anciennes* 83 (2009): 39–63.

Habinek, Thomas. *The Politics of Latin Literature: Writing, Identity, and Empire in Ancient Rome*. Princeton, NJ: Princeton University Press, 1998.

Habinek, Thomas. *The World of Roman Song: From Ritualized Speech to Social Order*. Baltimore: Johns Hopkins University Press, 2005.

Habinek, Thomas. "The Wisdom of Ennius." *Arethusa* 39, no. 3 (2006): 471–88.

Habinek, Thomas. "Tentacular Mind: Stoicism, Neuroscience, and the Configurations of Physical Reality." In *A Field Guide to a New Meta-Field: Bridging the Humanities-Neuroscience Divide*, edited by Barbara Stafford, 64–83. Chicago: University of Chicago Press, 2011.

Habinek, Thomas. "Rhetoric, Music, and the Arts." In *The Oxford Handbook of Rhetorical Studies*, edited by Michael J. McDonald, 289–300. Oxford: Oxford University Press, 2017.

Habinek, Thomas, and Hector Reyes. "Distributed Cognition and its Discontents: A Dialogue across History and Artistic Genre." In *A History of Distributed Cognition*, edited by Miranda

Anderson, Douglas Cairns, and Mark Sprevak, 229–43. Edinburgh: Edinburgh University Press, 2018.

Habinek, Thomas, and Hector Reyes. *Methodical Fire: The Physics of Art and Art Theory from Zeno to Baudelaire*. Forthcoming.

Hadot, Pierre. *Philosophy as a Way of Life: Spiritual Exercises from Socrates to Foucault*. Translated by Michael Chase. Oxford: Oxford University Press, 1995.

Hadot, Pierre. "Réflexions sur la notion de 'culture de soi.'" In *Michel Foucault philosophe: rencontre international, Paris, 9, 10, Il janvier 1988*, edited by the Association pour le Centre Michel Foucault, 261–70. Paris: Seuil, 1989.

Hajdu, Péter. "The Mad Poet in Horace's *Ars Poetica.*" *Canadian Review of Comparative Literature/Revue Canadienne de Littérature Comparée* 41 (2014): 28–42.

Hall, Jonathan M. *Ethnic Identity in Greek Antiquity*. Cambridge: Cambridge University Press, 1997.

Halliwell, Stephen. *The Poetics of Aristotle: Translation and Commentary*. Chapel Hill: University of North Carolina Press, 1987.

Halliwell, Stephen. *Plato, Republic 10: Translation and Commentary*. Warminster: Aris & Phillips, 1988.

Halliwell, Stephen. *The Aesthetics of Mimesis: Ancient Texts and Modern Problems*. Princeton, NJ: Princeton University Press, 2002.

Halliwell, Stephen. "Aristotelian Mimesis between Theory and Practice." In *Rethinking Mimesis: Concepts and Practices of Literary Representation*, edited by Saija Isomaa, Pirjo Lyytikäinen, Sanna Nyqvist, Merja Polvinen, and Riikka Rossi, 1–22. Newcastle upon Tyne: Cambridge Scholars Publishing, 2012.

Halliwell, Stephen. "Beyond the Mirror of Nature: Plato's Ethics of Visual Form." In *Plato on Art and Beauty*, edited by Alison Denham, 173–204. New York: Palgrave Macmillan, 2012.

Halliwell, Stephen. "Fiction." In *A Companion to Ancient Aesthetics*, edited by Pierre Destrée and Penelope Murray, 341–53. Oxford: Blackwell, 2015.

Hamilton, John T. *Security: Politics, Humanity, and the Philology of Care*. Princeton, NJ: Princeton University Press, 2013.

Hanink, Johanna. "Archives, Repertoires, Bodies, and Bones: Thoughts on Reperformance for Classicists." In *Imagining Reperformance in Ancient Culture: Studies in the Tradition of Drama and Lyric*, edited by Richard Hunter and Anna Uhlig, 21–41. Cambridge: Cambridge University Press, 2017.

Harper, Donald. *Early Chinese Medical Literature: The Mawangdui Medical Manuscripts*. London: Kegan Paul International, 1998.

Harris, William V. *Restraining Rage: The Ideology of Anger Control in Classical Antiquity*. Cambridge, MA: Harvard University Press, 2001.

Harrison, Thomas. "Greek Religion and Literature." In *A Companion to Greek Religion*, edited by Daniel Ogden, 371–84. Oxford: Wiley-Blackwell, 2010.

Harrison, Thomas. "Belief vs. Practice." In *The Oxford Handbook of Ancient Greek Religion*, edited by Esther Eidinow and Julia Kindt, 21–8. Oxford: Oxford University Press, 2015.

Havelock, Christine Mitchell. *The Aphrodite of Knidos and her Successors*. Ann Arbor: University of Michigan Press, 1995.

Havelock, Eric. *Prologue to Greek Literacy*. Cincinnati, OH: University of Cincinnati, 1971.

Hawes, Greta. *Rationalizing Myth in Antiquity*. Oxford: Oxford University Press, 2014.

Heath, Malcolm. "Aristotle and the Value of Tragedy." *British Journal of Aesthetics* 54 (2014): 111–23.

Heidegger, Martin. *Being and Time*. Translated by John Macquarrie and Edward Robinson. Oxford: Blackwell, 1962. (= *Sein und Zeit*. In Edmund Husserl, ed., *Jahrbuch für Philosophie und phänomologische Forschung*, vol. 8, 1–438. Halle a. d. S.: Max Niemeyer, 1927.)

Heidegger, Martin. "What Is Metaphysics? (1929)." Translated by David Farrell Krell. In *Martin Heidegger: Pathmarks*, edited by William McNeill, 82–96. Cambridge: Cambridge University Press, 2010. (= "Was ist Metaphysik?" In *Martin Heidegger: Gesamtausgabe: Band 9, Wegmarken*, edited by Friedrich-Wilhelm von Herrmann. Frankfurt: Klostermann, 2004.)

Herder, Johann Gottfried. "Das Kind der Sorge" (1787). In *Johann Gottfried von Herder. Volkslieder, Übertragungen, Dichtungen* (Bibliothek deutscher Klassiker 60), edited by Ulrich Gaier, 743–4. Frankfurt: Deutscher Klassiker-Verlag, 1990.

Hickey, Todd M. *Wine, Wealth, and the State in Late Antique Egypt: The House of Apion at Oxyrhynchus*. Ann Arbor: University of Michigan Press, 2012.

Hölkeskamp, Karl-Joachim. *Die Entstehung der Nobilität: Studien zur sozialen und politischen Geschichte der Römischen Republik im 4. Jh. v. Chr.* Stuttgart: Steiner, 1987.

Hölkeskamp, Karl-Joachim. *Reconstructing the Roman Republic: An Ancient Political Culture and Modern Research*. Translated by Henry Heitmann-Gordon. Princeton, NJ: Princeton University Press, 2010.

Hopkins, Keith. *Death and Renewal*. Sociological Studies in Roman History 2. Cambridge: Cambridge University Press, 1983.

Horden, Peregrine, and Nicholas Purcell. *The Corrupting Sea: A Study of Mediterranean History*. Malden, MA: Blackwell Publishers, 2000.

Horky, Philip Sydney. "The Imprint of the Soul: Psychosomatic Affection in Plato, Gorgias and the 'Orphic' Gold Tablets." *Mouseion* 6 (2006): 371–86.

Horky, Philip Sydney. *Plato and Pythagoreanism*. Oxford: Oxford University Press, 2013.

Hornblower, S. *Thucydides*. Baltimore: Johns Hopkins University Press, 1987.

Hsu, Elisabeth. *Pulse Diagnosis in Early Chinese Medicine: The Telling Touch*. University of Cambridge Oriental Publications 68. Cambridge: Cambridge University Press, 2010.

Huffmann, Carl. *Archytas of Tarentum: Pythagorean, Philosopher, and Mathematician King*. Cambridge: Cambridge University Press, 2005.

Hunter, Virginia J. *Past and Process in Herodotus and Thucydides*. Princeton, NJ: Princeton University Press, 1982.

Hurwit, Jeffrey M. *Artists and Signatures in Ancient Greece*. Cambridge: Cambridge University Press, 2015.

Hussey, Edward. "Aristotle and Mathematics." In *Science and Mathematics in Ancient Greek Culture*, edited by C. J. Tuplin and T. E. Rihll, 217–29. Oxford: Oxford University Press, 2002.

Hyland, Drew A. "Caring for Myth: Heidegger, Plato, and the Myth of Cura." *Research in Phenomenology* 27 (1997): 90–102.

Imbert, Claude. "Stoic Logic and Alexandrian Poetics." In *Doubt and Dogmatism: Studies in Hellenistic Epistemology*, edited by Malcolm Schofield, Myles Burnyeat, and Jonathan Barnes, 182–216. Oxford: Oxford University Press, 1980.

Immerwahr, H. R. "Ergon: History as a Monument in Herodotus and Thucydides." *American Journal of Philology* 81 (1960): 261–90.

Inwood, Brad. *Reading Seneca: Stoic Philosophy at Rome*. Oxford: Oxford University Press, 2005.

Irwin, Terence H. *Aristotle's First Principles*. New York: Oxford University Press, 1988.

Jacoby, Felix. "Hekataios." *RE* 7.2 (1912), coll. 2667–750.

Jacoby, Felix. *Fragmente der griechischen Historiker*. Leiden: Brill, 2013.

Jacoby, Felix. "On the Development of Greek Historiography and the Plan for the New Collection of the Fragments of the Greek Historians. The 1956 text with the editorial additions of Herbert Bloch." Translated by Mortimer Chambers and Stephan Schorn. *Histos* (Suppl. 3) (2015).

Jakab, Eva. "Inheritance." In *The Oxford Handbook of Roman Law and Society*, edited by Paul Du Plessis, Clifford Ando, and Kaius Tuori, 498–509. Oxford: Oxford University Press, 2016.

Jakubiec, Alexandre. "Rites and Religious Beliefs of Socrates according to Xenophon (Apology of Socrates 11 and Memorabilia 1.1.2)." *Classical Quarterly* 67, no. 1 (2017): 291–3.

Johnston, Sarah Iles. "Animating Statues: A Case Study in Ritual." *Arethusa* 41 (2008): 445–77.

Johnstone, S. "A New History of Libraries and Books in the Hellenistic Period." *Classical Antiquity* 33 (2014): 347–93.

Jolivet, Régis. *Les doctrines existentialistes de Kierkegaard à J.-P. Sartre*. Abbaye Saint-Wandrille: Editions de Fontenelles, 1948.

Jones, David. *The Bankers of Puteoli: Finance, Trade and Industry in the Roman World*. Stroud: Tempus, 2006.

Jones, Nathaniel B. *Painting, Ethics, and Aesthetics in Rome*. Cambridge: Cambridge University Press, 2019.

Kalmo, Hent, and Quentin Skinner, eds. *Sovereignty in Fragments: The Past, Present and Future of a Contested Concept*. Cambridge: Cambridge University Press, 2010.

Kaster, Robert. "The Taxonomy of Patience, or, When Is 'Patientia' Not a Virtue?" *Classical Philology* 97 (2002): 133–44.

Kaster, R. A. "Terentius Varro, Marcus." *Oxford Classical Dictionary* online. https://doi-org/10.1093/acrefore/9780199381135.013.6699.

Kehoe, Dennis. *The Economics of Agriculture on Roman Imperial Estates in North Africa*. Göttingen: Vandenhoeck & Ruprecht, 1988.

Kehoe, Dennis. *Management and Investment on Estates in Roman Egypt During the Early Empire*. Bonn: R. Habelt, 1992.

Kehoe, Dennis. *Law and the Rural Economy in the Roman Empire*. Ann Arbor: University of Michigan Press, 2007.

Ker, James. *The Deaths of Seneca*. New York: Oxford University Press, 2009.

Klima, Ursula. *Untersuchungen zu dem Begriff Sapientia: von der republikanischen Zeit bis Tacitus*. Habelts Dissertationsdrucke, Reihe klassische Philologie, 10. Bonn: Rudolf Habelt, 1971.

Koenen, Ludwig. "The Ptolemaic King as a Religious Figure." In *Images and Ideologies: Self-Definition in the Hellenistic World*, edited by Anthony Bulloch, Erich S. Gruen, A. A. Long, and Andrew Stewart, 25–115. Berkeley: University of California Press, 1993.

König, Jason, Katerina Oikonomopoulou, and Greg Woolf, eds. *Ancient Libraries*. Cambridge: Cambridge University Press, 2013.

Konstan, David. *Friendship in the Classical World*. Cambridge: Cambridge University Press, 1997.

Konstan, David. "Socrates in Aristophanes' *Clouds*." In *The Cambridge Companion to Socrates*, edited by Sara Abel-Rappe and Rachana Kamtekar, 75–90. Cambridge: Cambridge University Press, 2011.

Kraus, Christina Shuttleworth. "The Language of Latin Historiography." In *A Companion to the Latin Language*, edited by James Clackson, 408–25. Malden, MA: Wiley-Blackwell, 2011.

Kristeller, Paul Oskar. "The Modern System of the Arts: A Study in the History of Aesthetics (I)." *Journal of the History of Ideas* 12 (1951): 496–527.

Kristeller, Paul Oskar. "The Modern System of the Arts: A Study in the History of Aesthetics (II)." *Journal of the History of Ideas* 13 (1952): 17–46.

Kristensen, Troels Myrup. "Embodied Images: Christian Response and Destruction in Late Antique Egypt." *Journal of Late Antiquity* 2 (2009): 224–50.

Lacoste, Jean. "'L'œil clairement ouvert sur la nature': Heidegger et Goethe." *Littérature* 120 (2000): 105–27.

Lacrosse, Joachim. "Plotinus, Porphyry, and India: A Re-Examination." In *Late Antique Epistemology: Other Ways to Truth*, edited by Panayiota Vassilopoulou and Stephen R. L. Clark, 103–17. London: Palgrave Macmillan, 2009.

Lada-Richards, Ismene. *Silent Eloquence: Lucian and Pantomime Dancing*. London: Duckworth, 2007.

Lape, Susan. "Solon and the Institution of the 'Democratic' Family Form." *Classical Journal* 98 (2002–2003): 117–39.

Lape, Susan. "Racializing Democracy: The Politics of Sexual Reproduction in Classical Athens." *Parallax* 9, no. 4 (2003): 52–63.

Larivée, Annie, and Alexandra Leduc. "Le souci de soi dans Être et Temps. L'accentuation radicale d'une tradition antique?" *Revue Philosophique de Louvain*, quatrième série, 100, no. 4 (2002): 723–41.

Lateiner, Donald. *The Historical Method of Herodotus*. Toronto: University of Toronto Press, 1989.

Ledentu, Marie, and Romain Loriol, eds. *Penser en listes dans les mondes grec et romain*. Bordeaux: Ausonius, 2020.

Leese, Michael. "An Economic Perspective on Marriage Alliances in Ancient Greece." In *Ancient Law, Ancient Society*, edited by Dennis P. Kehoe and Thomas A. J. McGinn, 32–45. Ann Arbor: University of Michigan Press, 2017.

Lesher, J. H. "Archaic Knowledge." In *Logos and Mythos*, edited by William Wians, 13–28. New York: State University of New York Press, 2009.

Levene, David S. "Pity, Fear and the Historical Audience: Tacitus on the Fall of Vitellius." In *The Passions in Roman Thought*, edited by Susanna Braund and Christopher Gill, 128–49. Cambridge: Cambridge University Press, 1997.

Lévi-Strauss, Claude. "Introduction à l'œuvre de Marcel Mauss." In Marcel Mauss, *Sociologie et anthropologie*, IX–LII. Paris: Presses universitaires de France, [1950] 2013.

Liddel, Peter, and Andrew T. Fear. *"Historiae mundi": Studies in Universal History*. London: Duckworth, 2010.

LiDonnici, Lynn R. *The Epidaurian Miracle Inscriptions: Text, Translation and Commentary*. Atlanta, GA: Scholars Press, 1995.

Liebert, Rana Saadi. *Tragic Pleasure from Homer to Plato*. Cambridge: Cambridge University Press, 2017.

Lloyd, G. E. R. *Early Greek Science: Thales to Aristotle*. New York: Norton, 1970.

Lloyd, G. E. R. *Magic, Reason, and Experience*. Cambridge: Cambridge University Press, 1979.

Lloyd, G. E. R. *Science, Folklore, and Ideology: Studies in the Life Sciences in Ancient Greece*. Cambridge: Cambridge University Press, 1983.

Lloyd, G. E. R. *Methods and Problems in Greek Science*. Cambridge: Cambridge University Press, 1991.

Lloyd, G. E. R. *In the Grip of Disease: Studies in the Greek Imagination*. Oxford: Oxford University Press, 2003.

Lloyd, G. E. R. *Being, Humanity, and Understanding*. Studies in Ancient and Modern Societies. Oxford: Oxford University Press, 2012.

Lloyd, G. E. R., and Nathan Sivin. *The Way and the Word: Science and Medicine in Early China and Greece*. New Haven, CT: Yale University Press, 2002.

Long, Anthony A. *Epictetus: A Stoic and Socratic Guide to Life*. Oxford: Oxford University Press, 2002.

Long, Christopher P. "Saving 'ta legomena': Aristotle and the History of Philosophy." *Review of Metaphysics* 60, no. 2 (2006): 247–67.

López Ruiz, Carolina. *When the Gods Were Born: Greek Cosmogonies and the Near East*. Cambridge, MA: Harvard University Press, 2010.

Loraux, Nicole. *The Invention of Athens: The Funeral Oration in the Classical City*. Translated by Alan Sheridan. Cambridge, MA: Harvard University Press, 1986.

Loraux, Nicole. "Thucydide et la sédition dans les mots." *Quaderni di storia* 12 (1986): 95–134.

Loraux, Nicole. *Born of the Earth: Myth and Politics in Athens*. Translated by Selina Stewart. Ithaca, NY: Cornell University Press, 2000.

Lord, Carnes. "Damon and Music Education." *Hermes* 106 (1978): 32–43.

Luce, Jean-Marc. "L'observateur implicite dans l'art de l'Antiquité." *Pallas* 105 (2017): 115–47.

Luraghi, Nino, ed. *The Historian's Craft in the Age of Herodotus*. Oxford: Oxford University Press, 2001.

Luraghi, Nino. "Meta-'historiē': Method and Genre in the 'Histories'." In *The Cambridge Companion to Herodotus*, edited by Carolyn Dewald and John Marincola, 76–91. Cambridge: Cambridge University Press, 2006.

Ma, John. *Statues and Cities: Honorific Portraits and Civic Identity in the Hellenistic World*. Oxford: Oxford University Press, 2013.

MacLean, Rose. *Freed Slaves and Roman Imperial Culture: Social Integration and the Transformation of Values*. Cambridge: Cambridge University Press, 2018.

Mango, Cyril, Michael Vickers, and E. D. Francis. "The Palace of Lausus at Constantinople and its Collection of Ancient Statues." *Journal of the History of Collections* 4 (1992): 89–98.

Mansfeld, Jaap. "*Technê*: A New Fragment of Chrysippus." *Greek Roman and Byzantine Studies* 24, no. 1 (1983): 57–65.

Marincola, John. *Authority and Tradition in Ancient Historiography*. Cambridge: Cambridge University Press, 1997.

Marrou, Henri-Irénée. *Histoire de l'éducation dans l'antiquité*. Paris: Éditions du Seuil, 1965.

Martin, Richard. "The Seven Sages as Performers of Wisdom." In *Cultural Poetics of Archaic Greece: Cult, Performance, Politics*, edited by Carol Dougherty and Leslie Kurke, 108–30. Cambridge: Cambridge University Press, 1993.

Matthews, William. "Ontology with Chinese Characteristics." *HAU: Journal of Ethnographic Theory* 7, no. 1 (2017): 265–85.

Mayor, Adrienne. *The Poison King: The Life and Legend of Mithradates, Rome's Deadliest Enemy*. Princeton, NJ: Princeton University Press, 2010.

McGinn, Thomas A.J. "Cui bono? The True Beneficiaries of Roman Private Law." In *Ancient Law, Ancient Society*, edited by Dennis P. Kehoe and Thomas A. J. McGinn, 133–66. Ann Arbor: University of Michigan Press, 2017.

McIlwain, Charles Howard. *Constitutionalism Ancient and Modern*. Ithaca, NY: Cornell University Press, 1940.

McNamara, Charles Joseph. "Quintilian's Theory of Certainty and Its Afterlife in Early Modern Italy." PhD dissertation, Columbia University, 2016.

Mendelson, Michael. "Saint Augustine." *The Stanford Encyclopedia of Philosophy*, edited by Edward N. Zalta. Winter 2016. Available online: https://plato.stanford.edu/archives/win2016/entries/augustine (accessed January 9, 2022).

Menn, Stephen. "Plotinus on the Identity of Knowledge with its Object." *Apeiron* 34, no. 3 (2001): 233–46.

Millar, Fergus. *Rome, the Greek World, and the East, Volume 1: The Roman Republic and the Augustan Revolution*. Edited by Hannah M. Cotton and Guy M. Rogers. Chapel Hill: University of North Carolina Press, 2002.

Moatti, Claudia. *The Birth of Critical Thinking in Republican Rome*. Translated by Janet Lloyd, with the collaboration of G. Rowe, J. Prim, and J. Harris. Cambridge: Cambridge University Press, 2015.

Moles, J. L. "Truth and Untruth in Herodotus and Thucydides." In *Lies and Fiction in the Ancient World*, edited by Christopher Gill and T. P. Wiseman, 88–121. Exeter: University of Exeter Press, 1993.

Momigliano, Arnaldo. "The Theological Efforts of the Roman Upper Classes in the First Century BC." *Classical Philology* 79, no. 3 (1984): 199–211.

Momigliano, Arnaldo. *The Classical Foundations of Modern Historiography*. With a foreword by R. Di Donato. Berkeley: University of California Press, 1990.

Moss, Judith. "What is Imitative Poetry and Why is it Bad?" In *The Cambridge Companion to Plato's* Republic, edited by G. R. F. Ferrari, 414–44. Cambridge: Cambridge University Press, 2007.

Mouritsen, Henrik. *The Freedman in the Roman World*. Cambridge: Cambridge University Press, 2011.

Murphy, Trevor. "Privileged Knowledge: Valerius Soranus and the Secret Name of Rome." In *Rituals in Ink: A Conference on Religion and Literary Production in Ancient Rome Held at Stanford University in February 2002*, edited by Alessandro Barchiesi, Jörg Rüpke, and Susan Stephens, 127–37. Stuttgart: Franz Steiner Verlag, 2004.

Murray, Penelope. "The Muses and their Arts." In *Music and Muses: The Culture of "Mousikê" in the Classical Athenian City*, edited by Penelope Murray and Peter Wilson, 365–89. Oxford: Oxford University Press, 2004.

Murray, Penelope. "The Muses in Antiquity." In *The Muses and their Afterlife in Postclassical Europe*, edited by Kathleen Christian, Clare Guest, and Claudia Wedepohl, 13–32. London: The Warburg Institute, 2014.

Nehamas, Alexander. "Plato on Imitation and Poetry in Republic 10." In *Plato on Beauty, Wisdom, and the Arts*, edited by Julius Moravcsik and Philip Temko, 47–78. Lanham, MD: Rowman and Littlefield, 1982.

Netz, Reviel. *Scale, Space and Canon in Ancient Literary Culture*. Cambridge: Cambridge University Press, 2020.

Neudecker, Reinhard. "Archives, Books and Sacred Space in Rome." In *Ancient Libraries*, edited by Jason König, Katarina Oikonomopoulou, and Greg Woolf, 312–31. Cambridge: Cambridge University Press, 2013.

Newby, Zara. "Absorption and Erudition in Philostratus' *Imagines*." In *Philostratus*, edited by Ewen Bowie and Jaś Elsner, 322–42. Oxford: Oxford University Press, 2009.

Nicolet, Claude. *The World of the Citizen in Republican Rome*. Translated by P. S. Falla. Berkeley: University of California Press, 1980.

Nightingale, Andrea. *Genres in Dialogue: Plato and the Construct of Philosophy*. Cambridge: Cambridge University Press, 1995.

North, J. A. "Caesar at the Lupercalia." *Journal of Roman Studies* 98 (2008): 144–60.

Nuffelen, Peter Van. "Varro's Divine Antiquities: Roman Religion as an Image of Truth." *Classical Philology* 105, no. 2 (2010): 162–88.

Obbink, Dirk. "Craft, Cult, and Canon in the Books from Herculaneum." In *Philodemus and the New Testament World*, edited by John Fitzgerald, Dirk Obbink, and Glenn Holland, 73–84. Leiden: Brill, 2004.

Ober, Josiah. *Democracy and Knowledge: Innovation and Learning in Classical Athens*. Princeton, NJ: Princeton University Press, 2008.

O'Neill, Peter. "Going Round in Circles: Popular Speech in Ancient Rome." *Classical Antiquity* 22 (2003): 135–66.

Orlin, Eric. *Foreign Cults in Rome: Creating a Roman Empire*. Oxford: Oxford University Press, 2010.

Osborne, Catherine. *Rethinking Early Greek Philosophy*. Ithaca, NY: Cornell University Press, 1987.

Osborne, Robin. *Demos: The Discovery of Classical Attika*. Cambridge: Cambridge University Press, 1985.

Papageorgiou, Nikolaos. "Prodicus and the Agon of the 'Logoi' in Aristophanes' 'Clouds.'" *Quaderni urbinati di cultura classica* 78, no. 3 (2004): 1000–9.

Parpola, Simo. *Letters from Assyrian and Babylonian Scholars*. State Archives of Assyria, 10. Helsinki: Helsinki University Press, 1993.

Pascatore, Russell. "Zeus' Plan in Early Greek Poetry's Construction of Political and Social Identity." PhD dissertation, University of Southern California (in progress).

Pelttari, Aaron. *The Space that Remains: Reading Latin Poetry in Late Antiquity*. Ithaca, NY: Cornell University Press, 2014.

Peponi, Anastasia-Erasmia. *Frontiers of Pleasure. Models of Aesthetic Response in Archaic and Classical Greek Thought*. New York: Oxford University Press, 2012.

Peponi, Anastasia-Erasmia. "Choral Anti-Aesthetics." In *Performance and Culture in Plato's Laws*, edited by A.-E. Peponi, 212–40. Cambridge: Cambridge University Press, 2013.

Peponi, Anastasia-Erasmia. "Aristotle's Definition of Dance." In *Choreutika: Performing and Theorising Dance in Ancient Greece*, edited by Laura Gianvittorio, 215–43. Pisa: Fabrizio Serra, 2017.

Perelmutter, Zeev. "'Nous' and Two Kinds of 'epistēmē' in Aristotle's Posterior Analytics." *Phronesis* 55 (2010): 228–54.

Perkins, Judith. *The Suffering Self: Pain and Narrative Representation in the Early Christian Era*. New York: Routledge, 1995.

Pfeiffer, Rudolph. *History of Classical Scholarship from the Beginnings to the End of the Hellenistic Age*. Oxford: Clarendon, 1968.

Piketty, Thomas. *Capital in the Twenty-First Century*. Translated by Arthur Goldhammer. Cambridge, MA: The Belknap Press of Harvard University Press, 2014.

Pizzi, Aurian Delli. "Impiety in Epigraphic Evidence." *Kernos. Revue internationale et pluridisciplinaire de religion grecque antique* 24 (2011): 59–76.

Plass, Paul. *The Game of Death in Ancient Rome*. Madison: University of Wisconsin Press, 1995.

Platt, Verity. *Facing the Gods: Epiphany and Representation in Graeco-Roman Art, Literature and Religion*. Cambridge: Cambridge University Press, 2011.

Platt, Verity. "Sight and the Gods." In *Sight and the Ancient Senses*, edited by Michael Squire, 161–79. London: Routledge, 2016.

Pocock, J. G. A. "The Origins of the Study of the Past: A Comparative Approach." *Comparative Studies of Society and History* 4 (1962): 209–46.

Pocock, J. G. A. *The Machiavellian Moment: Florentine Political Thought and the Atlantic Republican Tradition*. Princeton, NJ: Princeton University Press, 1975.

Pocock, J. G. A. "The Ideal of Citizenship Since Classical Times." *Queen's Quarterly* 99 (1992): 33–55.

Pocock, J. G. A. "Classical and Civil History: The Transformation of Humanism." *Cromohs* 1 (1996): 1–34.

Pocock, J. G. A. *Barbarism and Religion, Volume 3: The First Decline and Fall*. Cambridge: Cambridge University Press, 2003.

Pollitt, Jerry J. *The Ancient View of Greek Art: Criticism, History, and Terminology*. New Haven, CT: Yale University Press, 1974.

Pollitt, Jerry J. *The Art of Ancient Greece: Sources and Documents*. 2nd edition. Cambridge: Cambridge University Press, 1990.

Porter, James I. "Content and Form in Philodemus: The History of an Illusion." In *Philodemus and Poetry: Poetic Theory and Practice in Lucretius, Philodemus, and Horace*, edited by Dirk Obbink, 97–147. Oxford: Oxford University Press, 1995.

Porter, James I. *The Origins of Aesthetic Thought in Ancient Greece: Matter, Sensation and Experience*. Cambridge: Cambridge University Press, 2010.

Porter, James I. "Why Art has Never been Autonomous." *Arethusa* 43 (2010): 165–80.

Porter, James I. "Why are there Nine Muses?" In *Synaesthesia and the Ancient Senses*, edited by Shane Butler and Alex Purves, 9–26. Durham, UK: Acumen, 2013.

Porter, James I. *The Sublime in Antiquity*. Cambridge: Cambridge University Press, 2016.

Poster, Carol. "The Task of the Bow: Heraclitus' Rhetorical Critique of Epic Language." *Philosophy and Rhetoric* 39 (2006): 1–21.

Potter, David S. *Prophets & Emperors: Human and Divine Authority from Augustus to Theodosius*. Cambridge, MA: Harvard University Press, 1994.

Price, Jonathan J. *Thucydides and Internal War*. Cambridge: Cambridge University Press, 2001.

Prioux, Evelyne. *Petits Musées en vers: Epigramme et discours sur les collections antiques*. Paris: CTHS-INHA, 2008.

Pucci, Pietro. *Hesiod and the Language of Poetry*. Baltimore: Johns Hopkins University Press, 1977.

Pulleyn, Simon. *Prayer in Greek Religion*. Oxford: Oxford University Press, 1997.

Purzycki, Benjamin G., Daniel N. Finkel, John Shaver, Nathan Wales, Adam B. Cohen, and Richard Sosis. "What Does God Know? Supernatural Agents' Access to Socially Strategic and Non-Strategic Information." *Cognitive Science* 36 (2012): 846–69.

Ramelli, Ilaria. "The Philosophical Stance of Allegory in Stoicism and its Reception in Platonism, Pagan and Christian: Origen in Dialogue with the Stoics and Plato." *International Journal of the Classical Tradition* 18, no. 3 (2011): 335–71.

Rappaport, Roy. *Ritual and Religion in the Making of Humanity*. Cambridge: Cambridge University Press, 1999.

Ravisi, Thea. "Displaying Sculpture in Rome." In *A Companion to Ancient Aesthetics*, edited by Pierre Destrée and Penelope Murray, 248–61. Oxford: Blackwell, 2015.

Rawson, Elizabeth. *Intellectual Life in the Late Roman Republic*. Baltimore: Johns Hopkins University Press, 1985.

Reich, Warren T. "History of the Notion of Care." In *Encyclopedia of Bioethics*, revised edition, edited by Warren T. Reich, 319–31. New York: Simon and Schuster Macmillan, 1995.

Revermann, Martin. "The Competence of Theatre Audiences in Fifth- and Fourth-century Athens." *Journal of Hellenic Studies* 126 (2006): 99–124.

Reydams-Schils, Gretchen. *The Roman Stoics: Self, Responsibility, and Affection*. Chicago: University of Chicago Press, 2005.

Rhodes, Peter J., with David M. Lewis. *The Decrees of the Greek States*. Oxford: Clarendon Press, 1997.

Richlin, Amy. "Pliny's Brassiere." In *Sexuality and Gender in the Classical World: Readings and Sources*, edited by Laura K. McClure, 225–52. Oxford: Blackwell, 2002.

Robins, Robert Henry. "The Initial Section of the *Tékhnê grammatikê*." In *Ancient Grammar: Content and Context*, edited by Pierre Swiggers and Alfons Wouters, 3–15. Leuven: Peeters, 1996.

Rocconi, Eleonora. "La dottrina aristossenica dell' 'ethos' musicale nel 'de musica' dello Ps.-Plutarco." *Seminari romani di cultura greca* 8 (2005): 291–7.

Rochberg, Francesca. *Before Nature: Cuneiform Knowledge and the History of Science*. Chicago: University of Chicago Press, 2016.

Roller, Matthew B. *Constructing Autocracy: Aristocrats and Emperors in Julio-Claudian Rome*. Princeton, NJ: Princeton University Press, 2001.

Roller, Matthew B. "Exemplarity in Roman Culture: The Cases of Horatius Cocles and Cloelia." *Classical Philology* 99 (2004): 1–56.

Rotstein, Andrea. "*Mousikoi agones* and the Conceptualisation of Genre in Ancient Greece." *Classical Antiquity* 31 (2012): 92–127.

Rouveret, Agnès. *Histoire et imaginaire de la peinture ancienne (Ve siècle av. J.-C.–Ier siècle ap. J.-C.)*. Rome: Ecole Française de Rome, 1989.

Rouveret, Agnès. "Painting and Private Art Collections in Rome." In *A Companion to Ancient Aesthetics*, edited by Pierre Destrée and Penelope Murray, 109–27. Oxford: Blackwell, 2015.

Rubel, Alexander, and Michael Vickers. *Fear and Loathing in Ancient Athens: Religion and Politics During the Peloponnesian War*. London: Routledge, 2014.

Rüpke, Jörg. *Religion in Republican Rome: Rationalization and Ritual Change*. Philadelphia: University of Pennsylvania Press, 2012.

Rüpke, Jörg. *Religious Deviance in the Roman World: Superstition Or Individuality?* Cambridge: Cambridge University Press, 2016.

Saetta Cottone, Rossella. "Agathon, Euripide et le thème de la mimèsis dramatique dans les Thesmophories d'Aristophane." *Revue des études grecques* 116, no. 2 (2003): 445–69.

Salmon, John. "Political Hoplites?" *Journal of Hellenic Studies* 97 (1977): 84–101.

Santangelo, Federico. "Whose Sacrilege?: A Note on Sal. 5.14." *Classical World* 104, no. 3 (2011): 333–8.

Santangelo, Federico. *Divination, Prediction and the End of the Roman Republic*. Cambridge: Cambridge University Press, 2013.

Scheid, John. "Polytheism Impossible; or, the Empty Gods: Reasons Behind a Void in the History of Roman Religion." *History and Anthropology* 3, no. 1 (1987): 303–25.

Schiefsky, Mark. *Hippocrates: On Ancient Medicine*. Leiden: Brill Academic Publishers, 2005.

Schironi, Francesca. *The Best of the Grammarians: Aristarchus of Samothrace on the Iliad*. Ann Arbor: University of Michigan Press, 2018.

Schlapbach, Karin. *The Anatomy of Dance Discourse: Literary and Philosophical Approaches to Dance in the Later Graeco-Roman World*. Oxford: Oxford University Press, 2018.

Schlefer, Jonathan. *The Assumptions Economists Make*. Cambridge, MA: The Belknap Press of Harvard University Press, 2012.

Schofield, Malcolm. "Cicero For and Against Divination." *Journal of Roman Studies* 76 (1986): 47–65.

Schofield, Malcolm. *The Stoic Idea of the City*. Cambridge: Cambridge University Press, 1991.

Sciarrino, Enrica. *Cato the Censor and the Beginnings of Latin Prose: From Poetic Translation to Elite Transcription*. Columbus: Ohio State University Press, 2011.

Scott, Mary. "Some Greek Terms in Homer Suggesting Non-Competitive Attitudes." *Acta Classica* 24 (1981): 1–15.

Scourfield, David H. *Consoling Heliodorus: A Commentary on Jerome Letter 60*. Oxford: Oxford University Press, 1993.

Sedley, David. "Epicureanism in the Roman Republic." In *The Cambridge Companion to Epicureanism*, edited by James Warren, 29–45. Cambridge: Cambridge University Press, 2009.

Segal, Charles P. "Gorgias and the Psychology of the Logos." *Harvard Studies in Classical Philology* 66 (1962): 99–155.

Sellers, Mortimer N. S. *American Republicanism: Roman Ideology in the United States Constitution*. New York: New York University Press, 1994.

Shaw, Brent D. "The Divine Economy: Stoicism as Ideology." *Latomus* 64 (1985): 16–54.

Simon, Gérard. *Le regard, l'être et l'apparence dans l'optique de l'antiquité*. Paris: Seuil, 1988.

Singer, P. N. "Galen." *The Stanford Encyclopedia of Philosophy*, edited by Edward N. Zalta. Winter 2016 Edition. Available online: https://plato.stanford.edu/archives/win2016/entries/galen/ (accessed January 25, 2022).

Sissa, Giulia. "Le Peuple philosophe. Le souci du bien dans la République de Platon et chez les Athéniens." *Chôra. Revue d'études anciennes et médiévales* 15/16 (2017/2018): 203–18.

Sissa, Giulia. "Caregivers of the Polis, Partygoers and Lotus-Eaters. Politics of Pleasure and Care in Plato's Republic." In *Philosophie für die Polis. Akten des 5. Kongresses der Gesellschaft für antike Philosophie 2016*, Beiträge zur Altertumskunde 380, edited by Christoph Riedweg, 175–201. Berlin: De Gruyter, 2019.

Sissa, Giulia, and Marcel Detienne. *The Daily Life of the Greek Gods*. Translated by Janet Lloyd. Stanford, CA: Stanford: University Press, 2000. (= *La vie quotidienne des dieux grecs*. Paris: Hachette, 1989.)

Sizgorich, Thomas. *Violence and Belief in Late Antiquity: Militant Devotion in Christianity and Islam*. Philadelphia: University of Pennsylvania Press, 2009.

Sloterdijk, Peter. *You Must Change Your Life: On Anthropotechnics*. Translated by Wieland Hoban. Cambridge, UK: Polity, 2013.

Snell, Bruno, Richard Kannicht, and S. L. Radt, eds. *Tragicorum Graecorum Fragmenta*. Göttingen: Vandenhoeck & Ruprecht, 1971–2004.

Snodgrass, Anthony. "The Hoplite Reform and History." *Journal of Hellenic Studies* 85 (1965): 110–22.

Snodgrass, Anthony. *Archaic Greece: The Age of Experiment*. London: J. M. Dent, 1980.

Sörbom, Göran. *Mimesis and Art*. Stockholm: Svenska Bokförlaget, 1966.

Sörbom, Göran. "Aristotle on Music as Representation." *Journal of Aesthetics and Art Criticism* 52 (1994): 37–46.

Spiegler, Peter. *Behind the Model: A Constructive Critique of Economic Modeling*. Cambridge: Cambridge University Press, 2015.

Squire, Michael. "Making Myron's Cow Moo? Ecphrastic Epigram and the Poetics of Simulation." *American Journal of Philology* 131 (2010): 589–634.

Squire, Michael. "Conceptualizing the (Visual) 'Arts.'" In *A Companion to Ancient Aesthetics*, edited by Pierre Destrée and Penelope Murray, 307–26. Oxford: Blackwell, 2015.

Squire, Michael. *Sight and the Ancient Senses*. London: Routledge, 2016.

Stafford, Barbara. *Echo Objects: The Cognitive Work of Images*. Chicago: University of Chicago Press, 2007.

Steiner, Deborah. *Images in Mind: Statues in Archaic and Classical Greek Literature and Thought*. Princeton, NJ: Princeton University Press, 2003.

Stephens, Susan A. *Seeing Double: Intercultural Poetics in Ptolemaic Alexandria*. Berkeley: University of California Press, 2003.

Stewart, Peter. "Gell's Idols and Roman Cult." In *Art's Agency and Art History*, edited by Robin Osborne and Jeremy Tanner, 158–78. Oxford: Blackwell, 2007.

Stock, Brian. *Augustine the Reader: Meditation, Self-Knowledge, and the Ethics of Interpretation*. Cambridge, MA: Harvard University Press, 1996.

Strathern, Marilyn. "No Nature, No Culture: The Hagen Case." In *Nature, Culture and Gender*, edited by Carol MacCormack and Marilyn Strathern, 174–222. Cambridge: Cambridge University Press, 1980.

Straumann, Benjamin. *Crisis and Constitutionalism: Roman Political Thought from the Fall of the Republic to the Age of Revolution*. New York: Oxford University Press, 2016.

Struck, Peter T. *Birth of the Symbol: Ancient Readers at the Limits of their Texts*. Princeton, NJ: Princeton University Press, 2004.

Struck, Peter T. *Divination and Human Nature: A Cognitive History of Intuition in Classical Antiquity*. Princeton, NJ: Princeton University Press, 2016.

Suny, Ronald Grigor. "Constructing Primordialism: Old Histories for New Nations." *Journal of Modern History* 72 (2001): 862–96.

Tanner, Jeremy. *The Invention of Art History in Ancient Greece: Religion, Society and Artistic Rationalisation*. Cambridge: Cambridge University Press, 2006.

Tanner, Jeremy. "Aesthetics and Art History Writing in Comparative Historical Perspective." *Arethusa* 43 (2010): 267–88.

Tanner, Jeremy. "Sight and Painting: Optical Theory and Pictorial Poetics in Classical Greek Art." In *Sight and the Ancient Senses*, edited by Michael Squire, 107–22. London: Routledge, 2016.

Thomas, Rosalind. *Oral Tradition and the Written Record in Classical Athens*. Cambridge: Cambridge University Press, 1989.

Thomas, Rosalind. *Herodotus in Context*. Cambridge: Cambridge University Press, 2000.

Thomas, Rosalind. "Herodotus' 'Histories' and the Floating Gap." In *The Historian's Craft in the Age of Herodotus*, edited by Nino Luraghi, 198–210. Oxford: Oxford University Press, 2001.

Thomas, Rosalind. "Thucydides and his Intellectual Milieu." In *Oxford Handbook of Thucydides*, edited by S. Forsdyke, E. Foster, and R. Balot, 567–86. Oxford: Oxford University Press, 2017.

Tilly, Charles. *Coercion, Capital, and European States: AD 990–1990*. Cambridge, MA: Blackwell, 1990.

Toner, Jerry. *Popular Culture in Ancient Rome*. Cambridge, UK: Polity Press, 2009.

Trachsel, Alexandra. "Démétrios de Scepsis et son Τρωικὸς διάκοσμος, ou comment ordonner le passé mythologique de la Troade au IIe siècle av. J.-C." *Polymnia* 3 (2017): 1–25.

Traill, John. *The Political Organization of Attica: A study of the demes, trittyes and phylai.* Toronto: Athenians, 1986.

Trimpi, Wesley. "The Meaning of Horace's Ut Pictura Poiesis." *Journal of the Warburg and Courtauld Institutes* 36 (1973): 1–34.

Trundle, Matthew. *Greek Mercenaries: From the Late Archaic Period to Alexander.* London: Routledge, 2004.

Tuck, Richard. *The Sleeping Sovereign: The Invention of Modern Democracy.* Cambridge: Cambridge University Press, 2015.

Tuplin, C. J., and T. E. Rihll, eds. *Science and Mathematics in Ancient Greek Culture.* Oxford: Oxford University Press, 2002.

Van der Eijk, P. J. "The 'Theology' of the Hippocratic Treatise on the Sacred Disease." *Apeiron* 23 (1990): 87–119.

Várhelyi, Zsuzsanna. "Political Murder and Sacrifice." In *Ancient Mediterranean Sacrifice*, edited by Jennifer Wright Knust and Zsuzsanna Várhelyi, 125–41. Oxford: Oxford University Press, 2011.

Vassilopoulou, Panayiota. "Introduction." In *Late Antique Epistemology: Other Ways to Truth*, edited by P. Vassilopoulou and Stephen R. L. Clark, 1–17. London: Palgrave Macmillan, 2009.

Ventrella, Francesco. "Art and Aesthetics." In *A Companion to Intellectual History*, edited by Richard Whatmore and Brian Young, 358–76. Oxford: Wiley Blackwell, 2015.

Versnel, H. S. *Coping with the Gods: Wayward Readings in Greek Theology.* Leiden: Brill, 2011.

Veyne, Paul. *Le pain et le cirque: sociologie historique d'un pluralisme politique.* Paris: Seuil, 1976.

Villard, Laurence. "L'essor du chromatisme au IVe siècle: quelques témoignages contemporains." In *Couleurs et matières dans l'Antiquité: textes, techniques et pratiques*, edited by Agnès Rouveret, Sandrine Dubel, and Valérie Naas, 43–53. Paris: Editions rue d'Ulm, 2006.

Viveiros de Castro, Eduardo. "Cosmological Deixis and Amerindian Perspectivism." *Journal of the Royal Anthropological Institute*, n.s., 4 (1998): 469–88.

Viveiros de Castro, Eduardo. *Cannibal Metaphysics.* Edited and translated by Peter Skafish. Minneapolis, MN: Univocal, 2014.

Volk, Katharina. "Signs, Seers and Senators: Divinatory Expertise in Cicero and Nigidius Figulus." In *Authority and Expertise in Ancient Scientific Culture*, edited by Jason König and Greg Woolf, 329–47. New York: Cambridge University Press, 2017.

Wagner, Roy. *The Invention of Culture.* 2nd edition. Chicago: University of Chicago Press, [1975] 2016.

Walbank, F. W. *Polybius.* Berkeley: University of California Press, 1972.

Walbank, F. W. "Profit or Amusement: Some Thoughts on the Motives of Hellenistic Historians." In *Purposes of History: Studies in Greek Historiography from the 4th to the 2nd Centuries B.C.: Proceedings of the International Colloquium Leuven, 24–26 May 1988*, edited by H. Verdin, G. Schepens, and E. de Keyser, 253–66. Leuven: Katholieke Universiteit, 1990.

Wallace, Robert W. *Reconstructing Damon: Music, Wisdom Teaching, and Politics in Perikles' Athens.* Oxford: Oxford University Press, 2015.

Wallace-Hadrill, Andrew. *Rome's Cultural Revolution*. Cambridge: Cambridge University Press, 2008.

Walsh, G. B. "Philodemus on the Terminology of Neoptolemus." *Mnemosyne* 40 (1987): 56–68.

Walzer, Richard. *Galen on Jews and Christians*. London: Oxford University Press, 1949.

Webb, Ruth. *Demons and Dancers: Performance in Late Antiquity*. Cambridge, MA: Harvard University Press, 2008.

Webb, Ruth. *Ekphrasis, Imagination and Persuasion in Ancient Rhetorical Theory and Practice*. Burlington, VT: Ashgate Publishing, 2009.

Webb, Ruth. "Reperformance and Embodied Knowledge in Roman Pantomime." In *Imagining Reperformance in Ancient Culture: Studies in the Tradition of Drama and Lyric*, edited by Richard Hunter and Anna Uhlig, 262–80. Cambridge: Cambridge University Press, 2017.

Weil, Raymond. *Aristote et l'histoire: Essai sur la "Politique."* Paris: Klincksieck, 1960.

West, M. L. *The Hesiodic Catalogue of Women: Its Nature, Structure and Origins*. Oxford: Clarendon Press, 1985.

West, M. L. *The East Face of Helicon: West Asiatic Elements in Greek Poetry and Myth*. Oxford: Oxford University Press, 1997.

Whelan, Frederick G. "Democratic Theory and the Boundary Problem." *Nomos* 25 (1983): 13–47.

Whitmarsh, Tim. *Greek Literature and the Roman Empire: The Politics of Imitation*. Oxford: Oxford University Press, 2001.

Whitmarsh, Tim. "Atheism as a Group Identity in Ancient Greece." *Religion in the Roman Empire* 3, no. 1 (2017): 50–65.

Wigodsky, Michael. "Horace and (Not Necessarily) Neoptolemus. The *Ars poetica* and Hellenistic Controversies." *Cronache Ercolanesi* 39 (2009): 7–27.

Wilson, Emily. *The Death of Socrates*. Cambridge, MA: Harvard University Press, 2007.

Woodruff, Paul. "Mimesis." In *A Companion to Ancient Aesthetics*, edited by Pierre Destrée and Penelope Murray, 329–40. Oxford: Blackwell, 2015.

Wyles, Rosie. "The Tragic Costumes." In *The Pronomos Vase and its Context*, edited by Oliver Taplin and Rosie Wyles, 231–53. Oxford: Oxford University Press, 2010.

Zagdoun, Mary-Anne. *L'esthétique d'Aristote*. Paris: CNRS Editions, 2011.

Zanker, Graham. *Herodas: Mimiambs*. Oxford: Aris and Phillips, 2009.

Zeitlin, Froma. *Playing the Other: Gender and Society in Classical Greek Literature*. Chicago: University of Chicago Press, 1996.

Zhao, Jingyi Jenny. *Aristotle and Xunzi on Shame, Moral Education and the Good Life*. Oxford: Oxford University Press, forthcoming.

Zhmud, Leonid. *The Origin of the History of Science in Classical Antiquity*. Translated by A. Chernoglazov. Berlin: De Gruyter, 2006.

CONTRIBUTORS

Clifford Ando is David B. and Clara E. Stern Professor and Professor of Classics, History and in the College at the University of Chicago. He is the author, editor, or translator of more than twenty books, including *Imperial Ideology and Provincial Loyalty in the Roman Empire* (2000), *Roman Social Imaginaries. Language and Thought in Contexts of Empire* (2015), and, with Myles Lavan, *Roman and Local Citizenship in the Long Second Century* (2021). He is also Senior Editor of *Bryn Mawr Classical Review*.

Sean Gurd is Professor in the Department of Classics at the University of Texas at Austin. He is the author of *Iphigenias at Aulis: Textual Multiplicity, Radical Philology* (2006); *Work in Progress: Literary Revision as Social Performance in Ancient Rome* (2012), *Dissonance: Auditory Aesthetics in Ancient Greece* (2016), and *The Origins of Music Theory in the Age of Plato* (2019), and has edited *Philology and its Histories* (2010), and co-edited *Pataphilology, an Irreader* (2018). With Pauline LeVen he edited the Bloomsbury *Cultural History of Western Music in Antiquity* (forthcoming).

Thomas N. Habinek (d. 2019) was Dean's Professor of Classics at the University of Southern California, having taught previously at UCLA and Berkeley. He is the author of *The Colometry of Latin Prose* (1985), *The World of Roman Song: From Ritualized Speech to Social Order* (2005), *Ancient Rhetoric and Oratory* (2005), and, with Alessandro Schiesaro, editor of *The Roman Cultural Revolution* (1997). His work laid the foundations for this volume.

Lucas Herchenroeder is Associate Professor (Teaching) of Classics at the University of Southern California, where he teaches broadly on topics in the literature and culture of the ancient Mediterranean world. He currently is writing a book that considers late classical and Hellenistic historiography in relation to broader developments in the culture of science in the period.

James Ker is Associate Professor of Classical Studies at the University of Pennsylvania. He is the author of *The Deaths of Seneca* (2009) and other books and articles on Roman literature and culture. His recent work has concerned Roman conceptions of time, in a book project entitled *The Ordered Day: Quotidian Time and Forms of Life in Ancient Rome*.

Geoffrey Lloyd is Emeritus Professor of Ancient Philosophy and Science at the University of Cambridge where from 1989 to 2000 he was Master of Darwin College. His interests in ancient Greek and Chinese philosophy, science, and medicine have increasingly drawn him into comparative studies drawing on social anthropology, evolutionary psychology, ethology, and cognitive science, as for example in his *Cognitive Variations: Reflections on* *the Unity and Diversity of the Human Mind* (2007), *Being, Humanity and Understanding* (2012), and most recently *Expanding Horizons in the History of Science* (2021). He was knighted for "services to the history of thought" in 1997.

Giulia Sissa is Distinguished Professor in the departments of Political Science and Classics at the University of California Los Angeles. She is the author of *Greek Virginity* (1990); *The Daily Life of the Greek Gods* (with Marcel Detienne, 2000); *Le Plaisir et le Mal. Philosophie de la drogue* (1997); *L'Âme est un corps de femme* (2000); *Sex and Sensuality in the Ancient World* (2008); *Jealousy: A Forbidden Passion* (2017); *Le Pouvoir des femmes: Un défi pour la démocratie* (2021); and co-editor of *Utopia 1516–2016: More's Eccentric Essay and its Activist Aftermath* (with Han van Ruler, 2017).

Zsuzsanna Várhelyi is Associate Professor of Classical Studies at Boston University, where she teaches courses on Roman history, religion, and the good life. She is the author of *The Religion of Senators in the Roman Empire* (2010), co-editor of *Ancient Mediterranean Sacrifice* (2011), and wrote, most recently, an essay "Statuary and Ritualization in Imperial Italy," in the collection *Ritual Matters: Material Residues and Ancient Religions* (2017).

Ruth Webb is Professeure des Universités, Langue et littérature grecques, at the Université de Lille. She is the author of *Demons and Dancers: Performance in Late Antiquity* (2008) and *Ekphrasis, Imagination and Persuasion in Ancient Rhetorical Theory and Practice* (2009), and co-editor of *Dion Chrysostome: Ilion n'a pas été prise: Discours "Troyen" 11* (2012), *Théorie et Pratique de la fiction à l'époque impériale* (2013) and *Faire voir: Etudes sur l'énargeia de l'Antiquité à l'époque moderne* (2021).

INDEX